Global Migration, Ethnicity and Britishness

Edited by

Tariq Modood
University of Bristol, UK

and

John Salt
University College London, UK

palgrave
macmillan

First published 2011
Published in paperback 2013 by
PALGRAVE MACMILLAN

Palgrave Macmillan in the UK is an imprint of Macmillan Publishers Limited, registered in England, company number 785998, of Houndmills, Basingstoke, Hampshire RG21 6XS.

Palgrave Macmillan in the US is a division of St Martin's Press LLC, 175 Fifth Avenue, New York, NY 10010.

Palgrave Macmillan is the global academic imprint of the above companies and has companies and representatives throughout the world.

Palgrave® and Macmillan® are registered trademarks in the United States, the United Kingdom, Europe and other countries.

ISBN 978–0–230–29687–9 hardback
ISBN 978–1–137–28595–9 paperback

This book is printed on paper suitable for recycling and made from fully managed and sustained forest sources. Logging, pulping and manufacturing processes are expected to conform to the environmental regulations of the country of origin.

A catalogue record for this book is available from the British Library.

A catalog record for this book is available from the Library of Congress.

10 9 8 7 6 5 4 3 2 1
22 21 20 19 18 17 16 15 14 13

Printed and bound in Great Britain by
CPI Antony Rowe, Chippenham and Eastbourne

Global Migration, Ethnicity and Britishness

Palgrave Politics of Identity and Citizenship Series

Series Editors: **Varun Uberoi**, University of Oxford; **Nasar Meer**, University of Southampton and **Tariq Modood**, University of Bristol

The politics of identity and citizenship has assumed increasing importance as our polities have become significantly more culturally, ethnically and religiously diverse. Different types of scholars, including philosophers, sociologists, political scientists and historians make contributions to this field and this series showcases a variety of innovative contributions to it. Focusing on a range of different countries, and utilizing the insights of different disciplines, the series helps to illuminate an increasingly controversial area of research and titles in it will be of interest to a number of audiences including scholars, students and other interested individuals.

Titles include:

Heidi Armbruster and Ulrike Hanna Meinhof (*editors*)
NEGOTIATING MULTICULTURAL EUROPE
Borders, Networks, Neighbourhoods

Fazila Bhimji
BRITISH ASIAN MUSLIM WOMEN, MULTIPLE SPATIALITIES AND COSMOPOLITANISM

Derek McGhee
SECURITY, CITIZENSHIP AND HUMAN RIGHTS
Shared Values in Uncertain Times

Tariq Modood and John Salt (*editors*)
GLOBAL MIGRATION, ETHNICITY AND BRITISHNESS

Nasar Meer
CITIZENSHIP, IDENTITY AND THE POLITICS OF MULTICULTURALISM
The Rise of Muslim Consciousness

Ganesh Nathan
SOCIAL FREEDOM IN A MULTICULTURAL STATE
Towards a Theory of Intercultural Justice

Michel Seymour (*editor*)
THE PLURAL STATES OF RECOGNITION

Katherine Smith
FAIRNESS, CLASS AND BELONGING IN CONTEMPORARY ENGLAND

Palgrave Politics of Identity and Citizenship Series
Series Standing Order ISBN 978–0–230–24901–1 (hardback)
(*outside North America only*)

You can receive future titles in this series as they are published by placing a standing order. Please contact your bookseller or, in case of difficulty, write to us at the address below with your name and address, the title of the series and the ISBN quoted above.

Customer Services Department, Macmillan Distribution Ltd, Houndmills, Basingstoke, Hampshire RG21 6XS, England

Contents

List of Tables and Figures

Tables

Figures

List of Contributors

Claire Dwyer is Senior Lecturer in Social and Cultural Geography at University College London and Deputy Director of the Migration Research Unit. Claire's research interests are in geographies of 'race', ethnicity and religion; transnationalism and diasporas; and feminist theory. She has undertaken research on Muslim identities in Britain, British South Asian diaspora commodity cultures and new religious landscapes in Britain. Recent publications include co-editing *Transnational Spaces* (2004) and *New Geographies of Race and Racism* (2008).

Steve Fenton is Professor Emeritus, Sociology, at the University of Bristol where he is attached to the Centre for the Study of Ethnicity and Citizenship. His recent work has been on the question of majoritarian sentiments and national identity, and he published a revised and updated edition of *Ethnicity* in 2010.

Ron Johnston is Fellow of the British Academy and Professor in the School of Geographical Sciences at the University of Bristol, having previously worked at Monash University and the Universities of Canterbury, Sheffield and Essex. Alongside his work on the geography of ethnicity in cities he has published extensively in electoral studies and on the history of geography.

Nabil Khattab is Senior Lecturer at the Hebrew University of Jerusalem and Honorary Research Fellow at the University of Bristol. Prior to this he was an RCUK research fellow in quantitative sociology, and a lecturer in sociology, both at the University of Bristol. His research interests fall within the field of ethnicity, social inequality, labour market, educational attainment and quantitative sociology.

Khalid Koser, formerly a Senior Lecturer at UCL, is Associate Dean and Head of the New Issues in Security Programme at the Geneva Centre for Security Policy. He is also Non-Resident Senior Fellow at the Brookings Institution, Research Associate at the Graduate Institute of International and Development Studies in Geneva, Visiting Fellow at the Lowy Institute in Sydney and Associate Fellow at Chatham House. Dr Koser is chair of the UK's Independent Advisory Group on Country Information. He is co-editor of the *Journal of Refugee Studies* and on the editorial board for *Global Governance; Ethnic and Racial Studies; Population, Space, and Place*; and *Forced Migration Review*.

Robin Mann is Research Fellow at the Wales Institute of Social and Economic Research, Data and Methods (WISERD), Bangor University, having been a Research Fellow at Bristol and Oxford Universities. His main research interests include nationalism, majority ethnicity and the politics of language and national identity in Wales. He is the author of numerous articles in these fields.

Nasar Meer is Senior Lecturer in the School of Arts and Social Sciences at the University of Northumbria. Previously he was a lecturer in the School of Social Sciences at the University of Southampton, and a researcher in the Centre for Study of Ethnicity and Citizenship at the University of Bristol. His publications include *Citizenship, Identity and the Politics of Multiculturalism* (2010). He is presently researching ideas of racism, anti-Semitism and Islamophobia, has a forthcoming monograph on *Race and Ethnicity* with Sage, and edits and co-edits special issues of the journals *Ethnic and Racial Studies*, and *Ethnicities*.

Tariq Modood is Professor of Sociology, Politics and Public Policy and the founding Director of the Centre for the Study of Ethnicity and Citizenship at the University of Bristol, and Co-Director of the Leverhulme Programme on Migration and Citizenship. He has extensive academic publications, has worked on numerous research projects and is a regular contributor to the media and policy debates in Britain. He was awarded an MBE for services to social sciences and ethnic relations in 2001 and elected a member of the Academy of Social Sciences in 2004.

John Salt is Emeritus Professor of Geography at University College London. He has been Director of the Migration Research Unit at UCL since 1989 and is Co-Director of the Leverhulme Programme on Migration and Citizenship. He has been a Consultant to the OECD, EU, Council of Europe, Australian government, UK Home Office, National Audit Office and Office for National Statistics. He received the Royal Geographical Society's Edward Heath Award for contributions to the study of population and migration in Europe. His principal research interests are in the field of international migration, especially by the highly skilled.

Gurchathen Sanghera is Lecturer at the School of International Relations, University of St Andrews, having previously been a Research Fellow at the University of Bristol. His current research interests are international relations and UN Peace Support Operations; the politics of race and ethnicity in contemporary Britain, particularly post-9/11 and 7/7; and critical approaches to human rights as strategy. Geographical areas of interest are the UK, Haiti, India and Liberia. He has published in a number of international refereed journals.

Bindi Shah is Lecturer in Sociology in the School of Social Sciences, University of Southampton, having previously been a Research Fellow at UCL. She holds a PhD in Sociology from the University of California, Davis, USA. Her research interests focus on how race, gender, class and religion construct belonging and citizenship among the second generation. Previously, she has published on second-generation Laotians in the USA. Her current project is a comparative study of the role of religion and religious institutions in shaping community, belonging and citizenship among young Jains in the UK and USA, funded by the Economic and Social Research Council.

Ibrahim Sirkeci is Professor of Transnational Studies at the European Business School London, Regent's College. Previously he worked at the University of Bristol. His recent research focus is the marketing of business schools, transnational mobile consumers, and the financial crisis and remittances and is funded by the British Academy, the Higher Education Academy and the World Bank. His most recent book, *Cultures of Migration*, is published by the University of Texas Press. He is the editor of *Migration Letters* and serves on editorial and review boards of many other journals.

Claire Smetherham is Associate Lecturer with the Open University, having previously worked as Research Associate at the Centre for the Study of Ethnicity and Citizenship, Department of Sociology, University of Bristol. Her research interests focus on the relationship between higher education and the labour market, in both a national and international context. Her publications include 'How Global is the UK Academic Labour Market?', *Globalisation, Societies & Education* (with Tariq Modood and Steve Fenton, 2010) and 'Firsts Among Equals?: Evidence on the Contemporary Relationship between Educational Credentials and the Occupational Structure', *Journal of Education and Work* (2006).

Suruchi Thapar-Björkert is Senior Lecturer in the Department of Government, University of Uppsala in Sweden. Previously she was Senior Lecturer at the Department of Sociology, University of Bristol. Her research interests are gendered discourses of colonialism and nationalism; gendered violence in India and Europe; gender, social capital and social exclusion; and feminist qualitative research methodologies. She has published widely in refereed journals and her first book, *Unseen Faces: Unheard Voices: Women in the Indian Nationalist Movement 1930–1942*, was published in 2006.

Varun Uberoi is Lecturer in the Department of Politics and History, Brunel University, having worked as a Research Fellow at the Centre for Ethnicity and Citizenship, University of Bristol, and the Department of Politics and International Relations, University of Oxford. His work combines normative political theory and public policy to examine the theory and practice of fostering unity amongst the culturally diverse citizens of modern polities. He co-edits Palgrave Macmillan's Politics of Identity and Citizenship Series, has published in key journals and has a forthcoming book, *Nation-Building Through Multiculturalism*.

Peter Wood is Emeritus Professor of Geography at University College London. He is an economic geographer with broad interests in regional and urban economic development. His research has focused on the international growth of knowledge-intensive services and their significance for national and regional access to business expertise. Most recently, he has acted as consultant in government-sponsored projects on the 'knowledge base' of major English cities and on the international mobility of corporate staff.

Preface to the Paperback Edition

In the year since the publication of the hardback edition of this book, events have made its findings even more pertinent. Continuing downward government pressure on labour migration, together with continuing poor economic conditions, has reduced numbers of migrants and increased selectivity. New measures have been taken to reduce international student numbers; routes to settlement have been restricted; family migration has come under greater scrutiny. The UK may be on the verge of a new migration paradigm which makes the prescience of the research reported here more important.

In the six months of late 2010 and early 2011, seven European premiers, including Prime Minister Cameron, made a high profile speech to the effect that 'multiculturalism is dead'. That such speeches continue to be made is evidence of the continuing potency of multiculturalism and the discursive hostility to that fact. The only policy consequence of Cameron's speech to date (April 2012) is the British government's decision, as spelled out by Eric Pickles, the Minister at the Department of Communities and Local Government, to not speak to those identified as 'extremists' or not sharing certain core values with the government. This was a policy that New Labour at times also espoused and so is part of a pattern of zig-zagging. The more important and deeper continuity is of anti-multiculturalist, pro-diversity speeches which do little to reverse multiculturalism in relation to existing citizens but confine policy change to security matters, immigration and citizenship acquisition. A related development has been that the radical secularist reaction to Muslim political assertiveness which amongst other things has led to the banning of the full face veil (niqab) in public in certain European countries, is stimulating a Christianist response in Britain (as well as elsewhere). Pope Benedict's high-profile visit to Britain in September 2010 included warnings against 'aggressive secularism'. At Christmas 2011 David Cameron argued that it was time to proclaim again that Britain is a Christian country, the first time that a major politician has spoken like that for a long time. While it was dismissed by many commentators it was welcomed by Ibrahim Mogra, the Chairman of the Mosque Committee of the Muslim Council of Britain and Baroness Warsi, the first Muslim to be a full member of the British Cabinet. The development of this triangular relationship between political Muslims, secularists of moderate and radical persuasions, and Christian identarians, as outlined on pp. 53–59 below, continues to be central to British, indeed, European multiculturalism.

Preface

This book presents some of the major findings from a programme of research into migration and ethnicity funded from 2003 by the Leverhulme Trust. The programme supported eight projects, carried out over six years. Some were completed several years ago, others more recently. The programme was undertaken jointly by the University Research Centre for the Study of Ethnicity and Citizenship at the Department of Sociology in the University of Bristol and the Migration Research Unit at the Department of Geography in University College London. The Co-Directors of the programme were Professor Tariq Modood (Bristol) and Professor John Salt (UCL).

The last decade has seen major perturbations in the UK migration scene. It began with substantial increases in inflows of highly skilled workers, especially in the IT and health sectors. These were accompanied by a rise in asylum seeking and then an unprecedented flow from Eastern Europe as new members joined the European Union. Meanwhile, international student numbers surged as they were actively courted by educational institutions. The Morecambe Bay disaster focused attention on the harm created by people smuggling and trafficking. Changes in political and social attitudes to migration occurred. Politicians embarked on a steady stream of immigration legislation. At the same time multiculturalism came under attack. In the popular mind, the turning point seems to be the terrorist attacks on 9/11, but actually hostility to multiculturalism predates this. In Britain, it was the riots that took place a few months earlier that led to the government saying that multiculturalism led to segregation and community cohesion was to be a new priority. Since then there has been a string of controversies involving Muslims, who have been particularly scrutinised by the media, with calls for the need to update and/or assert British national identity. In short, our research programme took place in a very dynamic context.

In bringing together two related but discrete academic disciplines, bodies of theory and approaches, we feel we have been able to throw light into some of the corners of the migration process which frequently escape comment or even detection. In particular, as the programme unfolded it became more apparent to us of the need to view international migration as a holistic process. Much past research has tended to regard movement and settlement as separate. What we have tried to show in this book is that migrants, hosts and intermediary agencies are participants in an unfolding process. For example, employers and educational institutions play a major role in both the movement of migrants and in shaping the attitudes of both hosts and the progeny of migrants. Our overall intention is to present our considerable empirical research findings to a wide range of interests. The chapters in this book represent only part of the output from the projects, but we have tried to ensure that they contain most of the main results. A list of the programme's publications to date is included in the Appendix.

We are extremely grateful to the Leverhulme Trust for funding the programme and for their continuing encouragement. We particularly applaud their policy of allowing us to chase what seemed interesting, without knowing where it would lead, and to adapt a timetable to the exigencies of multiple intellectual commitments on the part of the key researchers – such being the nature of academic life today.

We are also indebted to many people who helped us carry out the research. These include not only the researchers themselves, but numerous assistants who acted as translators, surveyors or transcribers. Particular thanks are owed to the many individuals who were willing interviewees, either migrants and their families or representatives of various organisations. 'Research fatigue', manifest in refusing invitations to be surveyed, is a growing problem in social science and we are most grateful to those who nevertheless provided us with the information without which this book would not have been possible. Our confident hope is that our findings will be useful to them too.

Part 1

1
Migration, Minorities and the Nation

Tariq Modood and John Salt

1. Introduction: immigration to the UK

The migration streams to the UK during the twentieth century flow almost entirely independently of each other. Within the immigration settlement system different countries have predominated at different times and brought to the UK people of varied character (Coleman and Salt, 1992: 444). In popular perception immigration into the UK since the Second World War has consisted mainly of poor non-white people from the New Commonwealth, supplemented more recently by asylum seekers from Africa and parts of Asia and finally by labour migrants from Eastern Europe. In reality, the largest long-standing group is the Irish who have created chains of migration since the mid-nineteenth century. Unlike the Irish, most other Europeans came to work, not settle. In the late 1940s and early 1950s they were actively recruited by British employers. The main exceptions are those who entered as refugees or who remained in the UK at the end of the Second World War. Immigrants from the New Commonwealth, a diverse group, came in waves from the late 1940s, first from the Caribbean, then India and Pakistan, Bangladesh and more recently Africa. Their arrival was accompanied by the first serious legislation aimed at immigration control, a process that continued with quickening speed until the last 10–15 years has seen an almost annual addition to the government's legislative immigration arsenal. Much of the legislation has been steered towards entry controls but significant also has been a legislative stream designed to promote both social and civic integration. This twofold approach of entry control (now 'migration management') and measures to encourage integration has persisted regardless of which political party was in power.

The research reported in our book should be seen against this background. There have been varied streams of movement, some with similar, others with different rationales. Migrants from particular origins have tended to arrive in waves, creating new diasporas, chains and networks. They have led to a range of consequences, many unintended, for both migrants and host populations. They have tested our theories and forced new thinking. Much of the theoretical debate has been dichotomised between understanding flows and understanding the settlement process and its relationships between communities. Large-scale population flows into and out of a country have many social and economic implications in both the short and long term. In spatial terms, different types of migrants have implications at both national and local levels. To some extent the implications reflect geographical distributions, degrees of concentration affecting, for example, health or educational provision, housing availability and quality, unemployment or skill shortages. There are also implications for particular organisations such as employers, schools and hospitals and trade unions which function as migration drivers, facilitators or avenues of integration. These agencies may have a positive or negative effect on the scale and nature of movement. Hence, a process of 'negotiation' occurs between the individuals in a particular migration stream, the various agencies such as health, housing, educational and labour market institutions and the host communities, leading to some form of 'consensual' relationship between them.

We may thus hypothesise that each migrant has a unique migration experience which cannot be represented by a view of international migration as a homogeneous flow of people. Migrants entering a host country through a particular migration route share, by definition, some common characteristics and are engaged in similar interactions with the host environment. Each of these migrant groups will interact with the agencies of settlement in the host country, sometimes in similar fashion, sometimes differently. For example, the outcomes in the labour market for a mature, highly skilled worker are different from those of a young trainee seeking work experience. A child migrant will have different health requirements to those of an elderly relative. A migrant student will participate in a different area of the housing market from an intra-company transferee. But there are also similarities: for example, young migrants, whatever their routes of entry, usually make less call on health systems. Those with a similar cultural background, such as strong religiosity, may exhibit a unity which cuts across dissimilar routes of entry. Conversely, class distinctions frequently transgress cultural and ethnic backgrounds.

The study of population movements requires the expertise both of disciplines which emphasise the measurement and documentations of large flows of people and the processes creating them and also of disciplines which examine the cultural, economic and political co-ordinates and consequences of migration. In our research, these approaches are linked and complementary leading to a more integrative analytical approach that links together movement and its consequences. We acknowledge that simple economic motors – disadvantage in the homeland, opportunity in the new land – play an important part, as do migrations impelled by civil war and economic collapse. But we argue that these migrations – and their cultural and political consequences – must also be seen as managed and negotiated by a range of agencies, each of which has a vested interest in maximising its returns from population movement.

2. The nature of migration

The last decade or so has seen an explosion of academic, policy and media interest in international migration. Unfortunately much of that interest has been characterised by a reductionism that has led to oversimplification and misunderstanding, prompting the question: what do we mean by migration? The answer to this question is by no means straightforward. There is an increasing diversity of flows that challenges traditional notions of 'migration'. Indeed, it is probably true to say that that there is no such person as a 'typical' migrant. Rather, a wide range of people exhibit different forms of and rationales for mobility which constitute a variety of migration streams on a continuum from commuting to permanent emigration. What we define as 'migration' becomes a choice, which may seem arbitrary but is usually dependent on the purpose of the definition, about where we draw the line. Furthermore, mobility streams are dynamic, involve different types of people and motivations, have different roles and different implications for host and sending societies and are influenced and managed by different agencies and institutions.

Each of these streams has a corresponding 'route of entry', based on the rules which are designed to regulate entry and allow governments to fine-tune overall migration flows. In devising and implementing these rules, governments are presented with a range of management challenges. For example, asylum seekers come to the UK for a variety of reasons; they originate in a wide range of countries; they have diverse educational backgrounds and skills; some come alone and others with family members; and there are increasing numbers of unaccompanied minors claiming asylum. There are similar diversities affecting other migration streams. Family reunion and formation, for instance, are generally accepted as fundamental human rights so that government actions are circumscribed by international human rights legislation, agreements and norms. Other types of movement have quite different roots and proceed in different ways. Retirement migration usually occurs on the basis of personal decisions, tempered by social security and pension arrangements. Educational institutions rather than governments play a leading role in the promotion and selection of foreign students and usually there are no numerical limits imposed. In contrast, for some years now the UK government has established quotas for entries of (often seasonal) low-skilled workers in the agriculture, hospitality and food-processing industries, with intermediary institutions such as gangmasters playing a pivotal role. The new Coalition government, formed in May 2010, has gone further by imposing a cap on most labour immigration from sources beyond the European Economic Area (EEA). Employers are usually the driving force behind the migration of the highly skilled, many of whom are intra-company transferees within large transnational corporations and for whom special entry arrangements are made.

3. The emergence of a global migration market

The last two decades have seen the emergence of a global migration market in which the UK is an active participant. It affects all levels of skill, but the real competition is for those with high levels of human expertise and there is now a complex pattern of movement by professional, managerial and technical staff (OECD, 2002). Since these movements are multi-directional, involving most states to a greater or lesser degree, we may call them 'international brain circulation'. Some countries are now more active than others in seeking to make net gains from this movement (OECD, 2008, 2010).

A major stimulus for competition in the global migration market has come from governments, either directly through quotas and management programmes or indirectly by providing a conducive framework for employers. Competition was led in the 1980s by Australia and Canada, followed in the 1990s by the USA. Europe held itself largely aloof until very recently, with little action and almost no debate about competition in the migration skills market. Employers worldwide are now facing the problem of integrating new processes and technologies which require specific skills but are finding they must compete internationally, where the main competitors are the USA, Australia and Canada and a growing number of European states (McLaughlan and Salt, 2002; OECD, 2008, 2010). The migration market for expertise has two main drivers. The first is the attempt to increase the national bank of expertise through the acquisition of high-level human resources; the other is the development of policies to counter specific skill shortages. Underlying the first of these is evidence that highly skilled migrants bring economic benefits to the host economy. Although some of the results are ambiguous or contradictory, studies from as far afield as the UK, Denmark, Germany, Australia, Singapore and the USA have shown that the higher the skill level of immigrants, the greater the likelihood of net fiscal gains to the economy (Gott and Johnston, 2002; Birrell, Hawthorne and Richardson, 2006). Put bluntly, the more skilled a country's immigrants, the greater the economic benefit.

A relative newcomer in the debate about labour immigration policy is the perceived shortage of specific skills and the need for new schemes to deal with it. Work permit systems have long existed to bring in skills from abroad that are in short supply. Mostly they have been seen as short-term measures to deal with temporary shortages, or to bring in specialists and corporate assignees. Nowadays, many developed countries have shortage lists for specific skills and have adopted new government schemes or programmes to deal with them. The UK, Denmark and the Netherlands have already followed Australia, Canada and New Zealand in developing points-based systems to aid in selection and other European countries are following suit.

For the most part, the strategies and procedures used to recruit specific skills in shortage occupations have been predominantly employer-led, with governments acting as facilitators. Although the theoretical basis for explaining international labour mobility has developed substantially over the last quarter century (Massey et al., 2005), a particular weakness is the lack of attention to the role of employers, whose decision making with respect to labour recruitment and deployment can be fundamental in the orchestration of movement, and to other institutions which are involved in setting the context in which movement occurs. In order to understand how migration is managed, an explanatory framework is needed that allows consideration of all the relevant actors.

The key question, then, is how do these different interests accommodate each other and what systems of movement are created? Several chapters in the book develop these points. Movement is conceptualised as including a migration for settlement through to shorter-term and flexible movements in internationalised labour markets, each capable of metamorphosing into something else through a set of processes which are increasingly institutionally driven. A useful starting point is to conceptualise international labour migration as a business, populated by a range of institutions, each of which has some influence on the processes, patterns and outcomes of movement. These institutions include employers and trade unions, government, regulatory bodies, migrant organisations and facilitators such as lawyers and smugglers. They each have their own operational strategies, and to achieve their objectives they negotiate with each other in order to reach compromise accommodations that produce migration outcomes. They also constitute networks of interrelationships, some of which are more important than others (Koser and Salt, 1997). Among the institutions influencing migration patterns, employing organisations play a key role through their acquisition and deployment of human skills. Their actions in this regard are determined by their business models, as well as by a suite of constraints and opportunities which impinge upon them, including such matters as welfare state arrangements, regulatory frameworks and the policies and actions of other institutional actors. For most commercial employers, recruitment and mobility decisions and processes are determined by the need to maximise profitability. Transnational corporations seek to make best use of their internal expertise and add to it through recruitment in the external labour market. However, it is clear that circumstances vary between sectors and by type of employer because of the nature of each organisation's predominant activities. Every employment sector has its own distinguishing characteristics in size, skill mix and training requirements, geographical spread of operations, ownership, nature of service or product and trends in product/service demand, all of which are relevant to international recruitment.

4. From migrants to minorities

Public attitudes to migrants and migration are frequently polarised, often ill-informed. The media tends to focus on specific issues, such as irregular migration (see the publicity attached to cockle pickers, Sangatte and the closure of the 'Calais Jungle', asylum seekers), the threat to UK workers from the influx of Eastern Europeans or issues surrounding arranged and forced marriage. After 9/11 and 7/7 in particular, popular and government attention refocused on integration, what it means to be a citizen and how individual and group identities are formed. New discourses and policies around social capital, social cohesion and citizenship were used to critique or remake previous understandings of integration, equality and multiculturalism. These topics have assumed a high political salience and interestingly there is much agreement today across the political spectrum, especially when they are linked to the idea that Muslims pose a cultural threat to British values and national identity. That there is this high degree of agreement should perhaps not be surprising, as for decades there has been a similar agreement on the need for managing immigration and embedding racial equality in British society.

The post-war migration to Britain from the Caribbean and the Asian sub-continent, while based upon imperial ties, was very much driven by economic imperatives. The rebuilding of the war-shattered economy created a demand for labour that could not be satisfied by the British population alone. Early studies of these migrants in the British economy show that regardless of their social origins and qualification levels, Caribbean and Asian people were very largely confined to low-paid manual work, and that racial discrimination in recruitment was widespread, even after being outlawed (Daniel, 1968; Smith, 1977). Later studies, such as the Fourth Survey of National Minorities in the 1990s, showed that the non-white minorities had much higher levels of unemployment than whites but they were also upwardly mobile and expanding in self-employment (Jones, 1993; Modood et al., 1997). They also showed that each of these conditions applied to some rather than all Caribbean and Asian ethnic groups. Increasingly, economic differences between migrants have become much more pronounced and much better substantiated by statistical data.

In the 1970s and 1980s theorists sought to explain racial inequality; the Fourth Survey made clear that what needs to be explained is racial inequality *and* ethnic diversity. For in so far as there is a fundamental divide in employment by ethnicity, it is not a black–white divide, but a divide between white, Chinese, African Asian and Indian men, on the one hand, and Bangladeshi,

Pakistani and Caribbean men, on the other. There are difficulties in creating a single measure of equality that encompasses both sexes, but if both sexes are taken into account, there seems to be a tripartite division. The Chinese and African Asians are in broad parity with whites; the Indians and Caribbeans are somewhat disadvantaged; and the Bangladeshis and Pakistanis are extremely disadvantaged (Modood et al., 1997; for latest data with slightly different ethnic categories, see NEP, 2010).

That these migrants were marked out as 'racial' groups and understood as racialised ethnicities (Modood, Berthoud and Nazroo, 2002) has three implications. Firstly, migrants were perceived as a collectivity or more precisely as collectivities rather than merely as individuals, neighbours, fellow workers, citizens and so on. Secondly, they were perceived by the white British and publicly labelled in terms of specific collectivities, such as black or Asian, whether they approved or not and, consequently, minority groups were forced to accept, resist or negotiate these labels and their implied identities. Thirdly, they had to draw attention to and resist various forms of discrimination and unfavourable treatment, whether in personal interactions or through mobilising and organising public protest and campaigns. Indeed, ethnic identities as publicly projected self-concepts have proved to be unexpectedly popular in Britain amongst members of ethnic minorities, certainly compared to earlier migrant groups and their descendants, say, Jews from Eastern Europe. Minority groups have played a major role in determining the public character of these identities, as well as in relation to the prevalence and decline of specific labels such as 'black', 'Asian' and 'Muslim'.

While racial discrimination legislation was introduced in the 1960s, until late 2003 it was lawful, except in Northern Ireland, to discriminate against religious minorities unless they were recognised as ethnic groups within the meaning of the law. The latter was the case with Jews and Sikhs but the courts did not accept that Muslims were an ethnic group and so it was possible, for example, to deny a Muslim a job *qua* Muslim. In such a circumstance, Muslims only had some limited indirect legal protection *qua* members of ethnic groups such as Pakistanis, Arabs and so on.

Yet, in the last decade Muslims have become central in Britain to what used to be called 'race relations'. How has this happened? Even before issues of international terrorism and foreign affairs intruded into domestic matters, religion in the form of Muslim politics was reshaping the terms of minority–majority relations (Modood, 2005). While initially unremarked upon, the long-standing exclusive focus on race and ethnicity and the exclusion of Muslims but not Jews and Sikhs came to be a source of resentment amongst some Muslims. At the same time the analyses, campaigns, policies and legislation associated with racial and ethnic equality and diversity were the principal source of precedence and legitimacy as Muslim activists began to make political claims upon British society and the polity. In short, one of the principal ways of seeing the emergence and development of ethno-religious equality is in terms of a grievance of exclusion from the existing equality framework and its utilisation in order to extend it to address the felt exclusion and to develop and seek public recognition for a minority subjectivity ignored by liberal legislators (Modood, 1993).

The emergence of Muslim identity politics and the placing of Muslims as a group at the centre of post-immigration minority–majority relations, and the politics of pro- and anti-multiculturalism that has accompanied it, has had an effect on how the majority white British population think of themselves. The last decade has witnessed an increased interest in 'Britishness' across a variety of domains. During this period the 'break up of Britain' (Nairn, 1977) has proceeded through the devolution of government to two regional assemblies and one Parliament. Post-immigration minorities too, alongside historically established minority nations, have come to symbolise a variety of anxieties surrounding forms of unity signalled in the ambiguities and ambivalences proposed in ideas of nationhood. One outcome is that accounts of Britishness in contemporary political and public discourse are proceeding through the critique of a variety of British Muslim cultural practices and characterisations of British Muslim norms and values.

Those writing on ethnic identities have for the most part focused on minority identities, whilst multiculturalists have stressed the tacit 'whiteness' of national identity in Britain, calling at the same time for a more inclusive national narrative. In all this social scientists have paid less attention to identities expressed by the ethnic majority. This is an important intellectual omission and of profound political consequence as evidence grows of a grumbling resentment on the part of the ethnic majority, especially in England. There is a feeling of an absence of the kind of national identities that are flourishing in Scotland and Wales and confusion over whether that identity should be England or Britain. Relatedly, there is an anger towards metropolitan elites for allegedly honouring minority cultures and identities at the expense of those of the majority.

5. Structure of the book

The rest of Part 1 consists of two macroscopic chapters. Chapter 2 is an overview of recent migrations to (mostly) and from the UK. It provides an empirical and statistically based context for the rest of the book by identifying the main migration streams affecting the UK currently and in the recent past.

Chapter 3 is an overview of some of the political challenges posed to British and other European societies by the mass immigration from outside Europe, especially former colonies, that took place in the third quarter of the twentieth century. Drawing on American experience, there is a discussion of whether the 'fault-line' in Europe will be a 'colour-line', xenophobia or Islamophobia. A key consideration in relation to this is what contemporary

Europeans will perceive to be the legitimate role of Islam and Muslim identity in public life. This is part of the wider question about secularism and the role of religion which the presence of Muslims has opened up, and is discussed in that chapter.

Part 2 contains four chapters which provide case studies of migrant workers at both the 'bottom' end as well as the 'top' of the labour market. They are rooted in the principle that there is a migration business which is institutionally organised. All these cases can be seen as examples of movements which are managed and operated partly by individuals and states, but also by a set of mediating institutions. Chapter 4 is a study of human smuggling and trafficking networks between Pakistan and Britain. Smuggled migrants are only one set of actors in a business directed by well-organised agencies. It poses two main questions: how far are states able to control irregular movement and to what extent are smuggled migrants different from those coming by legal routes? In contrast, Chapter 5 looks at how the large transnational corporations, for whom movement of staff is routine, are being globalised and a new elite of internationalised workers has emerged. It argues that in recruiting and allocating the staff expertise vital to their global operations, companies combine their mobility options into portfolios of moves according to their needs and those of their employees. Companies allocate human resources as circumstances dictate in ways that resolve constraints and that fit in with the desires and aspirations of their workforce. At the same time, overseas academic staff and researchers have become a significant feature of British higher education and Chapter 6 explores in what way and which kinds of universities can be said to be globalised. UK universities have increasingly set themselves to compete in a global educational marketplace. Concentration of research funding in an elite band of universities allows them to attract applications from 'global academics' who choose, temporarily or more permanently, Britain as the locus for the pursuit of their career. This not only meets the shortages in the production of postgraduates and postdoctorates in certain subjects but allows certain British universities to be globally 'excellent'. Chapter 7 is strongly linked to the two preceding chapters. It introduces a new trend which links corporate and educational globalisation. This is an emerging policy among transnational companies to target international students in order to recruit them into their global labour markets.

Part 3 consists of five chapters which focus on identity and integration. They concentrate on post-immigration social formations and on second and third generational issues. They are linked to questions of social, political and cultural change and introduce the topic of ethnic inequalities and hierarchies while continuing the earlier themes of education and labour markets. The place of Muslims is a recurrent feature, whether in relation to the labour market or to the over-visibility of Islamic identity and questions about whether Muslims want to be and are capable of being British.

The desire to improve their own or their children's educational attainments and thereby to achieve upward mobility is a central motive of migrants and patterns of social segregation are often established in the early phase of a migration. Social capital may be transported from the country of origin and mobilised globally and can result in upward mobility and/or closed communities. Thus Chapter 8 with its focus on segregation and returns on education and Chapter 9 on social capital are on areas closely related to migrations. Research on ethnicity and returns on education in Britain has revealed that non-white minorities are likely to face 'ethnic penalties' when entering the labour market, whereby members of ethnic minority groups fail to get into occupations commensurate with their qualifications. These studies, however, do not look at the effects of residential location and segregation. Moreover, often these analyses of occupational attainment by education treat ethnic minority groups as homogeneous, not clearly recognising that in several there is substantial heterogeneity on other criteria, such as religion, which may also influence occupational attainment. Typically, ethnicity and religion are not analysed together. Chapter 8 seeks to remedy these deficiencies. Chapter 9 discusses the research findings on the educational aspirations and experiences of a range of young British Pakistani men and women. It introduces the concept of 'ethnic capital' to explain why the working class amongst these groups seems to be more committed to finishing school education and going on to higher education than is generally true of working-class young people. The analysis also draws out the differences between the most and least educationally successful respondents and suggests the ways in which ethnicity intersects with gender, class, religiosity and place to produce differences in opportunity and experience.

Most western societies now, in both symbolic and material terms, are becoming accommodative of cultural 'difference'. The longer-standing theme of racial equality and universal human rights has been joined by a politics of (cultural) recognition, as some of the new citizens argue citizenship rights do not solve problems of cultural difference. At the same time, especially since about 9/11, there is a sense that Muslims are not integrating and will be more difficult to integrate than other groups. Chapters 10 and 11 look at aspects of this backlash against multiculturalism and new discourses of British national identity. Chapter 10 examines what senior politicians in the Labour and Conservative parties said about Muslims and British national identity and also offers an analysis of media discourses in relation to a specific national controversy focused on the wearing of the face veil by some Muslim women. Chapter 11 seeks to uncover orientations to the nation, disclosed in general talk amongst the ethnic majority about 'the country'. It uses the concept of 'resentment', a broadly detected sense of loss of entitlement among some of the majority population, to highlight that the evolution of a post-immigration multicultural Britishness is unlikely without specifically attending to the sense of grievance amongst a significant section of the white majority population.

We hope that the evidence presented in the book will go some way towards a more informed debate of migration and citizenship issues and away from the strident shouting across barricades that characterises much of the public discourse.

References

Birrell, R., Hawthorne, L. and Richardson, S. (2006) *Evaluation of the General Skilled Migration Categories*. Canberra: Department of Immigration and Multicultural Affairs, Commonwealth of Australia.

Coleman, D. and Salt, J. (1992) *The British Population: Demographic Patterns, Trends and Processes*. Oxford: Oxford University Press.

Daniel, W.W. (1968) *Racial Discrimination in England*. London: Penguin.

Gott, C. and Johnston, K. (2002) *The Migrant Population in the UK: Fiscal Effects*. RDS Occasional Paper 77. London: Home Office.

Jones, T. (1993) *Britain's Ethnic Minorities*. London: Policy Studies Institute.

Koser, K. and Salt, J. (1997) 'The Geography of Highly Skilled International Migration', *International Journal of Population Geography*, 3: 285–303.

Massey, D.S., Arango, J., Hugo, G., Kouaouci, A., Pellegrino, A. and Taylor, J.E. (2005) *Worlds in Motion. Understanding International Migration at the End of the Millennium*. Oxford: Oxford University Press.

McLaughlan, G. and Salt, J. (2002) *Migration Policies Towards Highly Skilled Foreign Workers, Home Office*, 156pp. London.

Modood, T. (1993) 'Muslim Views on Religious Identity and Racial Equality', *New Community*, 19(3): 513–519.

Modood, T. (2005) *Multicultural Politics: Racism, Ethnicity and Muslims in Britain*. University of Minnesota Press and University of Edinburgh Press.

Modood, T., Berthoud, R., Lakey, J., Nazroo, J., Smith, P., Virdee S. and Beishon S. (1997) *Ethnic Minorities in Britain: Diversity and Disadvantage*. London: Policy Studies Institute.

Modood, T., Berthoud, R. and Nazroo, J. (2002) '"Race", Racism and Ethnicity: A Response to Ken Smith', *Sociology*, 36(2): 419–427.

National Equality Panel (NEP) (2010) *An Anatomy of Economic Inequality in the UK* (Chaired by Professor John Hills). London: Government Equalities Office.

Nairn, T. (1977) *The Breakup of Britain; Crisis and Neo-nationalism*. London: New Left Books.

OECD (2002) *International Migration of the Highly Skilled*. Paris: Organization for Economic Cooperation and Development.

OECD (2008) *International Migration Outlook*. Paris: Organization for Economic Cooperation and Development.

OECD (2010) *International Migration Outlook*. Paris: Organization for Economic Cooperation and Development.

Smith, D.J. (1977) *Racial Disadvantage in Britain*. London: Penguin.

2
Migration To and From the UK

John Salt

1. Introduction

The Leverhulme research programme has coincided with interesting, even unprecedented, times for the British international migration scene. The period witnessed the highest ever annual net migration gain (245,000 in 2004), coming on top of a run of large net gains that have put migration in pole position as the leading component of national population change. Opening up the labour market to citizens of the new member states of the European Union (EU) from May 2004 initiated what is almost certainly the largest ever single wave of immigration (with Poles the largest ever single national group of entrants) that the British Isles have ever experienced. Furthermore, the Home Office launched the single biggest change in migration policy of recent times, a points-based management strategy for economic migration, which came into operation from 2008.

The purpose of this chapter is to provide a statistical context for the research projects reported upon in the ensuing text. Although it presents some historical data, it does not attempt to rehearse the story of immigration into the UK, most of which occurred in modern times from the middle of the twentieth century. Indeed, the bookshelves are replete with texts which document the patterns of international migration since the Second World War which 'have brought a whole new society, politics and vocabulary to the UK' (Coleman and Salt, 1992: 433). Nor does it attempt to review the policy developments of the last 10–15 years, or the various assessments of fiscal and labour market effects of migration flows (see, e.g., Glover et al., 2001; Gott and Johnston, 2002; Coleman and Rowthorne, 2004; Lilley, 2005; Sriskandarajah, Cooley and Reed, 2005; Dustmann, Glitz and Frattini, 2008; House of Lords, 2008; Lemos and Portes, 2008).

The chapter uses a range of data sources to present a wide-ranging picture of recent trends in migrant flows and stocks. Particular attention is paid to estimating the scale and nature of flows, with a focus on the different movement streams that compose the overall pattern. Aggregate migration statistics cover a multitude of rationales and processes behind a set of diverse movements that are the product of different processes and circumstances. For example, the right of a migrant to family reunion is commonly accepted as a basic human right and this facilitates the flow of spouses and children. Overseas student recruitment is usually left to educational institutions which are bound by no specific limits on numbers beyond the purely local and work on the basis of attracting as many fee payers as possible. In contrast, the movement of seasonal or low-skilled workers is often managed by state-imposed quotas such as those in the agriculture, hospitality and food-processing industries. Highly skilled migrants come by other routes, such as corporate assignments and may have to comply with the rules and regulations of professional organisations. Quite different circumstances surround retirement migration, where moves are usually personal decisions, tempered by social security and pension arrangements. In short, migration flows are extremely varied. People come for different reasons, stay for different periods and fulfil different roles. Simultaneously, thousands of people each year return to their country of origin or migrate elsewhere. UK nationals are part of the movement in both directions. Although some important advances have been made in devising better data on international migration, the picture remains incomplete (UK Statistics Authority, 2009).

The chapter is focused on identifying and quantifying the broad trends over the last 10–15 years in the main routes of entry and on the resultant migrant stock. The emphasis is on immigration, for which there are vastly more data, although the significance of emigration is also recognised. The account is not exhaustive and its selectivity reflects the themes developed in the later chapters, particularly in the emphasis on labour migration. It draws on various official statistical sources and it is recognised that the picture they present is incomplete. Where there are different data sources on the same subject, for example, in the measurement of labour flows, it is impossible to achieve definitive results. Indeed, it is best to regard most migration statistics as estimates, especially when they come from sample surveys like the International Passenger Survey (IPS) and the Labour Force Survey (LFS). The chapter begins with a review of the main flows, followed by a summary of the main characteristics of the migrant stock.

2. Flows of migrants to and from the UK

The only source of both immigration and emigration data is the IPS, a sample survey of passengers arriving at and departing from UK air and sea ports and the Channel Tunnel. Immigrants and emigrants are defined as those intending to stay in the UK or be away from there for a year or more, having lived out of the UK (for immigrants) or in the UK (for emigrants) for a year or more. Other data sources give estimates of immigration but not emigration.

2.1. How many people enter and leave the UK?

Table 2.1 uses unadjusted IPS data to show the main long-term trends, with flows aggregated at five-year intervals, except for 2005–08, to smooth over annual variations. The data illustrate the high turnover of population. Since 1975, 9.8 million people entered the UK and 8.3 million left. There was a net loss of 1.7 million British and a net gain of 3.2 million non-British. However, there has been a marked shift in trend, from substantial net losses overall in 1975–84 to even larger net gains since 2000. Annual average gains of non-British people during 1975–94 were relatively stable, since when they have risen dramatically to over a quarter of a million since 2005. In contrast, net losses of British people were high between 1975 and 1984, fell to a relatively low level for the next 15 years and then rose after 2000. Since the beginning of the millennium, total net migration has been positive and of a much higher order than in the preceding century. Hence, during the period of our research programme, migration flows have been historically very high and might in some measure justify the epithet 'mass migration'.

The Office for National Statistics (ONS) suggests that the overall totals derived from the IPS should be adjusted to provide a more accurate estimate.

Table 2.1 International migration flows, 1975–2008, thousands

All				British			Non-British		
	In	Out	Net	In	Out	Net	In	Out	Net
1975–79	932	1037	−105	396	701	−306	535	336	200
1980–84	930	1065	−136	415	724	−308	516	342	171
1985–89	1159	1038	120	521	635	−114	638	402	235
1990–94	1176	1133	42	507	654	−148	669	478	191
1995–99	1441	1104	336	491	629	−140	952	475	475
2000–04	2062	1457	606	487	792	−303	1574	665	909
2005–08	2090	1424	666	321	695	−374	1768	728	1039
Annual average				**British**			**Non-British**		
	In	Out	Net	In	Out	Net	In	Out	Net
1975–79	186	207	−21	79	140	−61	107	67	40
1980–84	186	213	−27	83	145	−62	103	68	34
1985–89	232	208	24	104	127	−23	128	80	47
1990–94	235	227	8	101	131	−30	134	96	38
1995–99	288	221	67	98	126	−28	190	95	95
2000–04	412	291	121	97	158	−61	315	133	182
2005–08	523	356	167	80	174	−94	442	182	260

Source: IPS.

IPS data are based on stated intention on entering and leaving the country and so it is likely that they exclude most people seeking asylum and dependants of asylum seekers. An adjustment is made for these. Further adjustments are made for other people who intend to be migrants but who in reality stay in the UK or abroad for less than a year and for those who state an initial intention to stay for more than a year but actually leave before this. These adjustments are used to produce Long-Term International Migration (LTIM) statistics. However, it is not possible to provide breakdowns by migrant characteristics using LTIM data, so Section 2.2 is based on IPS unadjusted statistics.

In the past, IPS data have not covered routes between the Irish Republic and the UK but estimates were made of movement between the two countries using Irish data. In 2008 the ONS stopped using Irish data and now uses the IPS for estimating migration between the UK and the Republic of Ireland. At the same time ONS has started to use data from the Northern Ireland Statistics and Research Agency (NISRA) to estimate international migration between Northern Ireland and the rest of the world. This is to ensure that the estimates of international migration are the same as those NISRA uses for its population estimates.

The picture since the early 1990s is presented in Figures 2.1–2.4. Total in- and outflows have both generally risen, with minor fluctuations, the

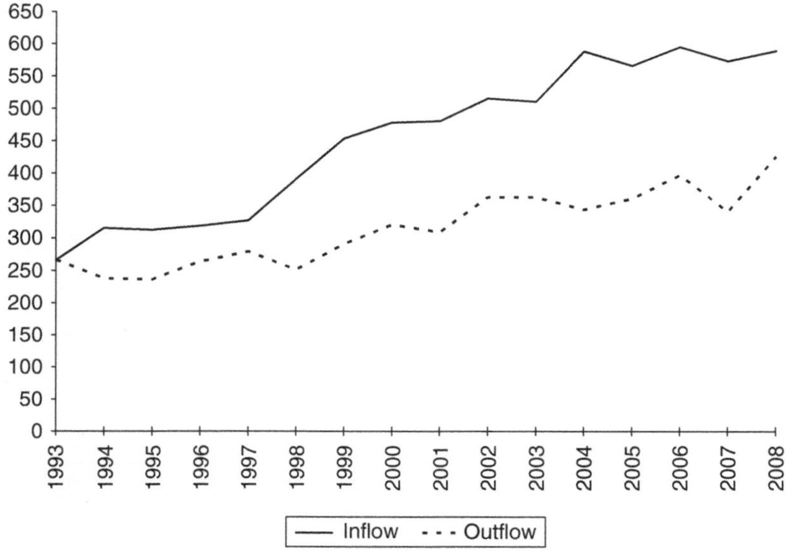

Figure 2.1 Long-term international migration, total in- and outflows, 1993–2008, thousands
Source: IPS, ONS.

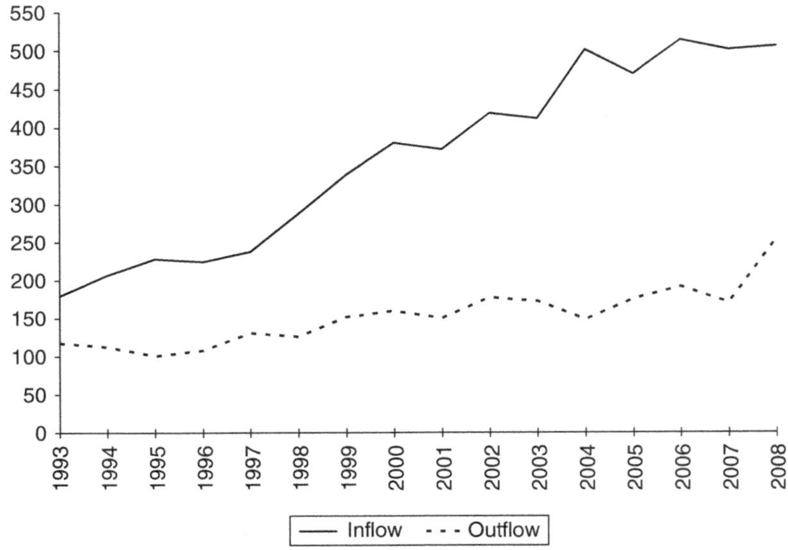

Figure 2.2 Long-term international migration, non-British citizens in- and outflows, 1993–2008, thousands
Source: IPS, ONS.

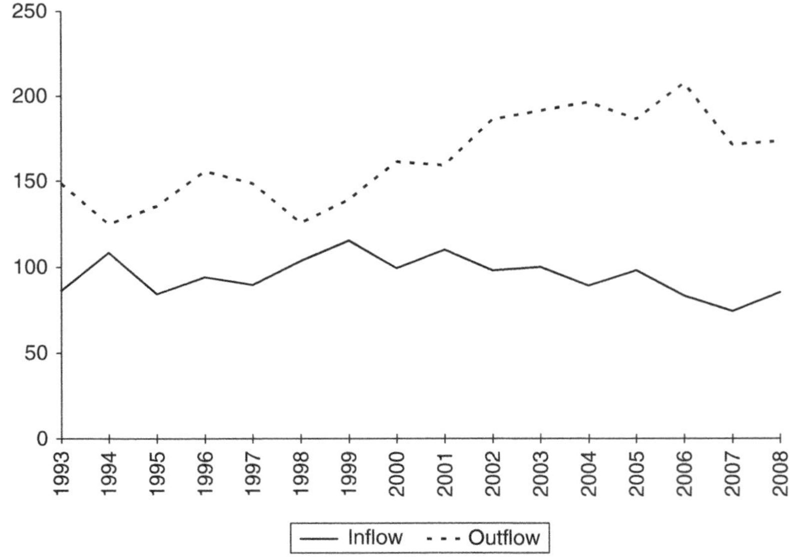

Figure 2.3 Long-term international migration, gross flows by citizenship, 1993–2008, thousands
Source: IPS, ONS.

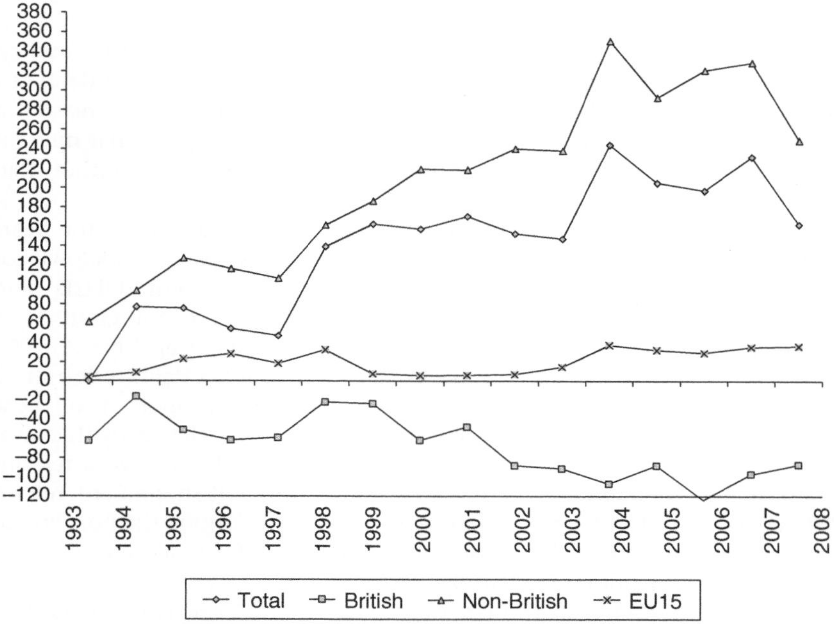

Figure 2.4 Long-term international migration, net flows by citizenship, 1993–2008, thousands
Source: IPS, ONS.

difference between them tending to increase until the last year (Figure 2.1). The number of non-British coming to the UK has also risen, although in four years since 2000 it fell. The number of non-British leaving has also tended to rise, although much less steeply until the last year (Figure 2.2). Fluctuations in flows of non-British do not always synchronise: both inflows and outflows fell in 2000–01, 2002–03 and 2006–07, but in 2004–05 inflows fell while outflows rose and in 2007–08 both flows rose. The size of flows for the British population is less than that for the non-British (Figure 2.3). Inflow has tended to fluctuate around the 100,000 mark for most of the period, dipping in the last three years. The main trend of British outflow has been upward for most of the period, falling back in the last couple of years. The net result of these trends is in Figure 2.4. Fluctuating total net gains have tended generally to mirror those of the non-British population, although during the present decade the behaviour of the British population has increased in importance as net losses among this group have increased. It is important to recognise that the overall flow pattern for the UK is thus a product of two sets of inflows and two of outflows and that a marked change in any of them affects the overall picture from year to year.

2.2. Why do people migrate to and from the UK?

The IPS asks a question on the reason for moving in or out of the country. Since it is not possible to identify reasons for moving from LTIM data, raw IPS figures are used. Because the survey asks only for the priority reason, it provides only a partial picture of the motivations of any particular migrant stream defined. Hence, the data should be taken as indicative rather than definitive.

Figure 2.5 shows the reasons for international migration for the years 2004–08 for British and non-British people. There is also a breakdown for Organization for Economic Cooperation and Development (OECD) and non-OECD countries, to provide a rough distinction between migrants from richer and poorer countries (Figure 2.6). In 2008, for all citizenships, 207,000 said their main reason for coming to the UK was for a definite job or to look for work, 38.5 per cent of all entrants. A higher proportion of those leaving, 53.3 per cent, did so primarily for work reasons. Hence, by this measure a smaller proportion of immigrants came to the UK for work reasons than that of emigrants leaving for work. Among the British, half entered for work reasons and 54.8 per cent left for work reasons. Among the non-British 38 per cent said their main reason for coming was for work and a similar proportion came primarily to study.

Reasons for coming to the UK vary between OECD (excluding the UK) and non-OECD area citizens. Whereas 47.8 per cent of OECD citizens came for work reasons in 2008, only 26.3 per cent of non-OECD citizens did so. In contrast, only 21.5 per cent of those from OECD states came primarily to study, compared with 48.6 of non-OECD citizens. The latter were much more

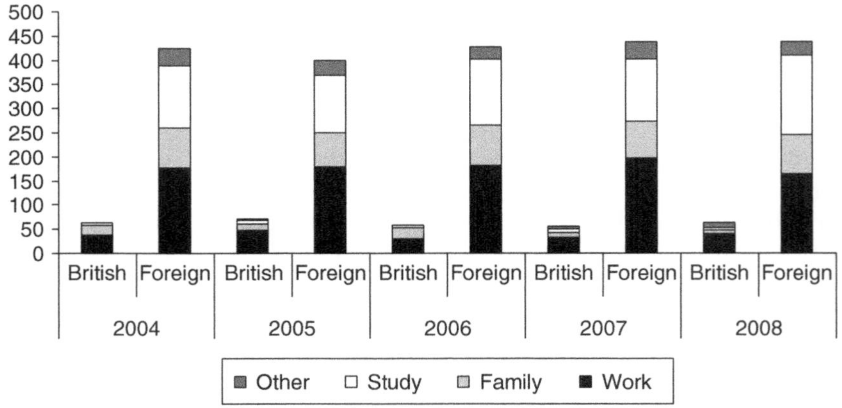

Figure 2.5 International migration: inflows of British and foreigners, by reason for visit, 2004–08, thousands
Source: IPS.

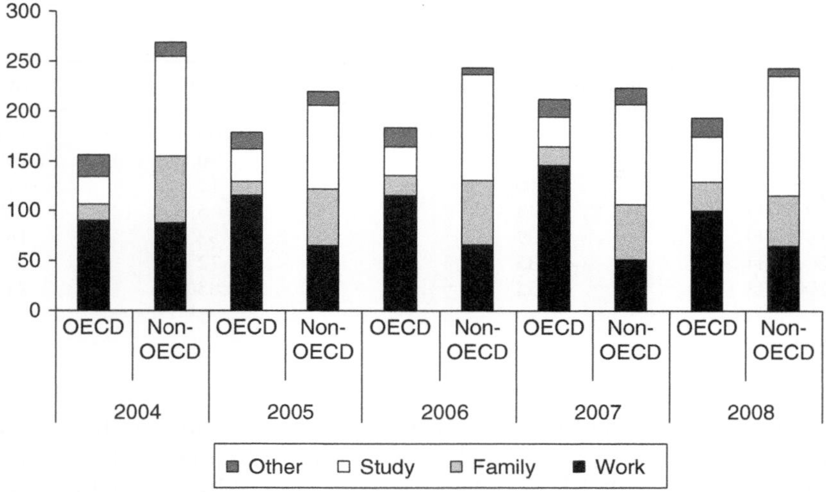

Figure 2.6 International migration: inflows of OECD (excluding UK) and non-OECD citizens by reason for visit, 2004–08, thousands
Source: IPS.

likely than the former to come primarily as family members accompanying or joining someone else. In general, those from richer (OECD) countries say they are predominantly work motivated, though more are now coming for study, while those from elsewhere are more likely to express study or family reasons for coming to the UK.

2.3. What is the scale and rationale for short-term movement?

A major shortfall in UK migration data has been the lack of information on short-term movement. The definition of migration traditionally used in British statistics has been that of the United Nations (UN), based on a stay length of 12 months or more. The ONS has recently produced estimates of numbers of short-term migrants staying in England and Wales or abroad for periods of 3–12 months. On average England and Wales received 324,000 short-term immigrants during the period mid-2004 to mid-2007, sent 413,000, giving a net balance of –89,000. Employment and study each accounted for around a quarter of the inflow, but employment was a more important cause of outflow.

2.4. What does the IPS tell us about labour migration?

A better measurement of the scale of labour migration than data on reason for movement is occupation prior to moving, since it records whether or not a person was in the labour market at that time. In 2008, 58 per cent of

Table 2.2 Net international migration, 1975–2008, by occupational group, thousands

	Professional and managerial	Manual and clerical	Total
1975–79	−68	−103	−171
1980–84	−53	−96	−149
1985–89	10	−12	−23
1990–94	13	5	19
1995–99	109	53	161
2000–04	185	72	257
2005–08	155	83	238

Source: IPS.

the inflow and 73.6 of the outflow were people who had been in employment prior to entry or leaving. This again implies that more of the inflow was coming into the UK to work, not having worked before entering, than was the case with the outflow. It is consistent with the tendency for young people to come for training or to learn English, gain employment and then leave.

The IPS breaks down migrants occupationally into two categories: (a) professional and managerial and (b) manual and clerical. Professional and managerial workers have traditionally accounted for the majority of gainfully employed migrants. Table 2.2 provides a long-term view of the net flows of each. During the period 1975–84 the UK experienced a net loss of professional and managerial workers which was subsequently turned into a substantial net gain. There was a similar pattern for manual and clerical workers.

Trends in numbers of British and non-British differed. Overall, in 2008 the country lost 39,000 highly skilled British workers and gained 79,000 non-British. In the same year, there was a net loss of 33,000 British manual and clerical workers, a net gain of 5000 non-British and an overall net loss of 29,000.

Thus, since the late 1990s the UK has seen rising inflows of non-British more than compensating for rising outflows of the domestic population. However, there seems to have been a shift in the balance between the two skill levels. In 1999 professional and managerial workers accounted for 82 per cent of the net gain of non-British workers, but by 2007 this proportion had fallen to 62 per cent. In 2008 there was another major change as the balance of manual and clerical workers fell into deficit. This may be explained largely by the emigration of A8 citizens who were performing low-skilled jobs. Overall, a gross (in- and out-) flow of 613,000 by both British and non-British led in 2008 to a net increase of only 11,000 on the IPS definition, a migration efficiency of less than 2 per cent.

2.5. Managing labour immigration: the work permit system

The main source of entry to the labour market over which the government exercises a large measure of control is the work permit system which became Tier 2 of the new points-based managed migration system (PBS) in November 2008. The work permit system was designed to bring in skilled workers in short supply from non-European Economic Area (EEA) countries. Employers must first have carried out a resident labour market test to ensure there were no suitable applicants in the EEA. Figure 2.7 shows how the four main elements of the system have evolved since 1995. Numbers of permits approved rose sharply until the early 2000s, since when there has been a levelling off with minor fluctuations. Amongst the categories of applications, work permits and first permissions are of particular interest as they were sought for foreign workers newly entering the labour market and can be used as an indicator of international labour migration from countries outside the EEA. Their numbers rose from about 24,000 in 1995 to peak at 96,740 in 2006, falling in the next two years to 77,660 in 2008. Although a permit is granted for a defined period, there are no statistics on how long permit-holders actually stay in the UK.

Figure 2.8 shows a breakdown of work permits and first permissions approvals for the main industry groups using the system since 1995. Just a few industries account for most issues with the dominance of computer

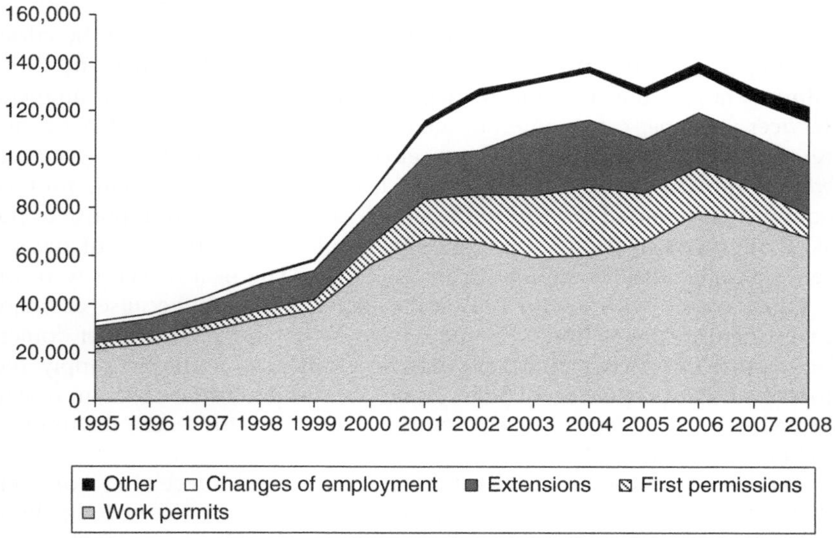

Figure 2.7 Work permit applications approved by type, 1995–2008
Source: UK Border Agency.

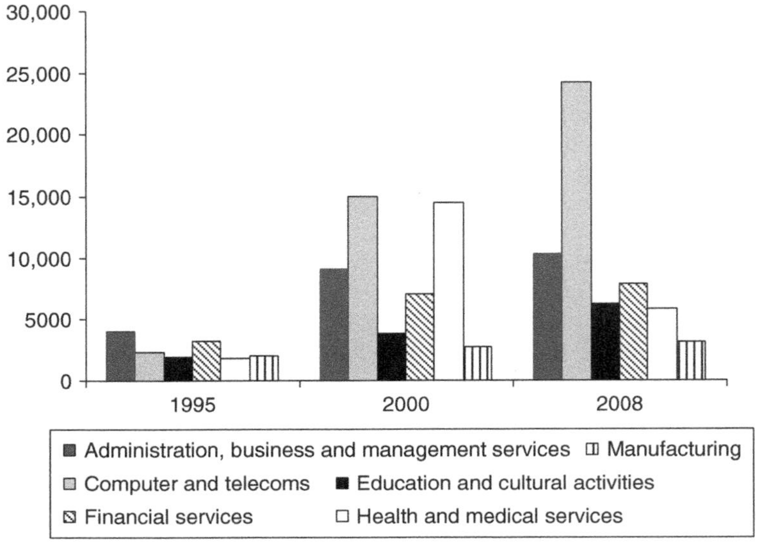

Figure 2.8 Work permits and first permissions approved by industry for 1995, 2000 and 2008
Source: UK Border Agency.

services now unchallenged, with 27.9 per cent of the total. Permits for health and medical staff have moved decisively in the opposite direction. A comparison with 1995 and 2000 shows substantial change. In 1995, administration, business and managerial services (16.7 per cent), financial services (13.2 per cent), entertainment and leisure services (12.1 per cent), retail and related services (11.7 per cent) and manufacturing (8.2 per cent) were dominant. There followed a shift from the traditional domination of commercial-oriented services to the health and IT sectors in response to the skills shortages in the UK over the last decade and, in the case of the latter especially, cheaper supplies from elsewhere. The health sector went on a roller-coaster, with a very substantial increase initially because of major investment in the National Health Service (NHS) and a shortage of domestic supply. Overseas recruitment has now fallen as domestic supply has increased. The proportion in financial services declined after 1995 but rose in more recent years. Given the economic downturn in this sector, the number held up relatively well in 2008.

There has also been a shift in the major nationalities receiving work permits (Figure 2.9). The most striking change has been the rise of India, both absolutely and relatively, to over 40 per cent of all issues in 2008. Numbers from the Philippines and South Africa rose sharply until 2001–02 when recruitment of nurses was at its height, since when they have fallen back.

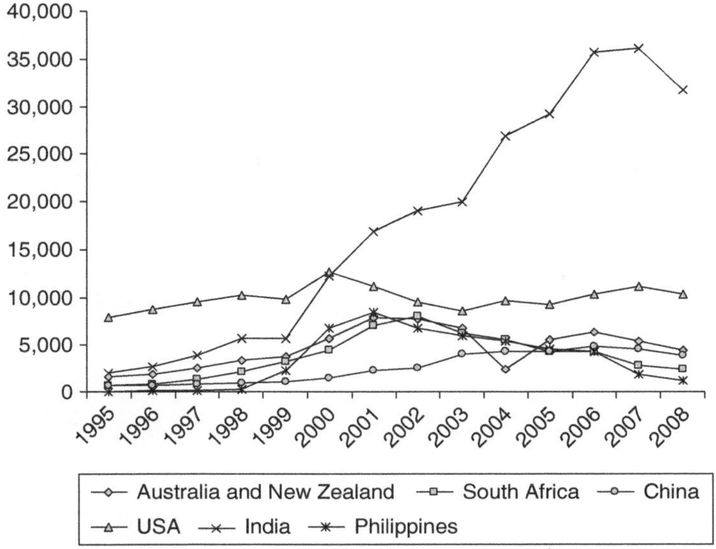

Figure 2.9 Work permits and first permissions issued in the UK by nationality, 1995–2008
Source: UK Border Agency.

In contrast, although numbers from the USA have risen overall, their proportion of the total has dropped steadily. Numbers from all countries depicted fell between 2007 and 2008.

2.6. Managing labour migration: National Insurance statistics

An alternative source of data on the number of foreign nationals newly entering the UK labour force comes from the allocation of National Insurance Numbers (NINos). Every foreign worker who is legally employed requires a NINo so the allocation of new numbers should give an indication of the annual (year running April–March) increment to the workforce. Comparisons of NINo data with those of other flow sources demonstrate the difficulty of putting together an accurate picture of labour migration into the UK. NINo data take no account of the length of time an individual allocated a number spends working in the UK and so they may include equally people who work for 1 week in the year with those working 52. Overall, they probably present a fuller picture of the overall foreign increment to the UK workforce than any other single source but should be used only with appropriate caveats. For example, the temporary nature of many of the A8 migrants may lead to difficulties when comparing recent increments to the workforce with past years. The data in Table 2.3 relate to year of registration,

Table 2.3 Overseas nationals entering the UK and allocated a National Insurance Number (NINo), thousands

(a) By year of registration and continent of origin

	2002–03	2003–04	2004–05	2005–06	2006–07	2007–08	2008–09
All	**346.2**	**373.5**	**435.4**	**663.1**	**705.8**	**733.1**	**686.1**
Europe – EU excluding Accession Countries	80.1	85.5	80.7	97.8	102.8	107.5	120.1
Europe – EU Accession Countries	17.7	28.7	116.8	276.7	317.5	332.4	257.0
Europe – non-EU	14.7	15.9	14.0	15.5	16.1	17.2	16.1
Africa	66.0	70.7	64.1	74.0	60.7	59.6	63.3
Asia and Middle East	113.6	116.0	109.4	134.4	143.8	149.9	163.0
The Americas	26.3	31.4	26.5	31.5	31.5	32.6	36.5
Australasia and Oceania	27.1	24.5	23.2	32.5	33.0	33.4	29.5
Others and Unknown	0.8	0.7	0.6	0.6	0.5	0.5	0.5

(b) By year of registration and age

	2002–03	2003–04	2004–05	2005–06	2006–07	2007–08	2008–09
All	**346.2**	**373.5**	**435.4**	**663.1**	**705.8**	**733.1**	**686.1**
<18	4.8	5.2	3.9	5.0	5.9	8.8	9.5
18–24	108.0	116.7	150.7	240.5	264.7	279.9	265.5
25–34	169.2	174.5	203.8	297.4	312.2	307.7	279.6
35–44	47.8	52.4	55.4	79.4	85.3	88.3	82.9
45–54	15.6	17.8	21.1	33.0	37.2	39.3	37.5
55–59	2.8	2.9	3.4	5.1	5.7	6.4	7.2
60+	1.2	1.3	1.5	2.1	2.5	2.7	3.6

(c) Top ten countries each year of registration

2002–03		2003–04		2004–05		2005–06		2006–07		2007–08		2008–09	
India	24.8	India	31.5	Poland	61.1	Poland	171.1	Poland	220.4	Poland	210.7	Poland	134.3
Australia	18.7	South Africa	18.5	India	32.5	India	45.9	India	48.8	India	49.8	India	59.3
South Africa	18.5	Australia	17.3	Pakistan	20.2	Lithuania	30.9	Slovak Rep.	28.6	Slovak Rep	30.0	Slovak Rep	24.0
Pakistan	16.7	Pakistan	16.8	South Africa	19.2	Slovak Rep.	27.5	Pakistan	25.0	Pakistan	24.8	France	24.0
France	13.7	Portugal	14.1	Australia	16.5	South Africa	24.0	Australia	24.2	Australia	24.1	Romania	23.9
Philippines	11.6	China Peoples Rep.	13.4	Lithuania	15.5	Australia	23.8	Lithuania	23.9	Romania	23.0	Pakistan	23.4
Spain	11.6	France	13.1	France	13.2	Pakistan	22.3	France	20.0	France	21.8	Australia	21.3
Zimbabwe	10.1	Spain	12.0	China Peoples Rep.	12.6	France	17.2	South Africa	16.8	Lithuania	19.0	Italy	18.6
Iraq	10.0	Poland	11.3	Portugal	12.2	Latvia	14.4	Germany	15.1	Germany	15.5	Lithuania	17.6
Portugal	9.6	Philippines	10.9	Slovak Rep.	11.1	Germany	13.4	China Peoples Rep.	13.0	Italy	15.4	Nigeria	17.4

Source: 100 per cent extract from National Insurance Recording System.

not year of arrival in the UK, and so may inflate the number compared with the two survey sources.

In the most recent year, 2008–09, there were 686,000 new registrations. The EU A12 accession countries accounted for 257,000 new registrations, 37.5 per cent of the total.

The vast majority allocated NINos are young, 38.7 per cent of them aged 18–24 and a further 40.8 per cent aged 25–34 (Table 2.3b). There have been some notable shifts in the main nationalities since 2003–04 but in recent years the pattern has been fairly stable (Table 2.3c). Poland, the clear leader in 2008–09 with 19.6 per cent, and India have been the top two each year since 2004–05, while Slovakia has held third place for the last three years. France and Italy are also in the top ten. Outside Europe, the leading origins are Pakistan, Australia and Nigeria.

2.7. Summary of labour immigration by routes of entry

In addition to work permits, there are other routes of entry for foreign workers. These include the free movement provisions of the EU and the 'light touch' management through the Workers Registration Scheme of citizens of the eight Eastern European accession countries (A8) since 2004. In 2008, the total number of labour immigrants coming into the UK through all routes of entry was about 390,000 (Table 2.4). The figures in the table take

Table 2.4 Foreign labour immigration by major routes of entry, 1999 and 2008

	1999		2008	
	Number	**Per cent**	**Number**	**Per cent**
WRS[a]	–	–	158,340	40.6
Work Permits[b]	55,494	30.2	77,660	19.9
EU15&EFTA[c]	30,000	16.3	49,000	12.6
Working Holiday Makers[d]	45,800	25.0	32,725	8.4
HSMP[b]	–	–	17,760	4.6
SAWS[b]	9,760	5.3	16,594	4.3
Domestic Servants[e]	14,900	8.1	11,500	3.0
UK Ancestry[e]	11,900	6.5	6,690	1.7
SBS[b]	–	–	1,570	0.4
IGS[a]	–	–	16,171	4.2
Au Pairs[e]	14,600	8.0	865	0.2
Ministers of Religion[e]	1,050	0.6	655	0.2
Total	183,504	100.0	389,530	100.0

Note: WRS – Worker Registration Scheme; WP – Work Permits; WHM – Working Holiday Makers; HSMP – Highly Skilled Migrant Programme; SAWS – Seasonal Agricultural Workers Scheme; SBS – Sectors Based Scheme; IGS – International Graduate Scheme; EU – European Union; EFTA – European Free Trade Agreement.

Source: [a] Home Office; [b] Work Permits (UK), UK Border Agency; [c] IPS; [d] UK Visas; [e] Inland Revenue and Social Security.

no account of duration of employment, so they will include an unknown number of short-term migrants. They also exclude an unknown number of self-employed people from the A8 states. Overall, however, they provide the best available estimate of total labour immigration into the UK. Even so, the number is below the 686,000 National Insurance Number allocations for foreign citizens in 2008–09.

2.8. Family migration

There is no simple way of estimating family related migration into the UK. Estimates based on IPS reasons for moving can provide only part of the answer, as indicated above.

For the most part, administrative data on those granted settlement are used to estimate the scale of family immigration. The number of family members granted settlement has fluctuated in recent years, from 66,000 in 1999 to 102,685 in 2008 when they accounted for 69 per cent of all settlement (Figure 2.10). A substantial proportion of these were already in the country and the number includes grants to dependants of persons granted settlement in their own right (e.g., employment- and asylum-related dependants) as well as those on the basis of family formation and reunion. Until 2003, wives were the largest group but since then children have taken their place; numbers of husbands have generally risen but those of

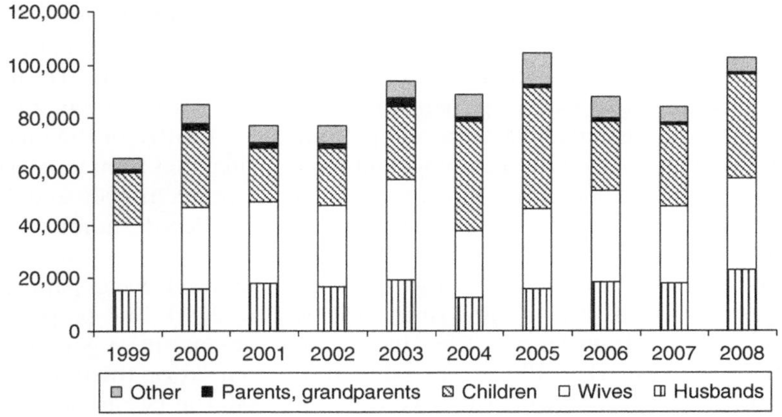

Figure 2.10 Family migration, 1999–2008

Notes:

1. Includes reconsideration cases and the outcome of appeals.
2. In 2002 includes nationals of the Czech Republic, Cyprus, Estonia, Hungary, Latvia, Lithuania, Malta, Poland, Slovakia and Slovenia before 1 May, but excludes them from this date.
3. From 2007 excludes Bulgaria and Romania.
4. In Other category data from 1999–2002 include husbands, wives and children of port asylum seekers given indefinite leave to remain.

Source: Home Office.

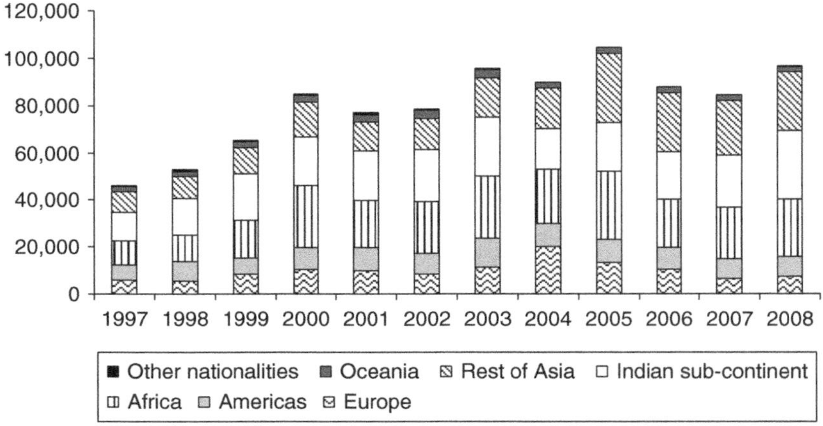

Figure 2.11 Spouses and dependants granted settlement, 1997–2008
Source: Home Office.

grandparents have tended to fall in the last few years. Grants of settlement on the basis only of family formation and reunion in 2008 were 55,325.

Acceptances for settlement are frequently used as an indicator of permanent immigration. In the long term, numbers have fluctuated with broadly three phases. Between the early 1960s and late 1970s, acceptances were relatively high, commonly in the 60,000–80,000 range. From the early 1980s to the mid-1990s, numbers dipped to below 60,000 in most years, the trough coinciding with the period of Conservative government. From the late 1990s they rose steeply, peaking in 2005. In most cases, particular peaks were for administrative reasons: examples include a change in the qualifying period for settlement in employment-related categories from four to five years in April 2006 which affected the number of grants in 2006 and 2007 or attempts to clear backlogs. During much of the last decade, numbers have run at about double those two decades earlier.

The increase in acceptances for settlement has been accompanied by a geographical shift in origins since 1997 (Figure 2.11). The proportions of acceptances from Europe, the Americas and Oceania have gone down, collectively from 31 to 18 per cent, while those from Africa, the Indian subcontinent ISC and Rest of Asia have risen. In 2008, the ISC accounted for 30 per cent and Africa and the Rest of Asia about a quarter each.

2.9. Immigration by students

The internationalisation of education has led to substantial numbers of young people moving between countries in order to improve qualifications and enhance career prospects (Chapter 7). In fact, they form a disparate group which includes those coming for secondary and tertiary education

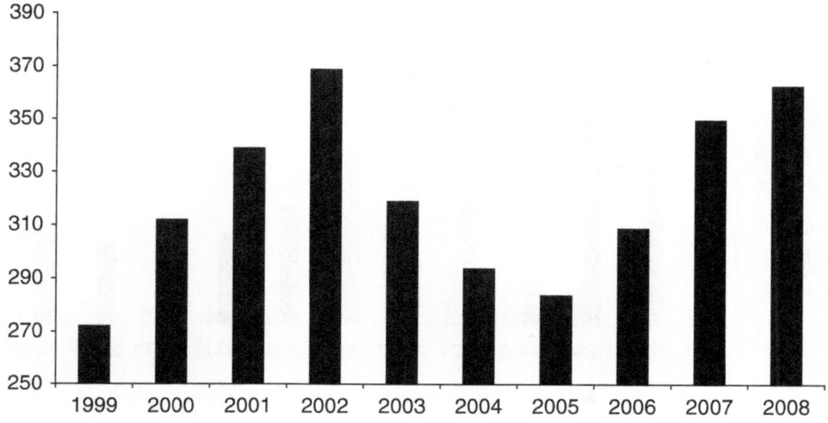

Figure 2.12 Students given leave to enter the UK, 1999–2008, thousands
Source: Home Office.

and for a range of vocational courses including language instruction. Statistics which break down this totality into its component parts do not exist.

Data exist for first-year enrolments by non-UK domiciled students from the Higher Education Statistics Agency. For academic year 2008–09 the total for postgraduates and undergraduates doing either full- or part-time courses was 205,000. Some of these would be living in the UK, although not domiciled there. Even so, this figure is considerably less than student entries measured by the UK Border Agency (UKBA). In 2008, 363,000 students were given leave to enter the UK, almost as many as in the peak year of 2002 (Figure 2.12). After a fall in the mid years of the decade, the last three years have seen a rising trend. From 2010, student entry is governed by the points-based system (Tier 4).

2.10. Trends in numbers of asylum seekers

The number of asylum seekers has fluctuated dramatically since the late 1990s (Figure 2.13), from around 30,000 to a peak of over 80,000 in 2002 and then back to about 26,000 in 2008. Including dependants, the number of asylum applications was 31,300 in 2008. Most applications are made in-country (i.e., by persons who had already entered the UK, rather than applications at port), 90 per cent in 2008. Africans constituted the largest group (40 per cent of all applications, excluding dependants, in 2008); 37 per cent were from Asia and Oceania, 19 per cent from the Middle East. The number of positive decisions (granted full asylum or humanitarian status) shows a similar pattern to that of applications, but they constitute a minority of total decisions: in 2008, 70 per cent were refusals.

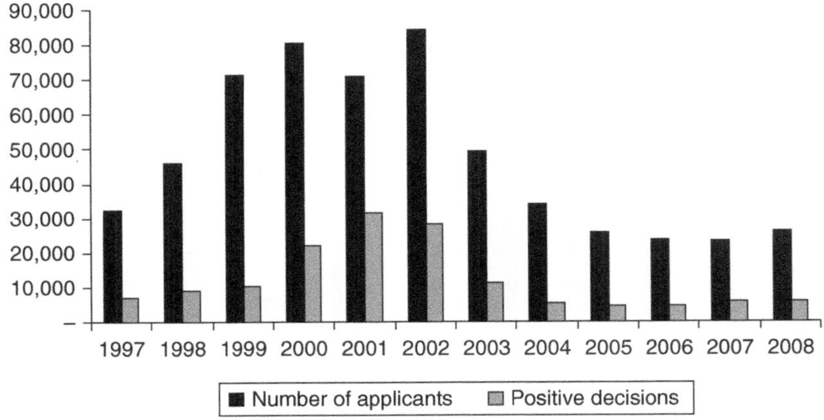

Figure 2.13 Asylum applications and positive decisions in the UK, excluding dependants, 1997–2008
Source: UK Border Agency.

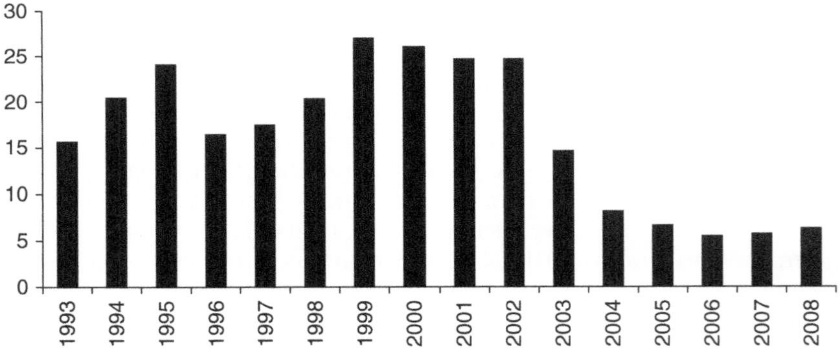

Figure 2.14 Asylum applications (including dependants) as a proportion of total non-British immigration into the UK, 1993–2008
Source: UK Border Agency.

Figure 2.14 relates the scale of asylum seeking (including dependants) to total adjusted immigration by the non-British for the period 1993–2008 in the form of a ratio of the two. During 1999–2002 the ratio was around 25 per cent but it fell sharply thereafter to 6.2 per cent in 2008 due to a combination of falling asylum applications and rising immigration flows.

3. Stock of foreign population

The LFS is the only source of data on the nationality of the foreign population and workforce in the UK. The survey includes all UK and foreign citizens, but the relatively small size of the sample (broadly speaking, one sample interviewee is weighted up to 300 people in total) means that disaggregation by nationality and migrant characteristics cannot be detailed. Partly for this reason, LFS data on international migration are not regularly published. Annual fluctuations may reflect sampling errors.

Because the results of the 2001 census indicated a total population over 900,000 fewer than anticipated from the annual population estimates, the ONS decided to regross the LFS to meet the new census population figure. This resulted in a reduction in the total LFS population for 2004 compared with that for 2003 of over a million people. In order to obtain a time series, ONS regrossed the LFS figures back over the last decade.

The data presented here refer to the spring quarter of each year. Those on foreigners in employment exclude armed forces and unpaid family workers.

3.1. How many foreign citizens are there in the UK?

During the period 1992–97 stocks of foreign nationals in the UK fluctuated around the 2 million mark, then rose with each succeeding year to reach 4.363 million in 2009 (Figure 2.15) when they accounted for 7.2 per cent of the total UK population, compared with 7 per cent in 2008 and 4.5 per cent in 2002. Europe was the largest source of foreign residents, topping 2 million (2.053) for the first time, 47.1 per cent of the total. Around

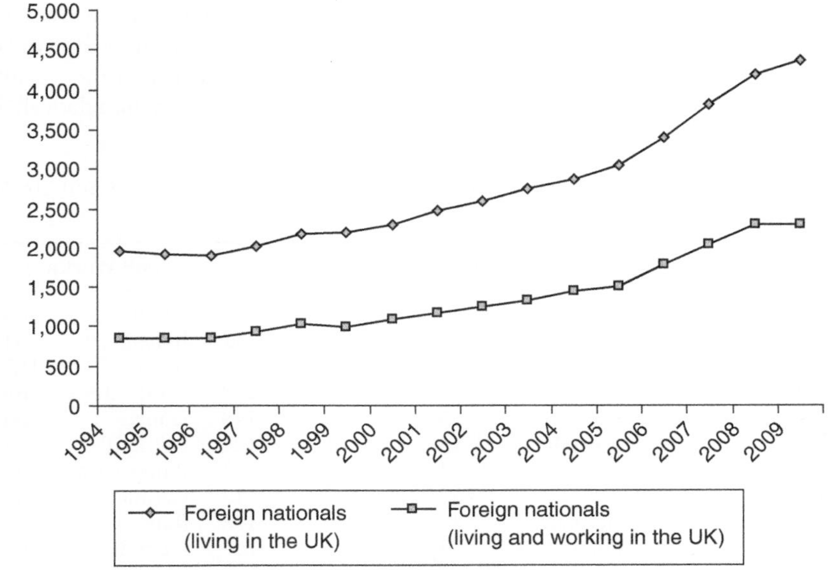

Figure 2.15 Foreign nationals, 1994–2009, thousands
Source: LFS.

a quarter of foreign citizens were from the EU (15)/EFTA (European Free Trade Association) states; citizens of the ten new Eastern European accession countries as a whole now account for 19 per cent of all foreigners. The dominance of the Irish has been waning for some time but in 2007, for the first time, they were no longer the largest national group when Poland took that position. Numbers of foreign nationals working in the UK fluctuated until 1996, after which they rose strongly, to top a million for the first time in 1998 (3.9 per cent of the total in employment), continuing this trend in subsequent years. By 2009, there were 2.293 million, 8 per cent of the total in employment.

Table 2.5 shows the top ten national groups living and also living and working in the UK in 2003 and 2009. The long-standing domination of Ireland has been replaced by Poland, both in the home and workplace, while India holds third place. The French, Germans and Italians remain significant groups but Americans have become less so.

3.2. What is the foreign population by country of birth?

The successive arrival in the UK of the different immigrant groups is summarised in Table 2.6. About half of those people born in the Irish Republic and a similar proportion of those from other European countries outside the then European Community (principally Poland) had entered the UK by the mid-1950s. In contrast, of those people born in the New Commonwealth and Pakistan (NCWP) who stated their year of entry, only 10 per cent – mostly white people born in the Mediterranean Commonwealth or India – entered before 1955. The majority of those born in the West Indies came into the UK between the mid-1950s and mid-1960s and the corresponding peak for people born in India came in the late 1960s and early 1970s. Bangladeshis

Table 2.5 Living and working in the UK, by citizenship and sex, 2003 and 2009, thousands

2003 Living		2003 Working		2009 Living		2009 Working	
Ireland	367	Ireland	179	Poland	546	Poland	369
India	154	India	82	Ireland	342	Ireland	163
USA	120	South Africa	67	India	293	India	152
France	102	USA	62	Pakistan	178	South Africa	85
South Africa	95	France	59	France	148	France	80
Italy	91	Australia	55	Germany	121	Pakistan	68
Portugal	88	Italy	53	South Africa	113	Philippines	63
Pakistan	83	Portugal	52	USA	113	Germany	62
Australia	73	Germany	39	Nigeria	108	Italy	62
Germany	70	Philippines	34	Italy	107	Australia	62

Source: LFS.

Table 2.6 Persons born outside the UK, by year of entry and country of birth, pre-1955–84, thousands

Country of birth	Pre-1955		1955–64		1965–74		1975–84		No reply		Total
	Number	%	Number	%	Number	%	Number	%	Number	%	Entrants
Irish Republic	243	44.7	136	25.0	61	11.2	27	5.0	76	14.0	544
Old Commonwealth	32	25.6	15	12.0	27	21.6	46	36.8	5	4.0	125
New Commonwealth and Pakistan	147	10.5	379	27.1	509	36.4	288	20.6	77	5.5	1,400
East African CW	6	3.1	16	8.3	113	58.9	49	25.5	9	4.7	192
Rest of African CW	7	9.3	9	12.0	22	29.3	30	40.0	7	9.3	75
Caribbean CW	18	7.4	146	60.3	52	21.5	8	3.3	18	7.4	242
India	61	16.0	87	22.8	148	38.7	64	16.8	23	6.0	382
Bangladesh	0	0.0	5	13.2	10	26.3	20	52.6	2	5.3	38
Far East CW	10	8.5	23	19.5	44	37.3	38	32.2	3	2.5	118
Mediterranean CW	33	29.5	40	35.7	30	26.8	7	6.3	3	2.7	112
Remainder of New Commonwealth	8	15.7	12	23.5	19	37.3	9	17.6	4	7.8	51
Pakistan	5	2.6	41	21.7	72	38.1	63	33.3	9	4.8	189
Other European Community	92	28.2	70	21.5	62	19.0	78	23.9	23	7.1	326
Other Europe (excluding USSR)	105	45.9	37	16.2	47	20.5	25	10.9	14	6.1	229
Rest of the world (including USSR)	88	22.0	39	9.8	75	18.8	181	45.3	18	4.5	400
All outside UK*	769	23.2	746	22.5	863	26.1	718	21.7	213	6.4	3,310

Note: * Includes 287,000 persons who gave a year of entry but did not state their country of birth.
Source: LFS. Coleman and Salt (1992), table 11.4.

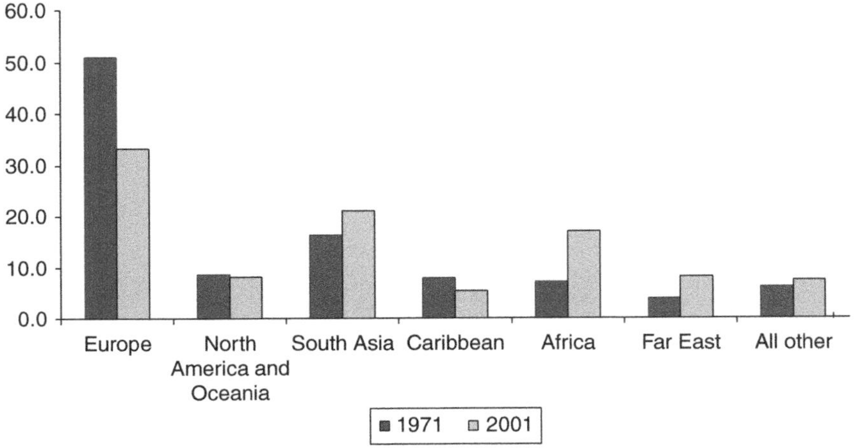

Figure 2.16 Countries of birth of the foreign-born population in 1971 and 2001, per cent
Source: Census.

came later, over a third of them during and after the 1980s (Coleman and Salt, 1992).

The most complete count of the foreign population by country of birth comes from the Census. Figure 2.16 compares the situation in 2001 with that in 1971, between which dates the number rose from about 3 million to almost 5 million. The geographical pattern changed substantially. Europe's proportion fell from half to a third of the total; that of South Asia rose from 16 to 21 per cent, Africa's from 7 to 17 per cent. The proportionate contribution of North America and Oceania was more or less unchanged while that of the Caribbean fell (Chappell, 2005).

The LFS provides annual statistics on country of birth as well as nationality, although the sample size means that numbers can fluctuate from year to year. In 2009 there were 6.890 million people living in the UK and born outside the country. Of these, 3.7 million were working, double the number in 1992. There are considerable variations in labour market participation by country of birth and nationality (Figure 2.17). Non-UK born and foreign citizens have lower employment rates than the indigenous population and this is especially the case for Pakistanis, Bangladeshis and Africans (excluding South Africa).

3.3. What is the size of the population by ethnic group?

Much of the debate surrounding the immigration issue in the UK focuses on ethnicity rather than nationality or country of birth. Ethnicity is perceived to be more enduring than immigration status, not least because many with

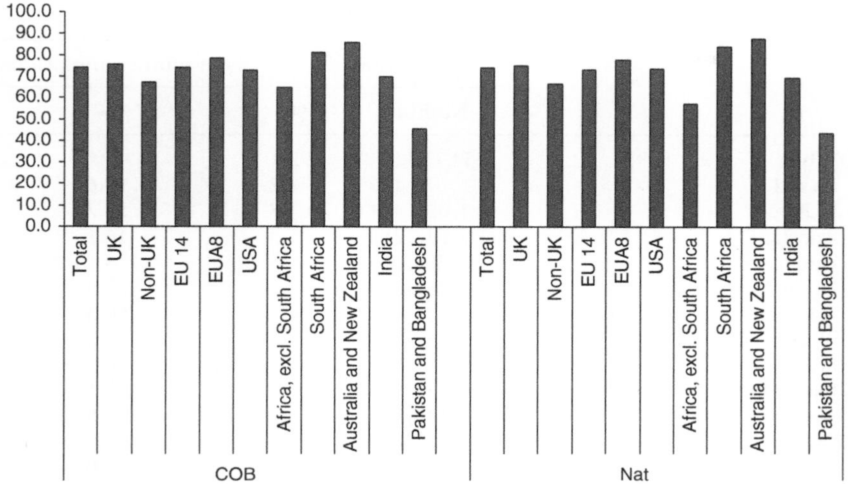

Figure 2.17 Employment rates by country of birth and nationality, fourth quarter average, 2003–09
Source: LFS.

an ethnic minority background were born and raised in the UK. The ethnicity concept is discussed in more detail in Chapter 3. In fact, the UK is one of the few countries to categorise its population by ethnic group. During the 1980s the LFS produced an ethnic count but not until 1991 did the Census ask an ethnic question, based on self-ascription. By 2001, the ethnic minority population was 4.6 million, half of whom were Asian or Asian British and about a quarter Black or Black British (Table 2.7).

3.4. What do we know about the numbers of irregular migrants?

Most irregular migrants will have entered the country legally but then shifted their status to become irregular. The one widely accepted set of estimates of the size of the irregular population was that of Woodbridge (2005) for the Home Office and the ONS. It uses a 'residual' method that compares the total de facto foreign-born population derived from the 2001 Census with estimates of the lawfully resident foreign-born population. The resulting overall estimate was between 310,000 and 570,000 with a central estimate of 430,000, as at Census day 2001. In addition there were at that time 175,000 quasi-legal migrants, whose right to remain depended on future determination of their asylum status and also an unknown number of children born to irregular migrants in the UK. Another important group are those whose applications for an extended stay were refused, but who nevertheless remained in the country. This group could account for

Table 2.7 Population of the UK, by ethnic group, April 2001

	Total		Non-white population
	Number	%	%
White	**54,153,898**	**92.1**	
Mixed	**677,117**	**1.2**	**14.6**
Indian	1,053,411	1.8	22.7
Pakistani	747,285	1.3	16.1
Bangladeshi	283,063	0.5	6.1
Other Asian	247,664	0.4	5.3
All Asian or Asian British	**2,331,423**	**4.0**	**50.3**
Black Caribbean	565,876	1.0	12.2
Black African	485,277	0.8	10.5
Black Other	97,585	0.2	2.1
All Black or Black British	**1,148,738**	**2.0**	**24.8**
Chinese	**247,403**	**0.4**	**5.3**
Other ethnic groups	**230,615**	**0.4**	**5.0**
All minority ethnic population	**4,635,296**	**7.9**	**100.0**
All population	**58,789,194**	**100.0**	

Source: Census (2001).

perhaps 50,000–80,000 irregulars (Gordon et al., 2009). The stock of irregular migrants will have changed since 2001 for a number of reasons: the continued arrival of asylum seekers; the clearance of the backlog of asylum cases; further illegal migrants entering and leaving the country; further migrants overstaying their permission; and the regularisation of previously irregular migrants, including those from EU accession countries whose status has become legal. Taking all these factors into account, Gordon et al. (2009) estimate the likely stock of irregular migrants at end 2007 to be in the range of 373,000–719,000 with a central estimate of 533,000. Including children born in the UK to irregular migrant couples, they estimate the number of irregular residents to be 618,000, with a range of 417,000–863,000.

4. Summary and conclusions

The chapter indicates the difficulty of providing either a simple or a comprehensive picture of the UK's international migration pattern and its associated trends, yet it is important to make these numerical assessments. Much of the debate in politics, the media and the wider public plays the 'numbers game', a pastime which greatly influences perceptions about the nature of migration, its causes and consequences. Further, our qualitative analyses as researchers need to be placed into a quantitative context. This point will be returned to in the concluding chapter.

The researcher seeking to quantify migration is faced with numerous data sources, concepts and definitions in use, most of which have not been developed to provide migration statistics. Most important, there is no measurable aggregate migration flow, but instead a series of different migration streams which can be conceptualised by their routes of entry. A simple fourfold breakdown of these – labour, family, student, asylum – is an essential starting point for analysis. On that basis, we may say that recently the best broad recorded estimate of annual foreign labour inflow has been around 400,000, that of students around 350,000, of family members 50,000 and asylum seekers 30,000. However, labour inflow may be more than half as much again (National Insurance Numbers), family inflow towards twice as many (all family members granted settlement) and asylum seeker numbers raised by several thousand dependants.

References

Chappell, R. (ed.) (2005) *Focus on People and Migration*. London: Palgrave Macmillan.

Coleman, D. and Rowthorne, R. (2004) 'The Economic Effects of Immigration into the United Kingdom', *Population and Development Review*, 30(4), 579–624.

Coleman, D. and Salt, J. (1992) *The British Population: Demographic Patterns, Trends and Processes*. Oxford: Oxford University Press.

Dustmann, C., Glitz, A. and Frattini, T. (2008) 'The Labour Market Impact of Immigration', CreAM Discussion Paper Series CDP 11/08, University College London.

Glover, S., Gott, C., Loizillon, A. et al. (2001) 'Migration: An Economic and Social Analysis', RDS Occasional Paper 67, Home Office, London.

Gordon, I., Scanlon, K.,Travers, T. and Whitehead, C. (2009) *Economic Impact on London and the UK Economy of an Earned Regularisation of Irregular Migrants to the UK*. London: Greater London Assembly.

Gott, C. and Johnston, K. (2002) 'The Migrant Population in the UK: Fiscal Effects', RDS Occasional Paper 77, Home Office, London.

House of Lords (2008) *The Economic Impact of Immigration*. London: Select Committee on Economic Affairs.

Lemos, S. and Portes, J. (2008) *The Impact of Migration from the New European States on Native Workers*. Department of Work and Pensions Working Paper No. 52. London: Department of Work and Pensions.

Lilley, P. (2005) *Too Much of a Good Thing? Towards a Balanced Approach to Immigration*. London: Centre for Policy Studies.

Sriskandarajah, D., Cooley, L. and Reed, H. (2005) *Paying Their Way: The Fiscal Contribution of Immigrants in the UK*. London: Institute for Public Policy Research.

UK Statistics Authority (2009) *Migration Statistics: The Way Ahead*. London: UK Statistics Authority.

Woodbridge, J. (2005) *Sizing the Unauthorised (Illegal) Population of the United Kingdom in 2001*. London: Home Office.

3
Multiculturalism, Ethnicity and Integration: Some Contemporary Challenges

Tariq Modood

1. Introduction

This chapter offers an overview of some of the political challenges posed to British and other European societies by the mass immigration from outside Europe, especially former colonies, that took place mainly in the third quarter of the twentieth century (as shown in Table 2.6 in Chapter 2). As Chapter 2 makes plain immigration is ongoing. The concern here, however, is on settled minorities. While the focus is on Britain, some of these challenges are shared by other European countries and it is helpful to bear that in mind. In identifying the key issues and some of the key options, a brief look at the American twentieth-century experience in relation to immigrant integration is offered as it is suggested that the ethnic diversity characteristic of urban America has emerged as a growing feature of Europe, albeit with two major differences. Firstly, the deep white-black divide that was a feature that predated modern immigration in the USA is not matched by a comparable 'fault-line' in British or European societies, either in terms of its specificity (i.e., 'race' or 'colour') or in its singular magnitude. Western European countries such as Britain, France and the Netherlands practised forms of racism but as very few non-whites were present in these countries until the post-war migrations, the racial divide primarily manifested itself in overseas colonies. Secondly, the majority of post-war immigrants to Europe, unlike the USA at any point in its history, were Muslims. They now constitute a significant proportion of the population of European cities and are raising social, cultural and, above all, political issues that have no direct parallel in the USA.[1]

There then follows a discussion of whether the 'fault-line' in Europe most associated with post-immigration social formations and groups will be a 'colour-line', or a more culturalised form of racism or simply Islamophobia. A key consideration in relation to this is what contemporary Europeans will perceive to be the legitimate role of Islam and Muslim identity in public life. This is part of the wider question about secularism and the role of religion which the presence of Muslims has opened up. Accommodation of Muslims into existing public spaces or policy fields occupied by religion, with some appropriate institutional adaptations or innovations, is taking place. Yet at the same time there is a growing hostility to Muslims, especially to their visibility and to the political demands made by or on behalf of some of them. This can take various forms. Two worth noting are a reactive renewal of Christianity, especially as a cultural identity marker, on the one hand, and an intellectual reassertion of radical secularism, on the other. It is not yet clear which of the options and trends mentioned above, or what combination of them, will be dominant, but the discussion underlines how the immigration of ethnically marked populations in their 'second generation' (or later) can be sites of conflict as well as transform polities and national identities.

2. The new European diversity

In the twentieth century the USA was conceived as a land of racial and ethnic diversity but Europeans thought of themselves as a continent of white nation-states. From the early West European colonisation of the Americas, the 'ethnic cleansing' of native populations and the large-scale transportation of enslaved Africans, the USA has seen several large waves of immigration. In the nineteenth century and the first half of the twentieth century this was mainly from various parts of Europe and, to a much lesser extent, the Pacific (Fuchs, 1990). Since the Second World War, however, the USA has seen large-scale immigration from many parts of the world, especially from the developing countries of the global 'South'. The same has occurred in Western Europe, though with one very significant difference that may have profound consequences. While the largest post-immigration minority in the USA is the Hispanics, in Western Europe it is Muslims (hence the whimsical but illuminating title of the American article 'Why Islam is Like Spanish' by Zolberg and Woon, 1999). This means that twenty-first century Europe is going to be more like the USA than it has ever been except that the, or one of the, principal fault-line(s) may not be black-white or even a European version of ethnic diversity like the new ethnoracial pentagon suggested by David Hollinger for contemporary USA (Hollinger, 1995). He writes critically of a popular perception of a five-sided division consisting of whites, blacks, reds (Native Americans), yellows (East Asians) and browns (South Asians). A third possibility for Europe is that the dividing line may take a religious or a religious-secular character, with the valorisation of Muslims by Christians and/or 'secular' people. What form should integration take in this socio-political landscape? What implications are there for a continent that thinks it is 'secular' but where state support for religion is routine, and for Christianity as a cultural marker of Europe?

Currently most of the largest, especially the capital, cities of Northwest Europe, are about 20–35 per cent non-white (i.e., people of non-European descent). Even without further large-scale immigration, being a young, fertile population, these proportions will grow for at least one generation more before they stabilise, reaching or exceeding 50 per cent in some cities in the next few years onwards, especially where 'indigenous', white Europeans are not fully reproducing themselves (Lutz, Skirbekk and Testa, 2007). The trend includes some of the larger urban centres of Southern Europe. A high degree of racial/ethnic/religious mix in its principal cities will be the norm in the twenty-first century Western Europe, and will characterise its national economic, cultural and political life, as it has done in twentieth- (and will do so in twenty-first) century USA. As has been said, there are important differences between Western Europe and the USA. Amongst these is that the majority of non-whites or people of non-European origins in most of the countries of Europe are Muslims (though in the UK they are only about a third of non-whites or ethnic minorities). With estimates of 12 to over 17 million Muslims in Western Europe today, the Muslim population in the former EU15 is only about 3–5 per cent and is relatively evenly distributed across the larger states (Peach, 2007; Pew Forum, 2010); in the larger cities the proportion which is Muslim, however, is several times larger.

In this context, with sharp recurring conflicts over freedom and offence (e.g., the Rushdie affair, the Danish Cartoons affair) and Muslim female dress (*hijab, niqab, burqa*), as well as serious violent disturbances as in the northern English cities in the summer of 2001 and in the banlieues of Paris and elsewhere in late 2005, questions about integration, equality, racism and Islam are becoming central to European politics. We need, however, to be clear about what are the important questions; we can also usefully learn – positively and negatively – from the American experience.

3. Models of integration

A good place to start is to clarify the key terms of assimilation, integration and multiculturalism. I propose the following (Modood, 2007). The concern here is not primarily in relation to socio-economic integration, for which see Loury, Modood and Teles (2005) and Heath and Cheung (2007).

3.1. Assimilation

Assimilation is where the processes affecting the relationship between social groups are seen as one-way, and where the desired outcome for society as a whole is seen as involving least change in the ways of doing things of the majority of the country and its institutional policies.[2] This may not necessarily be a laissez-faire approach – for the state can play an active role in bringing about the desired outcome, as in early twentieth-century 'Americanisation' policies towards European migrants in the USA – but the preferred result is one where the newcomers do little to disturb the society they are settling in and become as much like their new compatriots as possible. From the 1960s onwards, beginning with Anglophone countries but spreading to others, assimilation as a policy has come to be seen as impractical (especially for those who stand out in terms of physical appearance), illiberal (requiring too much state intervention) and inegalitarian (treating indigenous citizens as a norm to which others must approximate). It was as early as 1966 that Roy Jenkins, the UK Home Secretary, declared that in the view of the British government integration is 'not a flattening process of assimilation but equal opportunity accompanied by cultural diversity in an atmosphere of mutual tolerance' (Jenkins, 1967: 267).[3] While 'assimilation' as a term has come to be dropped in favour of 'integration' yet, even today, when some politicians use the term 'integration', they actually, consciously or not, mean what has here been defined as assimilation, so the use of these terms in public discourse must not be taken at their face value but critically inspected.

3.2. Integration

Integration is where processes of social interaction are seen as two-way, and where members of the majority community as well as immigrants and ethnic minorities are required to do something; so the latter cannot alone be blamed for 'failing to or not trying to integrate'. The established society is the site of institutions – including employers, civil society and the government – in which integration has to take place, and they accordingly must take the lead.

3.3. Multiculturalism

Multiculturalism is where processes of integration are seen both as two-way and as working differently for different groups. In this understanding, each group is distinctive, and thus integration cannot consist of a single template (hence the 'multi'). The 'culturalism' – by no means a happy term either in relation to 'culture' or 'ism' – refers to the understanding that the groups in question are likely not just to be marked by newness or phenotype or socio-economic location but by certain forms of group identities. The latter point indeed suggests that better, though longer, terms might be 'pluralistic integration' or multicultural citizenship.

The concept of equality is central to multiculturalism but it may also be so for certain conceptions of integration. The key difference between integration and multiculturalism is that the concepts of group and of 'multi' are essential to the latter. Post-immigration minorities are groups differentiated from the majority society or the norm in society by two kinds of processes. On the one hand, by the fact of negative 'difference': with alienness, inferiorisation, stigmatisation, stereotyping, exclusion, discrimination, racism and so on. On the other hand, by the senses of identity that groups so perceived have of themselves. The two together are the key data for multiculturalism. The differences at issue are those perceived both by outsiders or group members – from the outside in and from the inside out – to constitute not just some form of distinctness but a form of alienness or inferiority that diminishes or makes difficult equal membership in the wider society or polity. There is a sense of groupness in play, a mode of being, but also subordination or marginality, a mode of oppression, and the two interact in creating an unequal 'us–them' relationship. I do not, however, mean terms such as 'groupness', 'mode of being', 'subordination', 'identity' and so on to denote univocal, internally undifferentiated concepts (see Modood, 2007: 93–97).

4. Multiculturalism

Multicultural accommodation of minorities, then, is different from integration because it recognises the social reality of groups, not just of individuals and organisations.[4] As I have indicated, there may be considerable complexity about what is meant by social reality or groupness here, and ideas of groups as discrete, homogeneous, unchanging, bounded populations are not realistic when we are thinking of multicultural recognition. Such recognition may have a legal dimension but for the most part will be at the level of civic consultations, political participation, institutional policies (e.g., schools and hospitals), discursive representations, especially in relation to the changing discourses of societal unity or national identity and their remaking. Regardless of the extent to which recognition of minority identities in this way is formal or informal, led by the state or the semi-autonomous institutions of civil society, it does not challenge, let alone displace individual rights and the shared dimensions of citizenship. Rather, such respect for minority groups, normatively and for its feasibility, assumes a robust framework of individual rights and citizenship identity. Multicultural theorists do, however, emphasise that individual rights always need to be interpreted and qualified by other rights and normative requirements, including other individual rights, and so have to be understood contextually and dialogically (Parekh, 2000; Xanthaki, 2010), and the same point applies to citizenship (Modood, 2007). Hence, for example, the right to freedom of expression always has a contextual rather than an absolute character, a context which may include the need to protect certain vulnerable groups from incitement to hatred, thus incitement to religious and/or racial hatred is against the law in most liberal democracies.

This leads us to the second point of difference between the concepts of integration and multiculturalism. It is that the groups in question, the post-immigration minorities, are not of one kind but are a 'multi'. For example, some people will identify with a 'colour' identity like 'black' but there will be others for whom national origin identities (like Turkish), or a regional heritage (like Berber) or a religious identity (like Sikh) may be much more meaningful, expressing forms of community and ethnic pride that are struggling for recognition and inclusion. And of course these minority identities will interact with wider, societal identities – woman, working class, Londoner, British – in differing ways, expressing the different experiences, locations and aspirations of different groups.

Moreover, the 'multi' does not just refer to cultural or self-definitional diversity. The groups in question may have different socio-economic positions, (dis)advantages, trajectories in, say, US, Canadian or British society (Loury, Modood and Teles, 2005; Heath and Cheung, 2007). Nor is it true that they are all worse off than their white co-citizens. The point is not that some, say, individual Indians in the West are better off than individual whites – that is trivially true. Rather, that groups such as the Indians, Chinese, Koreans and some other East Asians, for example, are developing a more middle-class profile than whites. Socio-economic integration, if it is to be anything more than inclusion into the working classes, must involve social mobility and so the appropriate multicultural position on socio-economic integration is to allow and support different groups of people – with different priorities, networks and forms of social capital – to become parts of different sections of the economy in a fair and egalitarian but non-uniform way. One consequence of this may of course be that as the socio-economic gap, measured in terms of aggregates, between ethnic or ethno-religious groups narrows, the gap between members in any one group widens to reflect the socio-economic structural inequalities within a society like Britain (NEP, 2010). So that as, for example, Indians develop a more middle-class position than the white population, the gap between the well-off and worst-off Indians may grow (NEP, 2010).

The multi has to apply also to concepts such as racism: there is not a singular racism but multiple racisms. There are of course colour/phenotype racisms but there are also cultural racisms which build on 'colour', a set of antagonistic or demeaning stereotypes based on alleged or real cultural traits. In the USA, the ways in which racism works with Latinos, for example, both in terms of representations but also in terms of treatment – perhaps more likely to be hired than a black job seeker but more vulnerable in terms of immigration policing and the possibility of being deported – will be different to how it is for African-Americans. Similarly, American-Asians may be admired in distinctive ways (e.g., for their academic and occupational achievements) but may also be racialised as 'nerds' and 'geeks', not to mention as foreign and un-American (Song, 2001). The most important cultural racism today, at least in Western Europe, is, as I explain below, anti-Muslim racism, sometimes called Islamophobia. A multicultural approach, recognising the plurality of racisms and the distinctive needs and vulnerabilities of different groups, is therefore what is needed to tackle racial and religious discrimination (Modood, 2005; Meer and Modood, 2009).

5. Multiculturalism: some further unpacking

The very last point I have just made is an explicitly political or policy point and illustrates how the term 'multiculturalism' (no less than the terms 'integration' or 'assimilation') operates at or combines different levels. There is the sociological level which acknowledges the fact of groupness (in terms of exclusionary difference as well as subjectivity); this is sometimes termed 'multicultural society' in order to distinguish it from political concepts. Then, secondly, there is the question of what should the political response be to that social reality. Assimilation is one response; liberal integration based on respect for individuals but no political recognition of groups is another; and multiculturalism is yet another response based not just on the equal dignity of individuals but also on the political accommodation of group identities as a means of challenging exclusionary racisms and practices and fostering respect and inclusion for demeaned groups. Moving beyond a focus on exclusion and minorities is a third level of multiculturalism, which is not just about positive minority identities but a positive vision of the whole remade so as to include the previously excluded or marginalised on the basis of equality and belonging. It is at this level that we may speak of multicultural integration or multicultural citizenship (Taylor, 1994; Parekh, 2000; Modood, 2007).

This third level of multiculturalism, incorporating the sociological fact of diversity, groupness and exclusion but going beyond individual rights and political accommodation, is perhaps the level that has been least emphasised. Or at least that is how it seems to many whose understanding of multiculturalism, sometimes polemical but sometimes sincere, is that multiculturalism is about encouraging minority difference without a counterbalancing emphasis on cross-cutting commonalities and a vision of a greater good. This has led many commentators and politicians to talk of multiculturalism as divisive and productive of segregation.

This popular, as well as academic, critique of multiculturalism was evident in the 1990s, not just in countries that had never embraced multiculturalism, such as France and Germany, but also in those that had, such as the Netherlands and Britain. After the terrorist attacks in America on 11 September 2001 and their aftermath, including the London bombings of 7 July 2005 and other failed or prevented attacks in Britain, fears about international Islamist and associated wars and conflict coalesced with anxiety about Muslims failing to integrate in Britain and other countries. The anti-multiculturalism discourses came not just to dominate the relevant policy discourses but to be at the forefront of politics. Discourses of 'community cohesion' and 'integration' were prominent in this politics, which overlooked the fact that no major theorist or advocate of multiculturalism, nor any relevant policy or legislation, had promoted 'separatism'. Theorists of multiculturalism, such as Taylor (1994) and Parekh (2000), related policy documents such as the *Report of the Commission on the Future of Multi-Ethnic Britain* (CMEB, 2000) and enactments such as those in Canada, universally regarded as a pioneer and exemplar of state multiculturalism, all appealed to and built on an idea of national citizenship. Certainly some urge a 'post-national' analysis of society and advocate transnationalism or cosmopolitanism (for example, Soysal, 1994; Held, 1995; Jacobson, 1997), but they are not multiculturalists in the sense being discussed here. Hence, from a multiculturalist point of view, though not from that of its critics, the recent emphasis on cohesion and citizenship is a necessary rebalancing of the political multiculturalism of the 1990s (Meer and Modood, 2009).[5] It has largely taken the form of what I have called above the second level of multiculturalism (Meer and Modood, 2009). The emphasis on cohesion cannot be understood as simply a move from multiculturalism to integration, as it not only continues to understand exclusion and identity as sociological facts but also to continue with group consultations, representation and accommodation. The latter have actually increased. The British government has found it necessary to increase the scale and level of consultations with Muslims in Britain since 9/11, though it has been dissatisfied with existing organisations and has sought to increase the number of organised interlocutors and the channels of communication (McLoughlin, 2010). Avowedly anti-multiculturalist countries and governments have worked to increase corporatism in practice, for example, with the creation by Nicholas Sarkozy of the French Council of the Muslim Faith (*Conseil Francais du Culte Musulman*) in 2003 to represent all Muslims to the French government in matters of worship and ritual; and by the creation of the Islam Confrenz in Germany in 2006, an exploratory body, yet with an extensive political agenda. It cannot be denied that these bodies are partly top-down efforts to control Muslims or to channel them into certain formations and away from others; but nevertheless it is quite clear that such institutional processes cannot be understood within the conceptual framework of assimilation or individualist integration.

We can better appreciate some of these developments if we step back a bit and consider what the American experience has been and what in the light of that we can identify as the main options and tendencies in Britain and Western Europe more generally, which constitute the context of some of the studies in this book.

6. The American experience

While the nineteenth and first half of the twentieth centuries' Europe has been a continent of emigration and nation-states, nineteenth and twentieth centuries' America was a continent of immigration and continental federation, the creation of a super-state. From about the middle of the twentieth century, however, new processes were initiated in Europe both in relation to emigration/immigration and to national/supra-national formations. Europe began to move in the direction of American processes; though even today it is still some way short of the USA, this is more so in relation to continental federation than levels of immigration and of immigration as a source not just of labour but of citizens. Large-scale immigration is not wholly new to countries such as Britain and France but it has not been on a scale comparable to the USA, for which it has been a significant source of new citizens and co-nationals, so it is worth briefly considering what the key features of the American experience have been. Two features are particularly worth emphasising. Firstly, constitutional nationalism or nation-building, and secondly, an acceptance of ethnic diversity.

In relation to the first, the USA is sometimes taken to lack a European-style nationalism and to be simply a country of immigrants (Walzer, 1997). Yet, with its, until very recently, intolerance of dual-nationality, self-belief that it is the biggest and best, with the raising of the Stars and Stripes at the start of every school-day and a culture of national flag-waving, the USA, both at a governmental and everyday level seems to be more openly nationalistic than some European countries, certainly Britain. It may be that Britain has a more implicit, understated form of nationalism (see Chapters 10 and 11 of this book) while the USA, with its history of immigration, has a more emphatic and unembarrassed emphasis on continuous nation-building, of inculcating pride in being American as a basis of cohesion. The early twentieth-century policies of assimilation gave way to a hyphenation (Irish-American, African-American and so on), but a conscious focus on integration has been a feature of American society in the way it has recently become so in most of Western Europe – which has to cope without the aspirational power of 'the American dream', of economic expansion and the pull of being part of a supremely successful nation, indeed, a superpower.

In relation to the second point, ethnic diversity, it is true that the USA has only limited governmental or legal recognition of ethnic groups such as the special status for Native Americans, affirmative action for African-Americans and routine, official and unofficial categorising and collecting data by ethnicity and race.[6] Yet, there are and have been for generations widespread societal discourses of race and ethnicity formed by immigration and continuing into second and third generations and beyond. This is not just about discourses but has a material reality in, for instance, the relatively laissez-faire attitude to the formation of residential concentrations, to ethnic community-based churches as a major basis for integrating new populations into an existing social landscape (Foner and Alba, 2008; Casanova, 2009), to ethnic blocs in politics (e.g., Tammany Hall, New York: Burrows and Wallace, 1999), and to various minorities actively campaigning in 'homeland' politics and exercising influence on US foreign policy (e.g., Jews in relation to Israel, Cubans in relation to Cuba). This has been labelled the 'Ethnicity Paradox': the allowing, even the encouraging of ethnic identity maintenance in the form of community organisations and cultural pride displays as a way of not damaging the self-esteem of migrants and non-coercively achieving civic integration and national loyalty (Lal, 1990).

This patriotic integration in a context of laissez-faire ethnic diversity was primarily the experience of 'white ethnics', of European migrants and their progeny. For native blacks, the primary experience has been that of 'the colour-line'. Their job opportunities, social acceptance and even legal rights until the 1960s were marked by strong racial exclusion, not intergenerational social mobility and full equality. Hence the USA has had not one but two dominant ways of dealing with 'difference': expanding the nation to integrate whites, initially with, later without top-down assimilation; and secondly, the perpetuation of racial segregation and inequality in relation to native-born blacks. Both ways, however, allow for a degree of ethnic/racial explicitness within the socio-political system that is greater than has been the norm or regarded as wholly acceptable in even contemporary Europe. Moreover, when racial equality policies began to be enacted in the second half of the twentieth century, they too appealed to a conception of citizenship and civil rights. Moreover, they may initially have implied a colour-blindness but soon gave way to not just racial explicitness in the employment policies of affirmative action or reverse discrimination in respect of meritorious black individuals but also the (re)creation of a quasi-ethnic grouping (Omi and Winant, 1994), which was not only 'proud to be black' but which sought affirmation in an ethnic-hyphenated group label, 'African-American', and not just the racial category of 'black'.

Different again from the (later) experiences of white ethnics and blacks is that of the post-1965 migrant groups, which consist principally of Hispanics and Asians. Their experience is somewhere in the middle of the other two, though with perhaps different groups exhibiting divergent trajectories. East and South Asians have been developing an entrepreneurial/professional profile and Mexicans a disadvantaged profile (Fuchs, 1990; Portes and Zhou, 1993; Zhou, 2005). While it is probably the case that no non-black group is likely to end up having a socio-economical profile as disadvantaged as blacks, nevertheless some Americans fear the threat of linguistic division and for many the greatest contemporary multicultural challenge is seen as having to do with Hispanics (Huntington, 2004).

7. What kind of integration in Europe?

Following from the above brief discussion I shall raise three important questions, which identify the larger context in which topics studied in this book can be situated. They are profound questions of public philosophy and policy but also require social science inquiry in relation to trends, possibilities and feasibilities, and are ranked from least to most challenging in my opinion. They are questions about integration and identities; about long-term cleavages; and about religion and secularism.

Will Europe insist on assimilation, the dominant historical pattern, or allow some space for private cultural difference within a model of civic integration (the current French ideology but not comprehensive practice) or some degree of multicultural integration (found to some degree in the Netherlands, Britain and Sweden)? The latter was becoming influential in the English-speaking world until 9/11, since when the perception has grown that unassimilated migrants, especially if Muslim, are a potential security threat, a fifth column.

Nevertheless, there is a strong ideology of diversity in the air, for example, in relation to sexuality and to historically squashed nationalisms (such as the Catalonian, Scottish, Flemish and so on) and it is unlikely to fade in the current context of globalisation, which seems to create identity movements in reaction to perceptions of global, usually Americanised, cultural homogeneity (Castells, 1997). Thus migration-based second and third generations who breathe this atmosphere may continue to mobilise around identities of cultural difference and demand equality of respect, especially when those identities are the basis of discrimination and structural inequalities – as was so evident in the banlieues of France in late 2005. Moreover, at what level(s) is integration to take place (especially in relation to identity-building): city/region or national or European? Another way of posing the question is: what is the hyphenation on offer? What will work? In the USA, the hyphenation always refers to America (not Texas, California and so on), but in contemporary Europe, integration policies are directed to developing a sufficiently strong sense of national citizenship. Indeed, in countries like France and Britain a (hyphenated) national identification is quite strong amongst the 'second generation' (and thus often a basis for complaints of unequal treatment as co-nationals), but identification with Europe is much weaker than amongst white/indigenous peers. While European identity as a platform for equality/belonging and lever for equality/belonging at the national level may or may not be helpful in some countries, it is probably the case that ethnic minority identification with the city one lives in (e.g., Liverpool or Rotterdam) may be easier to identify with than 'British' or 'Dutch' because of all the national, cultural, historical and political (including foreign policy adventures like Iraq) baggage that go with the latter. For example, one can say one is proud to be a Liverpudlian without feeling that this implicates you in the US–UK occupation of Iraq. Moreover, co-citizens may say of you 'You are not really Dutch' even if you were born in the Netherlands but are less likely to say 'You are not a Rotterdammer' if you are a long-term resident of that city.

8. Dividing lines

A second question is where will the major dividing line in Europe be in relation to post-immigration social formations? Will it, for example, be a colour-line? In Britain we have come to approach issues to do with integration through what used to be called – and in other countries the language will not always have a natural resonance or fit – 'race-relations', itself an American term. People saw the issue as primarily one of racial discrimination or colour racism, which of course had a historical legacy: slavery, colonialism, empire and so on. In the Leverhulme Programme and in this book part of our focus is on recent and current migration: on smuggling of people, the mobility of expertise, on the globalisation of British higher education. Our other focus and the one I am particularly addressing in this chapter is on post-immigration settlement, on social exclusion and national integration. In relation to these topics our attention is on the experiences of and discourses about Pakistani-origin Muslims in Britain, and other Muslims more generally. The whole issue to do with Muslims, which dominates the headlines today, only became a feature of majority-minority relations from the early 1990s. In Britain virtually nobody – policymakers, the media nor academics – talked about Muslims throughout most of the 1980s. The big dramatic crisis that brought the idea of Muslims into public political discourse was the *Satanic Verses* or the Salman Rushdie affair that began in late 1988 and became one of the biggest national and international stories, following the fatwa of the Ayatollah Khomeini in February in 1989.

For some decades up to that time, and to some extent beyond that time, in relation to the post-war immigration of peoples from the West Indies and South Asia, the dominant post-immigration issue was colour racism. One consequence is that the legal and policy framework in Britain still reflects the conceptualisation and priorities of racial dualism, of black–white dualism. Muslims and issues about Muslims arose in that context, and have struggled to seek clarity and a distinctive set of priorities, by counterposing themselves in that context, against that agenda. This dependence upon a 'race' framework has meant, at least initially, that Muslims have been marginalised. To some extent the assertiveness of Muslims in Britain has to be understood in the context of trying to move themselves from a marginalised position where things were seen in terms of black and white, to one where they as it were say 'talk to us as Muslims, treat us as Muslims, not just as people who are not white' (cf. the British Muslim magazine *Q-News*; Bari, 2005).

In the Anglo-American or Atlantocentric version of racism, which is certainly one of the classical and enduring versions, it is phenotype which is alleged to explain the existence of certain, mainly negative cultural traits (Miles, 1989: 71–72). Yet while the physicality of people of African descent is taken to be enough to fill out the image of them as a group, as a 'race' – as, for example, strong, sensual, rhythmical and unintelligent – the racialised image of South Asians, such as the Pakistanis, is not so extensively linked to physical appearance. It very soon appeals to cultural motifs such as language, religion, family structures, exotic dress, cuisine and art forms (Modood, 2005: 6–18, chapter 1; Meer and Modood, 2009). These are taken to be part of the meaning of 'Asian' and of why Asians – which in Britain means South Asians – are perceived by some as alien, backward and undesirable. Such motifs are appealed to in excluding, harassing or discriminating against Asians; in both constituting them as a group and justifying negative treatment of them. Muslims too are being generalised about in these and other ways in Europe (and elsewhere) at the moment. For the most part they are visually identified by a phenotype (primarily Arab or South Asian appearance) though also by dress and name and sometimes by accent. To this identification or image are attached stereotypes about religious fanaticism, separatism, not wanting to integrate, lack of national feeling or even disloyalty and association with or sympathy for terrorism. They are being perceived not just as neighbours, citizens and so on but as Muslims; and it has to be said that many Muslims – like some blacks, Jews, gays, women, Scots and so on in parallel situations before them – are vociferously challenging the negative perceptions but not the underlying logic that Muslims are a group. They are responding to the negative perceptions by offering positive images, stories and generalisations about Muslims; less often by saying Muslims are not a group but only a variety of individuals, citizens and so on. Thus a process of group formation has been underway for about two decades in Britain and, though with less intensity and visibility, in other parts of Western Europe.

We can call this process 'racialisation' and the negative dimension of it 'anti-Muslim racism' because the 'otherness' or 'groupness' that is being appealed to and is being developed is connected to the cultural and racial otherness that is connected to European/white peoples' historical and contemporary perception and treatment of people that they perceive to be non-European or non-white. How Muslims are perceived today is both connected to how they have been perceived and treated by European empires and their racial hierarchies, as well as by Christian Islamophobia and the Crusades in earlier centuries (Daniel, 1960, 1967). The images, generalisations and fears have both a continuity as well as a newness. Moreover, these perceptions and treatments overlap with contemporary European/white peoples' attitudes and behaviour towards blacks, Asians, immigrants and so on. The perception and treatment clearly has a religious and cultural dimension but equally clearly it has a phenotypical dimension. Given a number of images – photographs or, say, cartoons – of people and asked to pick out a Muslim, most white people would probably have a go and not reply, but I do not know what any of these people believe, just as if they were asked to identify Jews they would have a go (though probably less today than in the past – because Jews are becoming de-racialised, normalised as 'white', in some ways in Britain and similar countries). It is true that racists do not accuse Muslims of a deficient biology but of being aliens, of not belonging in 'our country', of 'taking over the country' and so on, but a racial image is used to identify Muslims as an 'Other'. This is the reason that the chapter in this book which discusses the negative perception of a minority is about Muslims in relation to British national identity.

One should perhaps also note the presence of a more general xenophobia, which can include white victims, as recent East European and South American labour migrants have discovered.[7] There is little evidence so far that the long-term 'fault-line' will be here (perhaps because it is too early to tell). The likely candidates, therefore, are a black-white divide, or one based on cultural-racism, combining 'race' and 'culture', especially in the form of an anti-Muslim racism. Or, relatedly, a Muslim/non-Muslim divide, in which amongst Muslims are included those of European phenotype, and amongst non-Muslims are Jews, Hindus, black Christians and so on. Perhaps it is simply wise to stress that, as in the USA, it does not just have to be one division; nevertheless, it is just as, if not more, likely that one of these three or four divisions will be more salient and more intractable than the others, as has been the case in the USA.

9. Religion and secularism

The sociological fact of 'secularisation', the decline of religious authority in the public sphere and decline of participation in religious activity in the private sphere, is strong in Europe but religious observance continues to be high in many places in the world, including the USA and including where it has been forcibly suppressed as in the area of the former USSR and China, and in many places religion's public significance is on the rise, not decline (Berger, Davie and Fokas, 2008). In most if not all European countries, 'secularism' – the political idea that politics, and especially the state, and religion should be independent of each other – if not in theory, certainly in practice, allows some space for one or more churches in the public/national space – symbolically, institutionally and in terms of subsidies and resources. The historical and geographical trend has been for this space to have been decreasing for some centuries. Yet secularism has been institutionalised in many different ways and in the main is not hostile to nor characterised by an absolute determination to expel religion from the political sphere, let alone expunge it from the world. While all Western countries are clearly secular in many ways, interpretations and the institutional arrangements diverge according to the dominant national religious culture and the differing projects of nation-state-building. The result is that what is taken to be the practice of secularism in one country is thought to be overly permissive or overly restrictive in another.

For example, the USA has as its First Amendment to the Constitution that there shall be no established church and there is wide support for this, and in the last few decades there has been a tendency amongst academics and jurists to interpret the church–state separation in continually more radical ways (Sandel, 1994; Hamburger, 2002). Yet, not only is the USA a deeply religious society, with much higher levels of church attendance than in Western Europe (Greely, 1995), but there is a strong Protestant, evangelical fundamentalism that is rare in Europe. This fundamentalism disputes some of the new radical interpretations of the 'no establishment clause', though not necessarily the clause itself, and is one of the primary mobilising forces in contemporary American politics; it is widely claimed that it decided the presidential election of 2004. The churches in question – mainly white, mainly in the South and mid-West – campaign openly for candidates and parties, indeed raise large sums of money for politicians and introduce religion-based issues into politics, such as positions on abortion, HIV/Aids, homosexuality, stem-cell research, prayer at school and the teaching of creationism at school. It has been said that no openly avowed atheist has ever been a candidate for the White House and that it would be impossible for such a candidate to be elected. It is not at all unusual for politicians – in fact for President George W. Bush, it was most usual – to publicly talk about their faith, to appeal to religion and to hold prayer meetings in government buildings and as a prelude or epilogue to government business. On the other hand, in 'establishment' Britain, bishops sit in the upper chamber of the legislature by right and only the senior archbishop can crown a new head of state, the monarch, but politicians rarely talk about their religion. An indication of the latter is how Tony Blair, when prime minister, was asked, following a visit to the White House, if he and President George Bush had prayed together, and the question was dismissed by his press officer, Alastair Cambell, by a curt 'We do not do God.' Questioned later about this, Blair, one of, if not the most openly religious prime ministers the UK has ever had, said: 'I don't want to end up with an American-style type of politics with us all going out there and beating our chests about our faith' and that while people were defined by their faith, it was 'a bit unhealthy' if it became used in the political process (BBC, 2005).

France draws the distinction between state and religion differently again. Like the USA, there is no state church but unlike the USA, the state actively promotes the privatisation of religion. While in the USA, organised religion in civil society is powerful and seeks to exert influence on the political process, French civil society does not carry signs or expressions of religion. This is particularly the case in state schools where the radical secularist idea of laicite is interpreted as the production of future citizens in a religion-free zone, hence the popular banning of the *foulard*, the headscarves worn by some Muslim girls and prospect of legislation to ban the covering of the face.[8] Yet, the French state, contrary to the USA, confers institutional legal status on the Catholic and Protestant Churches and on the Jewish Consistory, albeit carefully designating organised religions as *cultes* and not communities. Through state-sponsored institutions such as the Jewish Consistory and the recently formed French Council of the Muslim Faith (*Conseil Francais du Culte Musulman*) the state gives some recognition to organised religions but largely on its own terms: selected religious leaders

Table 3.1 Religion vis-à-vis state and civil society in three countries

	State	**Civil Society**
Britain	Weak establishment; with state funding and incorporation of faith schools	Weak but churches can be a source of political criticism and action
USA	No establishment; tax relief for private faith schools	Strong and politically mobilised
France	Actively secular but offers top-down recognition and control; state payments to private faith schools	Weak and it is rare for churches to be political

Source: Adapted from Modood (2007).

have regular meetings with the state but on narrowly religious and non-political set of issues. Indeed, such an institutional framework is as much a form of state control as it is of recognition and falls far short of any kind of social partnership. We might want to express these three different national manifestations of secularism as in Table 3.1.

So, political secularism means quite different things in different countries, depending on their history and political culture. The key thing to recognise is that in Western countries, certainly in Europe, there are points of symbolic, institutional, policy and fiscal linkages between the state and aspects of Christianity. Secularism has increasingly grown in power and scope, but a historically evolved and evolving compromise with religion are the defining features of Western European secularism, rather than the absolute separation of religion and politics. Secularism today enjoys a hegemony in Western Europe, but it is a moderate rather than a radical, a pragmatic rather than an ideological, secularism (Modood, 2010).

Yet, in the very recent decades the presence of Muslims and Islamic claims-making upon European societies and states has resulted in a (temporary?) reversal of aspects of secularisation and the decline of collective religion. While there are also increased assertions of Enlightenment secularism, there are also increased assertions of (cultural) Christianity. Each of these is a direct reaction to the growing presence of Muslims and claims for recognition by Muslims and so can be seen as a domestic version of a 'clash of civilisations' thesis which under some circumstances is and could be projected more internationally, even globally.

9.1. Accommodation into existing or novel compromises

An example of accommodation is the development of a religious equality agenda in Britain, including the incorporation of some Muslim schools on the same basis as schools of religions with a much longer presence. It also includes the recommendations of The Royal Commission on the Reform of the House of Lords (2000) that in addition to the Anglican bishops who sit in that House by right as part of the Anglican 'establishment', this right should be extended to cover those of other Christian and non-Christian faiths.[9] The same point can be made in relation to the fact that as early as 1974 the Belgian state decided to include Islam within its Council of Religions as a full member, or to the way that Muslims in the Netherlands have long had state-funded religious schools and television channels as a progressive step in that country's traditional way of institutionally dealing with organised religion, namely, 'pillarisation'.[10] Similarly, a 'Muslim community' is becoming recognised by public authorities in Germany by appealing to the historic German idea of a 'religious community' (*Religionsgemeinschaft*). Again, a series of French Interior Ministers have taken a number of steps to 'normalise' Islam in France by creating an official French Islam under the authority of the state in ways that make it identical to other faiths (for more on these cases see Cesari, 2004; Modood and Kastoryano, 2006). An institutionalisation of Islam, and of religious pluralism in general, is taking place but it is in a context in which neither political Christianity nor radical secularism are dominant but where the status quo is an accommodative, moderate secularism.

9.2. Renewal of Christian and radical secular identities

As has been noted there is a considerable negative reaction to Muslims. While in the main this is to do with a racialisation of Muslims in terms of culture, politics and terrorism, it is also manifested in relation to religion, secularism and the institutional accommodation of Muslims. Several trends can be identified. An example of an institutional accommodation resulting from Muslim pressure is that the 2001 UK Census included a religion question for the first time in its 150 years history; it was also exceptional in being a voluntary question, unlike the rest of the Census form. Despite misgivings that the question would be declined, 94 per cent answered it. The real surprise, however, was the number of people who ticked themselves in as 'Christian' (rather than 'no religion'). It was considerably higher than recorded in most surveys. For example, while in the British Social Attitudes (BSA) survey of 1992, 31 per cent did not profess a belief in god(s) and in the latest BSA survey 43 per cent self-identified as non-religious (indeed 59 per cent did not describe themselves as religious) (Park et al., 2010), in the 2001 Census 72 per cent identified themselves as Christians and less than 16 per cent as without a religion. While there is no one explanation for these variations, it is quite possible that the presence and salience of Muslims is stimulating a Christian identity. Voas and Bruce (2004) found that in neighbourhoods with high Muslim populations, the percentage of white Britons who chose 'Christian' is considerably higher than in similar, less mixed, neighbourhoods, even after controlling for various factors such as income. The emergence of a new, sometimes politically assertive cultural identification with Christianity has been noted in Denmark (2006) and perhaps also in Germany (2004).[11] It was politically apparent in the EU Constitution debate as well as in the ongoing debate about Turkey as a future EU member (Casanova, 2009). Some of the exponents of the former wanted a declaration to include a reference to Christianity as the religion of Europe. Even some of those who did not favour this openly reject Turkey as a possible EU member because it is not a Christian country, and worse, would bring a massive 70 million Muslims into the EU. These assertions of Christianity are not necessarily accompanied by any increase in expressions of faith or church attendance, which continue to decline across Europe. Giscard d'Estaing, the former President of France, who chaired the Convention on the Future of Europe, the body which drafted the (abortive) EU Constitution, expresses nicely the assertiveness I speak of: 'I never go to Church, but Europe is a Christian continent.' It has to be said, however, the political views about Europe referred to are held not just by cultural Christian identarians but also by many practising Christians, including the Catholic Church. It has been argued that Pope John Paul II 'looked at the essential cleavage in the world as being between religion and unbelief. Devout Christians, Muslims, and Buddhists had more in common with each other than with atheists' (Caldwell, 2009: 151). Pope Benedict XVI, the same author contends, 'thinks that, within societies, believers and unbelievers exist in symbiosis. Secular Westerners, he implies, have a lot in common with their religious fellows' (Caldwell, 2009: 151). The suggestion is that secularists and Christians in Europe have more in common with each other than they do with Muslims. That many secularists do not share Pope Benedict's view is evident from the fact that the proposed clause about Christianity was absent from the draft of the EU Constitution.[12] While there is little sign of a Christian Right in Europe of the kind that is strong in the USA, there is to some degree a reinforcing or renewing of a sense that Europe is 'secular Christian', analogous to the term 'secular Jew' to describe someone of Jewish descent who has a sense of Jewish identity but is not religiously practising and may even be an atheist.

Besides this secular Christian identity assertiveness which is to be found, albeit not exclusively, on the centre-right, there is also a more radical secularism which is more characteristic of the left. It is a tradition that goes back to the Enlightenment (though more the French rather than the British or German Enlightenment) and is not only non-religious but is often anti-religion. It has been most epigrammatically captured by Karl Marx's famous 'religion is the opium of the masses' and Nietzsche's 'God is dead.' Post-9/11 has seen the emergence of a radical discourse referred to as 'the new atheism'; see Beattie (2007) who has authors such as Dawkins (2006), Harris (2004) and Hitchens (2007) in mind.

Its political manifestation is found amongst intellectuals and political commentators such as A.C. Grayling, Kenan Malik and Polly Toynbee, organisations such as the National Secular Society and the British Humanist

Association. They interpret political secularism to mean that religious beliefs and discourse should be excluded from the public sphere and/or politics and certainly activities endorsed or funded by the state. Thus they argue, for example, for the disestablishment of the Church of England, the removal of the Anglican bishops from the House of Lords and the withdrawal of state support for faith schools (the greatest beneficiary of which in terms of secondary schooling is the Catholic Church). With groups like Muslims, Sikhs and Hindus pressing to have some of these benefits extended to themselves (as to some extent has already happened in the case of the Jews) and religious groups more involved in the delivery of welfare and urban renewal, it is clear that this radical political secularism is not only a break with the inherited status quo secularism in most parts of Western Europe (with France being something of an exception) but is at odds with the current institutionalisation of religious pluralism.

Which of these will become dominant, or how these trends may develop, interact and synthesise is not clear. The critical issue of principle is not how but *whether* religious groups, especially those that are marginal and under-represented in public life, ought to be represented. The real problem today, however, is with an approach that eschews difference-blindness in general but would not dream of being anything other than religion-blind. Take the BBC – an organisation with a deserved reputation for public service and high standards, an aspect of which is manifested in the remark by a serving Director-General, Greg Dykes, that the organisation was 'hideously white' (Dykes, 2002). Relatedly, for some years now it has given political importance to reviewing and improving its personnel practices and its output of programmes, including its on-screen 'representation' of the British population, by making provision for and winning the confidence of women, ethnic groups and young people. Why should it not also use religious groups as a criterion of inclusivity and have to demonstrate that it is doing the same for viewers and staff defined by religious community membership? There is perhaps no prospect at present of religious equality catching up with the importance that employers and other organisations give to sex or race in the UK (outside Northern Ireland), but it is notable that despite initial governmental reluctance, in the new Equalities Act (2010) measures to address religious discrimination have been scaled up to match those of other unlawful forms of discrimination. This is partly related to the European historical experience of religion as a source of prejudice and conflict, a memory which has been reactivated by the presence of militant Muslims, not to mention networks of terrorists. It is a matter of concern that this fear of Muslims is strengthening intolerant, exclusionary politics across Europe. Specifically, that some people are today developing cultural Christianity and/or secularism as an ideology to oppose Islam and its public recognition is a challenge both to pluralism and equality, and thus to some of the bases of contemporary democracy. This is not just a risk to democracy as such but, in the present context of high levels of fear of and hostility to Muslims and Islam, threatens to create a long-term racialised-religious division in Europe.

Notes

1. Though the controversy about building an Islamic centre at 51 Park in New York, two blocks from Ground Zero, and the threat by a church pastor to burn 200 copies of the Qur'an on the ninth anniversary of 9/11 suggests that some may be too optimistic about the extent of religious tolerance in the USA (Foner and Alba, 2008). It is nevertheless unlikely that the presence of Muslims will become as central to American society as to some European countries.
2. When US sociologists use the term 'assimilation', they usually mean what is meant by integration in the UK (e.g., as in the 'segmented assimilation' proposed by Portes and Zhou (1993)).
3. Though in the light of the Rushdie Affair he wished 'we might have been more cautious about allowing the creation in the 1950s [*sic*] of a substantial Muslim community here' (*Observer*, 25 February 1989). It is also worth noting that despite his bold and pioneering stand on racial equality in the 1960s and 1970s in retrospect he only gave this topic a few sentences in his lengthy autobiography (Jenkins, 1991).
4. This is my key point of disagreement with some liberal conceptions of multiculturalism, for example, that of Anne Phillips (2007) (see Modood, 2008), and with conceptions of a multicultural society or 'multiculture' without groups, for example, Brubaker (2004) and Gilroy (2004) (see Modood, 2007 and Meer and Modood, 2009, respectively).
5. Even in the 1990s, multiculturalism in Britain was expressly linked to a national identity, to its modernisation, to, for example, 'Cool Britannia' and 'rebranding Britain' (Leonard, 2003).
6. Affirmative Action in relation to employment and entry to higher education was introduced in the 1960s and 1970s for African-Americans but began to be extended to other groups just as it became curtailed in scope by the law courts (e.g., only targets and not quotas were permitted).
7. The experience of East Europeans who came to Britain following the accession of their countries into the EU is currently being studied by my colleague, Dr Jon Fox.
8. The French lower house of parliament passed the bill with an overwhelming majority in July 2010, but before the upper house debated it, the bill was referred to the Conseil d'État for a ruling on whether it would violate individual freedoms (see http://www.guardian.co.uk/commentisfree/belief/2010/jul/13/france-burqa-ban-veil).
9. The former and current Chief Rabbis are both members of the House of Lords, and while this is no doubt related to their (former) office, the peerage is personal to them and not *ex officio*.
10. This principle that recognised that Protestants and Catholics had a right to state resources and some publicly funded autonomous institutions officially ended in 1960. It is or at least until recently, however, still considered as a 'relevant framework for the development of a model that grants certain collective rights to religious groups' (Sunier and von Luijeren, 2002) in such matters as state funding of Islamic schools. So, the accommodation of Muslims is or was being achieved through a combination of mild pillarisation and Dutch minority policies, though some of these policies have recently been discontinued.

11. In the general election of 2010, Nick Griffin, the leader of the BNP used a 'Christian nation' rhetoric, saying, 'I'm an Anglican. By blood, by descent, by the way I was brought up, by my schooling and so on' (Bartley, 2010a). Moreover, the new Christian Party endorsed the stand of the BNP on immigration (Bartley, 2010b).
12. Which was not ratified by the Council of Ministers and so was missing from the final document and the Lisbon Treaty.

References

Bari, A. (2005) 'Race, Religion and Multiculturalism', *Q-News*, 361(March).
Bartley, J. (2010a) 'Nick Griffin Expresses Support for Sentamu and Nazir Ali', http://ekklesia.co.uk/node/11599. Last accessed 28 December 2010.
Bartley, J. (2010b) 'Christian Party Endorses BNP Stance on Immigration from the EU, http://ekklesia.co.uk/node/11598. Last accessed 28 December 2010.
BBC (2005) 'Blair Shuns US Religious Politics', 22 March, http://news.bbc.co.uk/1/hi/uk_politics/4369481.stm. Last accessed 28 December 2010.
Beattie, T. (2007) *The New Atheists: The Twilight of Reason and the War on Religion*. London: Darton Longman & Todd.
Berger, P., Davie, G. and Fokas, E. (2008) *Religious America, Secular Europe: A Theme and Variation*. Aldershot: Ashgate.
Brubaker, R. (2004) *Ethnicity Without Groups*. Cambridge, MA and London: Harvard University Press.
Caldwell, C. (2009) *Reflections on the Revolution in Europe: Immigration, Islam and the West*. London: Allen Lane.
Casanova, J. (2009) 'Immigration and the New Religious Pluralism: A European Union-United States Comparison', in G.B. Levey and T. Modood, eds. *Secularism, Religion and Multicultural Citizenship*. Cambridge: Cambridge University Press, pp. 139–163.
Castells, M. (1997) *The Information Age: Economy, Society and Culture, Volume II. The Power of Identity*. Malden, MA and Oxford: Blackwell.
Cesari, J. (2004) *When Islam and Democracy Meet: Muslims in Europe and in the United States*. New York and Basingstoke: Palgrave Macmillan.
CMEB. (2000) *The Future of Multi-Ethnic Britain: Report of the Commission on the Future of Multi-Ethnic Britain*. London: Runnymede Trust.
Daniel, N. (1960) *Islam and the West. Vol. 1, The Making of An Image, 1000–1300 A.D.* Edinburgh: Edinburgh University Press.
Daniel, N. (1967) *Islam and the West. Vol. 2, Islam, Europe and Empire*. Edinburgh: Edinburgh University Press.
Dawkins, R. (2006) *The God Delusion*. London: Bantam Press.
Dykes, G. (2002) 'Diversity in Broadcasting: A Public Service Perspective', http://www.bbc.co.uk/pressofice/speeches/stories/dyke_cba.shtml.
Foner, N. and Alba, R. (2008) 'Immigrant Religion in the US and Western Europe: Bridge or Barrier to Inclusion?', *International Migration Review*, 42(2): 360–392.
Fuchs, L.H. (1990) *The American Kaleidoscope: Race, Ethnicity, and the Civic Culture*. Middletown, CN: Wesleyan University Press.
Gilroy, P. (2004) *After Empire: Melancholia or Convivial Culture?* London: Routledge.
Greely, A. (1995) 'The Persistence of Religion', *Cross Currents*, 45(Spring): 24–41.
Hamburger, P. (2002) *Separation of Church and State*. Cambridge MA and London: Harvard University Press.

Harris, S. (2004) *The End of Faith: Religion, Terror, and the Future of Reason*. New York: W.W. Norton & Co.

Heath, A.F. and Cheung, S.Y. (2007) *Unequal Chances: Ethnic Minorities in Western Labour Markets*. Oxford: Published for The British Academy by Oxford University Press.

Held, D. (1995) *Democracy and the Global Order: From the Modern State to Cosmopolitan Governance*. Cambridge: Polity.

Hitchens, C. (2007) *God Is Not Great: How Religion Poisons Everything*. New York: Twelve Books.

Hollinger, D.A. (1995) *Postethnic America: Beyond Multiculturalism*. New York: Basic Books.

Huntington, S.P. (2004) *Who Are We?: The Challenges to America's National Identity*. New York and London: Simon & Schuster.

Jacobson, J. (1997) 'Religion and Ethnicity: Dual and Alternative Sources of Identity Among Young British Pakistanis', *Ethnic and Racial Studies*, 20: 238–256.

Jenkins, R. (1967) 'Racial Equality in Britain', in A. Lester, ed. *Essays and Speeches by Roy Jenkins*. London: Collins.

Jenkins, R. (1991) *A Life at the Centre*. London: Papermac.

Lal, B.B. (1990) *The Romance of Culture in an Urban Civilisation: Robert E. Park on Race and Ethnic Relations in Cities*. London: Routledge.

Leonard, K. (2003) 'American Muslim Politics: Discourses and Practices', *Ethnicities*, 3(2): 147–181.

Loury, G.C., Modood, T. and Teles, S.M. (2005) *Ethnicity, Social Mobility, and Public Policy: Comparing the USA and UK*. Cambridge: Cambridge University Press.

Lutz, W., Skirbekk, V. and Testa, M. (2007) 'The Low-Fertility Trap Hypothesis: Forces that May Lead to Further Postponement and Fewer Births in Europe', *IIASA Reprint*.

McLoughlin, S. (2010) 'Race to Faith Relations, the Local to the National Level: The State and Muslim Organisations in Britain', in A. Kreienbrink and M. Bodenstein, eds. *Muslim Organisations and the State – European Perspectives*. Nürnberg: Bundesamt für Migration und Flüchtlinge, pp. 123–149.

Meer, N. and Modood, T. (2009) 'The Multicultural State We're in: Muslims, "Multiculture" and the "Civic Re-balancing" of British Multiculturalism', *Political Studies*, 57(3): 473–497.

Miles, R. (1989) *Racism*. London: Routledge.

Modood, T. (2005) *Multicultural Politics: Racism, Ethnicity and Muslims in Britain*. Edinburgh: Edinburgh University Press.

Modood, T. (2007) *Multiculturalism. A Civic Idea*. Cambridge: Polity.

Modood, T. (2008) 'Multiculturalism and Groups' *Social & Legal Studies*, 17(4): 549–553.

Modood, T. (2010) 'Moderate Secularism, Religion as Identity and Respect for Religion', *The Political Quarterly*, 81(1): 4–14.

Modood, T. and Kastoryano, R. (2006) 'Secularism and the Accomodation of Muslims in Europe', in T. Modood, A. Triandafyllidou and R. Zapata-Barrero, eds. *Multiculturalism, Muslims and Citizenship: A European Approach*. London: Routledge, pp. 162–178.

NEP (2010) *An Anatomy of Economic Inequality in the UK: Report of the National Equality Panel*. London: Government Equalities Office.

Omi, M. and Winant, H. (1994) *Racial Formation in the United States: From the 1960s to the 1990s*. New York and London: Routledge.

Parekh, B.C. (2000) *Rethinking Multiculturalism: Cultural Diversity and Political Theory*. Basingstoke: Palgrave Macmillan.
Park, A., Curtice, J., Thomson, K., Phillips, M., Clery, E. and Butt, S., eds. (2010) *British Social Attitudes. The 26th Report*. London: Sage.
Peach, C. (2007) 'Muslim Population of Europe: A Brief Overview of Demographic Trends and and Socio-Economic Integration', *Muslim Integration*, Washington, DC: Center for Strategic and International Studies.
Pew Forum (2010) Muslim Networks and Movements in Western Europe, http://pewresearch.org/pubs/1731/muslim-networks-movements-western-europe. Last accessed on 14 February 2011.
Phillips, A. (2007) *Multiculturalism Without Culture*. Princeton, NJ and Oxford: Princeton University Press.
Portes, A. and Zhou, M. (1993) 'The New Second Generation: Segmented Assimilation and Its Variants', *Annals of the American Academy of Political and Social Science*, pp. 74–96.
Sandel, M. (1994) 'Review of Rawls' Political Liberalism', *Harvard Law Review*, 107: 1765–1794.
Song, A. (2001) 'Comparing Minorities' Ethnic Options: Do Asian Americans Possess "More" Ethnic Options than African Americans?' *Ethnicities*, 1(1): 57–82.
Soysal, Y.N. (1994) *Limits of Citizenship: Migrants and Postnational Membership in Europe*. Chicago, IL and London: University of Chicago Press.
Sunier, T. and von Luijeren, M. (2002) 'Islam in the Netherlands', in Y. Haddad, ed. *Muslims in the West. From Sojourners to Citizens*. New York: Oxford University Press: 144–158.
Taylor, C. (1994) 'The Politics of Recognition', in A. Gutmann, ed. *Multiculturalism and 'The Politics of Recognition': An Essay*. Princeton, NJ: Princeton University Press, pp. 25–73.
The Royal Commission on Reform of the House of Lords (2000) *A House for the Future*. London, Cm 4534.
Voas, D. and Bruce, S. (2004) 'Research Note: The 2001 Census and Christian Identification in Britain', *Journal of Contemporary Religion*, 19(1): 23–28.
Walzer, M. (1997) *On Toleration*. New Haven, CT and London: Yale University Press.
Xanthaki, A. (2010) 'Multiculturalism and International Law: Discussing Universal Standards', *Human Rights Quarterly* 32(1): 21–48.
Zhou, M. (2005) 'Ethnicity as Social Capital: Community-Based Institutions and Embedded Networks of Social Relations', in G.C. Loury, T. Modood and S.M. Teles, eds. *Ethnicity, Social Mobility, and Public Policy. Comparing the USA and UK*. Cambridge: Cambridge University Press, pp. 131–159.
Zolberg, A. and Woon, L. (1999) 'Why Islam is like Spanish: Cultural Incorporation in Europe and the United States', *Politics & Society*, 27(1): 5–38.

Part 2

4

Why Take the Risk? Explaining Migrant Smuggling

Khalid Koser

1. Introduction

There is a clear legal distinction between migrant smuggling and human trafficking. The former involves a migrant voluntarily paying for clandestine transportation into another country; the latter involves people being coerced into moving against their will and exploited after arrival in their destination, either in their own or another country. While the risks associated with human trafficking are almost always greater, migrant smuggling is certainly not always risk-free. A large number of people die trying to cross land and sea borders without being detected by the authorities – as many as 2000 migrants each year trying to cross the Mediterranean from Africa to Europe and 400 trying to cross the Mexico–US border (GCIM, 2005). Smuggled migrants – especially women – can be confronted with discrimination, are obliged to accept the most menial informal sector jobs, can face specific health-related risks and are often at risk of exploitation by employers and landlords (Gencianos, 2004). Smuggled migrants with irregular status are barred from using the full range of services available to citizens and migrants with regular status and do not always make use of public services to which they are entitled, for example, emergency health care (Le Voy et al., 2004). Furthermore, migrant smuggling can effectively degrade into human trafficking, where a migrant is moved without fully paying off his or her debt to a smuggler, thus opening up the possibility for exploitation until the balance is repaid (Koser, 2007).

There are no accurate data on the global scale of migrant smuggling. The reasons are both conceptual – it can be hard to distinguish smuggled migrants from other undocumented migrants – as well as practical – by definition smuggled migrants enter a country clandestinely and their illegal status makes them reluctant to be known to authorities or researchers. A fairly commonly cited estimate is that between 2.5 and 4 million migrants cross international borders without authorisation each year (ICMPD, 2004). This includes people trafficked across borders, those who are smuggled, as well as some who move independently; but the proportions of each are not known. Estimates of between 500,000 and 1 million migrants smuggled annually are common, and many experts believe that the scale of the phenomenon is growing (de Tapia, 2004; Koser, 2007).

Similar inaccuracies surround estimates of the financial costs of migrant smuggling. A 2005 overview of smuggling costs reported in various sources over the preceding five years demonstrated an enormous range – from USD 203 to be smuggled across an African border to USD 26,000 to be smuggled from Asia to America (Petros, 2005). More recent media reports have estimated that being smuggled between mainland China and North America can cost up to USD 70,000 per person.

Data problems notwithstanding, what is clear is that despite the risks involved, each year hundreds of thousands of people at least probably pay billions of dollars between them to be smuggled around the world. This chapter tries to explain why.

In so doing it has two other ambitions. Like almost all other empirical research on migrant smuggling, this chapter is based on a small-scale and specific case study and its results are not necessarily more widely applicable. Furthermore, some of the findings presented here contrast quite significantly with smuggling research in other contexts. In response, a simple framework for comparative research on migrant smuggling in the future is developed. At the same time, one of the lessons learned from other research on migrant smuggling is the numerous problems associated with trying to sample, identify and interview smuggled migrants in destination countries. As a result the research for this chapter adopted a different approach by focusing on the families of smuggled migrants in countries of origin. An additional aim is therefore to assess the effectiveness of this alternative methodological approach.

The chapter forms part of the output from a wider research project on the geography of human smuggling and trafficking, the objectives of which were to try to understand how smugglers and traffickers are changing the geography of international migration; how migrant smuggling and trafficking are developing as a business; and what the implications of smuggling and trafficking are for migrants themselves. This was an interdisciplinary and 'two-ended' study, combining research in Afghanistan and Pakistan, covered in this chapter, with research among irregular Pakistani migrants in the UK, which has been published elsewhere (Ahmad, 2008a, 2008b).

The chapter is structured in four main sections. The next section reviews existing explanations for migrant smuggling and highlights the lack of research on how and why the decision to move with a smuggler is actually made. Then the methods used in the research on which this chapter is based are described, and the decision to focus on the origin rather than destination country explained. The next two sections together present empirical evidence on decision-making, emphasising that in this case study the decision was deliberate and deliberative, and considering the relative importance of motivation, information, return and risk in explaining the decision. The final substantive section of the chapter develops a basic framework for further comparative and longitudinal research, briefly flags policy implications and evaluates the effectiveness of the methodological approach adopted.

2. Explanations of migrant smuggling

From the recent surge in research and publications on migrant smuggling, three principal frameworks for explaining the phenomenon have emerged. One focuses on underlying causes (Koser, 2007; Castles and Miller, 2009). Growing developmental, demographic and democratic disparities provide powerful reasons to move, as does the global jobs crisis affecting a large part of the less developed world. The segmentation of labour markets in advanced economies is creating an increasing demand for migrant workers there. A revolution in communications has facilitated growing awareness of disparities and opportunities for would-be migrants; while transformations in transportation have made mobility cheaper and more readily accessible. Migration networks have expanded rapidly to facilitate migration, and the growth of a migration industry adds further momentum. For these sorts of reasons, it is argued, more people than ever before want to move, but because of restrictive asylum and immigration policies, there are proportionately fewer legal opportunities for them to do so. The demand for irregular migration has increased as a result, and migrant smugglers have cornered the emerging market.

A separate, but related explanation focuses specifically on the role of policies, and views the growth of migrant smuggling as an unintended consequence of restrictive asylum and immigration policies (Koser, 2000; Castles, 2004; Peixoto, 2008). Research in this vein has not been able to establish a causal link between restrictive policies and the growth of migrant smuggling. But it has shown how one of the principal functions served by smugglers is to overcome obstacles that have resulted directly from these policies, especially in the form of visa restrictions and border controls. The argument is that were these obstacles to be removed – for example, by increasing opportunities for legal migration – the services of smugglers would no longer be required, or at least demand for them would be reduced.

A third explanation expands the migration industry concept contained within the first. It draws on the 'business model' of migration published by British geographers John Salt and Jeremy Stein in 1997, who conceived of migration as a business comprising '...a system of institutionalized networks with complex profit and loss accounts, including a set of institutions, agents and individuals each of which stands to make a commercial gain' (Salt and Stein, 1997: 467). Migrant smuggling (and human trafficking) comprises the illegitimate side of this business. According to this model, the profit motive creates an almost irrepressible momentum within the migration business, and migrant smugglers actively recruit clients to turn a profit (Bilger, Hofmann and Jandl, 2006).

The first of these explanations might be characterised as macro-level (it concerns underlying structural features) and the second and third meso-level (respectively, the role of policy and intermediaries). What is striking is that explanations for migrant smuggling have not yet followed the conceptual funnel down to the micro-level of individual or family decision-making, even though there is a significant migration literature at this level upon which to draw (e.g., de Jong and Gardner, 1981; Boyd, 1989; Stark, 1991; Herman, 2006). Each of the above explanations implies why individuals decide to employ the services of smugglers: because they are desperate to escape poverty and repression, because policy changes leave them with little option or because they are actively recruited by the migration industry. But none really explains the decision.

Beyond the explanation that research on migrant smuggling has not yet matured enough for the development of a comprehensive explanatory framework, there are two other plausible reasons why most research to date seems to have ignored the migrants' decisions in the process. One might be that there is effectively no decision to be made – that people are forced into smuggling. This is wrong, and conflates migrant smuggling with human trafficking. Although in reality the two phenomena can merge into one another, legally they are distinct as explained in the introduction. So there is a decision that is made, and the research suggests that it can be a complex one including negotiating an acceptable cost; selecting between competing services; and choosing a route and final destination (van Liempt and Doomernik, 2006). A second possible reason why little attention has been paid to the decision to employ a smuggler might be the perception that there is little or no risk involved. Again the reason why this is wrong is explained in the introduction.

Indeed, it is the combination of its voluntary nature and the risks it entails that makes the decision by migrants to employ a smuggler so interesting and apparently different from other migration decision-making. Unless they are fleeing persecution, most migrants who pay smugglers are exercising a positive choice between staying and going. This choice characterises voluntary migrants and differentiates them from forced migrants who often have little option but to flee. At the same time, the choice to be smuggled entails significant risks. This is unlike most voluntary migrants, who do not risk as much whether they stay or go, and far more like forced migrants, for whom opting to stay at home is a high-risk strategy. In their decision-making, it appears that smuggled migrants lie somewhere between voluntary and forced migrants as usually conceived. The fact that smuggled migrants are paying for the privilege of exercising a voluntary choice that entails significant risk makes their decision even more unusual.

If engaging migrant smugglers really is voluntary, then ultimately the main reason that the phenomenon exists and continues to expand is that people continue to be willing to pay for it despite its risks. The remainder of this chapter tries to explain why.

3. Methods

The findings presented in this chapter draw on two discrete fieldwork periods, the first to both Pakistan and Afghanistan and the second to Pakistan alone, which took place between January and March 2004. The first visit had two main purposes. One was to understand the context for migrant smuggling from Afghanistan and Pakistan, and this was established through interviews with representatives from government, international organisations, non-governmental organisations and law enforcement agencies, as well as local researchers, journalists and activists in the field. The second purpose was to try to speak to smugglers themselves. This was achieved with limited success – in-depth interviews were conducted with five smugglers, and five more with agents variously involved in the process (e.g., forgers and intermediaries). To supplement this information, further in-depth interviews were conducted with eight people who had been smuggled out of Pakistan but had subsequently been deported. Together, these interviews took place in Islamabad, Karachi and Peshawar in Pakistan, and Kabul in Afghanistan. Most of the interviews were in English, but on occasion the assistance of an interpreter was required.

The main purpose of the second visit was to speak to the families of smuggled migrants. One reason was to try to understand the socio-economic context from which smuggled migrants originate. The second was to consider the implications of smuggling for those who presumably often were involved in the decision to migrate, had to raise the money to pay for migration, but did not actually move themselves. Relevant families were identified through a 'snowball' sampling procedure: an initial group of families was identified through a smuggler, and they in turn identified further families. These household interviews all took place in Karachi.

Pilot interviews quickly demonstrated the reluctance of many of these families to be interviewed in my presence, so most of the household surveys were conducted – individually – by a team of four researchers employed from the Aga Khan University in Karachi. I met the team each morning to overview the day's schedule, and every evening to review questionnaires, and I attended a handful of interviews. A total of 183 families were approached for interviews, in most cases at their front door. Of these, 133 refused to participate in the research, mainly citing concerns about exposing family members abroad. A structured questionnaire was used for the interviews, which lasted between 45 and 90 minutes, and normally took place with the head of the household – or in his or her absence the next most senior household member present.

Certainly not all the key actors involved in smuggling were interviewed during the first period of fieldwork, and equally the household survey was far from representative. It follows that the results presented here are indicative rather than conclusive. They provide an insight into the decision-making of migrants and their families, but by no means can they tell the whole story.

Understanding decision-making is notoriously difficult especially, as in this case, where there is a reliance on *post facto* rationalisation. As was observed by Bedford (1975), motives adduced by migrants for moves in the past may hide, as much as reveal, underlying causes for movement. Not only do memories get blurred; there may also be a tendency to emphasise a concrete objective or specific factor rather than the cumulative effect of hopes and fears that in reality underlie most migration decisions. Migrants may also be tempted to misrepresent their motivations for moving – if they are willing to participate in research at all – where they find themselves in a precarious legal situation in their destinations, as was the case for most of the migrants in this study, who were reported not to have legal status in the UK.

Road-testing an approach to try to overcome these sorts of methodological problems was one reason for the focus in this research on the families of smuggled migrants rather than the migrants themselves. A second reason was to try to widen understanding of the role in the smuggling process of the range of different 'actors' or 'stakeholders' involved. Most empirical research in this field to date has comprised interviews either with smuggled migrants or with policy-makers and practitioners in destination countries; and in general there has been very little research in countries of origin for smuggling rather than countries of destination. The discussion and conclusion to this chapter assesses the effectiveness of this methodological approach and makes recommendations for future research.

4. Making the decision

Before trying to explain the decision to pay a smuggler to migrate, it is important to understand the nature of the decision – who made it and in what circumstances? In almost all the cases covered by the research for this chapter, the decision to employ a smuggler to facilitate the migration of a family member was made jointly, often in consultation with family members outside the country; and with deliberation.

To try to understand who made the decision, respondents were asked two straightforward questions: 'Who made the decision to go?' and 'Who chose the destination?', and in each case the location of the key decision-maker at the time was also recorded. The results are tabulated in Table 4.1.

Table 4.1 Making the decision

Questionnaire number	Who took the decision?	Location at the time?	Who chose the destination?	Location at the time?
1	Elder brother	Ireland	Elder brother	Ireland
2	Uncle	UK	Father	Pakistan
3	Wife	Pakistan	Father-in-law	UK
4	Father	Pakistan	Father	Pakistan
5	Mother	Pakistan	Cousin	UK
6	Uncle	Italy	Uncle	Italy
7	Political party	Pakistan	Father	Pakistan
8	Wife	Pakistan	Friend	Ireland
9	Brother	Pakistan	Self	Pakistan
10	Uncle	Pakistan	Uncle	Pakistan
11	Father	Pakistan	Cousin	Pakistan
12	Self	Pakistan	Friend	Turkey
13	Self	Pakistan	Self	Pakistan
14	Father	Pakistan	Father	Pakistan
15	Self	Pakistan	Brother-in-law	UK
16	Self	Pakistan	Self	Pakistan
17	Self	Pakistan	Self	Pakistan
18	Father	Pakistan	Father	Pakistan
19	Political party	Pakistan	Friend	UK
20	Wife	Pakistan	Brother-in-law	Portugal
21	Uncle	Pakistan	Uncle	Pakistan
22	Wife	Pakistan	Wife	Pakistan
23	Brother-in-law	Pakistan	Self	Pakistan
24	Self	Pakistan	Friend	UK
25	Husband	Pakistan	Husband	Pakistan
26	Uncle	Pakistan	Father	Pakistan
27	Mother	Pakistan	Self	Pakistan
28	Cousin	Pakistan	Cousin	Pakistan
29	Father	Pakistan	Cousin	UK
30	Uncle	Pakistan	Uncle	Pakistan
31	Self	Pakistan	Self	Pakistan
32	Father	Pakistan	Brother	Spain
33	Self	Pakistan	Self	Pakistan
34	Brother	Pakistan	Brother	UK
35	Self	Pakistan	Self	Pakistan
36	Self	Pakistan	Self	Pakistan
37	Self	Pakistan	Self	Pakistan
38	Self	Pakistan	Self	Pakistan
39	Self	Pakistan	Self	Pakistan
40	Self	Pakistan	Husband	Pakistan
41	Mother	Pakistan	Aunt	Germany
42	Self	Pakistan	Friend	Germany

Table 4.1 (Continued)

Questionnaire number	Who took the decision?	Location at the time?	Who chose the destination?	Location at the time?
43	Self	Pakistan	Self	Pakistan
44	Self	Pakistan	Friend	UK
45	Self	Pakistan	Brother	Germany
46	Self	Pakistan	Self	Pakistan
47	Father	Pakistan	Father	Pakistan
48	Self	Pakistan	Self	Pakistan
49	Self	Pakistan	Uncle	UK
50	Brother	Pakistan	Brother	Pakistan

Source: Field data (2003).

The results indicate that the decision to migrate with a smuggler was not often an individual decision. In only 13 cases was it reported that the would-be migrant himself or herself both took the decision to migrate and chose the final destination. In eight other cases the would-be migrant decided to go, but the decision on a destination was made by another family member, in all but one case already living in the country in question. Indeed the transnational nature of the decision also stands out in the results: in 19 of the 50 cases one or both of the decision-makers was not in Pakistan at the time the decision to go and the choice of destination was made.

In the three cases where a woman migrated (questionnaire numbers 25, 29 and 40), five out of the six decisions were made by male relatives (husband, father or male cousin) although in one case the migrant apparently decided herself to go. Where decisions were made for male migrants there is no discernible pattern about who made the decision; and in particular the decision on the final destination was made by whichever relative (or in some cases friends) happened to already be living there. It is worth noting that in two cases (questionnaire numbers 22 and 41) women made the decision both whether and where to migrate for male migrants.

One reason why it is not surprising that other family members had a stake in the decision was the cost involved, which in almost all cases was beyond the means of the individual migrant. The costs reported varied from 80,000 Pakistani Rupees (PKR) (about GBP 620) to PKR 700,000 (approximately GBP 5400) (in two cases), and over the 50 households averaged just over PKR 408,000 (around GBP 3100). Explanations for the range are that smuggling took place at different times and to different destinations; and different smugglers apparently offered different deals.

Thirty households were willing to answer a question about how they raised the money to pay for the smuggler (Table 4.2). The most frequent response (16) was savings. A further 21 responses indicated that households

Table 4.2 Raising the money to pay smugglers

Source	**Frequency**
Savings	16
Sale of property	9
Sale of land	8
Sale of jewellery	4
Loans from relatives	4
Money lenders	3
Loans from friends	3
Bank loans	3
Community fund	1
Total*	51

Note: *30 households responded to this question; column totals exceed 30 as in some cases there were multiple sources of income.
Source: Field data (2003).

had sold possessions, particularly property, land or jewellery in order to raise sufficient funds. A further 14 responses showed a reliance for at least part of the capital on loans from a variety of sources. A number of households combined several sources to raise the money. A clear implication of these findings is that this was not a snap decision: mobilising resources in the ways indicated in Table 4.2 takes time.

A third way that the findings indicate that the decision to employ a smuggler was often a family decision was responses to the question 'Who identified the smuggler?' Forty-three households responded to this question; in 18 cases the smuggler was apparently identified by the would-be migrant himself (none of the women migrants located their own smuggler) and in the remaining 25 cases by family, friends and in two cases by a religious party.

5. Explaining the decision

On the basis of the preceding analysis, a first step in explaining the decision to employ a smuggler is to understand that it was normally a decision that involved family members in one way or another and that it was taken with due deliberation. If anything this makes the decision even more extraordinary. It is one thing to understand why an individual might choose to risk his or her own life by being smuggled; it is quite another to understand why a family would invest in some cases their life savings potentially to risk the life of a spouse or child. Similarly, rushing into an ill-informed decision might explain making a mistake, but this seems less likely where the decision has been thought through.

Drawing on further empirical data, this section considers four possible hypotheses: first, that the households or migrants were so desperate that they had no choice but to take the risk; second, that they did not understand the risk that was being taken; third, that the potential financial returns made the risk worthwhile; and fourth, that the risk involved was so minimal as not to count against the decision.

5.1. Desperation

The most common reason suggested in the existing literature for people to move out of desperation is that they are fleeing life-threatening circumstances as refugees (Kunz, 1973; Salt, 1986), although it has also been suggested that even refugees have some, albeit very limited, choices (Richmond, 1994). Arguably four of the 50 migrants covered by this survey might fall within this category. The main reason they were reported to have left was because of their affiliation with anti-government political (and in one case religious) groups that meant they felt that at the very least they might be arrested if they stayed. For this small minority paying a smuggler to get out of the country was probably worthwhile despite the associated risks.

In contrast, it is clear that most people moved for broadly economic reasons. The most common response to the question about motivations for migration was to earn more money (23) and next to set up a business (16). The remaining seven respondents reported motivations as education (4) and marriage (3).

To what extent might those who moved for economic reasons be described as desperate? Eight were unemployed before they left and in all their cases the main motivation to move was to find work. On the other hand, all of them had completed school education and all eight had been born in Karachi. The average income across their households was just over PKR 80,000 (approximately USD 1300) per year – considerably less than the average of PKR 156,000 (around USD 2500) across all 50 surveyed households, but by no means on the poverty line. These were not, then, desperate, landless peasants forced to move to survive; they were generally middle-class and relatively well-educated urban young men who were out of work. In any case, presumably even people desperate for work might consider a safer and cheaper option to find work – in the informal economy, in another city or perhaps even in the Middle East – than employing a smuggler to transport them to Europe.

Of the migrants who were employed when they left, their occupations varied considerably. Three were doctors and three laboratory assistants in hospitals; three had clerical jobs and a further three were shopkeepers. The rest were spread across a wide range of occupational categories, and five were students. The majority had completed school education and 16 also had university qualifications. Six of their families had moved to the city from a rural area in Pakistan. This is hardly the profile of a person desperate enough to risk their life to get to Europe.

A final set of indicators that the 'desperation hypothesis' does not adequately explain the decision to employ smugglers emerges from the status of the households from which migration took place. As has already been indicated, their average annual income was about PKR 156,000 (USD 2500); the majority had urban origins; and most had the wherewithal to raise significant sums of money to pay a smuggler. The mean number of household adults was 3.44. Most lived in middle-class Karachi 'towns' such as Gulshan-e-Iqbal, North Nazimabad and Federal B Areas; and a few in Malir and Orangi 'towns', which are among the poorest in the city. All 50 households owned a television, 45 owned a refrigerator, 24 had a telephone and 11 each had a car and a computer. Twenty-seven owned property, six owned land and one household owned a business.

5.2. A lack of knowledge

The availability of information, or lack thereof, has been shown to play a critical role in migration decision-making (Massey et al., 1987; Wilpert, 1992) and refugee decision-making too (Cuny and Stein, 1991). If they did not take the risk of moving with smugglers because of desperation, could it be that the migrants and households involved did not realise the risk they were undertaking?

Certainly, previous studies have found that smuggled migrants have very little knowledge about what they are getting themselves into. Interviews in another study with asylum seekers in the UK from Afghanistan, Colombia, Kosovo and Somalia, the majority of whom had been smuggled, found that very few had any prior knowledge about how they would be transported, where they would end up and what to expect when they got there (Gilbert and Koser, 2006). That study identified five specific reasons for the lack of knowledge among the respondents: many did not decide their own destinations; few had family or friends in their intended destination; some had been misled or given limited information; several left quickly and did not have time to gather sufficient information; and several were uneducated and spoke no English.

How do these reasons stack up in the present case study? First, as was implied by the results shown in Table 4.1, every respondent had a final destination in mind. In contrast to the asylum seekers in the study by Gilbert and Koser, who were characterised as having 'lost control' of their migration through their vulnerability as asylum seekers, for most of the families in this case study migration was a deliberate and deliberated strategy. Second, in 17 cases their final destination was chosen by family or friends already there. Third, and furthermore, fully 46 of the 50 households surveyed reported that another household member had migrated before the migrant in question. In other words, almost every household had access to a family member who either was still living abroad or who at least had experience of international migration. Fourth, as has already been established, while four migrants in this case study might have left in rushed circumstances to avoid arrest, the majority did not. Finally, and again as has been alluded, the majority of migrants in question had at least completed school education.

While these explanations probably prove that migrants and their families know about what to expect in destination countries, perhaps they did not realise the implications of smuggling. Only 16 of the 34 households willing to answer the question admitted that earlier migrants from their households had also employed smugglers, so it may be that even those households with friends and family abroad had no direct understanding of smuggling. On the other hand, these were generally relatively well-educated households which surely would have been aware of migrant smuggling, a very common and widely reported phenomenon in Pakistan. Furthermore of the 25 out of 43 cases where family and friends located a smuggler, in 15 cases the smuggler was reported to be a personal or business contact. It is especially striking that in three cases, migrants had been intercepted and returned to Pakistan en route to Europe, and their families had saved up to send them again. These migrants at least had first-hand experience of some of the risks and the potential for failure, but were willing nevertheless to try again.

5.3. Financial gains

The chance to earn more money – even if it means a reduction in job status – is one of the main incentives for people to migrate to richer countries. In as far as the money earned is made available to family members back home, for example, through remittances, supporting the migration of one household member can also be a family strategy (Stark, 1991; Poirine, 1997). A third possible explanation for the decision to migrate with a smuggler is that the prospective financial gains sufficiently outweigh the risks involved. The results tabulated in Table 4.3 lend some credence to this hypothesis.

On the one hand, these data reinforce just how significant an investment smuggling represented for most households – on average smugglers' fees amounted to 262 per cent of the households' annual income. Even the lowest ratio of fee to household income was 67 per cent; while in the most extreme case the fee represented over ten times the household's annual income.

On the other hand, on average, annual remittances from the smuggled migrant amounted to 52 per cent of the agents' fees – ranging from just 3 per cent in one case to 100 per cent in another case. Continuing to use mean values, this means that on average it would require just less than two years of remittances at a steady rate to repay the initial investment in smuggling – the range was from just one year in one case to over 31 years in another. Thereafter, assuming current rates of both, remittances would significantly increase household incomes – on average more than doubling them.

Table 4.3 Annual household incomes, smugglers' fees and annual remittances (PKR) for selected households

Questionnaire number	Annual household income	Smugglers' fees	Annual remittances
1	204,000	350,000	200,000
2	108,000	400,000	–
3	42,000	450,000	300,000
4	228,000	300,000	9,600
5	54,000	500,000	175,000
6	216,000	400,000	144,000
7	144,000	700,000	–
8	264,000	600,000	100,000
9	90,000	450,000	120,000
12	114,000	500,000	300,000
14	93,600	450,000	400,000
17	222,000	700,000	600,000
24	120,000	80,000	–
32	54,000	300,000	300,000
33	48,000	450,000	200,000
35	168,000	300,000	–
43	180,000	400,000	–
44	180,000	300,000	120,000
45	156,000	400,000	100,000
47	264,000	300,000	200,000
48	240,000	350,000	140,000
50	240,000	300,000	–
Mean	155,891	408,182	213,038

Note: – no answer provided.
Source: Field data (2003).

Clearly there are some important assumptions in this analysis: that the migrant can find and keep a job for at least a year; that he or she is able to earn sufficiently to send back a proportion of the income; that he or she is not arrested and deported as an irregular migrant and so on. But on the basis of this small case study it appears that these were reasonable assumptions for families to make, as is explained next.

5.4. Risk

The potential for relatively high financial returns probably combines with the fact that the risks involved were actually very small, to provide a reasonable explanation for paying smugglers. First, it is worth observing that all 50 of the migrants covered by this research were reported to have arrived safely in the destination of their choice. Clearly this study did not necessarily comprise a representative sample, and it may well be that some of those families that chose not to take part in the research did so because of the trauma of having lost a family member during the journey. But in none of the other contextual interviews carried out for this research – including with unsuccessful smuggled migrants who had been intercepted and returned – were there reports of direct experience of death or injury on the way.

Second, the families surveyed all reported that the migrants in question had found work in their destination. These families may have not have being telling the truth, and it is also quite feasible that the migrants were exaggerating their apparent success (Koser and Pinkerton, 2002). Nevertheless the fact that such a high proportion of families (35 of 50) reported receiving regular remittances indicates that at least a good number of migrants were earning a reasonable income somehow.

The remittance data presented in the last section, third, also suggests that on the whole this was a financial risk worth taking for the households involved. Many liquidated assets or invested their savings, some also lost the income of the member who migrated, but most relatively quickly recouped their investment and added substantially to their household income.

6. Discussion

The main aim for this chapter is to try to explain a migration decision that on the surface is irrational: why do people pay to undertake a migration that is risky at best and life-threatening at worst? The fact that in this case study the decision has been shown in most cases to have been made in consultation with family members and in a deliberate and deliberative manner makes it even more intriguing. The preceding analysis has largely discounted the possibilities in this particular case study that desperation drove people to take the risk or that they were simply unaware of what they were getting into. It suggested instead that a combination of high returns and low risks made the decision rational for those making it.

Like almost all other empirical research on migrant smuggling, however, the findings here cannot be extrapolated with any confidence to other situations. They are based on a small sample and may not even apply to other smuggling scenarios in the same geographical context. They are based on interviews that took place several years ago, and thus might not accurately describe the situation today. And it certainly cannot be assumed that research on migrant smuggling between another set of origin and destination countries would yield similar results.

Properly to understand the dynamics of migrant smuggling as a global phenomenon, what is required is both longitudinal and comparative research. The preceding analysis suggests a simple framework based on the four factors of motivation, information, return and risk. Each of the factors is dynamic and their changing interaction is likely to influence the scale and nature of migrant smuggling over time. In the above case study, for example, a transition from high return-low risk to low return-high risk would probably reduce the scale of smuggling significantly – apart from by those who were desperate to move or who had too little information to assess the risk. The outcome might therefore be predicted to be fewer smuggled migrants but with a concentration of those fleeing in refugee-like circumstances.

One of the principal dynamics likely to influence motivation is the political context in origin countries. In the above case study four respondents apparently moved because they feared reprisals on the basis of their political or religious affiliations and the current political climate in both Afghanistan and Pakistan is unstable enough not to discount the threat of further reprisals of this kind. Other research has demonstrated that asylum seekers – including a significant proportion of people who are eventually recognised as refugees – also increasingly employ smugglers (Schuster, 2004; Marfleet, 2006). For people fleeing for their lives their motivation to escape will outweigh the other considerations of information, return and risk in migrating with a smuggler.

The comparison between the findings about information and knowledge in this case study and those reported elsewhere highlights one of the most striking discrepancies revealed by different case studies on smuggled migrants. Some report that migrants are well informed, often by their smugglers (Koser, 1997); while others report that migrants know virtually nothing (Morrison, 2000). As explained above, Gilbert and Koser (2006) identified a series of factors that might combine to explain varying levels of information in the smuggling process. It would be a fair conclusion that in the above case study, nobody chose to migrate with smugglers because they were unaware of the risks entailed. But that is clearly not the case in other contexts. One reason may be that the migrants in this case study were urban and relatively well educated – in other words, they had access to information and in many cases they also had family and friends already living abroad. This is far less likely to be the case where smuggling originates in poorer and rural settings.

There are two main components that determine the return on migrant smuggling – the price charged by smugglers and the ability of the smuggled migrant to earn a sufficient income to send home remittances. Petros's (2005) review of smuggling costs found no clear trend, but did confirm that costs change over time. Interviews with smugglers in Afghanistan and Pakistan pointed to an increase in the amount they had charged over time, for three main reasons. First, many of the smugglers operating in Pakistan during the late 1990s were apparently Afghan nationals and their number decreased substantially once they were able to return home, thus reducing competition among the remaining smugglers. Second, most smugglers reported that at the same time demand for their services had increased markedly in the last few years before the interviews, apparently often from Afghans looking for alternatives to returning home. Third, smugglers increasingly have moved migrants by airplane rather than overland or by boat, the costs incurred by smugglers to facilitate migration thus increasing.

In the case study discussed above, it was reported that all 50 migrants had found employment, and that 35 of them were regularly sending home remittances. A whole host of variables is likely to influence both outcomes in other situations. The migrants in this study, for example, were relatively well educated and all spoke English; they were moving to a country where many already had friends and family who might help them find work; and also to a country with a buoyant economy and significant unregulated informal labour market. Most apparently earned sufficiently to be able to send home some money, and presumably in doing so were fulfilling a social obligation. All of these variables can change over time and are likely to vary between case studies.

Existing empirical evidence is too patchy and incomplete to make an assessment about whether certain smuggling routes entail greater physical risks for migrants than others. It seems reasonable to assume, however, that the mode of transport is a factor. All of the migrants covered in this research were reported to have flown either directly or indirectly to the UK, and as the smugglers indicated this is far less risky than travelling by boat or overland. The risk of death or physical harm is only one aspect of the risk involved in smuggling – as indicated in the introduction to this chapter it can also result in abuse and exploitation after arrival, and imprisonment and deportation. In this particular case study, for example, smugglers were paid in advance of the journey, thus negating the possibility of direct exploitation by smugglers after arrival; but this certainly is not the arrangement that has been reported in other situations. And one of the significant unknowns in all smuggling research is what proportion of people are still in transit, and what their experiences are.

The proposal that a combination of motivation, information, return and risk might begin to explain different migrant smuggling outcomes, and that each of these factors is dynamic, also opens up the potential for certain policy interventions. In the long term reducing global disparities in development, demography and the democratic process might remove the motivation for migrants to leave their countries in the first place. Opening up legal means for migration should reduce their dependence on smugglers. Perhaps rather more realistically and immediately, there is a role for information campaigns to try to make sure that people understand the risks they are taking in being smuggled. Origin country policies towards reducing smuggling might increase costs, while destination country policies in the informal labour market might reduce the possibility for smuggled migrants to work; a combination that might serve to reduce the returns on smuggling. While policy interventions certainly should not aim at increasing the physical risk for migrants (although it is often argued that they do as an unintended consequence), they can increase the risk that migrants will not be able to find work, or will be quickly arrested and deported.

Besides proposing a basic framework for comparative and longitudinal research on migrant smuggling, another aim for this chapter has been to road-test an alternative methodology for research in this area. Researching migrant smuggling in destination countries is notoriously difficult for the reasons stipulated earlier. To what extent has research in the origin country helped overcome some of the obstacles? The evaluation is mixed. The approach adopted here has focused the spotlight on the role of families in migrant smuggling, which has largely been ignored to date but appears at least in this case to be significant. It has proved an effective method for understanding the socio-economic context from which smuggled migrants originate. It has also begun to explain how migrant smuggling is financed and how money flows through the smuggling system, by permitting interviews directly with smugglers themselves.

It has not, however, overcome the recall problem associated with most research on migrant decision-making – rather than asking migrants to remember and explain their decisions it asked families to do so on their behalf. On the other hand, there is a possibility that families have less reason to mislead interviewers on this topic. The method has also relied on indirect information in that families were asked to report on what they had heard from migrants about their employment status and living conditions in the UK.

Ideally future research on migrant smuggling should take place both in origin and destination countries – and where appropriate and possible also in transit countries too. It should combine research with the migrants themselves, their family members and intermediaries including smugglers and policy-makers. The real challenge will be to try to match specific migrants to their own families and the smugglers who transported them: the families interviewed for this research resolutely refused to provide contact information for family members who had been smuggled to the UK and the smugglers would not name the families or migrants for whom they had worked.

In trying to explain migrant smuggling by answering the question 'Why take the risk?' this chapter has also charted some directions for future research on a significant – and probably growing – global phenomenon. It has suggested a basic framework for comparative and longitudinal research and demonstrated the potential value of extending the usual methodological approach to include origin country settings and wider coverage of those actually involved in the process.

References

Ahmad, A. (2008a) 'Dead Men Working: Time and Space in London's "Illegal" Migrant Economy', *Work, Employment and Society*, 22(2): 301–318.

Ahmad, A. (2008b) 'Human Smuggling and Illegal Labour: Pakistani Migrants in London's Informal Economy', *Journal of Ethnic and Migration Studies*, 34(6): 853–874.

Bedford, R.D. (1975) 'The Questions to be Asked of Migrants', in R.J. Pryor, ed. *The Motivation of Migration*. Canberra: Australian National University: 28–32.

Bilger, V., Hofmann, M. and Jandl, M. (2006) 'Human Smuggling as a Transnational Service Industry: Evidence from Austria', *International Migration*, 44(4): 60–93.

Boyd, M. (1989) 'Family and Personal Networks in International Migration: Recent Developments and New Agendas', *International Migration Review*, 23: 638–672.
Castles, S. (2004) 'Why Migration Policies Fail', *Ethnic and Racial Studies*, 27(2): 205–227.
Castles, S. and Miller, M. (2009) *The Age of Migration*, 4th edn. New York: Guildford Press.
Cuny, F.C. and Stein, B.N. (1991) 'Introduction', in M.A. Larkin, F.C. Cuny and B.N. Stein, eds. *Repatriation Under Conflict in Central America*. Washington DC: CIPRA and Intertect, pp. 1–8.
De Jong, G.F. and Gardner, R.W. (1981) *Migration Decision-Making*. New York: Pergamon.
de Tapia, S. (2004) *New Patterns of Irregular Migration in Europe*. Paris: Council of Europe.
Gencianos, G. (2004) 'International Civil Society Cooperation on Migrants' Rights: Perspectives from an NGO Network', *European Journal of Migration and Law*, 6: 147–155.
Gilbert, A. and Koser, K. (2006) 'Coming to the UK: What do Asylum-Seekers Know About the UK Before Arrival?', *Journal of Ethnic and Migration Studies*, 32(7): 456–471.
Global Commission on International Migration (GCIM) (2005) *Migration in an Interconnected World: New Directions for Action*. Geneva: GCIM.
Herman, E. (2006) 'Migration as a Family Business: The Role of Personal Networks in the Mobility Phase of Migration', *International Migration*, 44(4): 191–230.
Hugo, G. (2005) 'Migrants in Society: Diversity and Cohesion', Expert paper for the Global Commission on International Migration.
International Centre on Migration Policy and Development (ICMPD) (2004) 'Irregular Transit Migration in the Mediterranean: Some Facts, Figures and Insights', presented to the Dialogue on Mediterranean Transit Migration, Vienna, 5–6 February.
Koser, K. (1997) 'Social Networks and the Asylum Cycle: The Case of Iranians in the Netherlands', *International Migration Review*, 31: 591–611.
Koser, K. (2000) 'Asylum Policies, Trafficking and Vulnerability', *International Migration*, 38(3): 91–112.
Koser, K. (2007) 'Irregular Migration' , in B. Marshall, ed. *The Politics of Migration*. London: Routledge: 44–57.
Koser, K. and Pinkerton, C. (2002) *The Social Networks of Asylum Seekers and the Dissemination of Information About Countries of Asylum*. London: Home Office, Research Development and Statistics Directorate.
Kunz, E.F. (1973) 'The Refugee in Flight: Kinetic Models and Forms of Displacement', *International Migration Review*, (7): 125–146.
Le Voy, M., Verbruggen, N. and Wets, J., eds (2004) *Undocumented Migrant Workers in Europe*. Brussels: PICUM.
Marfleet, P. (2006) *Refugees in a Global Era*. London: Palgrave Macmillan.
Massey, D.S., Alarcon, R., Durand, J. and Gonzalez, H. (1987) *Return to Aztlan*. Berkeley, CA: University of California Press.
Morrison, J. (2000) 'The Trafficking and Smuggling of Refugees: The End Game in European Asylum Policy?', *New Issues in Refugee Research*. Geneva: UNHCR.
Peixoto, J. (2008) 'Migrant Smuggling and Trafficking in Portugal', in C. Bonifazi, M. Okolski and J. Schoorl, eds. *International Migration in Europe: New Trends and New Methods of Analysis*, Amsterdam: Amsterdam University Press, pp. 65–86.
Petros, M. (2005) *'The Costs of Human Smuggling and Trafficking', Global Migration Perspectives*, Vol. 31. Geneva: GCIM.
Richmond, A. (1994) *Global Apartheid*. Don Mills, ON: Oxford University Press.

Salt, J. (1986) 'International Migration: A Spatial Theoretical Approach', in M. Pacione, ed. *Population Geography: Progress and Prospect*. London: Croom Helm, pp. 163–193.
Salt, J. and Stein, J. (1997) 'Migration as a Business: The Case of Trafficking', *International Migration*, 35: 467–494.
Schuster, L. (2004) 'The Exclusion of Asylum Seekers in Europe', *COMPAS Working Paper*, 1, COMPAS, Oxford.
Stark, O. (1991) *The Migration of Labour*. Oxford: Basil Blackwell.
Van Liempt, I. and Doomernik, J. (2006) 'Migrant's Agency in the Smuggling Process', *International Migration*, 44(4): 165–189.
Wilpert, C. (1992) 'The Use of Social Networks in Turkish Migration to Germany', in M.M. Kritz, L.L. Lim and H. Zlotnik, eds. *International Migration Systems*. Oxford: Clarendon, pp. 177–189.

5

Acquisition and Mobility of Expertise in Global Corporate Labour Markets

John Salt and Peter Wood

1. Introduction: influences on international corporate labour mobility

Multinational enterprises (MNEs) employ various combinations of international exchange to deploy their staff expertise to where it is needed. Such 'portfolios of mobility', combining permanent staff transfers, expatriate residential assignments, business travel and commuting, help to sustain corporate functions across a variety of production and market environments (Koser and Salt, 1997; Salt, 1997; Goshall and Bartlett, 1998; Forsgren, Holm and Johanson, 2005; Faulconbridge and Beaverstock, 2008; Jones, 2008a; Millar and Salt, 2008).

The dynamics of production in transnational corporations focus attention on knowledge interchange, where the aim is to combine information from diverse sources and generate useful knowledge about designing, making and selling new products and services in particular locales. The potential added value from accumulating internationally mobile expertise comes from their prior immersion in a range of cultural, institutional and project-related communities (Forsgren, Holm and Johanson, 2005). From a company perspective, the learning imperative for international mobility is linked to a desire to create a cadre of executives and technicians who are able to think and act both globally and locally. However, the mere movement of expertise between institutions and countries is insufficient to ensure learning. Also important are the management processes which mediate the transfer and assimilation of expertise, synthesise it with existing knowledge and integrate it with current production methods (Millar, Demaid and Quintas, 1997).

A previous paper showed that different types of movement may be related to different forms of knowledge exchange (Millar and Salt, 2008). For example, significant programmes of business development or global integration usually require extended personnel ('embodied') movement. More routine exchanges, however, can usually be sustained by shorter-term and virtual (electronic) interactions (Collins, 1997; Williams, 2007). Companies develop and use different forms of mobility, combining them into more or less formal 'portfolios' of movements according to their business needs. They must also incorporate the training of internationally mobile staff, new communications systems, and often eventually the progressive transfer of technical and business expertise to 'host country' personnel. Portfolios of mobility in firms are therefore influenced by sector-specific characteristics and by a set of key factors which determine the types of mobility that may be used for particular purposes, in particular places and at certain times.

Much of this chapter focuses on specific sectoral characteristics which influence portfolios of mobility at any time. Historically, international corporate activity was first dominated by primary and processing industries, with associated investment and trading functions, relying heavily on expatriate expertise. By the later decades of the twentieth century, the internationalisation of manufacturing required a widening array of production and marketing skills and more complex combinations of expatriate and host country personnel. Today, primary and manufacturing production are still significant in the international exchange of MNE expertise. The most rapid recent growth has been in services, however, especially the knowledge-intensive business services including finance, accountancy, information technology (IT) and other business consultancies.

This chapter is about the acquisition and international movement of expertise within the internal labour markets of a sample of MNEs with substantial UK bases. It uses the findings of a survey of 35 such companies, in six economic sectors, undertaken during 2005–06.[1] It builds on existing analyses (Millar and Salt, 2006, 2008; Salt, 2009), which have identified the main factors underlying company portfolios of mobility, to focus on some key characteristics which affect how knowledge is moved internationally within particular industries and services. Its emphasis is on those business conditions which influence long- and short-term migratory assignments, but their implications for other forms of mobility are briefly discussed. Table 5.1 summarises the firms included in each of the six sectors.

2. Statistical background

2.1. The national level

The significance on intra-company transfers (ICTs) for the international migration patterns of the highly skilled into the UK is perhaps most directly indicated by work permit data. These show how strongly such labour immigration is influenced by recruitment and movement of staff by large companies within their global labour markets.[2] In 2006, 34.9 per cent of UK work permits and first permissions (excluding extensions and changes of employment) were ICTs; by 2008 the proportion had reached 46.5 per cent (Table 5.2). The bulk of these were in computer services, telecommunications, manufacturing, administration, business and

Table 5.1 Sectors and sample companies

Aerospace	This sector is capital intensive and, with one exception, the six companies in the research sample were large, 'post-mature' transnational companies. They are involved often as partners in consortia, producing and delivering large-scale, high value, long-term, engineering intensive and technologically complex product systems. The two major market elements of the sector, civil and military, shared many similarities but also some key differences.
Extractive	Two of the four companies in the sample were in oil exploration, production and distribution, one in gas and the other in minerals. Three were multi-product firms, with each product market presenting variable business cycles and competitive challenges. All four companies have experienced internationalisation through a series of mergers and acquisitions, creating marked changes in patterns of mobility.
Electronics	The sample is made up of five 'global' companies, three with US headquarters, one Dutch, and the other UK-based but recently taken over by a Swedish company. All companies are multi-product corporations focusing on microelectronics-based networking and communications products and services. Three had been particularly affected by market and employment contraction. All had experienced structural change through mergers and acquisitions.
Pharmaceuticals	Both companies in the sample were large, science-based, R&D-intensive, multi-product firms. They have UK headquarters, although one is US owned, with fewer UK-based employees than the other.
Information technology	There are eight firms in the sample. Three are Indian multinationals, with two focusing on IT, consulting and business process outsourcing, and the other delivering software solutions and integration services. Three have US headquarters, one European and one is Japanese owned. Their dominant activities reflect the main growth markets for software, IT and business services in the UK, in outsourcing and the public sector. One of the US companies is also engaged in a range of consultancy, and is also included in the consultancy sample.
Consultancy	The activities of the four consultancy companies in the sample were in many ways similar to, and overlapped with, the IT companies. Three were large and multi-functional, with one a smaller human resource consultancy. All had a wide international presence.

management services, and finance. In contrast, such in-migrant moves were rare in the public sector, including education, health, medical services and government, and in hospitality, entertainment and leisure services, and sporting activities.

Table 5.2 Intra-company transfers (ICTs) work permits and first permissions by sector, 2006 and 2008

	2006			2008		
	ICT	Total	ICT %	ICT	Total	ICT %
Administration, business and management services	4,895	12,006	40.8	4,943	10,249	48.2
Agriculture activities	20	419	4.8	21	304	6.9
Computer services	17,503	21,024	83.3	19,208	21,690	88.6
Construction and land services	891	3,367	26.5	615	2,338	26.3
Education and cultural activities	183	7,449	2.5	227	6,274	3.6
Entertainment and leisure services	171	4,598	3.7	175	4,770	3.7
Extraction industries	876	1,534	57.1	816	1,392	58.6
Financial services	4,061	8,695	46.7	4,024	7,852	51.2
Government	12	652	1.8	13	396	3.3
Health and medical services	337	17,162	2.0	336	5,883	5.7
Hospitality, hotels, catering and other services	135	7,246	1.9	78	3,865	2.0
Law-related services	275	1,157	23.8	266	1,004	26.5
Manufacturing	1,563	3,036	51.5	1,844	3,153	58.5
Real estate and property services	49	285	17.2	23	140	16.4
Retail and related services	388	1,594	24.3	394	1,092	36.1
Security and protective services	35	138	25.4	99	212	46.7
Sporting activities	4	1,953	0.2	7	2,677	0.3
Telecommunications	1,467	2,092	70.1	2,030	2,466	82.3
Transport	367	996	36.8	500	855	58.5
Utilities: gas, electricity, water	410	1,051	39.0	506	945	53.5
Total	33,642	96,454	34.9	36,125	77,660	46.5

Source: UK Border Agency.

2.2. The company level

All of the companies interviewed operated internationally, and most would describe themselves as global. Eight respondents were able to provide statistical information on the outcomes of their global mobility practices.[3] For these, Table 5.3 shows the number and proportions of annual secondments during *c.* 2004–05 between major geographical regions. The data show the importance of the transatlantic conduit between Europe and the USA and the continuing significance of the 'colonial' pattern of flows between the UK/USA and Rest of the World (RoW). For the most part, companies were not transferring large numbers of staff between locations outside these two major regions, or from the RoW to Europe and the USA. Hence, while flows are to some extent global, traditional routes dominate. Although the sample is too small to generalise, there are indications of sectoral difference. For example, the aerospace and electronics firms were

Table 5.3 Number of assignments by major geographical region, 2004–05

	EU_US to EU_US		EU_US to RoW		RoW to EU_US		RoW to RoW		Total
Pharmaceutical	77	53.1%	32	22.1%	16	11.0%	20	13.8%	145
Pharmaceutical	97	37.6%	108	41.9%	16	6.2%	37	14.3%	258
Aero	199	55.1%	154	42.7%	3	0.8%	5	1.4%	361
Extractive	791	38.5%	971	47.3%	291	14.2%	0	0.0%	2,053
Aero	78	54.5%	51	35.7%	14	9.8%	0	0.0%	143
Electronics	28	70.0%	4	10.0%	8	20.0%	0	0.0%	40
IT	290	28.7%	719	71.3%	0	0.0%	0	0.0%	1,009
Aero	88	73.9%	30	25.2%	0	0.0%	1	0.8%	119
Total	1,648	39.9%	2,069	50.1%	348	8.4%	63	1.5%	4,128

Source: Company data.

dominated by transatlantic exchange, the extractive firms were perhaps most dispersed in their global exchange, while the two pharmaceutical companies had higher proportions of moves between RoW locations.

3. General sectoral influences

In all companies, spatial mobility is to a large extent determined by the geographical distribution of corporate locations. Generally speaking, location influences the range of mobility options available, the mode of international moves employed and the company's recruitment strategies. Among manufacturing and extractive companies, the production process has important implications for industrial location and the physical mobility of expertise across sites and countries. The aerospace, extractives, pharmaceutical and electronics sectors have high capital intensity and, with one or two exceptions in the sample, are characterised by large-size, 'post-mature'[4] transnationalising companies. They face specific pressures associated with the need for corporate renewal and innovativeness which have implications for their evolving geographical and structural configurations, their levels of technological, procedural and capital sophistication and their strategies towards human resource management (Miller and Friesen, 1984; Sparrow and Braun, 2006). The companies are involved, often as partners in consortia, in the production and delivery of large-scale, high value, long-term and technologically complex product systems (Paoli and Prencipe, 1999; Acha et al., 2004). Their customers may include national governments that play active and multiple roles in product and project development, for example, as contractor, partner and regulator. The importance of each of these characteristics varies between companies and sectors.

In contrast, the business of companies in the IT and consultancy sectors is primarily client orientated and has grown rapidly over the past 30 years (Gallouj, 2002; Wood, 2002; Kolb et al., 2004; Beyers, 2007; Rubalcaba and Kox, 2007). This means that most mobility involves exchanging expertise with client locations which are themselves frequently widely distributed geographically. Corporate growth in parts of these sectors has been rapid in recent years, frequently including mergers and acquisitions. This is particularly the case in IT where offshoring and outsourcing have become widespread. Mobility is principally project based and relatively short term.

The portfolios of mobility across all these sectors are being affected by shifting corporate priorities and intensified competition among MNEs in general, reflecting four main factors.

1. Growing diversity in *production and market characteristics*. Established MNEs face a widening range of operational conditions and increased organisational complexity across a growing variety of global regions.

(Dicken, 2007; Forsgren, Holm and Johanson, 2005; Jones, 2008a). They are also encountering intensified competition, not just from the core economies of the USA, Europe and Japan, but increasingly from MNEs based in countries such as India, Korea, Malaysia, Russia, China and the Gulf States. These may be evolving networks of international exchange and control more attuned to commercial, cultural and political sensibilities in these and other growing markets.

2. Continuing *corporate restructuring*, including mergers and acquisitions, de-mergers, management buyouts and joint ventures, some specifically designed to ensure more effective international production and marketing. The outcomes of these processes also reflects the technology-based expansion of the volume and scope of international communications.
3. Particular *customers and customer relationships* including the many complex technical, relational and contractual issues requiring continued attention throughout the life of projects.
4. *Product, project and process-related* influences, notably the different balance of expertise required by each project, related to its location, purpose, life cycle, degrees of technological and process change, required levels of expert attention, and security and commercial confidentiality.

Additional factors include challenges to habitual patterns of expatriate exchange themselves, based on changing attitudes among expert personnel to extended overseas assignments or travel, and the declining attraction of the 'colonial model' of expatriation.

4. Types of mobility

Eight expertise mobility options, extending across overlapping time periods, were identified to support both career development and international projects. These types of mobility are discussed in more detail in Millar and Salt (2008):

- The occasional recruitment of new staff to work on particular projects from the external labour market (ELM) or from the other international subsidiaries or divisions of the same company. This is comparatively rare and is likely to involve either senior appointments or particular specialists in short supply.
- Long-term residential assignments of key managers/experts, extending from 12 months to 5 years: frequent.
- Short-term residential assignments, from 2 to 12 months, occasionally extending to 24 months: frequent.
- Commuter assignments of key experts. Usually commuting weekly, over periods from 1–2 months to 2 years: some growth, mainly around Europe.

- 'Rotators' (especially in extraction sectors), involving successive weeks on and off duty.
- Extended business travel, carried out over 30 day to 6-month periods: growing.
- Business travel, from a few days to three months: frequent.
- Virtual information exchange: a complement to, or substitution for, embodied forms of expertise exchange: rapidly growing.

In all companies, mobility arises from a combination of project management and career development goals. The balance varies across companies, although there is an element of career development in many if not most moves. For the older established, more capital-intensive employers, secondment moves are mainly for career development purposes or for setting up new production facilities. Most companies still prefer to 'grow their own' staff by equipping them with the necessary skill and experience to perform higher level jobs. Such moves are also important in spreading corporate culture globally to all company locations. This 'colonial model' remains the norm during the process of internationalisation, such as when a new production facility is established in an emerging market, until local staff are trained and available. Staff involved are mainly senior people, as indicated in Table 5.4. In IT and business services companies, where mobility is predominantly client orientated, the career development component is less obvious. Assignments are generally short term and for a specific purpose. Nevertheless, in normal circumstances there is usually some element of training or experience gaining involved which broadens the individual's expertise base.

5. Sectoral characteristics

The six sectors were chosen in the research design to reflect a range of conditions and circumstances affecting corporate mobility. There are many commonalities in the creation of mobility portfolios. They include both demand (corporate business requirement) and supply (individual career development and life cycle preference) driven reasons for mobility, stage of internationalisation, response to structural change and client facing roles. Some of these have been discussed in the earlier papers. Below, we attempt to identify the role of those factors which are either specific to the sector or are of predominant importance. The emphasis is on internal labour market assignments.

5.1. Aerospace sector

Companies are involved in both defence and civil projects which often use similar technologies to produce common products, such as undercarriages, engines or cockpit arrays. Markets are typically determined by the

Table 5.4 Assignments by seniority level for selected companies, 2003–05

	Number	Per cent
Extractive		
Executives	142	6.9
Senior level leaders	798	38.9
First level leaders, individual contributors	833	40.6
Graduate hires (during their first couple of years with the company)	150	7.3
Others	130	6.3
Total	2054	100.0
Pharmaceutical		
Senior VP	8	3.1
VP	60	23.5
Directors	74	29.0
Managers	83	32.5
Supervisors	22	8.6
Project managers, consultants	8	3.1
Total	255	100.0
Aero		
Senior management	85	23.5
Professional	130	36.0
Management	124	34.3
Technical	21	5.8
Work	1	0.3
Total	361	100.0

Source: Company data.

political spending priorities of national governments and/or the existence of internationally collaborative 'champion' projects, such as a new generation of commercial aircraft. The competitive dynamics of the civil and defence markets have similarities and differences, which mean that, to some extent, the mobility patterns associated with them vary. In the defence sector, companies produce military hardware and software. A major concern here is national security considerations which have the effect of frequently confining international movement to select nationalities.

The geographical location of a relatively small number of aerospace companies, located in a few highly developed countries, means that most assignment flows are within and between Europe and the USA. Mobile staff are relatively senior and/or likely to be engineering or research specialists. All four of the factors identified above are significant.

Product- and process-related influences. There is heavy upfront capital investment and long payback times through to eventual decommissioning.

Projects involve work on technologically complex product systems, with each sub-system component having its own life cycle and particular skill requirements. In general, the length of project life cycles expands the tenure and/or the volume of international movements, for example, converting a long-term assignment into the localisation of staff.

The complex nature of the end product means that competitors and customers are held in convoluted relationships. The penalties for inadequate relationship building are high in terms of loss of business and participation in complex supply chain networks. Maintaining trust and goodwill requires high volumes of (sometimes extended) business travel.

> Your competitor today could be your customer tomorrow; [and] can be your supplier the day after. So you don't want to spoil those relationships. It's cut throat, but not in the way that other industries work. (Aerospace 1)

Corporate restructuring in the form of mergers and acquisitions (M&As) has resulted in consequential moves. For example, it has given access by UK firms to the lucrative US market and, in the defence sector, limited the constraining influence of security regulations for both British and American nationals. M&As may therefore enable security clearance to be extended across the various country sites involved in the same programme. This has made it easier to assign some staff internationally without necessarily easing constraints on assignment for nationals of third countries.

Customer relations, which often require closer relationships with suppliers, are crucial in configuring patterns of mobility. Building trust is crucial because the penalties for loss of contracts are severe.

> It's really important to be close to the customer...in a business where it's all about relationships. [If] you get the relationship wrong, you don't get a big contract that lasts for 15 years, [and] 20–30 years in terms of after-market. (Aerospace 1)

The need to share and spread resources and practices has emphasised the focus on short-term international assignments while generating increasing volumes of business travel to attend meetings and build trust-based relationships

In the defence sector, where governments are the customers, national security regulations which affect the nationality of recruitment favour internal labour market (ILM) movements over international hires. In consequence, a lack of relational/political trust and a fear of information leakage and knowledge spillover in international relations can inhibit the mobility of expertise between companies and countries. Constraints on knowledge transfer, confined to certain groups, with consequent limiting of access to technology and expertise for others, means that preference is given to career-oriented moves.

> The first [consideration regarding international mobility] is going to be security. So is that individual cleared to the appropriate level to work on a project, and what level of security clearance? What nationalities can work on particular projects? (Aerospace 2)

> I think from the US side, the UK is part of Europe, I think there's a trust of the UK which probably doesn't extend to some of the other European countries and [a fear] that anything fed through into the UK will leak through into other countries in Europe. (Aerospace 3)

5.2. Extractive industries

Companies in extractive industries operate in a wide range of locations. For example, in the oil and gas industry, downstream operations are geographically broadly based. Upstream activities often are in places regarded as less hospitable, such as Angola, Azerbaijan or Kazakhstan. Such non-European and non-US assets are becoming increasingly important. The competitive dynamics of the upstream (exploration and production) industry, being based on process innovation, are different from those of the downstream industry where competition is based on price, market segmentation and product differentiation.

In some of the extractive companies, *restructuring and international reorganisation* has led to the creation of regional hubs as centres of excellence challenging the traditional headquarter dominance of expatriation. Moving work, rather than people, to such hubs has changed the tenure and geographical pattern of international mobility, for instance, allowing long-term moves to remote overseas locations to be substituted with short-term project-related moves among regionally based subject experts. There are different patterns of mobility among companies that have retained their international headquarters as a repository of expertise, and thus as vital components of career development moves by senior executives and future leaders.

Market development is important for mobility patterns. Traditional first-world markets for extractive industries are mature and tend to be self-sufficient in terms of skills, with limited international mobility among them. Such mobility therefore serves the growth of new resource regions and emerging markets. The eventual aim is to localise recruitment in these regions. During the early stages of market development, therefore, market growth depends on long-term and short-term assignments designed to transfer project-specific and production-related expertise, while also coaching and mentoring host-country staff.

A major trend in the oil and gas sectors is for production countries to create their own national companies to exploit resources in partnership with the global players. This is especially the case in emerging markets. In general, the volume of movement typically increases during the initial stages of market development. Short-term assignments and extended business travel are employed to establish trust, gain new business and build markets. Career expatriation is also associated with gaining the experience of setting up and running a fledgling operation.

> One of the reasons for using expats is . . . when you enter a new area you're doing it to get the corporate culture and to hire people . . . set up the systems, processes, . . . find your successors and then off to the next country. (Extractive 1)

For some companies, the traditional model of expatriation is incapable of sustaining the rate of growth required in emerging markets. Developing local staff instead of bringing in assignees is the common response, so the level of expatriation may be expected to decline over time.

> 10 years ago, the [country name] operation was 80 per cent British ex-pats and 20 per cent local . . . staff, now it is 50/50. (Extractive 2)

Also, various phases of each project may require different types of move, involving different specialists.

> You could have a project that would be in pre-feasibility for 2–3 years, . . . then, from pre-feasibility study you get into the pre-operational phase, which also starts off very much as a small project before it becomes operational. That can be up to four or five years. Then you move into life of a mine which then runs into anything from 20–30–40 years. (Extractive 3)

Typically, the initial planning phase is associated with extensive business travel among a wide range of specialists. The early development phases, where risk and uncertainty are high, require longer-term and more specialised mobility among (generally fewer) career expatriates and/or experienced project managers.

A peculiarity of the *production process* in extractive industries is the use of personnel rotation. Broadly speaking there are two types. The first consists of people who work on offshore/desert installations within the country on a shift cycle of several weeks on/off. They are usually local nationals and are transported by the company to/from their in-country base. The second group works internationally in remote or difficult locations on rotating shifts of 1–2 months on/off with the company flying them to and from their home country. Usually this is because they are working at a location where it is not feasible/desirable to provide family accommodation. The numbers of rotators may be quite considerable, running into many hundreds at any one time. They are always unaccompanied by family members and there is usually a special assignment package which includes a hardship allowance.

5.3. Electronics

The five 'global' companies in electronics were multi-business and multi-product organisations. In general, international mobility was used to share, standardise and spread best practice around the company to enhance overall cost-effectiveness. One of the main features of their staff mobility was the effect of *structural change* through M&As. In some cases this had resulted in decentralised structures which subsequently went through a process of centralisation, consolidation and the rationalisation of certain core functions.

> So traditionally [Company] had lots of separate companies that worked as individual organisations who had their own HR, finance operations. A lot of that is now being centralised. (Electronics 1)

Consolidation and rationalisation had affected the location of employment and patterns of mobility for some functions. This led to employment growth for certain types of skills in regions where they were competitively priced, and contraction elsewhere.

> I would certainly suggest that the reason you see so much more happening in China and the Far East has got a lot to do with the fact that it's cheaper to build factories and to run them over there. (Electronics 1)

This phase of expansion had led to an initial surge of extended business travel, as well as secondments for higher managerial roles.

Production and process-related changes in the electronics sector, with rapid technological developments, have led to the creation of regional centres of excellence and to a shift from hardware to software platforms. Centres of excellence in particular technological domains concentrate expertise into particular locations, redistributing employment between countries. To an extent, they enable particular branches of business to operate independently, servicing local customers with local staff, bringing in expertise (physically or virtually) from other groups and regions as and when required.

All companies had undergone a shift from growth based on demand for hardware to that based on value-added services (VAS). Growth of the VAS market provided opportunities for redeployment among companies facing declining fortunes. While this shift had increased the technological complexity of service offerings in two companies, this had not increased physical movements internationally. Instead, virtual exchange has been increasingly employed.

The shift from hardware to software has involved comprehensive organisational, cultural and managerial change. Such reorientation opens up opportunities for career development to different people. For example, it may involve a shift in managerial opportunities towards sales and marketing strategists and away from technology specialists.

> Sales and marketing is generally not [about] technology but strategic planning. You're seen as a future leader of the corporation and we want to give you as broad an experience as we possibly can so that you're a better all round manager of the company. (Electronics 4)

The patterns and directions of international mobility in electronics are also influenced by business cycles that affect profit and investment opportunities.

> People only send expats out when there's money available, ... So there's more business travel and there's more ex-pats. So it follows the cycle. If we were at the bottom of the cycle there would be less ex-pats and less business travel. (Electronics 4)

In some of the companies, *market expansion and development* has fostered all kinds of international movements – especially, in emerging regions where production is being built up. In one company this led to more moves for training purposes as well as an increase in long-term expatriation.

> At any one time we have between 3–5,000 ex-pats worldwide. Of those I would say 80 per cent are on training assignments and the other 20 per cent is the kind of strategic senior individual skill type movement. (Electronics 4)
>
> When we announce we're going to build a factory somewhere new, we'll ship in 50–60 people from – generally the US – to do the construction and they'll be there for 2–3 years. (Electronics 4)

Increasingly, these emerging regions are where production sites have grown up around pools of available, appropriate and competitively priced skills.

> So we put a software development centre in [Russia] purely because the universities there are focused on software development. And they've got a huge resource untapped, ... they are coming out of the university with some niche skills. (Electronics 4)

However, particularly in immature and rapidly evolving markets, long-term expatriation assignments are increasingly seen as insufficiently flexible to adjust to business needs.

> The business changes so quickly that you could be expecting something to develop one way today, and then in six to twelve months' time a completely different scenario will have emerged. So yes, the business changes quite organically very, very fast these days, and that's a major reason why you don't want to have committed great chunks of people to three or four years in one particular country. (Electronics 1)

Shorter-term assignments therefore tend to be used to support project-oriented movements, which may be substituted for on cost grounds by regular (often extended) business travel.

In international electronics, therefore, the increasing development of emerging markets, where there may be few suitable local candidates, provides opportunities for senior executives, strategic planners and/or potential future leaders to undertake career development assignments, sometimes in relatively 'hostile' locations. These moves enable the company to develop rapid responses to the market, while also spreading the corporate culture. They also form part of the traditional strategy to internationalise and then localise the workforce, as expatriate managers hire their replacements and staff, from the local community.

> But what we do when we set up a new entity, like we've done in Kazakhstan and Morocco, is to generally ship in somebody who's got experience in the company and they go and set up the office and hire the people and integrate them.... (Electronics 4)

5.4. Pharmaceuticals

The pharmaceutical business is based on specific knowledge, skills and research expertise, and requires a lot of movement of specialised staff, research scientists or manufacturing staff.

> We have to move these people around the world to where we have the global centres of that particular type of work .... We have research facilities in Norway and the USA, and we have a constant flow of people between those two R&D sites and the UK is the third major R&D site. We have a constant flow of scientists transferring their knowledge and skills to their global team and working in other teams because they have specific R&D knowledge to help them. (Pharmaceuticals 2)

Product and project-related moves, typically assignments for knowledge transfer, are common and may be either long or short term (less than one year).

An important characteristic of the industry is the need to work with government health services and regulation, which puts a premium on long-term assignments.

> If you're trying to form a relationship with a government as a country manager, you're not going to do that in three years. Four years is still a bit short... probably five years. (Pharmaceuticals 1)

Because the pharmaceutical industry is strongly affected by changing political and regulatory regimes, companies build expertise in government affairs, also requiring extensive business travel (particularly to the USA), especially among lobbyists.

Pharmaceuticals companies produce a wide range of products, each with associated project life cycles that call for various types of movements from people with different sets of skills. For example, R&D may take 20 or more years to reach the market whereas the consumer business development is near-market, taking about 3–5 years. Mobility, particularly business travel, is compelled by a desire to reduce complexity and minimise risk and uncertainty. Most project-related mobility was associated with the initial stages of a project. The different project and process-related activities required to establish a project will involve a variety of people travelling.

> We're setting up a manufacturing type of production in our Shanghai Plant, which is already used in our core plant. So at the beginning of the project, there will be people going over from the core plant who are familiar with the manufacturing process. Equally there will be people throughout the project, overseeing it and particularly when the US Drugs Agency authorities are going in to give their approval. Maybe more people will be going in around the time when everything is approved. (Pharmaceuticals 2)

The nature of their products and processes means that pharmaceutical companies need to acquire but also retain people with scarce and highly desirable skills.

> Our business is based on a very specific knowledge, skills, research. So it requires a lot of movement of the very highly specialised, maybe research scientists. Our manufacturing staff have very specific specialised knowledge. We have to move these people around the world to where we have global centres of that particular type of work.... (Pharmaceuticals 2)

International mobility represents a potential challenge to such retention, and the two companies adopted different approaches to handling this. The larger company reserved international assignments for the more elite and senior staff levels – those who had decided to make their career in the company. In contrast, the smaller company saw the assignment framework as a means of supporting retention by contractually tying people back to their home country:

> Our preference is to handle all international moves as an assignment, which ties them back to their home country. (Pharmaceuticals 2)

Both companies have experienced significant *structural change*. They were created out of a series of M&As involving large corporations that led to a drive for certain corporate functions to be centralised and rationalised. Nevertheless, some activities remain internationally scattered because of the effects of the legacy structure. There had been a marked structural shift in both companies towards the creation of consolidated centres of excellence in key global regions. This had stimulated international commuting as well as outward international mobility to spread expertise, either (in Pharmaceuticals 1 and 2) within particular business units, such as R&D or across different teams around the world.

Global operations had led to globally defined managerial roles involving extensive business travel for knowledge transfer purposes.

> Short-term assignments are generally used where the project is going to be for that short nature of time.... Short-termers generally will not be on a career path. Short-termers will be experts who will generally be going back to do the same job that they did before. (Pharmaceuticals 1)

5.5. Information Technology

Companies in this sector differ from those discussed above in that it is their core business to deploy human expertise to serve client needs wherever they arise, so that knowledge transfer assignments form the bulk of international movements. All companies in the sample focused on outsourcing and, to a greater or lesser extent, offshoring. Those operating exclusively in this market focus on providing services to large multinationals in industrialised countries, but they do not necessarily resource these locally.

> Essentially all we deliver is people and skills, we don't manufacture hardware or software products generally and ship those round the world. We deliver people and spawn it, grow it, but we've moved towards these low cost centres for certain types of services as a basis for helping them to grow. (IT 1)

Typically, such knowledge transfer (outflow) assignments are very short term – mainly for cost reasons.

> From a cost point of view the faster you can get the thing operating out of India compared with the UK, the better, you don't want to take time about it. (IT 1)

Career development moves are almost entirely for staff engaging with current and potential clients to develop leadership skills and to provide cross-cultural experience. Most moves are project related, generally over 85 per cent, and of staff with specific software skills. There is an element of career development in many client-orientated short-term moves which inevitably entail accumulation of experience while working on the client's premises.

The key to mobility in the IT sector is *client related*. Project-related moves are used for on-site working with clients. Because much of the work is for global clients in many sectors, there is a need for employees who have had experience of business in different markets, different technologies and different kinds of businesses. The rotation element in ICT mobility provides this experience and is a major element in enhancing the skills of the IT companies' workforces.

The normal pattern is for teams of migrants to be rotated through the UK client site to build up the necessary competencies in offshore locations. This results in a high volume of international mobility while the number of foreign nationals on-site in the UK may remain the same. One Indian-owned company commented

> We actively rotate people back to India ... we'd actively move them back to India and bring some of the offshore team on-site. ... The on-site team get a real appreciation of the client's needs – which the offshore team don't get unless we rotate them. Essentially, it's like a cultural training scheme with domain knowledge being rotated. Although you can write accurate specifications, what is missing from those specifications is the business context in which they sit and you can really only pick that up by actually working closely with the client. (IT 2)

Corporate reorganisation has also played a role in the sector. For non-Indian companies, establishing a base there typically involved managerial-level knowledge transfer (inflow) assignments to that country.

> As part of the set up [in preparation for offshoring] there was a huge influx of assignments to India .... There were a lot of HR people going out to set up the whole bit. ... so there have been a lot of assignments into India over the last three years and that's still continuing ... just to do with internal set up. (IT 3)

Usually, these were expected to decline in volume as well as length of tenure as the phase of market development matured, the preference being to localise such roles quickly rather than to use expatriates.

As offshoring became more common the flow of expatriates reversed direction. IT firms built up facilities in lower-cost overseas locations (notably India) in order to capitalise on the market for offshore service delivery. Indian staff, initially with 'generic' IT skills, were recruited to undertake short-term, project-related 'knowledge transfer' assignments at the premises of clients.

Market development underlies corporate growth and mobility in the sector. It comes from serving large clients in industrialised countries – mainly the US and the UK. Establishing a (sales and marketing) presence in client locations is, therefore, a pre-requisite for market development.

> As we grew we started off with having the sales and marketing arm spread across the world where our clients are, essentially. And as the client expectation increased then we had to set up centres for development worldwide. (IT 4)

In response to the pressure to grow, some IT companies have developed global sourcing strategies to recruit internationally. The global sourcing model typically involves the location and redistribution of IT production activities among on-site, near-shore and offshore locations that may, previously, have been undertaken domestically, including in-house, in client organisations. According to this model, a service provider may use its UK base – perhaps a customer facing sales and marketing division or a UK-based development centre – to sponsor overseas nationals to work for short periods at or near an end-client's site. The service provider uses the ICT route to rotate offshore staff through the client organisation and back overseas where they may help to build up repositories of client- and market-specific knowledge.

> Our main sales focus is in the US and Europe. Our main delivery centres where most of the coding work is done are in India in about 10 centres. We also have small local centres in the US and Netherlands and we've just opened up a small centre in China consisting of about 100 people to overcome the obvious pressures of wage inflation that will be coming from India over the next few years. (IT 2)

Thus the companies have become *global service providers*, using ICTs as core elements in their outsourcing business models. In essence, their businesses have been constructed around bringing in offshore staff to work with clients (Millar and Salt, 2007).

> So, in other words, if you were going to have somebody working in the UK it would cost the project twice as much which is why, in terms of cost, you want to move the work around among the people.... Assuming that you've got the quality, and you can sustain the quality that the customer wants then you're looking at doing it cheaper. Why are we doing it off-shore? The only reason we're taking it to India is for cost – otherwise we wouldn't be doing it. (IT 1)

5.6. Consultancies

The activities of consultancy companies are in many ways similar to and overlap with those of IT companies. Their core function is to move expertise to wherever it is needed by international clients. They rely less on longer-term assignments than primary and manufacturing MNEs and more on shorter-term business travel and commuting. There are two elements to mobility within the sector. One is between the constituent parts of the company and may, for example, involve different international offices collaborating on a project for a client. The other is directly between consultancy and client where staff locate themselves at the client's premises.

A major characteristic of international consultancy companies is their *corporate structure*, which determines much of their mobility portfolio. The firms included here offer a pool of talent, especially at senior levels, applying North American, British and European experience through internationally networked organisations, increasingly linking formerly competitive national entities. While the globalisation of markets may dominate their structural dynamics, unlike the other sectors above, the primary operational challenge facing international consultancies is to adapt this expertise to market and client conditions in many international localities (Jones, 2007). They therefore generally operate in a decentralised manner, through national or regional profit centres, primarily responsible for serving home market clients, although within financial and business guidelines set by international parent companies.

This combination of local partnerships and global responsibilities means that the organisation of mobility occurs at different geographical levels.

> We don't have a global scheduling system for (moving) our people, because at the end of the day we're not a global organization.... (Consultancy 2).

However, when it comes to international assignments, there is a need to have some level of commonality, and there are common policies.

> for example, our [senior staff management system] is the same globally. (Consultancy 2)

Tactical, including financial, priorities are therefore still largely determined at national levels. UK consultancies, however, have needed increasingly to support their international partners under terms established by the global organisation. Nowadays this involves supporting distributed, globally interconnected teams to serve the project requirements of multinational clients, and also developing service products that attract international clients.

Product and market characteristics are also crucial. The presence, at appropriate times in different locations, of strategically or technically experienced consultants is critical to the quality of their service, their ability to respond to unpredictable events and, perhaps most importantly, to the trust placed in them by their clients (Jones, 2008b). Their office networks must therefore serve these ends. Not constrained by the requirements of physical production, such offices may be established almost anywhere within the international, largely urban-based, network of business exchange. This gives them a flexibility which means that they might be expected to be in the vanguard of expert mobility practice as they adapt their structures and strategies to changing market opportunities and perhaps also exploit novel, including virtual, methods and patterns of interaction.

For the present, at least, these international consultancies maintain a decentralised labour supply structure, allowing them to draw on experience from mature business markets and networking with multinational clients. But they are increasingly more formally aligning their practices to *global markets*, partly because this is what their UK clients want, but also to respond to the market developments moulding structural change by their global parents. These changes are encouraging the movement of consultancy staff to become more internationally orientated.

> The majority of our assignments are for specific clients, for a specific purpose. Whatever grade of person is going, it's to fill a need for that particular project. We don't have many assignments that are somebody of a high level going out for broad management responsibilities. It does happen, but those people are more likely to be transferred permanently to that location ... or somebody will be recruited locally. (Consultancy 3)

Allocating and employing the expertise of senior consultants is a complex task, since they seldom work on only one project at any time, and become increasingly dependent on modern communications. Consultants for company 4, for example, are often engaged in interview-based work for which the critical mass of expertise cannot be locally available in many countries.

6. Conclusion

Growing competition in the global economy means that international employers need to ensure efficient allocation of their human resources. This may involve recruitment into permanent positions (including overseas localisation), long-term, short-term and commuting assignments, business travel and virtual forms of exchange. This chapter has examined some of the links between the processes of economic globalisation, human resource management and international movements by expert employees across a variety of sectors. It has shed light on the ways in which companies deploy their networks of expertise internationally in response to changing opportunities.

Our findings show that managing the mobility of expertise has become a key element in corporate globalisation. Companies formally develop and use different forms of mobility, according to their needs and those of their employees. Sector-specific characteristics, as well as the purposes that can best be served by different types of mobility, in particular places and at certain times, all affect the patterns of international mobility in firms.

Our analysis suggests that four main factors shape the international movement of expertise: production and market characteristics; corporate restructuring; customers and customer relationships; and product, project and process-related influences. While these are common to all sectors, they act in notably different ways. For example, customer-related and product-related factors dominate aerospace, while market-related factors and structural dynamics appear to be more significant in the extractive industries. Research and development-related moves are most critical in pharmaceuticals, and cost-related, client-based project mobility in IT and consultancy. These factors rarely act in isolation. Seemingly minor changes, for example, a new contract, can have far-reaching ramifications for the volumes of international movements, their origins and destinations, types and durations, as well as the characteristics of the mobile population.

In practice, however, the patterns of exchange are complex and resistant to integrated approaches. At any time, large companies may have numerous projects at various stages of development. Subsumed within the various patterns of project-related and market development moves is a range of career-oriented moves that span from the most senior to younger potential leaders. At the time of our survey, there appeared to be considerable 'slack' in the way mobility was managed, with relatively relaxed attitudes towards its costs, purposes and the scope given to younger and mid-career staff to gain experience. Mobility was traditionally regarded as a derived function, responding primarily to the type of business available, the time horizon of project planning, and client and market relationships. Mobility costs were generally regarded as necessary to support wider project management aims, and thus absorbed into larger budgets. Companies therefore seldom planned their overall portfolios of mobility. Assignments, business travel and virtual exchange were each responses to the needs of various international projects, often administered by separate offices or even devolved to business units. In these, some consideration was given to bilateral substitution, for example, between short-term assignments and business travel, or business travel and virtual communications. Such decisions, however, remained largely subject to the overriding demands of project managers.

Almost all governments wish to attract knowledge migrants because they are the lifeblood of the global economy. However, such migrants are largely managed by multinational corporations, usually within well-defined channels of movement which include recruitment to or moves between company 'centres of excellence' including head office, regional and research centres. This often creates tension between governments and large employers. These movements present challenges to governments seeking to manage migration through the identification of skill shortages, while also protecting the indigenous workforce.

Notes

1. The research was carried out jointly by the authors and Dr. Jane Millar.
2. Work permits were replaced at the end of 2008 by Tier 2 of the new points-based system (PBS – from 2009).
3. Data on numbers and patterns of moves were requested from all companies interviewed. Only the selection here were able and willing to provide statistics.
4. The authors consider these companies to be 'post-mature' because in a number of respects they would appear to be evolving beyond what Miller and Friesen (1984) have termed the 'mature phase' of the corporate life cycle and towards the 'revival phase'.

References

Acha, V., Davies, A., Hobday, M. and Salter, A. (2004) 'Exploring the Capital Goods Economy: Complex Product Systems in the UK', *Industrial and Corporate Change*, 13(3): 505–529.

Beyers, W.B. (2007) 'Services and Regional Development in the United States', in P. Daniels and J. Bryson, eds. *The Handbook of Service Industries*. Cheltenham: Edward Elgar, pp. 126–148.

Collins, H.M. (1997) 'Humans, Machines, and the Structure of Knowledge', in R.L. Ruggles, ed. *Knowledge Management Tools*. Boston, MA: Butterworth-Heinemann, pp. 145–163.

Dicken, P. (2007) *Global Shift: Reshaping the Global Economic Map in the 21st Century*, 5th Edition. London: Sage.

Faulconbridge, J.R. and Beaverstock, J.V. (2008) 'Geographies of International Business Travel in the Professional Service Economy', *GaWC Research Bulletin*, 252, University of Loughborough, http://www.lboro.ac.uk/gawc/rb/rb252.html. Last accessed December 2010.

Forsgren, M., Holm, U. and Johanson, J. (2005) *Managing the Embedded Multinational: A Business Network View*. Cheltenham: Edward Elgar.

Gallouj, F. (2002) *Innovation in the Service Economy: The New Wealth of Nations*. Cheltenham: Edward Elgar.

Goshall, S. and Bartlett, C.A. (1998) *Managing Across Borders: The Transnational Solution*. London: Random House.

Jones, A. (2007) 'More than "Managing Across Borders?" The Complex Role of Face to Face Interaction in Globalizing Law Firms', *Journal of Economic Geography*, 7, 223–246.

Jones, A. (2008a) 'The Rise of Global Work', *Transactions, Institute of British Geographers*, 33, 12–26.

Jones, A. (2008b) 'Beyond Embeddedness: Economic Practices and the Invisible Dimensions of Transnational Business Activity', *Progress in Human Geography*, 32(1), 71–88.

Kolb, H., Murteira, S., Peixoto, J. and Sabino, C. (2004) 'Recruitment and Migration in the ICT Sector', *IMIS-Beitrage*, 25, 147–177.

Koser, K. and Salt, J. (1997) 'The Geography of Highly Skilled International Migration', *International Journal of Population Geography*, 3(December), 285–303.

Millar, J. and Salt, J. (2006) 'In Whose Interests? IT Migration in an Interconnected World Economy', *Population, Space and Place*, 13, 41–58.

Millar, J. and Salt, J. (2008) 'Portfolios of Mobility: The Movement of Expertise in Trans-national Corporations in Two Sectors – Aerospace and Extractive Industries', *Global Networks*, 8(1), 25–50.

Millar, J., Demaid, A. and Quintas, P. (1997) 'Trans-organizational Innovation: A framework for Research', *Technology Analysis and Strategic Management*, 9(4): 399–418.

Miller, D. and Friesen, P.H. (1984) 'A Longitudinal Study of the Corporate Life Cycle', *Management Science*, 30(10): 1161–1183.

Paoli, M. and Prencipe, A. (1999) 'The Role of Knowledge Bases in Complex Product Systems: Some Empirical Evidence From the Aero-Engine Industry', *Journal of Management and Governance*, 3(2): 137–160.

Rubalcaba, L. and Kox, H. (2007) *Business Services in European Economic Growth*. London: Palgrave Macmillan.

Salt, J. (1997) 'International Movements of the Highly Skilled', Occasional Paper No. 3, International Migration Unit, OECD, Paris.

Salt, J. (2009) 'Business Travel and Portfolios of Mobility Within Global Companies', in B. Deruder, F. Witlox, J. Beaverstock and J. Faulconbridge, eds. *Business Travel in the Global Economy*. London: Ashgate, pp. 107–124.

Williams, A. (2007) 'Listen to Me, Learn With Me: International Migration and Knowledge Transfer', *British Journal of Industrial Relations*, 45, 361–382.

Wood, P., ed. (2002) *Consultancy and Innovation: The Business Service Revolution in Europe*. London: Routledge.

6
Academics and Globalisation

Steve Fenton, Tariq Modood and Claire Smetherham

1. Introduction

One of the constant themes of the recent sociology of higher education (HE) has been the globalisation of both knowledge and the transfer of scientists and researchers. Within this literature globalisation is often treated in terms of culture transfers, knowledge transfers and challenges to local identities. However, a key material feature is the intensification of competition – in all kinds of markets – from the local and regional to the global. This has happened in universities, nationally and internationally. A consequence of this has been the amplification of inequalities, marked in HE in the UK by the detaching of a small cluster of elite universities from the rest.

The chapter presents two core arguments. Firstly, we argue that there is a concentration in elite UK universities of research funding and research activity. These are typically relatively large, internationally known, prestige institutions. This concentration of research funding, especially in the form of time-limited programmes and projects, leads to the recruitment of large numbers of research only (RO) staff – and it is among these RO staff that we typically find large numbers of overseas researchers. This elite group of universities does not even extend to the 'Russell Group' as a whole but to only a handful of its members. Moreover, such research staff are most numerous in a number of subject areas, namely, engineering, physical sciences, mathematics and to a lesser extent medicine and social sciences. They are also likely to be young and employed on fixed-term contracts. Our second argument relates to the reasons that overseas academics are attracted to posts in UK higher education institutions (HEIs). We argue that there are three different labour markets in HE: the aforementioned for contract research staff; a further market for elite academic teaching and research (TR) staff; and another for replacement staff in under-supplied or shortage areas in both teaching and research. So, while some come to Britain as a 'reserve army of academic labour' into subject areas and types of posts which are under-supplied or less competed for by UK academics, others come to UK HEIs as part of a 'circulation' or 'progression' through high-prestige international institutions.

These three different labour market arguments can be referred to as 'the funding model', 'the elite university model' and 'the replacement labour model'. According to the funding model, overseas academic staff are attracted to posts advertised in research-rich departments with large funds. The UK has an important scientific and more broadly academic research industry which is key to the maintenance of a competitive position in global markets, both for knowledge production itself and for the more explicitly practical and commercial benefits of this knowledge. The research industry is supported by Research Councils and private sector funding and tends to be directed disproportionately to an elite group of universities and institutions. The extent of research funding in these universities creates a large number of research posts, not all of which can be filled by the domestic supply of graduates and postgraduates. Thus one part of the explanation of large numbers of overseas researchers in the UK HE sector is the demand for staff in highly research-intensive institutions, above all the 'golden triangle' of Oxbridge and London. We can expect to see overseas RO staff concentrated in elite, highly research-oriented HEIs.

The argument from the elite university model is that high-prestige universities attract staff because they are world-class universities through which 'high flying' staff members circulate. These same elite institutions contain academic units which see themselves and are seen by others (e.g., world competitive academics in, say, New England) as part of a global market in elite talent. Oxbridge history departments, for example, may expect to attract applications to posts from Harvard staff. Thus in TR posts, as well as RO posts, these elite institutions will attract significant numbers of academic staff from overseas sources. This labour market is therefore populated by high-prestige global-career academics. These post-holders may be older, in permanent posts, across more subjects and in higher-positions than RO staff.

We also argue that globalisation has a further face in relation to labour markets in HE: the deployment of overseas staff, particularly at an early career stage, in areas under-supplied by the British system. According to a replacement labour model, certain positions in the academic labour market are difficult to fill for one of two main reasons. These are first, under-production (i.e., not enough student through-put in the UK) and/or second, the attractiveness of commercial careers within the wider labour market. In these circumstances, academic staff from overseas act essentially as replacement labour. According to this model we would expect to find overseas staff concentrated in typically under-supplied areas or unattractive posts (fixed-term junior positions within some sub-fields of engineering, for instance). In some cases of course, several of these arguments will be operating at once.

2. Globalisation in higher education

Recent literature in the sociology of HE acknowledges that in an age of globalisation of commerce, mass culture and commodities the sector has been touched by these wider processes of globalisation, and in a variety of ways (Scott, 2000; Deem, 2001; Naidoo, 2003; Altbach, 2004; Teichler, 2004). Empirically, globalisation in HE has several possible manifestations. The term might refer to the presence of overseas academic staff in TR posts in UK universities. It could also mean the presence of overseas students, both undergraduate and postgraduate, on a global basis (Merrick, 2004).

Thirdly, globalisation may refer not just to the presence of overseas academics in universities but also to how they work, including how non-overseas individuals work. The phrase 'globalised academic' might equally refer, for instance, to overseas or UK staff who have collegial relationships with other academics in, say, New Zealand, the United States (USA), Denmark or India. This aspect of globalisation is something more than the presence of particular overseas academics in the labour market in the UK. Globalisation could also refer to global partnerships between institutions and the world base of some universities, for example, US universities with campuses in other countries. Our focus in this chapter is on the first of these definitions: the presence of overseas academic staff in UK universities, a simple indicator, but one which begins to tell the story of global academic markets in UK universities. Before describing and discussing recent patterns of academic migration to the UK, we briefly review some principal concerns in the field.

In relation to globalisation (understood essentially as the idea of global connectedness, alongside the technologies which make connectedness more possible), one of the debates in globalisation theory is the extent to which globalisation produces more 'sameness' (e.g., debates about the 'MacDonaldisation' of culture, social life or education) or produces more difference (see, e.g., Pieterse, 1996). A further dimension is that globalisation is 'willed', that is, it does not just happen but people do things to make it happen. For example, global changes promoted by economic and political elites (e.g., trade globalisation promoted through the World Trade Organization (WTO) and American and EU trade areas). Debates in globalisation theory also recognise that globalisation is 'unequal' – that is, the multiple exchanges and transfers that occur are on an unequal basis with global winners and losers.

All of these points are relevant to our chapter. Firstly, academic transfers, of people and knowledge, depend to a considerable extent on 'sameness'; the universality of scientific and engineering knowledge systems makes transfers more readily possible (higher maths, for instance, is pretty much the same game wherever you are). Mobile researchers must provide a reasonably ready-made fit to the work that they take up in the host country.

Secondly, people move partly because they are able to move and this means that their governments are willing to allow them, or indeed encourage them, to move. This is clearly the case with the mass movement of Chinese scholars who were previously confined to China but are now spread around the globe (or at least the rich parts of it) to help China benefit from Western knowledge or vice versa. Post 1989 a lot of new movements of academics became possible and occurred in large numbers (see, e.g., Alpion, 2008). There are 'artificial' restrictions on these kinds of movements. For example, the USA makes it quite difficult for foreign-trained medics and lawyers to work there with national and state registration systems acting as protectionisms for local professionals (Cheng and Yang, 1998). The global exchanges reflect, and by and large reinforce rather than break, global inequalities. Rich countries are big gainers in the importation of both high-skilled and lower skill labour.

A particular theme within the literature in this field has been the globalisation of knowledge and the professional transfer of scientists and researchers (Mahroum, 1999b; Casey et al., 2001; Ackers, 2005; Morano-Foadi, 2005). Alongside this, recent evaluation studies by the Higher Education Policy Institute (HEPI) (Sastry, 2005), Higher Education Funding Council for England (HEFCE, 2005) and Association for University Teachers (AUT, 2005) have all used national UK HESA (Higher Education Statistics Agency) data to pursue concerns with the increasing globalisation of the academic workforce in the UK. HEFCE (HEFCE, 2005) used data from the HESA individualised staff records for 1994–95 to 2002–03 and the HESA new individualised staff record for 2003–04. This report drew attention to an apparently important change in the numbers and proportions of groups of staff by nationality. The biggest growth was in the number of Eastern and Central European staff (which increased by 164 per cent since 1995–96). Western European and Scandinavian staff were the largest group after UK nationals and had also grown significantly over the period. The report also noted increases in levels of overseas staff across all grades. Of those permanent academic staff whose academic discipline was known in 2003–04, languages had the highest proportion of overseas nationality staff (19 per cent) and education the lowest (4 per cent). (Languages are though a special case because they hire staff as, for example, 'lecteurs' by dint of the nature of the subject.)

3. Brain drain

Two particular concerns evident in the literature and on the policy agenda concern expansion and demographic change in HE and the perceived losses to the system through emigration or 'brain drain', alongside an ongoing concern with the so-called marketisation of HE. Initial policy thinking in the 1950s and 1960s saw what was termed the brain drain as a damaging phenomenon. It was perceived as a threat to UK economic success. Historically, brain drain has become conceptualised in progressively more complex terms. Later consideration of compensating inflows of skilled immigrants brought 'brain gain' into the vocabulary.

Recent literature distinguishes between two main types of mobility: external, which involves losses from the system as a result of emigration, and internal, which refers to losses within the national system to other sectors. In the case of the labour market for academics, the most relevant types of internal and external mobility concern movement from the education system to the wider labour market; mobility within the public research sector and between public research and industry; mobility within industry; and international mobility which sheds light on the temporary and permanent migration of academic personnel. The most recent formulation speaks of the concept of a beneficial 'brain circulation' within a global community. Issues concerning the movement of academics and researchers have also more recently been conceptualised in terms of the recruitment of needed 'talent' within knowledge-driven economies.

Various sorts of geographical mobility exist, including short-term overseas visits, long-term stays and permanent stays. When highly skilled persons are involved in one of these *various* forms of mobility, various outcomes might result from it. Gaillard and Gaillard (1998) and Johnson and Regets (1998) talk of a notion of brain circulation. This form of mobility, which referred to longer-term subsequent expatriation of skilled personnel in and out of different locations, is often perceived as a positive mobility that provides a channel for knowledge transfer. Subsequent thinking seemed to coalesce around the notion of 'magnet' disciplines and research institutions. Mahroum (1998) emphasised the geographical clustering of European migrants to the USA in a few centres of excellence but noted that the magnetism is not simply generated by good science. Additional factors such as flexible and open career structures, high rewards, a strong entrepreneurial culture and a good quality of life are also key elements in the reputation of a magnet (Mahroum, 1999a). Evidence from Italian immigrants to the UK confirms the importance of magnets, with their mix of scientific and cultural attractions (Ackers, 2005).

In addition to domestic policies, programmes to ease or assist immigration are also influential. Mahroum (1999c) argued that countries with special legislation to attract highly skilled migrants are the best placed to benefit from the global talent pool, with measures to ease the entry and boost the post-training employment and entrepreneurial opportunities of overseas students being particularly significant.

4. The issue of supply

One reason that there might be shortages in an area that attracts overseas staff is that the British university system is under-producing them, an example being the lack of students or graduates in physics or other sciences. A major review of the supply of individuals with science, technology, engineering and mathematics skills (Roberts, 2002; see also Adams 2006) identified a number of problems concerning the supply of individuals at different educational levels, including A-Level, university and doctoral candidates. Indeed, the Roberts Review provided evidence of a marked decline in the number of students studying certain science subjects (Balakrishnan, 2007; Bond, 2007), compared to business studies, for example, which showed a strong progression rate from A-Level to degree. We cannot, however, be sure which academic specialties are poorly supplied by graduates in that subject. There is insufficient evidence about the 'progression' from studying the subject to the supply of academic staff.

What is clearer is that there is a market for professional expertise, such as engineers, business managers, lawyers and medical staff, within the private and public sectors outside academia. Social science researchers, for example, may be found in universities, research institutes, government departments or commercial organisations – in careers in marketing, for instance. Engineers, lawyers and chemists similarly inhabit jobs in both universities and outside the academy in private sector organisations. Some, like medical professionals, have posts which are shared across institutions, usually the National Health Service (NHS) and the universities. The commercial marketplace is therefore likely to be important in the competition for staff. Indeed, where there are professions with attractive labour markets outside universities (such as industries related to oil exploration, medicine or law), which attract highly qualified people and pay well because they are a lucrative area, this may mean that universities find it hard to recruit scholars (Merriman, 2008). Although we do not know for sure, it is reasonable to suggest that the more attractive and under-supplied those labour markets are the more UK people will gravitate to positions within them; and, in turn, the more likely that UK people will find university positions in the same area relatively unattractive. This leaves open shortage areas in universities. The available evidence shows that this is certainly likely to be the case in some engineering sub-fields and in the field of medicine (Sanders, 2004).

A review of human resource strategies (Ackers and Gill, 2005) highlighted a concern, in a number of research-intensive UK institutions in particular, about attractive pathways out of the academic sector. This was particularly the case in disciplines such as mathematics, biology, physiology and genomics where alternative routes into industry were very strong. One London-based institution reported that 'in some areas it is becoming increasingly difficult to recruit UK staff', referring to the impact of attractive alternatives both abroad and from other professions in London (Ackers and Gill, 2005: 285). Given the existing, often patchy evidence it remains difficult to know whether a particular shortfall is caused by under-supply or by qualified individuals entering other careers, or both.

5. Study and methods

The quantitative data on which the chapter draws are the annually collected employment data pertaining to staff working in HE institutions in the UK, hereafter referred to as the Higher Education Statistics Agency or HESA data.[1] We use data for the years 1998/99, 2001/02 and 2004/05 (HESA, 1999, 2002, 2005), concentrating on the key role of a small group of elite institutions.

5.1. HESA data and definition of key variables

The HESA staff record provides data in respect of the characteristics of members of all academic staff employed under a contract of employment by a HEI in the UK. In 2004–05 HESA collected data from 182 individual HEIs. This meant information on approximately 130,000 academic staff that year. Our introductory arguments indicate that we would be especially interested in differences, in the presence of overseas staff, between types of university institution, subject areas and different types of post. These key variables are defined below.

5.2. Institution type

By 'Golden Triangle' we mean Imperial College, King's College, the London School of Economics (LSE), University College London (UCL), Oxford and Cambridge Universities. These institutions not only receive a large section of the research budget in the UK, but also enjoy a worldwide reputation for excellence in their own right.[2] The Russell Group[3] is an association of 20 major research-intensive universities of the UK, which together receive a very large proportion (around two thirds) of research grant and contract funding in the UK. In the UK, those universities created in or after 1992 from former polytechnics and colleges of HE are commonly referred to as 'new' or 'post-1992' institutions – and they typically have a much lower proportion of research grant funding. Polytechnics were initially created in the UK towards the middle of the 1960s, when the then Secretary of State for Education initiated a new sector of HE. Polytechnics were intended to complement the older, more academically orientated universities and focus on professional and vocational programmes of study.

5.3. HESA cost centre

This refers to the broad group of subjects where staff are located for budget purposes. Individual cost centres (e.g., clinical medicine, biosciences, chemistry, social studies and modern languages) are assigned by HESA into groups, which reflect both academic similarities and comparable resource requirements. Engineering and technology, a broad cost centre group, includes general engineering, chemical engineering, mineral, metallurgy and materials engineering, civil engineering, electrical, electronic and computer engineering, mechanical, aero and production engineering, other technologies and IT and systems sciences, and computer software engineering. Staff must be in at least one cost centre per contract. The 2004–05 dataset includes cost centre for the contract with the most senior grade group (or the highest full-time equivalent (FTE) if two or more contracts are at the same grade level).

5.4. Academic employment function

There are large differences in overseas presence, in types of post, or what the HESA data code calls 'employment function'. In particular we will look at the employment of overseas staff in 'research only' (RO) as against 'teaching and research' posts (TR).[4]

We supplement the analysis of the HEFCE data with a web-based survey of overseas academics, which we conducted in six UK research-intensive HEIs (Sheffield, Bristol, Birmingham, Leeds and two London institutions). We explored the career and employment details of 981 respondents. We also undertook follow-up interviews with 40 of the respondents, questioning them about their personal narratives of their careers and future plans, collegial relationships and ways of working in their discipline. These two sets of data allow us an insight into what we call the processes of globalisation, or how globalisation actually works within HE. We report here on the data from junior staff in order to focus on early career decisions. We have selected 21 RO academics, aged under 30, typically in their first post after being educated overseas. They included 11 women, 8 individuals from Asia, 7 from the EU, 1 each from Canada and Australia, and 4 from elsewhere in the world. All were on fixed-term contracts and all major subject disciplines were represented.

6. Principal findings: the presence of overseas-born staff in UK higher education

In this first empirical section of the chapter we ask: where are overseas staff found and how significant is their presence? The HESA nationality variable defines the country of legal citizenship of a member of staff. Data are supplied to HESA in the form of country codes which are mapped on to geographical regions following consultation with the (then) Department for

Education and Skills. UK nationality staff are those whose country of legal nationality is the UK, including the Channel Islands and Isle of Man. Overseas nationality staff are those whose country of legal nationality is a country other than the UK. For the purposes of our own analysis, overseas nationalities were recoded to enable us to distinguish different regional groups of origins.

We now go on to look at three main variables: institution type, cost centre (i.e., academic discipline) and employment function (TR or RO posts) in order to give a descriptive account of the presence of overseas nationality staff in UK universities.

6.1. Institutional differences

Firstly, we consider the distribution of overseas staff among four categories of institution: Golden Triangle (GT), the rest of Russell Group (RRG), other pre-1992 and post-1992 institutions. The GT includes four of the main London institutions, to which overseas staff are almost certainly attracted both by prestige and the capital city. The LSE, which is unique in the UK in its concentration on teaching and research across the social, political and economic sciences, is an exception to other Golden Triangle institutions which include all the main subject areas. The universities of Oxford and Cambridge form the corners of the triangle.

Small in number, the RRG institutions lead in research income and have large staff complements. In 2006–07, all Russell Group universities, including the GT, accounted for 66 per cent (over £2.2 billion) of UK universities' research grant and contract income, 68 per cent of total Research Council income, 56 per cent of all doctorates awarded in the UK and over 30 per cent of all students studying in the UK from outside the EU. In the 2001 national Research Assessment Exercise, 78 per cent of the staff in Grade 5* departments and 57 per cent of the staff in Grade 5 departments were located in Russell Group Universities, and in 2007–08 Russell Group universities were allocated approximately 66 per cent of the total quality-related (QR) research funding from the Funding Councils (see www.russellgroup.ac.uk). It should be noted that for the purposes of our analysis we have separated out the six GT universities who are members of the organisation called 'The Russell Group' and so our refined 'Rest of Russell Group' (RRG) category contains only the remaining 14 universities. We have done this because the GT universities are critically different from the others and conform to our elite model, as analysed below, in ways that the other 14 do not. Thirty eight per cent of all staff in the dataset were in RRG universities in 2004–05.

We look first at the percentage of overseas staff by institution type (GT, RRG, other pre-1992, post-1992) for all three years. In the most recent year of data, in GT universities 33 per cent of all staff were overseas; in RRG 21.4 per cent; in other pre-1992 22 per cent; and in post-1992 10 per cent.

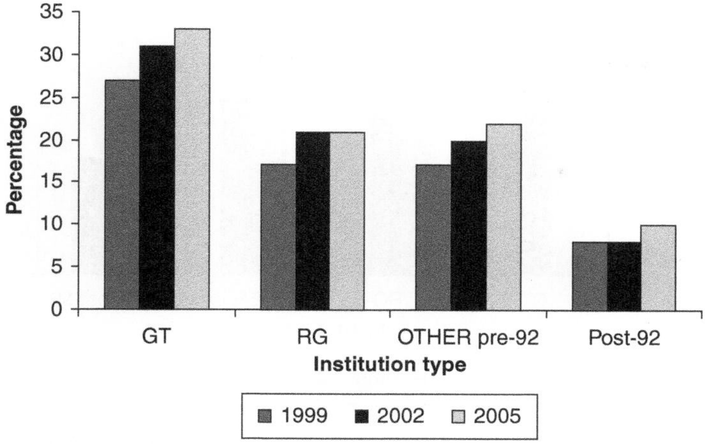

Figure 6.1 Percentage of overseas staff by year and institution type: all staff

The real stand-out, then, is GT with a third of its staff from overseas; and, at the other end, the post-1992 sector with only 10 per cent (Figure 6.1).

The percentage of overseas staff increased over the three years for all types of university. And even in post-1992 universities, by 2005 nearly one quarter of RO staff were overseas. This suggests that, despite the institutional differences identified above, the pressures to hire overseas staff have increased year on year across all types of institution. We shall see, though, that the post-1992 institutions do not typically have staff in the subjects which have large numbers of overseas staff such as large engineering faculties.

The larger institutions will of course soak up more of the total overseas staff because more of the staff total is in large institutions. The RRG and other pre-1992 are about the same in size with regard to total staff (although there are more institutions in the latter). In 2004–05 the total number of TR staff in the RRG was 17,189, and for the other pre-1992 institutions was 19,530. The total number of RO staff was 12,396 in the RRG and 9141 in the other pre-1992 universities, with little difference in the cost centres that these overseas staff were in. As the data testify, RG institutions are typically much bigger than others within the sector.

Overseas academic staff are disproportionately in RO posts. We should not therefore discuss the presence of overseas staff without also referring to the type of post held. Figures 6.2 and 6.3 show that the percentage of staff who were from overseas origins increased over the three years for all categories of academic post.

The RRG, then, often seems to differ little from all other non-Russell Group pre-1992 universities, despite the prevailing assumption that they are

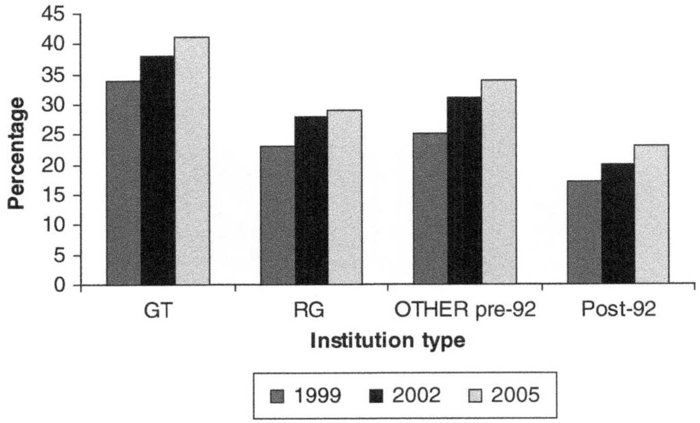

Figure 6.2 Percentage of overseas staff by year and institution type: research only staff

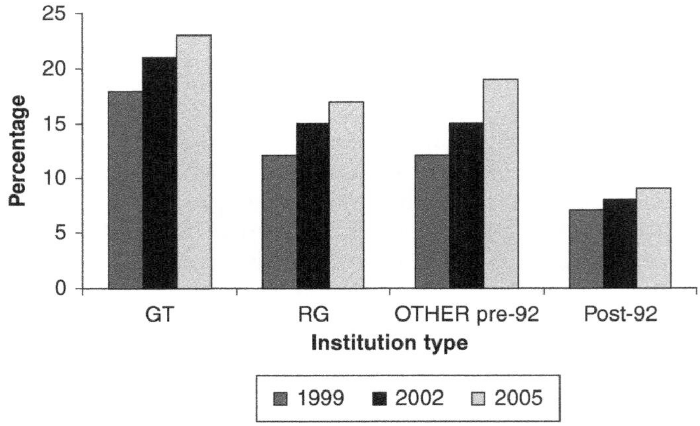

Figure 6.3 Percentage of overseas staff by year and institution type: teaching and research staff

closer to the GT whom Russell Group members regard as their peers. All pre-1992 institutions can be clearly distinguished from the post-1992 universities. The latter are clearly differently structured institutions since most do not have the large and expensive research subject areas. One of the distinguishing features of the RG universities is that they are on the whole larger than the other pre-1992 universities, so in terms of absolute numbers, on a per institution basis, more overseas staff are to be found in the RRG, as indeed are RO staff per se. Nevertheless and surprisingly, other pre-1992 universities have proportionately more overseas TR staff.

It may be thought there would be some difference between institutions, in the countries and regions from which staff come. This could be a clue to the speculation about 'funding' as against 'replacement labour' as explanatory factors. However, when we examine type of university by country of origin of staff there does not appear to be a big difference. The main difference is that GT institutions are much more able to attract US academics than anybody else, with no real difference between the RRG and other pre-1992 universities. For overseas TR staff in GT universities, 4 per cent (307 staff) were from the USA in 2005; 86.4 per cent (6684) were from EU-25 countries and 8 per cent (617) were from the rest of the world. In the other pre-1992 institutions in this year just 2.2 per cent (421) of overseas staff came from the USA; 89.3 per cent (17,443) were from the EU-25 countries and 7.1 per cent (1382) were from elsewhere in the world. Over time, there was a steady increase of ROs across all nationalities and institution types.

Not only is it true that in both TR and RO the 'other pre-1992' have slightly more overseas staff than RRG, but if we look at the RO staff by cost centre then it is also very clear that the other pre-1992 institutions have a higher *proportion* of overseas staff than those in the Russell Group (see section on cost centre below). However, the universities that recruit the majority of RO staff from overseas are still the big GT universities, which far outstrip both other pre-1992 and RRG in these terms. These data indicate that whilst there is a clear GT global effect, the RRG is no more global, in terms of its proportion of overseas staff, than the other pre-1992 institutions. The question then becomes how we account for this overseas presence. Because the GT institutions have such a relatively high proportion of overseas staff (33 per cent), this suggests there maybe something about the GT institutions that attracts or seeks or simply employs overseas staff; and it is that that we are interested in.

We know that some institutions have a high proportion of overseas staff (in some cases one in four staff are overseas). This means that every fourth time these institutions recruit a member of staff it is, in theory, a non-British national. In practice these odds must in fact be higher because a lot of the UK staff have been in post a long time and not recruited recently (the white – and male – staff are, for example, much older than others). Indeed the chances are very strong that overseas staff have been recruited much more recently. This would mean that, given their proportions in the total, the chances, per new post, of hiring an overseas person, must now be very high especially in some institutions. The younger age of overseas staff is indicative but not conclusive evidence of recency of appointment. While only 64 per cent of UK staff in RO posts are in the age group of 26–40 years, the proportion amongst overseas RO staff is 80 per cent. In TR the percentage of UK staff in the younger age groups was 26 per cent, compared to 48 per cent of overseas staff who are in the young age group.

Table 6.1 Origins of overseas academics in the UK

	Frequency	Per cent
W. Europe & Scandinavia	10,640	41.9
E. & Central Europe	3002	11.8
Australia, NZ, USA & Canada	4254	16.8
China, Japan & E. Asia	3140	12.4
Middle East & Central Asia	2199	8.7
Other non-European	2162	8.5
Total	25,397	100.0

Source: 2004–05 HESA data.

We have noted above how there have been some shifts in where overseas staff originate. The region and country of origin of overseas staff differ according to the subject area or recruitment, as shown in Table 6.1. In 2005, whilst for all subject areas about 42 per cent of academic staff are recruited from Western Europe, in social science subjects this is over 46 per cent and in arts 55 per cent. But in engineering subjects only 22 per cent are recruited from Western Europe. Engineering departments look further afield: 30 per cent of their overseas staff originate from China, Japan and East Asia. Even science only recruits 12 per cent from these East Asian countries and other subject areas recruit very few from this source. In arts and social science English language ability is clearly more of a factor: most of the overseas staff in these subject areas beyond Western Europe are recruited from Australia, New Zealand, the USA and Canada.

To recap, thus far we have shown that globalisation, measured in terms of proportions of overseas staff, is concentrated to a far greater extent in the research-intensive GT institutions. We suggest that this is the case for three main reasons. Firstly, the elite GT universities have been elevated into global rankings such that they attract a high share of overseas staff. Indeed, these institutions have been referred to as both 'magnets' (Mahroum, 1999a, 1999c) and as 'world-class' universities (Altbach and Balan, 2007; Mohrman, Ma and Baker, 2008). These institutions attract a huge and disproportionate share of funding – especially in research fields such as medicine, science and engineering (see below). Thirdly, in institutions which attract a large share of funding in select research areas a large market for contract researchers is created. In expensive research areas, only one centre is funded namely one nuclear research centre, one Jodrell Bank.[5] Such departments and research groups are international, and increasingly so.

In relation to funding, a central consequence of the government increasing competition within the HE sector, for example, through nearly two decades of the Research Assessment Exercise, has been the concentration of research funding, and of overseas academics in key institutions. This

Table 6.2 Higher education research funding for England, 2008–09

University	Research funding (£,000)
University of Cambridge	111,559
University of Oxford	110,134
University College London	104,114
Imperial College London	97,702
University of Manchester	81,867
King's College London	59,987
University of Leeds	48,831
University of Southampton	47,618
University of Sheffield	44,735
University of Bristol	44,582

has confirmed significant structural differences between pre- and post-1992 institutions. For instance, it is only the elite, large institutions, such as UCL, that have specialist space science laboratories. The Mullard Space Science Laboratory, part of the UCL Department of Space and Climate Physics, provides a good example.

Table 6.2 illustrates those universities with the greatest research funding received from HEFCE for universities in England in 2008–09. Total research funding differs from total teaching funding, and additional funding is also given to support very high-cost and vulnerable science subjects, particularly physics, chemistry, chemical engineering, and mineral metallurgy and materials engineering.

All of these institutions are Russell Group universities. The LSE (£18,306,000) was the only GT institution that failed to make it into the top ten, given its predominantly social science-based research work.

As part of HEFCE's funding package for universities and colleges in England for 2008–09, 47 out of the 130 English institutions receive additional funding. Of the £24,724,000 in additional funding given to HEIs, just four GT universities together secure almost one fifth of the total (£4,271,000). The concentration of funding is therefore confined to certain institutions. As we have demonstrated, these are also the universities with the highest numbers of overseas staff.

7. Cost centre and academic employment function

We look now at the presence of overseas academic staff in different cost centres within the elite GT institutions where we know that overseas staff are concentrated; and we examine their distribution by job function and by disciplinary location in these institutions. In the GT institutions the presence of overseas staff varies greatly by cost centre, with some high, some quite low.

Table 6.3 Percentage of all overseas staff by cost centre (1998–99, 2001–02 and 2004–05): Golden Triangle universities only

Cost centre	1998–99		2001–02		2004–05	
	N	%	N	%	N	%
Chemical engineering	128	60	133	59	71	50
Electrical engineering	117	39	187	46	162	47
Chemistry	258	36	338	44	241	42
Mathematics	190	36	218	41	206	41
Social studies	434	33	562	37	578	40
Physics	325	32	425	37	363	36

Within cost centres, some particular subjects have yet higher proportions of overseas staff (Table 6.3).

For all these cost centres the overseas presence is high; and it is growing, except for chemical engineering. In these cost centres in these elite institutions between 36 per cent and 50 per cent were overseas nationals in 2004–05. Over the long term there has therefore been concentration in these departments. This is a very high proportion of overseas and compares with 33 per cent overseas overall in these institutions: in one of our interviewees' research group (theoretical physics) there were no staff at all from the UK, and in several other research groups UK staff were in a minority. This evidence suggests that subjects or disciplines are absolutely critical to analysis. Indeed, the empirical actualisation of theoretical arguments about resourcing put forward above is that it is those groups of subjects that attract large research funding and overseas staff. The figures in Table 6.3 are all slightly higher than the figures for RG and pre-1992 universities, which broadly stand together. Figures for the post-1992 universities are a lot lower. Thus the data suggest that not only is the degree of globalisation (measured in terms of the proportions overseas) within the elite institutions growing, but so too is the gap between the GT and post-1992 institutions.

8. 'Golden Triangle' institutions

We look now at the importance of academic function when considering the overseas presence in particular cost centres in these institutions. If we look just at the GT universities, as the big magnets for overseas staff, then the cost centre distributions are very different by function, as can be seen in Table 6.4.

This cost centre split reveals two main things. Firstly, that overseas staff are concentrated in RO posts in these institutions. Further, the proportion of overseas RO staff in posts differs according to cost centre. There are some cost centres with very high percentages of overseas RO staff. There is also a

Table 6.4 Proportion of overseas staff in Golden Triangle by job function, 2004–05

	Research only (%)	Teaching and research (%)
Medicine and dentistry	38	16
Science	42	19
Engineering and technology	57	25
Social science	39	32
Arts	33	23
Total	41	23

Source: HESA, 2004–05 Staff Data.

relatively low presence of overseas TR staff. In all cases the percentage overseas is smaller for them. In 'hard' subjects, for example, engineering and mathematics, the ratio of RO to TR is higher. In engineering and technology almost 60 per cent of RO staff were foreign but this figure was only a quarter in TR positions. Social studies, on the other hand, stands out for remaining broadly similar in its numbers of overseas staff in each of these employment functions. This suggests that in the elite universities the social sciences are in the market for international staff where employment involves both teaching and research. Where, as in chemical engineering, overseas staff are quite well represented in TR posts, this may be more likely to highlight a lack of supply and the consequent need for overseas people for this kind of position.

It is not surprising that, in the elite GT institutions especially, there are very high percentages of overseas staff in RO posts. For this type of research work, the UK knowledge economy at the highest level depends very much on overseas staff. It is however notable that in TR posts the percentages of overseas are lower – in some cases quite significantly. It may be that overseas staff are less likely to be appointed in TR subjects because of an actual or perceived difficulty of language. And this will vary between subjects as in some subjects language will be less crucial, or the important language in question will be a scientific language. This would explain the wide variation between the 16 per cent in medicine and dentistry to double that proportion in the social sciences, while the higher figure of 23 per cent in the arts could be explained by expertise in languages other than English.

Employment function is critical. We now bring this together with cost centre and institution type in order to consider the academic function effect on the presence of overseas staff in RO and TR by cost centre in the different types of institution. What we are looking at here is whether the proportions of RO staff are bigger than TR. In the biosciences, for example, 47 per cent (569) of RO staff were overseas in 2004–05. This compared to 16.5 per cent (72) in TR posts. In the other pre-1992 universities the figures were 39 per cent (599) and 14 per cent (163). In chemistry 56.1 per cent (217) of RO staff were overseas in this year, compared to just 12.6 per cent (23) in

TR positions. In the other pre-1992 universities the comparable figures were 46.2 per cent (199) and 11.7 per cent (48).

Our analysis suggests that it is the GT universities that really stand out, particularly in terms of the percentage of overseas RO staff in these cost centres. It is also worth noting that the other pre-1992 institutions employ a higher proportion of overseas staff than the RRG. It is also clear that cost centre is critical to analysis, since in these particular cost centres differences between other pre-1992 institutions and the RRG are quite large, even though overall the difference is not great.

To probe these differences further we now examine the presence of overseas staff in different employment functions across the different types of institution that we are interested in. The post-1992 institutions still have over 4000 overseas staff. Our focus here is on what they do. In order to address this question we need to look at the relative concentration of overseas staff into RO or TR posts.

The data in Table 6.5 show us that the within the more elite institutional categories of GT and RRG, more overseas staff are concentrated in RO posts than in other types of post. Within the other pre-1992 and post-1992 institutions, on the other hand, more overseas staff are concentrated in TR posts. Post-1992 universities have 4188 overseas staff, of whom 70 per cent are in TR posts. This *is a very different picture* from the RO imports in the science-engineering-oriented GT universities, the latter of which have only 30 per cent of their overseas staff in TR posts.

The question then becomes what these overseas academics, working in the post-1992 universities, teach. The following cost centres accounted for more than half of all post-1992 overseas TR staff in 2004–05: nursing, IT, business, social studies, design and creative arts, modern languages. Except for the last there is nothing intrinsic to these subjects to suggest why they should have a high proportion of overseas staff. Yet business and IT alone accounted for 25 per cent of overseas TR staff in post-1992 universities. The high proportion of overseas staff in subjects such as nursing IT, business and so on is likely to be linked to the fact that these subjects have competing

Table 6.5 How non-UK staff are distributed through academic functions (non-UK staff only), by institution type, 2004–05

All non-UK	**RO (%)**	**TR (%)**
GT	67	30
RG	52	41
Other pre-1992	41	48
Post-1992	16	71

Note: Row totals do not add up to 100 per cent because teaching only and other are not shown.

commercial markets for potential UK-based staff (Ghosh, 2006). In addition to the large number of people in RO posts, GT universities attract top rank international academics and they too, like 71 per cent of the overseas staff in post-1992 universities, will be in TR posts.

Musselin (2004) mentions in passing (but without discussion as this was not a feature of her study) that academic 'stars' (circulating elites with international reputations in their subject fields) are a feature of the international dimension. We can confirm this in relation to our study, but highlight its significant scale in certain institutions and subjects in the UK.

9. What overseas staff give as their reasons for coming to the UK

The national data shows that overseas staff are attracted to work in British HE though not evenly across the sector, but concentrated in particular cost centres and the most prestigious institutions. These tend to be ROs and typically younger persons. We can explore further why younger overseas staff at the start of their career come to the UK by looking at our web survey and interviews.

Table 6.6 shows that the respondents to our web survey came principally for the purposes of developing their careers. Half of all respondents reported this as being the most important reason why they had come. A further 18 per cent reported intellectual opportunities as being most important, followed closely by research funding and facilities (15 per cent).

Our qualitative interviews with staff showed that the UK was seen as a generally attractive place to be, and for the following four main reasons. Firstly, the academic environment, particularly the freedom to pursue one's own research agenda and interests: 'The thing I particularly like about doing research in the UK is the working environment. Here I feel that research is really about research'; 'the relationship between me and my boss works really well.... She gives me a lot of freedom to manage what I'm doing so that is very satisfying'; 'When I tell my friends in Spain about the conditions of work I've got here I beat them in almost all the points.' The job opportunities

Table 6.6 Most important factor for coming to the UK (web survey)

	Frequency	**Per cent**
Career development	56	49.6
Intellectual opportunities	20	17.7
Research funding & facilities	17	15
Family reasons	8	7.1
Quality of life	7	6.2
Salary	5	4.4
Total	113	100

in UK universities were also perceived to be good, particularly in comparison to those in other EU countries, where opportunities for recognition and progression were seen as extremely difficult at the start of the career.

Secondly, the academic environment in the UK was seen as being more open to outsiders than many other countries. This was particularly the case for those from Germany, Italy and Spain. In recruitment procedures it was felt that professional networks (who one's PhD supervisor had been, or who one had worked with previously) would be more important than one's own work. Indeed the majority of our interviewees spoke of how they felt that UK institutions would be more welcoming, where interviewers for posts would judge them principally on their merit and academic record rather than more intangible factors.

Thirdly, certain UK institutions were seen to be highly marketable on a curriculum vitae (CV). Interviewees repeatedly told us how they saw UK experience as beneficial in its marketability in later CV moves. German and Austrian scholars in particular were of the view that it would be beneficial, if not an expectation or condition of progression, if they left their home country after having done their PhD and gained experience in another country. Fourthly, the reputation of particular institutions and research groups within the UK system was attractive. As one respondent said: 'This was my first choice. I had read a lot of the research work coming out of the Centre, which was one of the research teams here – so I knew them and I knew of them. It's a particularly famous institution so that was part of the attraction.'

Another important draw for overseas academics was the fact that working in the UK involved working in an English-speaking academic environment, which was seen to offer obvious advantages in publications and language, networking and intellectual opportunities.

Those who had come to the UK to take up a first postdoctoral position were generally very enthusiastic about gaining experience of the UK system, building up contacts, applying their existing knowledge, 'proving' that their investment in their education had been worthwhile; and gaining experience of working in a different environment, with different individuals. These staff came with high hopes of developing their careers, and the UK was seen as a good place to do that.

Elsewhere we have reported our findings that in the main our respondents are very satisfied with their professional experience despite the fact that the majority are on fixed-term contracts (Smetherham, Fenton and Modood, 2008). In order to assess to what extent overseas staff represent a 'global' workforce we will consider what our respondents said about their future plans. According to our online survey data, just 25 per cent of respondents (all aged under 30 and in RO positions) said that they were intending to stay permanently in the UK. There was very little gender difference in response, the proportions being 23 per cent of men and 25 per cent of women. The interviewees in our study typically articulated their thoughts about their future career plans in uncertain terms. Only 7 of our 21 interviewees responded that they had a definite and specific career plan at that point. The majority of researchers responded that they had no definite plans, or made very vague statements about their futures in terms of 'taking each day as it comes'. This in itself does not point to feelings of job insecurity or uncertainty regarding the future per se, but can arise from the position that fixed-term researchers find themselves in. Many did not feel the need to make specific plans (just yet, in any case), but would reassess their positions and projects when their current contract was nearing an end. Yet this orientation clearly did not necessarily stem from a position of job security either. Many of our researchers, who were not in secure employment as fixed-term contract researchers, also expressed contentment and a reluctance to plan too much for the future. In terms of their future careers, 3 saw themselves as definitely returning home in the near future; 4 as definitely returning home within the longer term; 14 were open on this issue, did not mention returning home, saw themselves as moving to a third country, or would by choice prefer to stay in the UK.

10. Conclusions

The chapter has shown that by and large, the percentage of overseas staff in all types of institutions, in all cost centres and in all employment functions has increased. Furthermore, globalisation is taking place predominantly in GT institutions. We have shown that these research-rich institutions are significantly different from others, with a much greater intensity of overseas staff. The other pre-1992 and RG institutions were not so different from each other in structure, and the data presented suggested that when they do have posts then they will attract, and employ, some staff from overseas.

Our study thus confirms the findings of Musselin (2004) in certain ways, but disconfirms them in bigger ways. In relation to the UK in the years of our data, we can confirm that the majority of overseas staff are fixed-term postdoctorals. However, the scale is much bigger than Musselin (2004) suggests. There is also significant differentiation between institutions and subjects. A focus on indices of the internationality of UK institutions and cost centres in our study clearly suggested that some institutions and cost centres were significantly more implicated in global labour exchanges than others. We argued that these two factors were closely linked in that those institutions which are most global (the elite GT universities) are also typically those with large departments and faculties in the more globalised cost centres (e.g., engineering, medicine).

There are certain factors that influence where overseas staff go. One is that they are attracted to high-prestige institutions and that these are seen as world class. Accordingly, we would have expected to see more overseas staff in the top six GT institutions – and the data presented in the chapter showed that this was indeed the case. Our web survey and qualitative interviews showed that these staff had typically come to the UK in order to develop strategically their future academic careers. Most had expected to be caught, at least initially, in somewhat precarious employment situations. But these staff had a mind on developing, in the longer term, more permanent academic careers – some on an international scale. Whilst the UK was seen as an excellent place to start careers, few saw themselves as staying in the UK longer term. The attractions of the UK included particular institutions and research teams, the marketability of the UK experience in later CV moves and positive perceptions of the academic environment. Interviewees mostly spoke positively about their academic experience in Britain, with only a small minority saying they were dissatisfied. Our qualitative evidence tended, therefore, to support the 'opportunity' model rather than the 'exploitation' model of academic careers in the UK. We also argued that prestige HEIs that have significantly sized physics, mathematics, chemistry and engineering departments will attract high-research funding. Subject areas that have large funding in turn imply large numbers of RO staff. These tend to be younger overseas staff that intend to develop their careers in the UK. If these staff were attracted to well-funded departments in elite high-research HEIs then we would have expected to see a concentration of overseas staff in RO positions. Again, the data show that this was indeed the case. However, certain subjects attract applicants from overseas, regardless of university type. If these institutions have less research funding, overseas academics are found in TR posts.

Thirdly, we referred to shortages. These indicate the ways in which the UK system is not meeting demand, and to the attractions of careers in the commercial world. The data show the presence of more overseas staff in areas where staff in the UK are generally under-supplied (for example, certain sub-fields of engineering). Here, a model of elite labour markets in HE was used to account for the presence of overseas TR staff in GT institutions. A replacement labour model was used to account for those overseas TR staff in HEIs outside the GT/RG; or to those working in under-supplied areas.

Acknowledgements

We are grateful to HESA for advice on the dataset. HESA cannot be held responsible for the analysis in this chapter.

Notes

1. The Higher Education Statistics Agency is the official agency for the collection, analysis and dissemination of quantitative information about higher education in the UK. The agency collects data on the characteristics of members of academic staff employed under a contract of employment by a HEI in the UK and include information on, for instance, mode of employment, terms of employment, grade

and employment function. Within our sample academic staff are defined as academic professionals who are responsible for planning, directing and undertaking academic teaching and research within HE institutions. They also include vice-chancellors, medical practitioners, dentists, veterinarians and other health care professionals who undertake lecturing or research activities. Atypical staff contracts are not counted in our population. Academic staff with less than 25 per cent full-time equivalent have also been excluded from the population. For 2004–05, when changes were made to the staff record, multiple contracts were reduced to the one with the most senior grade group (or the highest FTE if two or more contracts were at the same grade level).

2. http://www.guardian.co.uk/education/2003/jun/03/highereducation.research, last accessed 23 December 2010.
3. The Russell Group is an association of 20 major research-intensive universities of the UK. These are Birmingham, Bristol, Cambridge, Cardiff, Edinburgh, Glasgow, Imperial College London, Kings College London, Leeds, Liverpool, LSE, Manchester, Newcastle, Nottingham, Queen's University Belfast, Oxford, Sheffield, Southampton, UCL and Warwick.
4. The academic employment function of a member of staff relates to the contract of employment and not the actual work undertaken. HESA also use the groups 'teaching only' and 'neither teaching nor research'.
5. The Jodrell Bank Centre for Astrophysics comprises the research activities in astronomy and astrophysics at the University of Manchester, the world leading facilities of the Jodrell Bank Observatory and MERLIN/VLBI National Facility and public outreach via the Jodrell Bank Visitor Centre.

References

Ackers, L. (2005) 'Moving People and Knowledge: Scientific Mobility in the European Union', *International Migration*, 43(5): 99–131.

Ackers, L. and Gill, B. (2005) 'Attracting and Retaining "Early Career" Researchers in English Higher Education Institutions', *Innovation: The European Journal of Social Sciences*, 18(3): 277–299.

Adams, M. (2006) 'Industry Facing Critical Shortage of Engineers, Other Professionals', *Oil and Gas Financial Journal*, 3(1): 1–7.

Alpion, G. (2008) 'Brain Down the Drain – An Expose of Social Closure in Western Academia', in G. Alpion, ed. *Encounters with Civilizations: From Alexander the Great to Mother Teresa*. India: Meteor Books, pp. 181–204.

Altbach, P. (2004) 'Globalisation and the University: Myths and Realities in an Unequal World', *Tertiary Education and Management*, 10(1): 3–25.

Altbach, P. and Balan, J. (2007) *World Class Worldwide: Transforming Research Universities in Asia and Latin America*. Baltimore, MD: Johns Hopkins University Press.

AUT (2005) *The 'Brain Drain': Academic and Skilled Migration to the UK and its Impacts on Africa*. Report to the AUT and NATFHE.

Balakrishnan, A. (2007) 'CBI Seeks Bursaries to Boost Science and Engineering Studies', *Guardian*, 13 August.

Bond, J. (2007) 'UK Skills Gap Continues to Deteriorate Warn IET', The Institution of Engineering and Technology, 9 July, http://www.theiet.org/about/media-centre/press-releases/20070709_2.cfm. Last accessed 23 December 2010.

Casey, T., Mahroum, S., Ducatel, K. and Barre, R. (2001) *The Mobility of Academic Researchers: Academic Careers and Recruitment in ICT and Biotechnology*. Seville: Joint Research Centre, Institute for Prospective Technological Studies.
Cheng, L. and Yang, P.Q. (1998) 'Global Interaction, Global Inequality, and Migration of the Highly Trained to the United States', *International Migration Review*, 32(3): 626–653.
Deem, R. (2001) 'Globalisation, New Managerialism, Academic Capitalism and Entrepreneurialism in Universities: Is the Local Dimension Still Important?', *Comparative Education*, 37(1): 7–20.
Gaillard, J. and Gaillard, A.M. (1998) 'The International Circulation of Scientists and Technologists: A Win-Lose or Win-Win Situation?', *Science Communication*, 20(1): 106–115.
Ghosh, P. (2006) 'Computer Industry "Faces Crisis" ', BBC News website, 17 November, http://news.bbc.co.uk/1/hi/technology/6155998.stm. Last accessed 23 December 2010.
HEFCE (2005) *Staff Employed at HEFCE Funded HEIs: Trends, Profiles and Projections*, 2005/23. Bristol: HEFCE.
HESA (1999) *HESA Staff Record for the Academic Year 1998–1999*. Cheltenham: HESA
HESA (2002) *HESA Staff Record for the Academic Year 2001–2002*. Cheltenham: HESA, last accessed 23 December, 2010.
HESA (2005) *HESA Staff Record for the Academic Year 2004–2005*. Cheltenham: HESA.
Johnson, J.M. and Regets, M. (1998) 'International Mobility of Scientists and Engineers to the US – Brain Drain or Brain Circulation?', *National Science Foundation Issue Brief 98*, June 22, p. 316.
Mahroum, S. (1998) *Europe and the Challenge of Brain Drain*, IPTS Report, No. 29, November.
Mahroum, S. (1999a) 'Global Magnets: Science and Technology Disciplines and Departments in the United Kingdom', *Minerva*, 37(4): 379–390.
Mahroum, S. (1999b) 'Patterns of Academic Inflow into the Higher Education System of the United Kingdom', *Higher Education in Europe*, 24(1): 119–129.
Mahroum, S. (1999c) *UK Global Magnets of Excellence*, JRC Publications Bulletin No. 20.
Merrick, B. (2004) *Broadening Our Horizons: International Students in UK Universities and Colleges*. UKCOSA: The Council for International Education.
Merriman, J. (2008) 'Shortage of Engineers Plagues Oil Industry', *International Herald Tribune*, 3 June.
Mohrman, K., Ma, W. and Baker, D.P. (2008) 'The Research University in Transition: The Emerging Global Model', *Higher Education Policy*, 21: 5–27.
Morano-Foadi, S. (2005) 'Scientific Mobility, Career Progression, and Excellence in the European Research Area', *International Migration*, 43(5): 133–162.
Musselin, C. (2004) 'Towards a European Academic Labour Market? Some Lessons Drawn From Empirical Studies on Academic Mobility', *Higher Education*, 48: 55–78.
Naidoo, R. (2003) 'Repositioning Higher Education as a Global Commodity: Opportunities and Challenges for Future Sociology of Education Work', *British Journal of Sociology of Education*, 24(2): 249–259.
Pieterse, J.N. (1996) 'Globalisation and Culture: Three Paradigms', *Economic and Political Weekly*, 31(23): 1389–1393.
Roberts, G. (2002) *SET for Success: The Supply of People with Science, Technology, Engineering and Mathematics Skills*. London: HM Treasury.
Sanders, C. (2004) 'Lack of Medical Lecturers Threatens NHS Salvation', *Times Higher Education*, 16 January.

Sastry, T. (2005) *Migration of Academic Staff To and From the UK – An Analysis of the HESA Data*. Oxford: Higher Education Policy Institute.
Scott, P. (2000) 'Globalisation and Higher Education: Challenges for the 21st Century', *Journal of Studies in International Education*, 4, (1): 3–10.
Smetherham, C., Fenton, S. and Modood, T. (2008) 'The Experiences of International Staff Working in the UK', C-SAP conference, Edinburgh, November.
Teichler, U. (2004) 'The Changing Debate on Internationalisation of Higher Education', *Higher Education*, 48, (1): 5–26.

7
International Students and the Labour Market: Experience in the UK

John Salt

1. Introduction

It is only comparatively recently that the role of institutions in orchestrating migration has come under serious investigation. Most migration theories continue to emphasise migrants and their actions as a key to understanding processes of movement (Koser and Salt, 1997). In fact, international labour migration may be conceptualised as a business, populated by a range of institutions each of which has some influence on the processes, patterns and outcomes of movement. These institutions include employers and trades unions, government, universities, regulatory bodies, migrant organisations and facilitators such as lawyers. They constitute networks of interrelationships, some of which are more important than others. They each have their own operational strategies and, to achieve their objectives, they negotiate with each other in order to reach compromise accommodations which produce migration outcomes. This process leads to tensions that in turn may create the need for further negotiations and new migration outcomes.

Among the institutions influencing labour migration patterns, employing organisations play a key role through their acquisition and deployment of human skills. Their actions in this regard are determined by their business models, as well as by a suite of constraints and opportunities which impinge upon them, including such matters as regulatory frameworks, welfare state arrangements and the policies and actions of other institutional actors. For most commercial employers, recruitment and mobility decisions and processes are determined by the need to maximise profitability. Transnational corporations seek to make best use of their internal expertise and add to it through recruitment in the external labour market.

Universities are key actors in the internationalisation of education. It is increasingly in their business as well as intellectual interests to attract students from other countries. In response, most UK universities actively market themselves overseas, resulting in a complex network of flows of students. Over the last decade or so, increasing attention has been paid to the international migration of students. The dominant perspectives have been those of students themselves (Li, Jowett and Skeldon, 1996; Lewis, 2005; Waters, 2006a, 2006b, 2009; Christie, 2007; Findlay and King, 2010), governments and educational institutions (OECD, 2001, 2007). Governments have seen foreign students (hereafter referred to as international students) for the most part in economic terms, educational institutions in financial terms.

Employers are largely left out of the literature and discussions about the patterns and trends of flows of international students. Our recent research suggests that this omission is unwarranted and that the place of employers in discussions about the migration of international students needs to be given greater prominence.[1] This is particularly the case with respect to the transition of international students into the labour market.

This chapter builds upon earlier research, discussed in Chapter 5, to explore the interaction of two international migration systems. One is the international mobility of students for higher education purposes, the other is international recruitment and mobility within corporate labour markets. UK data for the academic year 2005–06 in which the research began suggest there were about a third of a million international students in higher education (UKCOSA, 2007). Estimates of their benefit to the economy in 2003–04 were around £4.6 billion in fees and other spending (Lenton, 2007) and £5.5 billion in 2004–05 (Vickers and Bekhradnia, 2007).

The chapter begins by presenting evidence from the earlier study that some employers value international students and are either targeting them for recruitment or thinking about doing so. By targeting we mean the deliberate selection of particular types of international students, for example, according to their nationality or disciplinary training. This is distinct from more general recruitment which may involve international students studying in the UK. The chapter then presents the results of a survey of university careers services which show that targeting exists and is becoming more common. This is followed by the principal findings from a survey of a sample of 15 employers in two sectors: finance and extractives. Finally, the significance of the findings is discussed from the perspective of employers, government and universities.

2. Establishing links between international student mobility and corporate labour markets

2.1. International student migration: changing paradigms

Until the mid-1980s the prevailing paradigm was 'education for aid'. Student mobility was predominantly from poorer (usually former colonies) to richer (colonial power) countries. It was characterised by a generally philanthropic (some might say paternalistic) approach, associated with low fees for overseas students. There was, of course, a sub-text in the assumption that on return to their own countries educational links would help strengthen economic ties. About 20 years ago, 'education for trade' started to be the prevailing paradigm (Baker et al., 1996). International students were seen as cash cows for educational institutions, reducing the need for state funding. Fees were increased and immigration rules amended to allow them to work while studying. They were seen as contributors to the economy instead of requiring subsidisation. Postgraduates especially were seen as new knowledge creators who could contribute to economic growth either directly or indirectly.

The logical development from this was for international students to be seen as 'probationary immigrants', in some countries at least (Kuptsch, 2006). For example, international students graduating from Australian universities are now a major source of permanent immigrants, with programmes designed to ease the transition from one status to the other (Birrell, Hawthorne and Richardson, 2006). In similar fashion, the Fresh Talent scheme in Scotland (Rogerson, Boyle and Mason, 2006) and the International Graduates Scheme (IGS) in the UK (later incorporated into Tier 1 of the points-based system) were designed to capitalise on international students at local universities by allowing them to stay after graduation to seek and take up work with the eventual possibility of a permanent stay.

In recent years several other countries have relaxed their rules on the recruitment of international students. In the Netherlands, they are allowed to stay and seek work up to three months after graduation. Austria allows them to change status to highly skilled workers and their employers are exempt from a resident labour market test. In Ireland they can remain for six months to find employment, while Slovakia allows them to stay for three months without a temporary residence permit (OECD, 2008).

It seems that we are now entering a potentially new paradigm in the mobility of international students, characterised by their perceived value to large employers as 'global human resources'. We are not yet in a position to determine the scale or nature of this phenomenon but, as we find in the rest of this chapter, there is enough evidence to suggest that it exists and is growing.

2.2. Corporate views of international students

Our earlier project was concerned with the international recruitment and mobility of expertise within transnational corporations (TNCs). It was carried out in 2004–06 and included interviews with 35 employers in 6 economic sectors (Millar and Salt, 2007, 2008; Salt, 2009). In the course of these interviews we became aware that some companies were increasingly attracted to the recruitment of particular international students at UK universities. There was a spectrum of interest. Some TNCs operating in the UK were deliberately targeting international students from specific countries studying in the UK for recruitment into their UK and global internal labour markets. Some were intending to do so or were thinking about it, others had not considered the matter. This information arose spontaneously in our interviews and was not part of our formal discussion guide.

Underlying many of the comments from employers was the more general recognition that international students at UK universities have much to offer large organisations.

> We recruit somewhere between 60 and 100 graduates in the UK every year through our graduate recruitment programmes, nearly 40–50 per cent of those, at least in recent years, are not Brits. The UK universities are a marvellous source of international talent. (Extractive)

Studying in another country means that international students have language and other cultural advantages.

> For all our graduates we try and make sure that they are multi-linguistic and they've got to have two languages at least, even if you're just in engineering or whatever. (Aerospace)

For companies with operations in particular countries, recruitment of international students from those locations is a matter of course. One company was quite clear about which international students it wanted. In this case operations in more remote parts of the world needed to be staffed but potential new recruits were thin on the ground locally and labour shortages could seriously undermine expansion and operational plans. Targeting was clear. Asked if it was targeting students from its growing market locations by recruiting them in the UK, the response of the company was emphatic:

> Oh yes, Russians, Chinese, the lot. That's a deliberate policy. (Extractive)

Sometimes specific technical expertise was required.

> I want to know every Kazak petrochemical person who's not in Kazakhstan at the moment because we'll get them home, if they want to come home, we'll get them home. (Extractive)

In this and in other cases, an important underlying reason for recruitment was to train and then send people back to their home countries.

> So they get hired and they go to work wherever they come from or some of them. Europeans work all over Europe, the other nationalities go to work wherever they come from. (Extractive 3)

As company human resources are now usually viewed in international terms, so employers are adopting a more international perspective towards the location of graduate recruitment.

> ...you look back to where all the vacancies are so you know Malaysia is looking for six of this and Nigeria is looking for seven of that and, if you spot a Russian doing an MBA who passes the requirements and is interested in going back to work in Russia, that's a prelude to an international career, so you know what your targets are and then you go out and see what applications you get. (Extractive)

This international perspective allows them to put in place and achieve international student recruitment quotas with a focus on what the business as a whole requires.

> In the future we're going to be much more managed about that.... We need to dovetail the needs of local businesses and allowing that continued relationship with local universities and then bringing in more of a headquarters view of access to talent that maybe graduated from the UK universities and that would like to repatriate one day. So we're starting to hire several dozen Chinese nationals from UK universities. (Extractive)

Sometimes government policy deters companies from targeting students from countries they are expanding into.

> We don't do that because often it's very difficult for those people to get work permits. (Aerospace)

Nevertheless, it is something that companies are looking to do:

> We currently don't do it... but it's something we recognise we need to do. (Aerospace)

These comments indicated that some companies were looking at international student recruitment in new ways – targeting particular nationalities and types of expertise as part of their global human resourcing initiatives. However, the results presented here offer only a snapshot of business practice and we have little idea how extensive is the targeting of international students by employers. The literature on this is minimal and although we can identify a rich seam of information relating to movements for education purposes and their international development implications, there seems little on the role that employers have in turning international students into global and local labour resources. There is some recent evidence that employers do value an international education. A survey of 233 employers suggested that

UK students do not adequately value an international dimension to their education but that global employers need graduates who have experience of different countries and cultures (Archer and Davison, 2008).

3. Survey of careers services

Of prime importance to us was to ascertain how far employers were actually targeting international students in the UK in their recruitment campaigns. In order to establish the extent of targeting we carried out a survey of university career services in the UK. It was designed to establish

- Whether and to what extent large companies are targeting specific international students for recruitment.
- If so, what sort of students, by discipline and nationality.
- What type of targeting is being employed.

3.1. Methodology

An electronic survey of Heads of Career Advisory Services in UK universities was conducted in the early summer of 2007. The aim was to identify the extent to which they were aware that employers using their services were deliberately targeting particular international students during recruitment. It was impressed upon respondents that it was important to return a negative response if they were not aware that targeting was going on.

Responses were received from 79 (57 per cent) of the 138 universities contacted. They represented a broad spectrum of universities as a whole: 15 per cent ($n = 12$) of respondents were from the Russell Group, 18 per cent ($n = 14$) were from the Higher Education and Research Opportunities in the UK (HERO)[2] institutions and 24 per cent ($n = 19$) were from the Coalition of Modern Universities (CMU)[3]. The majority of respondents, 43 per cent ($n = 34$), were from universities that are unclassified in these terms.

3.2. Awareness of targeting

The responses demonstrated that targeting of international students is a widespread phenomenon. Forty-one per cent of the sample (32 Heads of Service) were aware that companies deliberately targeted international students when recruiting at their institutions. Furthermore, almost two thirds (63 per cent, $n = 19$) of those considered deliberate targeting an increasing trend.

There is also evidence that employers were selective in deciding which universities to recruit from, with some institutions more likely to be used for targeted recruitment than others: for example, 34 per cent ($n = 11$) were Russell Group universities, more than double their proportion of total respondents. In the presentation of results below, the numbers and percentages relate to the 41 per cent of the sample that were aware of targeting.

3.3. Perceived characteristics of targeting companies

A key issue for us was the type of companies which are doing the targeting, particularly the degree to which those recruited are absorbed into large corporate internal labour markets as distinct from smaller organisations operating either locally or nationally. Over half (59 per cent) of the sample reported that multinational corporations were the main actors, including both foreign- (58 per cent) and UK-owned (55 per cent) companies.

Careers services were also asked about the industrial sector into which the targeted recruitment of international students was occurring. Responses indicated that a broad spectrum of the economy was involved. In all, 17 sectors were mentioned as ones in which targeting companies were active. Most frequently mentioned were the financial services sector (87 per cent), information technology (53 per cent), manufacturing (43 per cent), extractive industries and law (20 per cent each).

Another critical issue is the degree to which companies are recruiting from particular international student populations with specific recruitment quotas in mind. While two respondents (8 per cent) had experience of companies frequently specifying quotas when recruiting international students from their institutions, a further 54 per cent ($n = 14$) reported that companies only occasionally specified quotas. Although 39 per cent ($n = 10$) replied that they were unaware of these being used, this does not necessarily mean that the practice did not happen.

A majority of respondents were aware that quotas are being used on some occasions. Doing so implies that, with regard to certain operations, for example, in emerging markets, companies have a set number of jobs in their internal labour markets for international students and are not recruiting on an ad hoc basis. Practice varies and business requirements at particular times come into play, perhaps with a set target number given them by their overseas arm.

3.4. Characteristics of the targeted international student population

The survey asked a number of questions designed to elicit the main types of international students being sought. Given the interest expressed by companies in our earlier survey in how recruits would be used within their international labour markets, national origins were important. All respondents in the sample reported that companies were deliberately targeting students from particular geographic regions and nationalities. By far the most frequently mentioned region for targeted recruitment was among Asian students ($n = 30$, 97 per cent), particularly those from China ($n = 27$, 87 per cent), Malaysia ($n = 13$, 42 per cent) and Japan ($n = 12$, 39 per cent).

African students were mentioned by 13 respondents (42 per cent) and 8 more (26 per cent) reported that European students were targets for recruitment, particularly those from Greece ($n = 4$, 13 per cent) and Germany

($n = 4$, 13 per cent). Only two respondents (6 per cent) reported that companies were looking to target students from North America and just one (3 per cent) had observed targeting of Middle Eastern students. Overall, 20 individual countries were explicitly mentioned.

There was selectivity in the disciplines sought. Most (87 per cent, $n = 26$) reported that companies were deliberately targeting international students from particular disciplinary areas, especially management/economics (88 per cent, $n = 23$), information technology (62 per cent, $n = 16$) and engineering (58 per cent, $n = 15$).

The majority (89 per cent, $n = 25$) of respondents were aware that companies also sought international students to fill particular occupations. Most frequently mentioned were professional jobs (92 per cent, $n = 23$), managerial positions (72 per cent, $n = 18$) and technical occupations (64 per cent, $n = 16$).

Although much of the literature on 'staying on' has focused on encouraging postdoctoral graduates to remain (Borjas, 2005), the majority of employers were recruiting at the undergraduate and postgraduate level, seeking recruits with a Masters degree (90 per cent, $n = 27$) as well as undergraduates (83 per cent, $n = 25$). Recruitment at the postdoctoral level was relatively less common. Only 43 per cent of the sample ($n = 13$) reported deliberate targeting of international students studying for a PhD.

3.5. Initiating the link between international students and employers

In their targeting of international students, companies are working with careers services in a number of ways. They include both employer- and university-generated initiatives. The active involvement of universities indicates that they see the recruitment of their existing international students as a positive in attracting new generations of them.

University-initiated events

Typically, as mentioned by 65 per cent of the sample ($n = 20$), the university took the lead in laying on special recruitment events/presentations geared towards their international student population. Of these, 95 per cent (18 out of the 19 responses to the item) considered this to be an increasing trend at their institution and the remainder reported a stable trend in such university-initiated activities.

Over half of events (58 per cent, $n = 11$) had been geared to students from particular countries but only 16 per cent were oriented towards international students from specific disciplines.

Employer-initiated events

Just under half of the sample (45 per cent, $n = 14$) had experience of employers laying on special recruitment events and/or presentations that were specifically geared towards international students at their institutions. Of those, 80 per cent ($n = 12$) considered this route to international student recruitment to be increasingly used.

Of those events that had been laid on by employers, all were oriented towards international students from particular countries but very few (9 per cent) targeted students from particular disciplines.

3.6. Recruitment practices

There is a wide range of initiatives designed to support targeted recruitment. Furthermore, the number of these seems to be growing, indicating the importance employers attach to this form of recruiting. Overall, targeting of specific national groups seems to be more important than targeting of individual disciplines.

Overseas vacancy handling

Overseas vacancy handling involves, for example, alerting students who have expressed an interest in working overseas about relevant vacancies that arise in their preferred locations. Fifteen Heads of Service reported that they provided overseas vacancy handling services for their international students. Three quarters ($n = 12$) of these were oriented to students from particular countries and 40 per cent ($n = 6$) were discipline-focused. The majority of these respondents (75 per cent, $n = 12$) considered that there was an increasing trend towards the provision of overseas vacancy handling and 25 per cent ($n = 4$) that the trend was stable.

Targeted mail, email or post

Almost all of those providing targeted mailings ($n = 11$) to international students were orienting these mailings to particular national groups of students. Only 40 per cent ($n = 4$) were providing this facility for international students studying particular disciplines. Most respondents (70 per cent, $n = 7$) considered the provision of targeted mailings to be an increasing trend.

Special interview sessions

About one in three respondents ($n = 8$) mentioned that employers were deliberately targeting international students in their recruitment activities by hosting special interview sessions for them. Four of the eight respondents considered this approach to recruitment was increasing.

Departmental linkages

Although it seems to be increasingly common for employers to forge links with academic departments, for both recruitment and other purposes, only a minority of Heads of Service (19 per cent, $n=5$) were aware of companies deliberately targeting international students in this manner.

Other methods

University careers services and/or companies were providing various other methods to link international students and potential employers. These included recruitment events ($n=6$); international job databases ($n=4$); links with recruitment agencies abroad ($n=3$); presentations ($n=3$); informal methods, for example, via student unions ($n=2$); international employer directories ($n=1$); and industrial placements ($n=1$). In all cases, activities were more focused on delivering service to international students from particular countries than to those in specific disciplines.

3.7. Summary

Our survey has established that some employers are deliberately targeting international students from particular countries when recruiting at UK universities. Furthermore, the practice is increasing. As yet we do not know what proportion of companies engage in the practice. Multinational companies are the main, but not the only actors. While a broad range of universities is experiencing targeting, the research-led Russell Group seems more heavily involved than other groups. Recruitment occurs into a broad spectrum of the economy, with financial services and IT being the most heavily involved. Practice with respect to setting recruitment quotas varies.

National origins are important, with Asians as a whole and Chinese particularly being frequent targets. International students at Masters and undergraduate level are particularly desirable, the main disciplines being management/economics, IT and engineering. Recruits into professional, managerial and technical occupations are most often sought. In support of these practices, employers and universities are interacting, increasingly and in a growing variety of formal and informal ways.

These findings suggest that targeting of international students is a new and growing migration process. They also have a number of implications for employers, universities and governments as well as for students themselves.

4. Survey of employers

Based on the information from the careers survey, the heads of graduate recruitment in 12 major financial services and three extractives companies were interviewed in 2007–08 with the aim of finding out the extent of corporate practice and the reasons for it. Eight of the 15 companies were deliberately targeting international students at UK universities, three were in the process of changing their recruitment practice to do so, two recruited international students but did not target them specifically and two did not

Table 7.1 Targeting of international students by sample companies

	No. of companies
Targeting IS	8
Thinking/In process of changing	3
Recruit IS but don't target	2
Don't recruit IS	2
Total	15

Source: Author's Survey.

recruit international students (Table 7.1). Our analysis suggests eight main reasons for targeting.

First, companies are increasingly seeking to increase the diversity of their talent pool. It is part of a strategy allowing them to expand their global HR base with recruits whose international experience and mobility gives them extra flexibility when allocating expertise. In developing their businesses globally, companies seek to promote a common cultural attitude along with the international mindset deemed to be possessed by international students. As one company executive explained

> Diversity . . . it's now much more about inclusivity . . . . Without people who are from that cultural background who understand what's involved there, it's very difficult from a business perspective for the organisation to break into that market. (Finance)

Second, international students are attractive for their perceived proclivity for international mobility, particularly at a time when many companies are striving to achieve new diversity goals. For example, companies that place a high international mobility load on an ageing senior workforce may consider the recruitment of international students to provide one route towards meeting their diversity goals in the future. The retention and career development of people who from the outset have proved willing to be internationally mobile enables companies to increase the nationality mix of the internationally mobile executive population in their internal labour markets. Our employers agreed that international students are more willing to be globally mobile and companies see that having an international education might be an indication of their potential mobility in the future. Their international outlook means they are able to live in more than one country during their careers.

> The people who are more likely to take up that opportunity that comes up overnight . . . are those that are likely to have studied in a number of different countries. (Finance)

Third, they have language and cultural awareness. In one of the few pieces of research on the links between employers and international student recruitment, a study of Finnish employers (Garam, 2005) found that Finns returning to the country from overseas study were often preferred to those Finns who had not moved. There were three particular grounds for this: the occupational skills they picked up; how the experience affected them as individuals (their 'personal growth'); and the skills and abilities they obtained which allowed them to live and interact in an international environment (their 'internationalisation'). Awareness and experience are increasingly important in international business where the expectation is growing that rising staff will have more than one language and understand local ways of doing business.

> As an international employer, [company] values mobility and international thinking... some level of maturity – a greater level of maturity if they've lived outside of their home country. (Finance)

Fourth, they are needed to help develop emerging markets (usually their home countries). This is likely to be particularly important when companies are developing new and emerging markets where there may be a shortage of locally trained and available talent. Additionally, for both large and small/medium-sized employers, there is the option to employ international students in the UK, for example, in departments dealing with the client-base in their home countries. This may be a prelude to building up domestic capabilities in those countries. In this case, the balance between the employment of international students in the UK and in their home counties is likely to respond to a number of factors. These include the company's commitment to grow that market – linked to its projected rates of growth, its 'absorptive capacity' (Cohen and Levinthal, 1990) and its ability to assimilate new recruits – and the preferences of the students themselves. Ultimately, the precise details of who is recruited and where they are employed will reflect the location of global, European or other regional head office operations and changes to the distribution and relative importance of those sites.

Companies are thus seeking to develop a bank of expertise in new international locations and citizens from there are seen to be important agents for market growth.

> In that case, [company] will be looking out for Eastern Europeans (Hungarians, Polish, Ukrainians) to populate its Eastern European desks in the UK, but then when the 'local bank' populations in those markets grows, it becomes more important to have specific Eastern European nationalities in those business-facing markets. Targeting is driven by where the business is emerging. (Finance)

Fifth, some employers perceive international students to possess advantages that domestically educated students do not. There are skills deficits in the labour market which cannot be filled by domestic graduates. Some scarce skill sets are better represented among international students.

> In terms of targeting international students, we have one programme that particularly springs to mind and that's the China audit programme...we've had that programme running for about three years now and that was set up to recruit Chinese nationals, to bring them into the firm here in the UK, and then when they are qualified, to send them back to China.... It's interesting because, of all the firms that we have internationally, there's quite a lot of this starting to go on. I've had contact from Cyprus, looking to identify Cypriot students over here and then, again, recruit them, target them to take them back...get them qualified somehow and then take them back. So there seems to be a general movement around this. (Finance)

Sixth, they help to increase mobility in the company as a whole. As companies become more global they want to be able to allocate their human resources to where business demands. Seniority requires the experience of different cultures.

> I think it is more the softer skills, so they tend to be more rounded because they've had to go to another country, integrate into another culture, make friends, study, learn the system, learn the social context of how to operate more so than maybe your Brit A level students at a UK university. The actual transition [into a global company] isn't as great. (Finance)

Seventh, the reputation of UK institutions and courses means companies know what they are getting. Often the education systems of emerging markets do not produce the sort of graduates in demand while UK universities do. They are developing strategies to build broad and deep relationships with their target universities.

> [company] does target around 25 universities where we actively market ourselves and these are mainly Russell[elite research focused] group. (Extractive)

Finally, companies are seeking cost reductions in assignments leading to the demise of the 'colonial' model of expatriation. International graduates from UK universities can be trained to work in their home countries, replacing expensive expats from Europe or the USA.

> Rather than training people up, British, Dutch or American people and then get them to go to Nigeria or wherever – Singapore – isn't it better just to source quality graduates from these areas? (Extractive)

All companies targeting international students were of the opinion that the practice will continue to increase. For example,

> Overall then the issue of targeted international student recruitment is not going away. Not anytime soon, I don't see it going. In fact, if anything I would say in the ten years I've been at [company]it's really started growing in the past, say, three ... as we've expanded outside mainstream continental Europe into new jurisdictions, be it Russia or any of the other places I've talked about. With more expansion coming, we've been asked to look at a Sub-Saharan recruiting strategy for Nigeria, Kenya, South Africa. (Finance)

5. University and government perspectives on targeting

The recruitment of international students by companies located in the host education country is not new. What is new is the specific targeting of those students in the recruitment process. This has implications for both universities and governments seeking to manage immigration systems. Targeting allows companies to take advantage of national government investment in university systems, together with the use of the various careers services for graduates. Through public funding of higher education, government may be seen to be subsidising corporate operations.

Targeted recruitment of international students has several implications for UK universities. Most obviously there will be revenue gains to them if studying in the UK is seen by mobile students as an avenue into lucrative employment with prestigious employers. Those universities which are selectively being targeted by employers stand to gain a particular marketing advantage, further reinforcing their images as desirable places to study. As a result, employer and institutional links could be strengthened. This is particularly important as universities themselves 'go global'. They increasingly need global partners, especially for research, and there is some evidence that they are considering how they can offer a more global perspective to their treatment of students, the curriculum and the communities in which they are placed (Fielden, 2007).

However, there could be implications for domestic students if universities were to reflect the corporate demand for international students – generally as well as for particular nationality groups – in their student intake. For example, domestic students may find enrolment onto certain courses more difficult should places be taken by their international counterparts.

The main concern of governments in respect of the right to work of international students has traditionally been the number of hours and nature of work they could perform while studying. In some cases it was a condition of entry for study that international students returned home upon completion of their degrees (ICMPD, 2006). In recent years several governments have relaxed their rules and regulations on international student recruitment, particularly in respect of those with IT qualifications (McLaughlan and Salt, 2002).

Yet, if international students do stay on, domestic students may find that the graduate labour market becomes less open to them and that the availability of international students has an effect upon salary rates (Baker and Finn, 2003; Borjas, 2005), particularly for entry-level occupations. At the same time there may be wider economic effects. A more liberal policy towards the recruitment of international students may indirectly attract corporate investment and jobs, capitalising on access to international students. A more informed and balanced approach to the retention of international students in the UK may be required.

The practice of targeting international students has implications for broader labour immigration policy. If international students are from non-European Economic Area (EEA) countries and their recruitment is followed by a period of work in the UK, then they currently fall under sponsorship arrangements as part of the points-based migration management system. If these prove too restrictive or bureaucratic for employers, they may be less likely to recruit for employment in the UK but may be more prone to recruit directly into their operations outside the UK. In the latter case, the UK economy would lose their skills without necessarily strengthening the links with student origin countries that have traditionally been regarded as an advantage of engaging in the international student higher education market. Hence, targeting has implications for government labour immigration management policies.

There are other considerations for government, important when there are multiple demands on the public purse. Investment in universities may be seen as a UK government subsidy to employers. This becomes particularly contentious if the recruitment of international students is seen as deleterious to home-grown ones or if it supports recruitment to build up capabilities in non-UK based competitor companies. Targeting may also require a rethink of concerns about brain drain. If international students are recruited with a view to sending them back home to work in local operations, then employers are important conduits for this reverse knowledge transfer. Conversely, if employers treat their recruits as global resources to be deployed anywhere, then graduates may be lost to their home countries, along with the resources put into their early education or into scholarships funding their study abroad.

In summary, targeted recruitment of international students has the potential to lead to a series of tensions between the main institutional actors that comprise the migration business: between global corporate managed migration and national government policies towards labour migration; between universities and employers; between individual universities; between government departments; and between university departments.

6. Conclusions

The evidence presented in this chapter represents a very early phase in the analysis of a phenomenon about which little is so far known. At this stage we cannot be sure how important targeted recruitment of international students is going to be in explaining labour migration. All we can say is that it exists, is growing and is worthy of further study.

The discussion in Section 5 of the chapter encompasses a number of possible implications of the practice about which so far we have little systematic information. It does raise a number of issues which merit further reflection by scholars and policy-makers concerned with international migration and its ramifications.

First, targeted recruitment of international students is part of the globalisation process in international labour markets and mobility. It links two major elements in the international migration business: student mobility and corporate mobility. The two systems reinforce each other to create a powerful combination that will inevitably lead to a more mobile global labour market and a more cosmopolitan internationally mobile population.

Second, it is going to be a factor in increasing competition within the global education system. Global companies do not recruit only in the UK. A consequence of this is that student fee levels and quality of education provided are likely to be more heavily scrutinised, both nationally and internationally.

Third, it creates pressures for domestic graduates entering the labour market. Preference for more culturally and linguistically experienced international students may affect the career chances of the home-grown. The comment of the head of graduate recruitment at one of the major oil companies is very revealing, though one might hope not prophetic:

> UK home-grown students need to watch out – they may not have jobs in five years time.

Finally, for all three of the institutional groups – employers, universities and government – the practice presents management problems. Currently we know neither the scale of the practice nor its rate of growth. It may, indeed, be a passing occurrence involving only a handful of companies. At the moment, however, this scenario seems unlikely in the face of continuing globalisation of education and labour markets. Nor do we know the extent to which, as far as employers are concerned, targeting is an ad hoc response to the development of new markets, for example, to overcome temporary difficulties associated with assessing the quality of educational establishments, and the international equivalence of skills and qualifications gained, in different countries. If it is, how and to what extent can it be planned for by all institutional actors?

Notes

1. The research was carried out jointly by the author and Dr Jane Millar.
2. Higher Education & Research Opportunities in the UK.
3. Coalition of Modern Universities.

References

Archer, W. and Davison, J. (2008) *Graduate Employability: What Do Employers Think and Want?* London: Council for Industry and Higher Education.

Baker, J.G. and Finn, M.G. (2003) *Stay Rates of Foreign National Doctoral Students in U.S. Economics Programs*. Oak Ridge: Southern Utah University – School of Business and Oak Ridge Associated Universities.

Baker, M., Robertson, F., Taylor, A. and Doube, L. (1996) *The Labour Market Effects of Overseas Students*. Canberra: Bureau of Immigration, Multicultural and Population Research.

Birrell, B., Hawthorne, L. and Richardson, S. (2006) *Evaluation of the General Skilled Migration Categories Report*. Canberra: Australian Government Department of Immigration and Citizenship.

Borjas, G.J. (2005) 'Foreign-Born Domestic Supply of Science and Engineering Workforce: The Labour Market Impact of High-Skill Migration', *American Economic Review*, 95(2): 55–60.

Christie, H. (2007) 'Higher Education and Spatial (Im)mobility', *Environment and Planning A*, 39, 2445–2463.

Cohen, W.M. and Levinthal, D.A. (1990) 'Absorptive Capacity: A New Perspective on Learning and Innovation', *Administrative Science Quarterly*, 35: 128–152.

Fielden, J. (2007) *Global Horizons for UK Universities*. London: Council for Industry and Higher Education.

Findlay, A.M. and King, R. (2010) *Motivations and Experiences of UK Students Studying Abroad*. Research Report No. 8, Department of Business, Innovation and Skills, London.

Garam, I. (2005) *Study on the Relevance of International Student Mobility to Work and Employment*. Helsinki: Centre for International Mobility (CIMO).

ICMPD (2006) *Comparative Study on Policies Towards Foreign Graduates*. Vienna: International Centre for Migration Policy Development.

Koser, K. and Salt, J. (1997) 'The Geography of Highly Skilled International Migration', *International Journal of Population Geography*, 3(December): 285–303.

Kuptsch, C. (2006) 'Students and Talent Flow – The Case of Europe: From Castle to Harbour', in C. Kuptsch and E.F. Pang, eds. *Competing for Global Talent*. Geneva: International Institute for Labour Studies, pp. 33–61.

Lenton, P. (2007) *Global Value: The Value of UK Education and Training Exports: An Update*. Manchester: British Council.

Lewis, N. (2005) 'Code of Practice for the Pastoral Care of International Students: Making a Globalising Industry in New Zealand', *Globalisation, Societies and Education*, 3, 5–47.

Li, F.L.N., Jowett, A.J. and Skeldon, R. (1996). 'Migrating to Learn and Learning to Migrate', *International Journal of Population Geography*, 2, 51–67.

McLaughlan, G. and Salt, J. (2002) *Migration Policies Towards Highly Skilled Foreign Workers*. London: Home Office.

Millar, J. and Salt, J. (2007) 'In Whose Interests? IT Migration in an Interconnected World', *Economy, Population, Space and Place*, 13(1): 41–58.

Millar, J. and Salt, J. (2008) 'Portfolios of Mobility: The Movement of Expertise in Transnational Corporations in Two Sectors: Aerospace and Extractive Industries', *Global Networks*, 8(1), 25–50.

OECD (2001) 'Student Mobility Between and Towards OECD Countries: A Comparative Analysis'. Part II in *Trends in International Migration*. Paris: OECD.

OECD (2007) 'Matching Educational background and Employment: A Challenge for Immigrants in Host Countries'. Part II in *International Migration Outlook*. Paris: OECD.

OECD (2008) 'Migration Policy Development'. 93–121 in *International Migration Outlook*. Paris: OECD.

Rogerson, R., Boyle, M. and Mason, C. (2006) *Progress Report on the Fresh Talent Initiative*. Edinburgh: The Scottish Government.

Salt, J. (2009), 'Business Travel and Portfolios of Mobility Within Global Companies', in Deruder, B, Witlox, F., Beaverstock, J and Faulconbridge, J (eds.) *Business Travel in the Global Economy*. London: Ashgate.

UKCOSA (2007) 'Higher Education Statistics', http://www.ukcosa.org.uk/about/statistics_he.php. Last accessed December 2010.

Vickers, P. and Bekhradnia, B. (2007) *The Economic Costs and Benefits of International Students*. Oxford: Higher Education Policy Institute (HEPI).

Waters, J.L. (2006a) 'Geographies of Cultural Capital: Education, International Migration and Family Strategies between Hong Kong and Canada', *Transactions of the Institute of British Geographers*, 31, 179–192.

Waters, J.L. (2006b) 'Emergent Geographies of International Education and Social Exclusion', *Antipode*, 38 (5), 1046–1068.

Waters, J.L. (2009) 'In Pursuit of Scarcity: Transnational Students, 'Employability' and the MBA', *Environment and Planning A*, 41, 1865–1883.

Part 3

8

Ethnicity, Religion, Residential Segregation and Life Chances

Nabil Khattab, Ibrahim Sirkeci, Ron Johnston and Tariq Modood

There is a wide range of work on aspects of ethnicity in the UK, but in a number of cases little is done to integrate those separate studies. Variation in educational and labour market experience across ethnic groups is one such area and another is residential segregation; the degree to which members of various groups live apart from each other. But are those different aspects of the minority group experience linked; does segregation matter as an influence on individuals' labour market experiences? Much of the academic and related work has focused on the facts of segregation themselves, with some comparative studies showing that the British situation is considerably less extreme than that experienced in the USA, notably by African-Americans and Hispanics in recent decades.

This focus on describing the degree to which members claiming minority ethnicity – in almost all cases using census data and thus relying on its classification of ethnic groups – is valuable as it provides a picture of contemporary Britain. But that descriptive material is of value not only as an end in itself but also because it provides the context for studies of segregation's impact. Segregation matters, it is claimed; it has a range of impacts on individuals, and thus on the structure and operation of society itself.

To evaluate that claim, this chapter reports on research into the interactions between residential segregation and what has become known in the literature as the 'ethnic penalty' in labour market experience, which argues that members of most minority groups suffer relatively to the host society in their labour market experience. Using both quantitative and qualitative data, we explore the extent to which members of various groups (defined by their religion as well as their self-assessed ethnicity) are able to capitalise on their educational attainments in the labour market.

We begin this chapter by discussing the social and economic influences of segregation and its role in determining the life chances of people followed by a discussion of ethnic penalties in Britain and the place various ethnic and religious groups occupy in Britain's social structure. In the next section we focus on the way ethnicity and religion have been defined, outlining our new ethno-religious classification, on the one hand, and outlining our method of measuring the labour market experience, on the other.

Having discussed our research approach, we then move on to present our quantitative (multivariate) analysis followed by some conclusions.

1. Segregation matters

Segregation matters to people in a variety of ways – and not only to members of ethnic minorities; other groups, such as the poor whatever their ethnic background, are also segregated and experience the same outcomes (although perhaps not as intensively). It matters, for example, to people's life chances – in their neighbourhoods and schools, and their local labour markets; in the delivery of public services to their homes and districts, and the facilities made available to them by both the private and the voluntary sector. Where you live matters to your future because, for example, of the quality of the state primary and secondary education available to you (and its impact on individuals realising their potential through tertiary education, as indicated by analyses underpinning the widening participation policies being implemented by British universities: Hoare and Johnston, 2011). If the quality of teaching at local schools is poor, resources are relatively impoverished and the school and neighbourhood milieux do not stimulate educational ambitions, young people living in such areas may well not realise their potential. This will then impact on their ability to succeed in the labour market – and the local labour market for such people may well offer fewer opportunities than those available elsewhere. This suggests a cycle of under-achievement, of people living in areas where their abilities are not fostered and, as a consequence, they are unable to move to other areas where their children might flourish. Post-immigration minorities (i.e., immigrants and their descendants) are also joining in this system of uneven opportunities as they often take up residence in relatively deprived areas and also to some extent as their overseas qualifications are not recognised.

Segregation also matters with regard to lifestyle and the development of the ideology and attitudes that underpin how people behave in their daily lives. Much of what they learn – attitudes and behaviour patterns – is derived from socialisation and mobilisation processes that operate through their social networks, many of which (especially at certain life stages and for some groups more than others) are spatially structured with a clear focus on the local neighbourhood. Where you live matters because it influences who you come into contact with and how you choose to live your life.[1]

Segregation matters, too, because it can be a source – or at least an exacerbation – of identity and difference within society that can generate tension and occasional conflict, especially where the differences are linked with other aspects of society, notably economic, social and political disadvantage. As societies become increasingly multiethnic and multicultural, and as ethnicity becomes a major source of identity in an increasingly mobile and potentially anomic world, the role of segregation in many aspects of identity-formation – not least the 'us-and-them' images that are often associated with such divided societies – is an important topic of public and political as well as academic debate.

These various claims about segregation's roles in the development of life chances, lifestyles, personal and group identity, and inter-group relations have been presented here as assertions. But the literature about them all is massive and growing ever-more rapidly it seems – as is the literature on how the negative consequences may be countered (Hewstone, 2009). Of course, the relationships are not deterministic – every situation is in some way unique (some, such as *apartheid* South Africa, were undoubtedly singular) and local contingency, as well as individual characteristics, is crucial. In addition, greater mobility – and ease of contact by improved communication systems – means that proximity is not a necessary prerequisite for sustaining friendship ties and links to cultural institutions (as Zelinsky and Lee, 1998, have argued). Nevertheless, the arguments regarding the negative impacts of segregation are strong.

As well as being a constraint, segregation can also be an opportunity, however, with positive potential impacts – in the development of ethnic entrepreneurship, for example, and in sustaining cultural distinctions. With regard to the former, the cultivation of local businesses by members of ethnic minority groups within the areas where they are segregated offers employment opportunities and career trajectories for those living there that may enable them to realise their potential within the local context (see Khattab et al., 2010). And the presence in segregated areas not only of informal social networks that sustain personal development but also cultural institutions – churches, mosques, social, cultural and business associations and sports clubs, and retail facilities, for example – provides a range of support mechanisms that sustain communities. Some individuals may eventually reduce their dependence on such communities for social and cultural – even economic and political – sustenance, moving away from the segregated areas as they, and especially their offspring, become part of the wider society.

In what follows we present a brief summary of our qualitative data in which some of the above arguments in relation to the impact of segregation are well illustrated. Our qualitative data have been collected through in-depth interviews with 34 Bangladeshi men and women living in relatively segregated (concentrated) localities. Approximately 60 per cent of the interviewees were women and about 40 per cent were men in their 20s and early 30s. Most of them were economically active working mainly in non-manual jobs either within the Bangladeshi residential areas of Tower Hamlets and Newham in London or in Bristol.

This interview material underpins the argument that those living within segregated areas face tough conditions in obtaining jobs. For example, one London female respondent in Tower Hamlets stated:

> I don't think there are decent job opportunities in this area, not really, not to be honest with you there aren't. Where does a young person go to find work and what kind of jobs will they be doing? I don't know. (Bangladeshi, female, age 29, teacher, lives in Tower Hamlets, London)

A Bangladeshi doctor living in Tower Hamlets elaborates the importance of a lack of qualifications among Bangladeshi youngsters which bars their chances and drives them to social problems:

> I think job opportunities in this area are quite terrible to be honest with you; if you're looking from private sector jobs to public sector jobs there are not that many... so I think the job sector is quite difficult because what the private sector will pay will not match up to the lifestyle needs of the youngsters to buy £70 trainers, you know they can't earn that in a month, so that's why drug crimes go up, so I think there's a huge significant link with that. Umm public sector jobs are again a huge problem because if you're not educated you can't get a job because there are educated people that can't get jobs... so I'm afraid I don't think it's good and this area's particularly bad. (Bangladeshi, male, age 34, doctor, lives in Tower Hamlets, London)

Due to the lack of good job opportunities, many residents living inside the ethnically segregated areas might turn to self-employment to escape unemployment. Very often they do that by relying on ethnic connections and networks as one interviewee exemplifies:

> There's a lot of ethnic barbers and hairdressers now, there's a lot of shops, there's a lot of takeaways; quite a lot of them actually are self-employed... there's a lot of Asian shops selling saris and stuff like that, so there's quite a lot of self-employed people actually in Easton. (Bangladeshi, female, age 19, student, lives in Easton, Bristol)

Another Bangladeshi interviewee has explained how the lack of qualifications and language skills force people to seek low-paid jobs within the local labour market:

> A lot of people don't have access to good jobs you know they have access to low paid, low skilled jobs working in a post office, working in a grocers, in a restaurant you know sort of catering and restaurant industry. Umm people who end up in restaurants and sort of ethnic businesses are the

> ones that don't speak a lot of English; they usually end up in jobs like that. It's not helped by the fact that they haven't got an education to help them get better jobs because some of the youngsters mess about at school and won't get educated or didn't have the opportunity. These are the ones that find it much harder to get skilled jobs, so they end up getting jobs in retail you know working in a store or a restaurant and they continue to stay like that. (Bangladeshi, female, age 27, HR advisor, lives in Tower Hamlets, London)

The above quotations clearly illustrate how segregation matters, which is the axiom on which the work reported here has been built. It focused on one particular aspect of its impact – on individuals' life chances through the labour market. Previous work has suggested that there is what has been termed an 'ethnic penalty' in British cities (Heath and McMahon, 1997), whereby members of ethnic minorities – and some more than others – are disadvantaged in their career trajectories relative to others because they are unable to obtain occupational positions (and the consequent rewards – income, status and wealth) commensurate with their qualifications (Modood, 2005; Khattab, 2009). That body of research has not addressed the issue of labour market spatial segmentation, however, and whether those members of ethnic minority groups living in both relatively segregated and relatively deprived areas suffer greater disadvantage than those living elsewhere, although spatial concentration has been pointed as a cause in some studies (see Fieldhouse and Tranmer, 2001; Peach, 2005). The programme of research summarised here fills that lacuna, with a combination of quantitative and qualitative analyses exploring the extent and geography of ethnic penalties in the British labour market.

2. Ethnic penalties in the labour market

Members of ethnic and religious minorities in Britain follow different routes in terms of education, employment and residential patterns. Some minority groups are over-represented in higher education, for example, while others are over-represented among the unemployed and/or inactive populations. The nature of the inequality or ethnic penalty experienced in education and the labour market has shifted considerably between and within groups over the past three decades. On average, for example, most ethnic groups now outperform Whites in education (Modood, 2003; Wilson, Burgess and Briggs, 2005), but lag behind white people in terms of labour market outcomes (Heath and McMahon, 1999; Heath and McMahon, 2005).

Our work on ethno-religious background and its impact on educational and occupational achievement shows that some groups – such as Muslim Indians – were likely to suffer penalties in education only; some – such as Christian Black Caribbeans – were likely to experience penalties in employment but not also in education; and others – for example, Muslim Pakistanis and Bangladeshis, and Sikh Indians – scored negatively on both scales, being disadvantaged in both education and the labour market (Khattab, 2009). These differences parallel those of other work on the ethnic minority experience in Britain. Modood (2005), for example, argued that Muslims face the most severe and hostile discrimination due to their distance from the English way of life, experiencing racism that combines elements of not only cultural distance but also physical differences (having black or brown skin versus white skin). For Muslim women, such racism and discrimination might operate even more intensively, especially among those wearing the hijab (Dale, 2002; Dale et al., 2002; Ahmad, Lissenburgh and Modood, 2003): some employers discriminate against Muslim women on the grounds that the hijab does not 'fit' within the workplace.

How is this apparently persisting pattern – with a white/non-white divide but one which is dwarfed by the scale of the disadvantage of Muslims, especially Pakistanis and Bangladeshis – to be explained? Heath and his colleagues have conducted analyses that controlled for a number of key factors such as sex, age and educational qualifications and found that in relation to unemployment and occupational level all non-white groups suffered an 'ethnic penalty' (Heath and McMahon, 1997). Whilst they could not specify the causal factors accounting for this penalty, they were in no doubt that most of it resulted from forms of unlawful direct and indirect racial discrimination. Their later analyses showed a reduction in the scope of the ethnic penalty once a generational variable was introduced: both foreign-born ('the first generation') and the British-born ('the second generation') men of all ethnic minorities were more likely to be unemployed than white men (National Equality Panel, 2010: 225–226). However, in relation to broad occupational levels they found that the second generation men and women had similar chances (after allowing for age and qualifications) of working in professional and managerial jobs to their white peers. One problem for recent immigrants is that their educational qualifications are not recognised in the UK, so that they may then have to take jobs for which they are, ostensibly, over-qualified.That does not necessarily mean that they were in equally well-paid jobs within the broad occupational levels, however; another study found, after controlling for age, occupational classification, family circumstances and qualifications, that there were considerable pay penalties for all non-white groups (National Equality Panel, 2010: 228–231). While in raw terms on average, Chinese men earned 11 per cent more than white British men in 2006–08, after allowance was made for factors such as their qualification levels, there was a pay penalty of 11 per cent. Such apparent discrimination applies to those able to obtain work commensurate to their qualifications: a study by the Department of Works and Pension that found that even with identical curricula vitae (CVs), job applicants with Asian and African sounding names were about 60 per cent less likely than Whites to receive a positive response (National Equality Panel, 2010: 234–235).

That the disadvantaged position of some minority groups may have resulted from their spatial concentration in highly deprived areas has also been recognised (Fieldhouse and Tranmer, 2001; Peach, 2005, 2006a). Until recently the impact of both spatial segregation and the ethno-religious background of individuals at the same time was difficult to investigate because of the lack of information on religion in previous censuses and the inability to access datasets with both individual and spatial information. The 2001 UK Census and the availability of its individual Controlled Access Microdata Sample (CAMS) made it possible to study the impact of spatial segregation and deprivation levels at the tract (neighbourhood) level and other individual factors including ethnicity and religion. Spatially, some areas are better off than others in terms of their employment opportunities, social capital, and other material and non-material resources. The concentration of some ethnic and religious groups in exceptionally deprived areas would result in poor educational and occupational outcomes. The literature in the UK addressing issues of ethnicity and residential segregation has pointed out that ethnic minorities are relatively segregated with Bangladeshis and Pakistanis being the most segregated groups (Owen, 2003; Johnston, Wilson and Burgess, 2004; Johnston, Poulsen and Forrest, 2006; Peach, 2005, 2006a). While some of the ethnic and religious groups are residentially segregated but socially and economically very flourishing (such as the Jewish community), other groups are residentially concentrated in deprived areas, such as the concentration of Muslim Bangladeshis in Tower Hamlets and Newham in London. This suggests that segregation per se is not the problem, but the concentration in highly deprived and poor areas might indeed be a real problem for the people living there. In this chapter we focus on the interactions between ethno-religious background and the return on education (i.e., the relation between qualifications and occupational outcomes) and the extent to which this impact is shaped by the spatial location of individuals.

3. Defining ethnicity and labour market experience

To evaluate further the impact of segregation on ethnic penalties, the work summarised here has explored the relationships among individual characteristics, residential location, educational qualifications and occupational status. It uses quantitative data obtained from the CAMS of the 2001 Census of England and Wales. This comprises a 3 per cent representative sample containing information on 1,843,530 separate individuals, with details on employment, education, ethnic and religious backgrounds, country of birth, housing, health, transport, gender, age and more. The geographical information available in the file places each individual's household within a 'census tract' – an area containing on average some 46,000 people for which aggregated data were available and allowed measures of ethnic residential segregation to be computed; in addition, the CAMS data were linked to the 2004 Index of Deprivation scores (Office of the Deputy Prime Minister, 2004) for small areas within each tract, from which a measure of the area's relative poverty/disadvantage could be derived.

3.1. Ethnicity

In these analyses, we have been able – unlike almost all other studies of ethnic disadvantage in the UK – to use a more nuanced definition of ethnicity than one reliant on the census categories alone. The official definition of ethnicity used by the British Office for National Statistics (now National Statistics) is largely based on a combination of racial characteristics and place of birth/family origin (see Dixie, 1998; for critiques, see Ballard, 1996, 1998). The current classification of 16 categories (Table 8.1) has evolved over two or more decades (see, e.g., Sillitoe and White, 1992). Apart from the Whites (with the Irish separately identified within this category after considerable debate and pressure: Walter, 1998; Howard, 2006), it focuses almost entirely on two groups defined largely by geography and colour – Black Africans and Black Caribbeans; Asians subdivided by country of origin (India, Pakistan, Bangladesh) – plus Chinese and a general racial category. In the 2001 Census, four 'mixed' categories were introduced (Aspinall, 2000a), based on racial characteristics and place of birth/family origin.

Walter (1998) characterises this classification scheme as a black/white binary while Berthoud (1998: 54) delineates the role of heritage in this regard. He also argues that ethnicity is a 'multi-faceted phenomenon based on some or all of several possible ingredients: physical appearance, subjective identification, cultural and religious affiliation, stereotyping and social exclusion' (Berthoud, 1998: 54). The need to recognise these various ingredients in data collection has long been debated and a religious question is now included in the census for all parts of the UK (Aspinall, 2000b). However, most discussions of ethnicity still rely on the 16 categories produced from the self-identification ethnicity question.

Table 8.1 The 16-fold classification of ethnic groups used in the 2001 Census of England and Wales

White British	**White Irish**	**White Other**	
Mixed White Black Caribbean Indian Black Caribbean Chinese	Mixed White Black African Pakistani Black African	Mixed White Asian Bangladeshi Black Other Other	Mixed White Other Other Asian

Census categories are pragmatically designed instruments for statistical data collection (Walter, 1998: 74) and this process is highly politicised (Kertzer and Arel, 2002: 3) while also strongly influencing the racial discourse and direction in a country. In this study, to address the significance of defining appropriate minority groups, we reclassified diversity in the UK by combining the responses to the 2001 Census questions on religion and ethnicity to explore differences within as well as between the usually analysed groups. Using the individual data available in the CAM sample, we have combined self-assessed ethnicity with religion, which allows analysis of the potentially significant differences among different religious groups and their separate cultures within several ethnic groups. This cross-classification yielded 15 major categories, shown in Table 8.2. (Mixed and other heterogeneous ethnic groups – e.g., Black Other – are excluded, while undefined religion categories – i.e., 'Any Other Religion' or 'Religion Not Stated' – are grouped together.)

National figures, reproduced in Table 8.3, show the value of this cross-classification. Rows in the first block show the percentages of the members of each ethnic group according to their religious affiliation. In three cases (White Irish, Pakistanis and Bangladeshis), the great majority of the members of those ethnic groups is associated with a single religion; in three others

Table 8.2 A 15-fold cross-classification of ethnicity and religion derived from the CAMS sample of respondents to the 2001 Census of England and Wales

Ethno-religious group		*N*	per cent
Christian	Christian White British	634,799	63.3
	Christian Irish	10,597	1.1
	Christian Black Caribbean	8539	0.9
	Christian Black African	7096	0.7
Muslim	Muslim Pakistani	12,398	1.2
	Muslim Bangladeshi	4662	0.5
	Muslim Indian	2581	0.3
	Muslim Other	1951	0.2
	Jewish British	3932	0.4
	No religion White British	143,365	14.3
	Other White British	74,810	7.5
	Chinese	5333	0.5
	Hindu Indian	10,062	1.0
	Sikh Indian	6311	0.6
	Other	76,769	7.5
	Total	1,003,205	100.0

Table 8.3 A cross-classification of religion and ethnicity in England and Wales, 2001 (row percentages show religious breakdown for ethnic groups while column percentages are for ethnic breakdown of religious groups)

Row %	Christian	Buddhist	Hindu	Jewish	Muslim	Sikh	Other/none	Total
Column %								
White British	75.9	0.1	0.0	0.5	0.1	0.0	23.3	100.0
	92.6	34.9	1.1	84.0	4.1	1.9	89.4	87.5
White Irish	85.4	0.2	0.0	0.2	0.1	0.0	14.0	100.0
	1.5	0.8	0.0	0.4	0.1	0.0	0.8	1.2
White Other	62.7	0.3	0.1	2.4	8.6	0.0	25.9	100.0
	2.3	3.1	0.2	12.4	7.5	0.2	2.9	2.6
Indian	4.9	0.2	45.0	0.1	12.7	29.1	8.1	100.0
	0.1	1.3	84.5	0.3	8.5	91.5	0.7	2.0
Pakistani	1.1	0.0	0.1	0.0	92.0	0.0	6.7	100.0
	0.0	0.1	0.1	0.1	42.5	0.1	0.4	1.4
Bangladeshi	0.5	0.1	0.6	0.0	92.5	0.0	6.3	100.0
	0.0	0.1	0.3	0.0	16.8	0.0	0.1	0.5
Other Asian	13.4	4.8	26.8	0.3	37.3	6.2	11.1	100.0
	0.1	8.1	11.7	0.3	5.8	4.6	0.2	0.5

Black Caribbean	73.8	0.2	0.3	0.1	0.8	0.0	24.9	100.0
	1.1	0.7	0.3	0.2	0.3	0.0	1.2	1.1
Black African	68.9	0.1	0.2	0.0	20.0	0.1	10.7	100.0
	0.9	0.2	0.2	0.1	6.2	0.1	0.4	0.9
Other Black	66.6	0.2	0.4	0.1	6.0	0.1	26.7	100.0
	0.2	0.1	0.1	0.0	0.4	0.0	0.2	0.2
Chinese	21.6	15.1	0.1	0.0	0.3	0.0	62.8	100.0
	0.1	23.7	0.0	0.0	0.0	0.0	1.2	0.4
Mixed	52.5	0.7	0.9	0.5	9.7	0.4	35.4	100.0
	0.9	3.2	1.0	1.2	4.2	0.8	2.0	1.3
Other	33.0	15.5	1.3	1.0	25.7	1.0	22.5	100.0
	0.2	23.6	0.5	0.9	3.6	0.7	0.4	0.4
Total	71.7	0.3	1.1	0.5	3.0	0.6	22.8	100.0
Total	100.0	100.0	100.0	100.0	100.0	100.0	100.0	100.0
N	37,338,486	144,453	552,421	259,927	1,546,626	329,358	11,870,645	52,041,916

(White British, Black Caribbean, and Black African) between two thirds and three quarters are associated with Christianity. Among Indians, a more varied distribution can be seen in terms of religious background (as also noted by Heath and Yu, 2005). In the second block, the rows give the breakdown of religious categories by ethnicity. In most cases, the great majority of those associated with a particular religious group also share the same self-assessed ethnic identity. The main exception are Muslims, which comprise a large Pakistani component plus significant numbers of Bangladeshis, Indians, Black Africans and Others.

Treating a main ethnic or religious group as homogeneous is to oversimplify the phenomenon. There are important cross-cutting ethnic-religious cleavages which may have major cultural connotations important in appreciating some behavioural patterns. In his analysis of segregation in London, Peach (2006b) has shown that members of the various Muslim ethnic groups tend to live in separate areas, as do various religious groups within the Indian ethnic community. Other studies argue that treating Muslims as a single aggregate involves 'capturing the characteristics of a heterogeneous group' (Peach, 2006a: 653: see also Office of the Deputy Prime Minister, 2004). We elaborate such in-group diversity here.

3.2. Labour market experience

Most analyses of labour market experience focus on one of two measures: employment status and occupational class. The first generally deploys a small number of categories: in-work (either employed or self-employed); out-of work and seeking employment (usually termed unemployment); and economically inactive (not seeking work; retired). The second – occupational class – employs the various categories (professional, managerial and so on) deployed in the census returns.

Since human capital theory argues that one's occupational status should be determined by ability, as reflected in educational qualifications, the two are then compared (in most cases using regression models, as in Heath and McMahon, 1997; Andrews et al., 2001), and the relative performance of different ethnic groups contrasted, to identify whether there are any ethnic penalties. Some of these studies have identified a number of factors influencing differences in the extent to which individuals realise their potential in the labour market, including educational qualifications (Heath and McMahon, 2005), generational differences (Platt, 2005), and differences between migration streams (Münz, 2004). Some conclude that there are 'ethnic penalties' in the degree to which abilities and employment opportunities are matched (Richardson and Wood, 1999; Owen, 2003) – which may reflect racial and/or ethnic disadvantage if not discrimination (Peach, 2005).

In this work, we have adopted a slightly different approach by focusing on the occupational returns to education, measured as the distance between skill levels required by current occupations and skills obtained through education. People seek initial employment opportunities that match their educational qualifications (Nielsen et al., 2003), and their subsequent careers are founded on those original qualifications. Most studies of the relationships between the two relate occupational level to educational achievements, with no prior expectation as to the types of occupation that individuals with given educational qualifications might aspire to. To counter that, following earlier studies on returns to education measuring over- and under-achievement (Halaby, 1994; Alpin et al., 1998; Green et al., 1999), we use a method of quantifying the distance between skill levels gained in education and the skill levels required for occupations (Khattab et al., 2010). Instead of using single years spent in education converted from self-reported education, we use skill levels as identified in the census data. This provides an index of the degree of match/mismatch between individuals' potential and occupation by combining two variables obtained from the 2001 Census of England and Wales: level of *highest educational qualification* and *occupational level* (as defined by the International Standard Classification of Occupations – ISCO88).

The ten different occupational levels have been grouped into four categories based on required skill levels identified in ISCO88 (see Hoffmann and Scott, 1993): we have excluded several categories (i.e., 'others', 'armed forces' and 'unknown' as well as unemployed and inactive), whilst placing others into skill levels according to assumed educational requirements needed to practice in those occupations. Required educational levels for each have been identified using the 2001 UK Census classification of qualifications into five levels. The result is a fourfold categorisation of educational qualifications ranging from 0 to 4 and occupational class ranging from 1 to 4; individuals aspiring to work in the highest occupational level, for example, are expected to have a degree or its equivalent (Table 8.4).

Using the skills levels needed for particular jobs and the required educational qualifications shown in Table 8.4, an index of the distance between the two has been devised. We obtain a skill-level distance score (SD_i) for each individual i by subtracting her/his qualification score (LQ_i) from the occupational skills level (LO_i):

$$SD_i = LO_i - LQ_i \tag{8.1}$$

SD ranges from +4 to –3. A score of 0 indicates a match: the individual's educational qualifications match those required by the occupational category that he/she has attained – for example, a person with a degree who is in a professional post, or one with only minimal qualifications who is in an elementary occupation. A positive score indicates under-qualification, with somebody lacking the skills level required for the obtained occupation (such as a professional with only level 2 educational qualifications); a negative score indicates over-qualification. Thus we have created an eight-point scale

Table 8.4 The classification of skill levels by occupational group and educational qualifications

Occupational group	Educational qualifications	Skill levels	
		LO	*LQ*
Legislators, senior officials, managers and professionals	Levels 4/5 (e.g., first/higher degree)	4	4
Technicians and associate professionals	Level 3 (e.g., 2+ 'A' level passes, NVQ level 3)	3	3
Clerks, service, shop and sales workers; skilled agricultural/fisheries workers; crafts and related trades; plant and machine operators/assemblers	Level 2 (e.g., 5+ 'O'/GCSE level passes, NVQ level 2, School Certificate)	2	2
Elementary occupations	Level 1 (e.g., 1+ 'O' level passes, GCSE any grade, NVQ level 1)	1	1
	No qualification	–	0

Note: *LO* – occupational skill level; *LQ* – qualification skill level.

of skill-level distance (from +4 to −3) and then due to very small numbers in categories −3 and +4, we have merged them into −2 and +3, respectively to produce a six-point scale. This scale provides an approximate measure of occupational attainment in relation to education/qualification and can be used to evaluate the extent to which different groups are under- or over-qualified according to their positions in the labour market. The advantage of using such a scale over simply contrasting educational background indicators to employment outcomes lies in the fact that the scale is easier to apply quantitatively and enables comparisons across different skill-levels. The skill-level distances provide us virtually equal measurement intervals.

4. Disadvantaged minorities in geographies of deprivation

Using 2001 Census data, we have identified the nature and extent of any apparent ethnic (and ethno-religious) penalties, both in terms of employment status and the returns on education. Regarding the first, for example, Table 8.5 shows the percentage of each ethno-religious group's members in four main employment status categories – separately for men and women.

This table shows very substantial differences among the ethno-religious groups, for both males and females. Among the latter, for example, Muslims are much more likely to be economically inactive (in most cases home-makers) than are Christian White British women and so less likely to be employees (Khattab et al., 2010). Among males, both Muslims and members

Table 8.5 Employment status by ethno-religious group and gender (per cent), 2001, England and Wales – age: 16–64*

	Men				Women			
	Unemployed	**Employee**	**Self-employed**	**Inactive**	**Unemployed**	**Employee**	**Self-employed**	**Inactive**
Christian White British	4.5	70.0	14.2	11.3	2.8	70.6	5.5	21.1
Jewish British	4.0	57.6	31.4	7.0	3.3	59.9	14.1	22.7
No religion White British	6.2	72.0	14.1	7.8	4.4	70.8	5.8	19.1
Other White British	6.4	69.9	14.2	9.5	4.0	69.1	6.1	20.7
Christian Irish	5.1	61.4	16.7	16.8	3.1	69.4	6.0	21.5
Christian Black Caribbean	13.6	67.5	8.8	10.1	6.0	75.7	2.5	15.8
Christian Black African	11.6	71.5	12.2	4.7	11.4	71.4	3.6	13.6
Muslim Pakistani	13.0	54.2	20.3	12.4	10.6	50.7	5.6	33.1
Muslim Bangladeshi	17.0	57.0	14.2	11.8	13.6	47.8	2.9	35.8
Muslim Indian	10.0	63.1	15.9	11.0	7.5	53.0	9.0	30.5
Muslim Other	15.9	56.1	16.8	11.2	10.6	52.6	6.3	30.5
Hindu Indian	5.5	67.8	19.0	7.7	4.8	68.4	9.4	17.4
Sikh Indian	7.7	63.8	19.5	9.0	5.7	70.8	7.0	16.5
Chinese	6.1	61.0	26.0	6.8	4.9	61.6	14.3	19.2
Other	7.9	70.1	14.0	8.0	5.7	68.1	7.1	19.1
N	22,097	280,574	58,215	41,627	13,363	269,770	22,041	79,791
Total %	5.5	69.7	14.5	10.3	3.5	70.1	5.7	20.7
Total *N*				402,513				384,965
		X^2: 5089.066 Sig: 0.000				X^2: 3933.832 Sig: 0.000		

Notes: * Those on full-time education are excluded from this analysis.

of the Christian Black groups are more likely to be unemployed. South Asian males are also more likely to be self-employed than members of the Black ethnic groups, but the highest levels of self-employment (and also some of the lowest levels of unemployment – for women as well) are recorded for the Jewish British and the Chinese.

For particular minority groups, such high levels of unemployment and inactivity can be explained to some extent by cultural difference – women working away from the home are more restricted in some cultures than others, for example, as with Bangladeshi Muslims. However, Bangladeshi Muslims are also one of those minority groups who live in relatively impoverished areas – those with high values on the Index of Multiple Deprivation – and were more likely to be either unemployed or inactive (relative to employed) than those living in less deprived areas, the implication being that the cultural differences are accentuated in the more deprived areas. Overall most ethno-religious minority groups are outperformed by their Christian White British neighbours – members of the host society are more likely not only to gain employment than members of most ethno-religious minorities but also to obtain employment in occupations with a status commensurate with their educational qualifications. Christian White Irish come closest to Christian White British in most employment categories, however, it is only Jewish men and women who do better than Christian White Britons. In general, inactivity levels vary substantially not only between genders but also across ethno-religious groups with Muslim minority members registering the highest unemployment and inactivity levels among our 15 ethno-religious groups for both men and women.

In another analysis (Johnston et al., 2010), we have focused on differences among males claiming Indian ethnicity and also among Muslim men, from various geographical origins, with regard to the returns they obtained in the labour market from their educational qualifications. Among Indian men, Sikhs were much more likely than either Hindus or Muslims to be over-qualified in their occupations, suggesting that this, not insubstantial, community is disadvantaged and clearly less able to capitalise on their educational qualifications than the larger Hindu group (a conclusion also reached by Brown, 2000). Within the Indian population, in addition, unmarried males were more likely to be over-qualified than those who were married. Where they lived was also a significant influence on Indian's performance in the labour market relative to their educational qualifications. The more deprived and the more segregated the neighbourhood the greater the likelihood that Indian males were over-qualified for their jobs. Labour market disadvantage was greatest for those living in the most disadvantaged neighbourhoods.

Compared to Pakistanis, Indian Muslim males were significantly less likely to be over-qualified in their occupations whereas Bangladeshi and Other Muslims are observed to have similar chances; Black Africans and those of 'Other' ethnicity were also more likely to be over-qualified. There is thus a continuum of labour market experience within the Muslim male population: Indian Muslims perform much better than Pakistanis and Bangladeshis, whereas Black Africans perform worse. Treating Muslims as a homogeneous group when discussing occupational attainment in relation to education therefore ignores significant within-group differences, reflecting not only their ethnicity but also the characteristics of their home neighbourhoods; again those living in the most deprived and the most segregated neighbourhoods were most likely to be over-qualified and suffer an ethnic penalty.

5. Ethno-religious minorities and skills level mismatch

Regarding those who are in employment, in this section we report on a study comparing the labour market experience of all males in the 14 other ethno-religious groups with those of the Christian White British to explore variations among groups in the average returns on education (i.e., whether in general they were under- or over-qualified for their current occupations). Because of the clustering of individuals within areas, these analyses deployed multi-level modelling to explore within- and between-area variations. Table 8.6 gives the results of a multinomial logistic regression in which the characteristics of those who were under- and over-qualified were contrasted with those whose occupational situations matched their qualifications. In addition to the ethno-religious variable, the analysis also considered whether or not the individuals were born in the UK, whether they were married, whether they were self-employed, their age and the characteristics of the census tract in which they lived.

The results of a multinomial regression model contrasting those males who were under- and over-qualified with those who had jobs commensurate with their educational qualifications are reported in Table 8.6. The left-hand block of coefficients shows very considerable variation in the probability of individuals being over-qualified – that is, apparently being unable to obtain jobs commensurate with their educational qualifications. The *b* values for all but two of the ethno-religious groups are positive and statistically significant, indicating that in all cases save two – for Christian Irish and Jewish British – the group members were much more likely to be over-qualified than were members of the dominant society. Furthermore, the two significant and positive coefficients for the other individual-level variables show that over-qualification was more common among those born outside the UK (suggesting that they may have had greater problems getting their qualifications recognised than those born in the UK, whose qualifications were probably obtained there) and those who were not married. The overseas-born were 34 per cent more likely to be in jobs for which they were over-qualified than were the UK-born (an exponent of 1.34); the unmarried

Table 8.6 Multi-level logistic regression of the occupational returns on education among males, 2001

Variables	Over-qualified			Under-qualified		
	b*	SE*	OR*	b*	SE*	OR*
Constant	**−5.001**	**0.118**	**0.01**	**−3.464**	**0.059**	**0.03**
Individual level						
Overseas-born (comparator: born in the UK)	**0.291**	**0.094**	**1.34**	**0.317**	**0.073**	**1.37**
Unmarried (comparator: married)	**0.77**	**0.058**	**2.16**	0.305	0.208	1.36
Age	0	0.002	1	**0.031**	**0.001**	**1.03**
Ethno-religious group (comparator: Christian White British)						
Jewish British	0.52	0.312	1.68	0.281	0.15	1.32
No religion White British	**0.471**	**0.068**	**1.6**	**−0.24**	**0.037**	**0.79**
Other White British	**0.615**	**0.083**	**1.85**	**−0.179**	**0.048**	**0.84**
Christian Irish	0.203	0.256	1.23	0.073	0.11	1.08
Christian Caribbean	**0.644**	**0.233**	**1.9**	−0.037	0.177	0.96
Christian African	**1.976**	**0.17**	**7.21**	**−2.027**	**0.512**	**0.13**
Muslim Pakistani	**1.016**	**0.186**	**2.76**	−0.118	0.16	0.89
Muslim Bangladeshi	**0.825**	**0.3**	**2.28**	**−0.735**	**0.197**	**0.29**
Muslim Indian	**1.05**	**0.338**	**2.86**	0.211	0.264	1.23
Muslim Other	**1.507**	**0.18**	**4.51**	−0.115	0.191	0.89
Hindu Indian	**0.998**	**0.178**	**2.71**	0.232	0.131	1.26
Sikh Indian	**0.7**	**0.265**	**2.01**	0.101	0.175	1.11
Chinese	**1.057**	**0.271**	**2.88**	0.199	0.215	1.13
Other	**0.954**	**0.108**	**2.6**	**−0.146**	**0.084**	**0.86**
Neighbourhood level						
IMD	0.002	0.002	1	**−0.007**	**0.001**	**0.99**
MII	**0.604**	**0.155**	**1.83**	**−0.36**	**0.112**	**0.7**
N=*84,495*						

Note: Coefficients significantly different from zero at the 0.05 level or better are shown in bold.
* *b* – unstandardised regression coefficient; SE – standard error of the regression coefficient; OR – odds ratio associated with the regression coefficient.
Source: CAMS individual data drawn from the 2001 UK Census. Census output is Crown copyright and is reproduced with the permission of the Controller of HMSO and the Queen's Printer for Scotland.

were twice as likely as the married to be over-qualified. The overseas-born and the unmarried were also more likely to be under-qualified, suggesting that in general such people are less likely to find roles in the labour market commensurate with their educational qualifications than the UK-born and the married.

Among the various ethno-religious groups, the odds ratios in the first block of columns (over-qualified) show that only two groups – Christian Irish and Jewish British – were not significantly more likely to be over-qualified (rather than in jobs that match their qualifications) than were Christian White British, with ratios as high as 7.21 and with nine in all exceeding 2.0 (including all Muslim and South Asian groups). These results suggest very substantial ethnic penalties suffered by most of the country's ethnic minority groups relative to their host society; significantly more minority group members are unable to obtain positions in the occupational structure consistent with their educational qualifications. In contrast, the absence of significant relationships in the second block of columns indicates few differences among the groups in the degree of under-qualification. The main difference among ethno-religious groups is in their ability to find jobs consistent with their qualifications: members of all groups are as likely to be under-qualified – to be in jobs that they lack the qualifications generally associated with such roles; a characteristic that applies more to older people, to those born overseas and to those who are unmarried.

Finally, the coefficients for the neighbourhood level variables (IMD – the neighbourhood value on the index of multiple deprivation – and MII – its value on the index of ethnic segregation; the higher the values the more deprived and the more segregated the areas, respectively) show that those living in the more segregated tracts – where members of the various ethnic minority groups lived in relative isolation from members of the host society – were significantly more likely to be over-qualified. The ethnic penalty was exacerbated in those areas. The odds ratios for the under-qualified confirmed that interpretation: values of less than one indicated that residents of deprived and relatively segregated areas were less likely to be in jobs which normally required higher qualifications than they possessed.

People living in the more segregated and deprived parts of the country were thus more likely to be in jobs for which they were over-qualified, suggesting that they are less able to realise their full potential there than people living in the less deprived and segregated parts of the country. The disadvantage suffered by members of most ethno-religious groups, the overseas-born and the unmarried were compounded if they lived in certain areas (as in any such logistic regression analysis, the combined impact of the independent variables is cumulative). The deprived and segregated areas in general have the less buoyant labour markets, and people living there are less able, it seems from these aggregate analyses, to obtain jobs commensurate with their qualifications: the ethnic penalty is greatest in the areas of greatest disadvantage. Furthermore, the significant negative coefficients for the two area-level variables in the comparisons of those who were under-qualified with those in occupations commensurate with their qualifications indicate that, compared to those living elsewhere, people were much less likely to obtain jobs for which they were under-qualified, irrespective of their ethno-religious status.

Obtaining employment for which you lack the formal qualifications is much easier in relatively buoyant labour markets.

The various studies summarised here have thus extended the work on ethnic penalties in the British labour market. Those focusing on labour market status – illustrated by the data in Table 8.5 – have shown substantial differences among ethno-religious groups across as well as between genders. Those focusing on the quality of the job obtained relative to educational qualifications – illustrated by one of the detailed regressions reported in Table 8.6 – have shown that in addition there are variations according to where people live: those in the more disadvantaged parts of the country are less able to obtain the sorts of work for which they are qualified, let alone those for which they are under-qualified. The assertion that segregation matters is sustained.

6. Concluding remarks

Our main aim in this chapter was to uncover the impact of the ethno-religious background and the role of space (segregation) in shaping occupational returns on education in England and Wales. We have deployed both quantitative and to a lesser extent qualitative data to obtain a better understanding of these influences. We argued that combining both ethnicity and religion is important in examining the complex nature of the differences between groups. For example, to know that a person's ethnicity is Indian is limited in assessing his or her overall chances of obtaining academic qualification and getting a professional job. However, interacting the ethnicity with religion significantly improves our ability to predict the odds of success for this person. In the case of women, this interaction between ethnicity and religion is even more important due to the huge differences between men and women in some of the faith groups (i.e., Muslim Indians). This complexity of the differences between the ethno-religious groups, among other things, is associated with the patterns of residential segregation of many of the ethno-religious groups. For instance, Bangladeshis (mostly Muslims) exemplify the very complex nature of the relationship between ethnicity, religion and segregation along with very large gender differences (Khattab et al., 2010).

Our findings are in line with other recent studies (see Khattab, 2009), confirming that the ethno-religious differences are indeed complex and require a multidimensional approach to studying ethnic penalties rather than the unidimensional focus of other research (Heath and McMahon, 1997, 1999; Modood et al., 1997). Using a classification of groups combining religion and ethnicity proved very useful and important in exploring arguments of cultural and colour racism (Modood, 2005). Our findings in relation to the impact of ethno-religious background are in line with Modood's cultural and colour racism theory. There was solid evidence to suggest that a particular group (i.e., Muslims) suffer more than other groups in the labour market.

While the ethno-religious differences in the occupational returns on qualifications found in this study cannot be associated with different types and levels of discrimination on the grounds of colour and cultural differences, it is quite possible that some of these differences are associated with unmeasured factors in our study such as the length of stay in the UK, or whether the qualification has been obtained from a UK institution and, most importantly, the class background. In a recent study addressing the influence of ethnicity, religion and class on labour market outcomes amongst South Asians in the UK, we have shown that class background is an important force and operates in parallel and in conjunction with ethno-religious background (Khattab et al., 2008).

Living in segregated areas was found to be sometimes associated with low occupational returns on education. This is not a universal rule. Jews, for example, are one of the most residentially segregated groups in Britain and at the same time enjoy a high occupational return on education. Nevertheless, it appears that segregated neighbourhoods are likely to reinforce the disadvantage of their residents to convert their qualifications into suitable jobs, especially if these neighbourhoods are deprived or not. This finding largely confirms Clark and Drinkwater's (2002) conclusions about the negative impact of segregation on employment.

The findings of this research programme have shown that the so-called ethnic penalties reported by various scholars (e.g., Heath and McMahon, 1997) consist of various aspects of which ethnicity is only one aspect; other aspects of these penalties, such as religion and residential segregation, also impact upon the labour market experience. Indeed, it was found that religion does matter and segregation too. However, in order to sustain this conclusion, future studies will have to control for other factors such as class background, pre-history migration, time of arrival in the UK, language efficiency and whether the qualifications have been obtained in the UK. Only then, we can determine with a great deal of confidence that religion and segregation matter.

Note

1. A good example of such work is Bowyer (2009).

References

Ahmad, F., Modood, T. and Lissenburgh, S. (2003) *South Asian Women and Employment in Britain: The Interaction of Gender and Ethnicity.* London: Policy Studies Institute (PSI).

Alpin, C., Shackleton, J.R. and Walsh, S. (1998) 'Over- and Undereducation in the UK Graduate Labour Market', *Studies in Higher Education*, 23: 17–34.

Andrews, M.J., Bradley, S. and Stott, D. (2001) 'The School-to-Work Transition, Skill Preferences and Matching', WP 2001/001, Lancaster University Management School.

Aspinall, P. (2000a) 'The Challenges of Measuring the New Ethno-Cultural Diversity in Britain in the New Millennium', *Policy and Politics*, 28: 109–118.

Aspinall, P. (2000b) 'Should a Question on "Religion" Be Asked in the 2001 British Census? A Public Policy Case in Favour', *Social Policy and Administration*, 34: 584–600.

Ballard, R. (1996) 'Negotiating Race and Ethnicity: Exploring the Implications of the 1991 Census', *Patterns of Prejudice*, 30: 3–33.

Ballard, R. (1998) 'Asking Ethnic Questions: Some Hows, Whys and Wherefores', *Patterns of Prejudice*, 32: 15–37.

Berthoud, R. (1998) 'Defining Ethnic Groups: Origin or Ethnicity?', *Patterns of Prejudice*, 32: 53–63.

Bowyer, B.T. (2009) 'The Contextual Determinants of Whites' Racial Attitudes in England', *British Journal of Political Science*, 39: 559–586.

Brown, M.S. (2000) 'Religion and Economic Activity in the South Asian Population', *Ethnic and Racial Studies*, 23(6): 1035–1061.

Clark, K. and Drinkwater, S. (2002) 'Enclaves, Neighbourhoods Effects and Employment Outcomes: Ethnic Minorities in England and Wales', *Journal of Population Economics*, 15: 5–29.

Dale, A. (2002) 'Social Exclusion of Pakistani and Bangladeshi Women', *Sociological Research Online*, http://www.socresonline.org.uk/7/3/dale.html, (3). Last accessed 29 December 2010.

Dale, A., Fieldhouse, E., Shaheen, N. and Kalra, V. (2002) 'The Labour Market Prospects for Pakistani and Bangladeshi Women', *Work Employment and Society*, 16(1): 5–25.

Dixie, J. (1998) 'The Ethnic and Religious Questions for 2001: Research and Responses', *Patterns of Prejudice*, 32: 5–14.

Fieldhouse, E.A. and Tranmer, M. (2001) 'Concentration Effects, Spatial Mismatch, or Neighborhood Selection? Exploring Labour Market and Neighborhood Variations in Male Unemployment Risk Using Census Microdata From Great Britain', *Geographical Analysis*, 33(4): 353–369.

Green, F., McIntosh, S. and Vignoles, A. (1999) 'Overeducation and Skills - Clarifying the Concepts', DP 435, Centre for Economic Performance, London School of Economics.

Halaby, C.N. (1994) 'Overeducation and Skill Mismatch', *Sociology of Education*, 67: 47–59.

Heath, A. and McMahon, D. (1997) 'Education and Occupational Attainments: The Impact of Ethnic Origins', in A.H. Halsey, H. Lauder, P. Brown and A.S. Wells, eds. *Education*. Oxford: Oxford University Press, pp. 646–662.

Heath, A. and McMahon, D. (1999) *Ethnic Differences in the Labour Market: The Role of Education and Social Class Origins*. Oxford: University of Oxford, CREST.

Heath, A. and McMahon, D. (2005) 'Social Mobility of Ethnic Minorities', in G.C. Loury, T. Modood and S.M. Teles, eds. *Ethnicity, Social Mobility and Public Policy*. Cambridge: Cambridge University Press, pp. 393–413.

Heath, A. and Yu, S. (2005) 'Explaining Ethnic Minority Disadvantage', in A. Heath, J. Ermisch and D. Gallie, eds. *Understanding Social Change*. Oxford: Oxford University Press for the British Academy, pp. 187–224.

Hewstone, M. (2009) 'Living Apart, Living Together: The Role of Intergroup Contact in Social Integration', *Proceedings of the British Academy*, 162, 243–300.

Hoare, A.G. and Johnston, R.J. (2011) 'Widening Participation Through Admissions Policy: A British Case Study', *Studies in Higher Education*, 36(1):21–41. Available at http://pdfserve.informaworld.com/394102_906484679_926715231.pdf.

Hoffmann, E. and Scott, M. (1993) *The Revised International Standard Classification of Occupation*. Geneva: International Labour Office, http://www.ilo.org/public/english/bureau/stat/download/papers/short.pdf. Last accessed 23 December 2010.

Howard, K. (2006) 'Constructing the Irish of Britain: Ethnic Recognition and the 2001 Census', *Ethnic and Racial Studies*, 29, 104–123.

Johnston, R., Wilson, D. and Burgess, S. (2004) 'School Segregation in Multiethnic England', *Ethnicities*, 4(2): 237–265.

Johnston, R., Poulsen, M. and Forrest, J. (2006) 'Ethnic Residential Segregation and Assimilation in British Towns and Cities: A Comparison of Those Claiming Single and Dual Ethnic Identities', *Migration Letters*, 3(1): 11–30.

Johnston, R., Sirkeci, I., Khattab, N. and Modood, T. (2010) 'Ethno-Religious Categories and Measuring Occupational Attainment in Relation to Education in England and Wales: A Multi-Level Analysis', *Environment and Planning A*, 42(3): 578–591.

Kertzer, D.I. and Arel, D. (2002) 'Censuses, Identity Formation, and the Struggle for Political Power', in D.I. Kertzer and D. Arel, eds. *Censuses and Identity: The Politics of Race, Ethnicity, and Language in National Censuses*. Cambridge: Cambridge University Press, pp. 1–42.

Khattab, N. (2009) 'Ethnoreligious background as a determinant of educational and occupational attainment in Britain'. *Sociology*, 43(2): 304–22.

Khattab, N. Modood, T., Sirkeci, I. and Johnston, R. (2008) 'Economic Activity in the South Asian Population in Britain: The Impact of Ethnicity, Religion and Class', Mobility in International Labour Markets Conference, 15–16 May. University College London, UK.

Khattab, N., Johnston, R., Sirkeci, I. and Modood, T. (2010) 'The Impact of Spatial Segregation on the Employment Outcomes Amongst Bangladeshi Men and Women in England and Wales', *Sociological Research Online*, 15(1), http://www.socresonline.org.uk/15/1/3.html. Last accessed 29 December 2010.

Modood, T. (2003) 'Ethnic Differences in Educational Performance', in D. Mason, ed. *Explaining Ethnic Differences: Changing Patterns of Disadvantage in Britain*. Bristol: Policy Press, pp. 53–67.

Modood, T. (2005) *Multicultural Politics: Racism, Ethnicity and Muslims in Britain*. Edinburgh: Edinburgh University Press.

Modood, T., Berthoud, R., Lakey et al., Nazroo, J., Smith, P., Virdee, S. and Beishon, S. (1997) *Ethnic Minorities in Britain: Diversity and Disadvantage*. London: Policy Studies Institute.

Münz, R. (2004) 'Migration, Labour Markets and Migrants' Integration in Europe: A Comparison', Paper given at EU/US Seminar on Integrating Immigrants into the Workforce, 26–29 June, OECD, Washington, DC.

National Equality Panel (NEP) (2010) *An Anatomy of Economic Inequality in the UK* (Chaired by Professor John Hills). London: Government Equalities Office.

Nielsen, H.S., Rosholm, M., Smith, N. and Husted, L. (2003) 'The School-to-Work Transition of 2nd Generation Immigrants in Denmark', *Journal of Population Economics*, 16: 755–786.

Office of the Deputy Prime Minister (ODPM) (2004) *The English Indices of Deprivation 2004*. London: Office of the Deputy Prime Minister.

Owen, D. (2003) 'The Demographic Characteristics of People From Minority Ethnic Groups in Britain', in D. Mason, ed. *Explaining Ethnic Differences*. Bristol: The Policy Press, pp. 21–51.

Peach, C. (2005) 'Social Integration and Social Mobility: Spatial Segregation and Intermarriage of the Caribbean Population in Britain', in G.C. Loury, T. Modood and S.M. Teles, eds. *Ethnicity, Social Mobility and Public Policy*. Cambridge: Cambridge University Press, pp. 178–203.

Peach, C. (2006a) 'Muslims in the 2001 Census of England and Wales: Gender and Economic Disadvantage', *Ethnic and Racial Studies*, 29(4): 629–655.

Peach, C. (2006b) 'Islam, Ethnicity and South Asian Religions in the London 2001 Census', *Transactions of the Institute of British Geographers*, NS31: 353–370.

Platt, L. (2005) 'The Intergenerational Social Mobility of Minority Ethnic Groups'. *Sociology*, 39(3): 445–461.

Richardson, R. and Wood, A.G. (1999) *Inclusive Schools, Inclusive Society: Race and Identity on the Agenda*. Stoke on Trent: Trentham Books.

Sillitoe, K. and White, H.P. (1991) 'Ethnic Group and the British Census: The Search for a Question', *Journal of the Royal Statistical Society Series A*, 155, 141–163.

Walter, B. (1998) 'Challenging the Black/White Binary: The Need for an Irish Category in the 2001 Census', *Patterns of Prejudice*, 32: 73–86.

Wilson, D., Burgess, S. and Briggs, A. (2005) 'The Dynamics of School Attainment of England's Ethnic Minorities', CMPO Working Paper 05/130, CMPO: The Centre for Market and Public Organisation, Bristol.

Zelinsky, W. and Lee, B.A. (1998) 'Heterolocalism: An Alternative Model of the Sociospatial Behaviour of Immigrant Ethnic Communities', *International Journal of Population Geography*, 4: 281–298.

9

Educational Achievement and Career Aspiration for Young British Pakistanis

Claire Dwyer, Tariq Modood, Gurchathen Sanghera, Bindi Shah and Suruchi Thapar-Björkert

1. Introduction

In this chapter we report on research conducted between 2004 and 2006 in Slough and Bradford which investigated the educational aspirations and experiences of young British Pakistani Muslim men and women.[1] Our research, funded by the Leverhulme Trust within a wider programme on migration and citizenship, sought to understand the extent to which young British Pakistanis were making progress in terms of educational achievement and employment in relation to their peers and in relation to the wider findings of successive reports on the differential achievements of ethnic groups (Modood and Shiner, 1994; Modood et al., 1997). Our qualitative study explored the attitudes and dispositions towards education and career aspirations held by a range of young people including both those who had achieved a measure of success (entry into higher education, for example, or professional qualifications) and those who had left compulsory education with few qualifications including those who remained unemployed. One starting point for this research was work by Zhou (2000, 2005) on the high academic achievements of Asian-Americans (particularly those of Vietnamese and Chinese heritage) which posited the role of 'ethnic social capital' as being particularly significant in promoting academic achievement through the enforcement of familial and community norms. We wanted to see whether similar forms of 'ethnic capital' (Modood, 2004) also operated within Pakistani Muslim communities and whether they were significant in shaping improved educational outcomes for young people. As we discuss below, our research enabled us to make some claims for the operation of 'ethnic capital' amongst our sample populations. We also found evidence of the complex intersection of 'ethnicity' with other factors including gender, class, religiosity and place to produce differences in opportunity and experience.

We begin our discussion with a brief elaboration of the broader literature on educational achievement for young people from minority ethnic groups. We then provide further details of the research which was undertaken reflecting on the differences between the two sites chosen for the research and on how some of the challenges faced in recruiting informants were significant in shaping our findings and our analysis. We then discuss our findings about the factors shaping the educational experiences and achievements of the young people we interviewed, before drawing some conclusions about how our findings might contribute to wider debates about the integration and success of ethnic minority groups in Britain.

2. Educational experiences and achievements for young British Pakistanis: theoretical debates

The educational achievements and aspirations of children from ethnic minority groups remain significant causes of concern for academics (Dale et al., 2002a, 2002b; Francis and Archer, 2005; Platt, 2005; Archer and Francis, 2006; Crozier and Davies, 2006, Burgess, Wilson and Piebalga, 2009) and policy-makers (Cabinet Office, 2008) in the UK. Recent studies acknowledge the variations, first made prominent by Modood (1993), in the educational achievements and higher education participation of *different* ethnic minority groups. Modood (2004) noted that while South Asians as a group had the highest rates of participation in post-compulsory education for the 16–24 age range, Indian and African-Asian men were the most likely to possess degrees and Pakistani and Bangladeshi men were the least likely. However, if Pakistani young men do less well than some of their South Asian peers, both young Pakistani men and women are more likely to go to university than their white peers (Connor et al., 2004). At the other end of the spectrum young Pakistani boys continue to do worse than most other groups at GCSE. Existing data on the experiences of young people from Pakistani Muslim backgrounds, the focus of much of Modood's previous research, suggest several important research questions. First, why do young men and women from Pakistani Muslim backgrounds continue to under-perform at school? Second, why are there emerging gender disparities between young men and women from Pakistani Muslim backgrounds, particularly the way in which young women are beginning to outperform young men at GCSE level? Third, why do young people from Pakistani Muslim backgrounds have *higher* rates of participation in higher education than many of their peers despite coming from predominantly working-class backgrounds? Finally, to what extent might current theories of 'ethnic capital' (Modood, 2004; Zhou, 2005) explain these trends?

Existing research on the education experiences of young Pakistani Muslim men and women is disparate. There has been considerable interest in the educational experiences of young women from South Asian Muslim backgrounds (Basit, 1997; Haw, 1998; Archer, 2002; Shain, 2002) which has focused on how young women negotiate the expectations of teachers and peers as well as respond to family and community pressures. Research suggests that many young Muslim women are articulating 'high educational and career goals' (Basit, 1997: 429) which are often supported by their parents and which may challenge teachers' 'culturally held stereotypes' (Haw, 1998: 136). Several recent studies highlight the growing numbers of young South Asian Muslim women in higher education (Ahmad, 2001; Tyrer and Ahmad, 2006; Hussain and Bagguley, 2007) and celebrate the achievements of women who have overcome both institutional and communal pressures to pursue their education. As we discuss elsewhere (Dwyer and Shah, 2009: 56), there remains considerable diversity of experience and for some educational aspirations remain limited by patriarchal constraints (Mohammad, 2005). Earlier work on South Asian women and employment (Brah, 1993) argued that women faced barriers in entering the workforce because of both patriarchal attitudes and institutional discrimination. More recent work shows higher levels of labour market participation amongst the Pakistani Muslim women studied and cites the importance of increasing levels of education (Dale et al., 2002a, 2002b). The authors suggest that women with qualifications are more likely to work after marriage and, while the presence of children was a significant factor influencing whether or not women worked, as more qualified women entered the workforce they would choose to stay on after they had children. Dale et al. (2002b: 22) emphasise that 'negative and out-dated stereotypes of Muslim women held by employers' remains a significant barrier to employment, a concern also raised in a recent survey by the Equal Opportunities Commission (2007).

Research on young Pakistani Muslim mens' educational and employment experiences has had a rather different focus, shaped by discussions about the assumed deviancy and criminality of young Muslim men (Alexander, 2000) particularly in the specific context of the urban unrest in the Northern cities of Bradford, Oldham and Burnley in 2001 (Macey, 1999, 2002, 2007) and by fears about radical Islamism. As Archer (2001: 81) argues, 'Muslim young men are increasingly being defined as militant and aggressive, intrinsically fundamentalist, ultimate Others.' Archer's research on young Muslim boys finds evidence both of disengagement from education and the influence of peer cultures which valorise 'hard' masculinities (Archer, 2003: 86). Work in Bradford (Hussain and Bagguley, 2005; Alam and Husband, 2006; Hopkins, 2006) and Scotland (Hopkins, 2004, 2006, 2007a, 2007b) recognises diverse and multiple Pakistani Muslim masculinities, although the challenge of negotiating negative stereotypes of Muslim men was identified as an impediment for even those with good educational qualifications. While there is limited evidence of upward social mobility for Pakistani Muslim men (Ramji, 2005, 2007), concerns remain about low educational achievement, social exclusion and unemployment (Salway, 2008).

Our research was framed by these accounts but also by a broader literature examining the educational success of minority ethnic groups. In the UK research on minority ethnic groups has tended to prioritise social class as the most significant factor in determining educational outcomes (Ball, Reay and David, 2003; Reay, David and Ball, 2005), notwithstanding a recognition of the complex ways in which class intersects with 'race' and gender. Recent interest in social capital theory has raised the question of how ethnic groups might mobilise different forms of social capital (Anthias, 2007) particularly to achieve positive educational outcomes. Archer and Francis (2005, 2006) draw on Bourdieu (1977) to find evidence of the mobilisation of cultural capital by British Chinese families, while Crozier and Davies (2006) highlight the role of the extended family in supporting Pakistani and Bangladeshi pupils. In the USA, Zhou (Zhou and Bankston, 1994; Zhou, 2000, 2005) has argued that the high academic achievements of Vietnamese and Chinese immigrant children can be explained by social capital theory (drawing on Coleman, 1988). Thus, economic disadvantage is compensated by social capital in the form of family norms, values and networks, as well as a broader set of community values and networks which promote particular educational goals (also see Thapar-Björkert and Sanghera, 2010). Two dimensions of social capital are particularly relevant to immigrant families: 'intergenerational closure' and 'norms enforcement'. The presence of dense co-ethnic networks in immigrant communities forms a closed structure and creates a protective barrier particularly for second-generation youth in multiracial inner-city neighbourhoods. Tightly knit co-ethnic networks prevent these young people from assimilating into the underclass, provide resources that facilitate access to good schools and promote academic achievement through the enforcement of familial and community norms. Zhou (2000) also identifies ethnic community organisations as contributing to intergenerational closure by reinforcing values about education and assisting with upward social mobility for working-class Asian Americans. Zhou's concept of ethnicity as social capital collapses the distinction between cultural capital acquired through the family and social capital as benefits mediated through social networks and group membership and highlights the broad roles that ethnicity can play through 'ethnic capital' (Modood, 2004). This notion of ethnic capital identifies important and sometimes hidden mechanisms. In particular it suggests a triad of factors – familial adult–child relationships, transmission of aspirations and attitudes and norms enforcement that can facilitate educational achievement and social mobility among those with limited economic capital (Modood, 2004; for a more extended theoretical discussion, see Shah, Dwyer and Modood, 2010).

As we discuss below, our research found some evidence of the operation of these mechanisms and thus the identification of mobilisation of 'ethnic capital'. However, we found too that the influence of gender and class raised in other accounts remains significant, suggesting that assessment of the utility of ethnic capital in achieving social mobility must be carefully contextualised (Shah, Dwyer and Modood, 2010).

3. Research sites and methodology

Research was conducted in Bradford, West Yorkshire, and Slough in Berkshire to provide two contrasting areas. These sites were chosen as urban centres with comparable percentages of their population recorded as of Pakistani background in the 2001 Census, 15 per cent and 12 per cent, respectively, although the Bradford Metropolitan District has a total population (467,665) which is more than four times larger than the total population of Slough (119,067). Bradford and Slough also provide contrasting labour markets although the variation in unemployment between the two places is not as stark as might be expected. At the time of the study, unemployment rates for males were 4.4 per cent in Slough and 6.7 per cent in Bradford compared with a national average of 5.7 per cent.[2] However, these figures masked much higher rates for populations of Pakistani origin concentrated in inner-city wards with the highest indices of deprivation. The physical and social deprivation and high unemployment levels of the Manningham neighbourhood in Bradford, with a concentration of Asian Muslims, are well documented (Bradford Commission, 1996; Allen, 2003; Darlow et al., 2005; Phillips, 2006), while in Slough too, concerns have been raised by the local council about the lower achievement rates of young people in the poorer wards of the town in which the Pakistani Muslim population is over-represented (Davies, 2004).

Labour markets in Bradford and Slough provide contrasting opportunities. In Slough some manufacturing companies, including Mars and SmithKline Beecham (now GlaxoSmithKline), remain although the factory work which first attracted Asian migrants has declined. The main employment expansion in recent decades has been in IT for which recruitment is often national, as well as in the public sector, retailing and distribution (Bowlby, Lloyd Evans and Roche, 2004). In Bradford, the Pakistani Muslim population first came to work in the textile industry in places like Lister Mill in Manningham (Lewis, 1994). The process of de-industrialisation has disproportionately affected Bradford's Asian populations (Cantle, 2001; Ouseley, 2001). Bradford has struggled to develop a robust post-industrial economy and remains a low-wage economy with a significant emphasis still on employment in declining manufacturing industries, although the public sector is increasingly important (Darlow et al., 2005). Research on youth employment in Bradford's 'flexible' labour economy (Husband, 2000) emphasises that young people often move through a succession of low-paid, low-skill jobs.

We conducted 125 interviews with 58 young men and 67 young women (Table 9.1), ranging in age from 16 to 26. The sample was recruited at a range of locations: youth and community centres, schools, universities, voluntary

Table 9.1 Summary of interviews

Age/Status	Male	Female
School or FE (aged 16–20)	Slough: 10 Bradford: 17	Slough: 9 Bradford: 23
University (19–23)	Slough: 7 Bradford: 4	Slough:10 Bradford: 4
Employed or unemployed (16–20)	Slough: 10 Bradford: 0	Slough: 6 Bradford: 4
Employed or unemployed (19–26)	Slough: 6 Bradford: 4	Slough: 9 Bradford: 2
Total	58	67

organisations, sports facilities, job centres and through snowball techniques in order to get a range of respondents – both those who had been educationally 'successful' and those who were deemed 'less successful'. Our sample included those who were at school studying 'A' levels, college and university students at a range of different higher education institutes, professional and manual workers and those who were unemployed. We included those who had left school at 16 (even if they had subsequently returned to education) and those who had stayed on to gain further qualifications. Although we tried to speak to a wide range of different respondents with contrasting experiences of education and employment we do not claim that our sample is representative of all young Pakistani Muslims in either of our case study locations. We recognise that our recruitment strategies will have accessed some kinds of respondents and not others. In particular we probably have an under-representation of young women who are economically inactive and who are not actively seeking education or employment as our research methods did not provide easy ways to access these women. We mainly conducted individual interviews, although in a small number of cases we used group interviews and one focus group. Interviews were taped, transcribed and analysed with the aid of *Atlas.ti* software using a grounded theory approach.[3] We also conducted interviews with 19 parents and a small number of teachers and community leaders.

The research process itself raised complex methodological and ethical issues which shaped our findings and the analysis. From the outset it was clear that research in Bradford was challenging, reflecting a charged racialised political history against a backdrop of urban deprivation (Allen, 2003; Alexander, 2004; Hussain and Bagguley, 2005; Sanghera and Thapar-Björkert, 2007a) and an overburden of previous research (Darlow et al., 2005). Sanghera found that considerable negotiation was required with key gatekeepers to facilitate access to interviewees and complex ethical issues were raised about doing research in Bradford where 'wariness and weariness' (Sanghera and Thapar-Björkert, 2007b: 10) was exhibited by potential gatekeepers. In contrast, Shah found it easier to gain assistance from key gatekeepers in Slough, arguably a context where there has been much less media and policy focus. The gender and ethnicity of the interviewers was sometimes important in shaping access to respondents, although in general the fact that neither interviewer was an 'insider', in this context 'Pakistani Muslim', was seen as an advantage by many respondents. However, the notion of an 'insider'/'outsider' position for the researcher is complex, contradictory and fluid (Mohammad, 2001) and both researchers experienced incidents when their ethnicity was (mis)read or presumed in different ways and their gender sometimes shaped respondents' performance during interviews (Sanghera and Thapar-Björkert, 2007b; Shah, 2007). During the recruitment process both Shah and Sanghera found it was harder to find young men willing to participate in the interviews than young women and young men were often perfunctory in their involvement. The resistance of some of these young men to the interview process might be understood within the moral panics around young Asian men, highlighted above, and a 'general climate of fear and suspicion' (Sanghera and Thapar-Björkert, 2007b: 2). All of these issues inevitably shape the research findings which we now go on to explore.

4. Evidence for the operation of the ethnic social capital in shaping educational success

In this section we discuss the evidence for the operation of some of the forms of ethnic social capital identified by Zhou (2000) and Modood (2004). First, it was clear that there was plenty of evidence, both from the young people we interviewed and their parents, of high aspirations for educational success:

> It's only the most important thing in life, and especially being an Asian... to be something in life, you have to have education, otherwise you're just like everyone else, nothing really, a manual worker in a factory, whatever, but if you have an education, you have something to your name, you are something, you get respect from having an education, it's very important. (Shafi, A-level student from Slough)

Another young woman from Slough, a university student at Brunel University, echoes these sentiments:

> [to get a qualification] is very important, especially when I looked at people in Pakistan who are not educated and are having such tough lives, all they can do is cleaning, servants, so it built me up to think that education is important.... My mum said, 'look at your dad, working in the Mars factory, if he had studied more, it would have been easier for him.' (Sultana)

The young people we interviewed saw education as a means of social mobility, to get better jobs than their parents, who were overwhelmingly employed in manual jobs. Thus educational success also becomes a means to make parents proud and to gain respect from others within the wider community (Thapar-Björkert and Sanghera, 2010). Our respondents agreed that parents were always urging them to work hard and do well at school and parents too could gain enhanced status through their children. As Rana, a 22-year-old graduate who works for Slough Council, explains:

> When they meet up with their friends or whatever, he [Dad] will say to them 'my daughter did this degree', they all talk about their children, 'What did your children do?'

Similarly, Alia, a university student from Slough reported:

> I think because themselves, they've never been to university and now because I'm going, it's their way of achieving something themselves, and when my dad tells people that I'm doing a degree he's just so proud, so proud you know.

These views held by the young people we interviewed were also echoed by the parents we talked to. Noor, a single mother, explained, 'you get a lot of respect if you've got a good job' while Aziz, a taxi driver in Slough who was also chair of the Slough Pakistan Welfare Association, put it in broader terms:

> Education is not just to get a good job, education makes you a good citizen, a good person, part of the society, if you're educated...you always try to do the better things, you communicate better, you speak better, this is good for society.

For the mother of Bilal, a young man in Slough who had left school with few qualifications but had now returned to college to do youth work, education was simply about helping to keep young men away from the negative influences of street crime:

> it's all what a good parent does you know, what a Pakistani parent does, you know what I mean,...but at the end of the day, I don't want my son hanging on the street where I know there's drugs, I don't want my son hanging on the street where I know he'll get beaten up or robbed or mugged, I don't want any harm happening to my children,....

Our findings then concur with others who have argued that immigrant parents often hold high aspirations for their children (Francis and Archer, 2005), motivated by the desire for children to gain social mobility and escape the trap of poorly paid, unskilled employment. The evidence of a competitive spirit among some Pakistani parents cited above by Rana (see also Archer and Francis, 2006) is also an example of what Zhou identifies as ethnic social capital – the ways in which intergenerational closure works to enforce social norms about educational success.

Although such aspirations were significant in shaping the educational performance of many of our respondents, at least in their own view, particularly some of the young women, it was clear from the diversity of experience of our interviewees that such high aspirations were not achieved by all. As we have argued elsewhere (Dwyer, Shah and Sanghera, 2008), we saw particular variation between the young men we interviewed, some of whom felt the pressure of parental aspirations that might have been unrealistic given the limited qualifications their sons had achieved. It is not enough for parents simply to exhibit high aspirations for their children; we had to consider the processes by which such goals were achieved.

Educational theorists have pointed out that in the UK a 'new market' in education has created differentiated circuits of schooling requiring the interplay of social class, cultural capital and choice (Ball, Bowe and Gewirtz, 1995). The majority of the respondents in our sample came from poor backgrounds where, if a parent was working, it was in low-paid and unskilled work. Such social and economic disadvantages were compounded by the fact that respondents lived predominantly in inner urban neighbourhoods with the least well-performing schools. Mohammad left school in Slough with no qualifications and claimed he gained little from his time there:

> I didn't learn nothing in science for five years . . . because we kept on getting supply teachers and stuff like that, and every year we'd have a different teacher, no one would actually work in the class as well, no students were prepared to work.

Inequalities between different schools were compounded in Slough because of the competitive grammar school system which meant that those parents with more social and cultural capital were better able to access the best schools. However, in Bradford too there was evidence of the ways in which some of the most educationally successful respondents attributed their success to parental strategies to access the better suburban schools. Naim, a university student from Bradford, explained that his mother saved so that they could move out of the inner-city neighbourhood and he could attend a better school in the more ethnically diverse suburbs:

> Back in [inner city] [at my] all Asian school it was like 'spot the white boy' sort of thing. When I came here it was 'spot the Asian'.

We found evidence then for the operation of economic and social capital amongst the Pakistani families we interviewed. Almost all families mobilised some form of economic capital such as extra tuition or purchasing computers to help their children's education. Where our respondents often diverged was in how successful they were in reinforcing norms and values and creating a home environment where education was a priority. We found the parents who themselves had had more education, or had migrated from urban areas in Pakistan or were second-generation immigrants with an experience of education in the UK were all more likely to be actively involved in their children's education. Shireen, mother of two school-aged sons in Slough, explained that she imposed strict rules and boundaries on her sons as she was concerned to prevent the influence of the negative masculine street culture which she saw in Slough:

> I don't think Asim [her son] was ever allowed out, you know, even after his 16th birthday. It was only when he started doing his 'A' levels that I became a bit more lax about him going out in the evenings.

Some of the parents we interviewed, although from working-class backgrounds in terms of their current employment, were able to mobilise what we might define as a more 'middle-class' orientated cultural capital (Shah, Dwyer and Modood, 2010). They might be able to use the social networks of extended family members or co-ethnic friends who had professional or business success to support their children. Maya, studying for 'A' levels in Slough, wanted to be a dentist and had been able to arrange work experience with a family friend. In other families, older siblings were important in supporting younger children and providing knowledge about how to negotiate the educational system or acted as 'high status role models' (Crozier and Davies, 2006: 685). Respondents acknowledged that even when parents wanted to support their children it was difficult for them. Iram noted that her parents:

> tried their best, they came to all our parents' evenings, read our reports, did all that, but because they didn't go to school properly, they were in and out of school when they were young, it was difficult for them to kind of keep up with what we were doing at the time.

For many families the pressures of work and family, limited English and familiarity with the educational system meant that parents were ill-equipped to navigate the demands of a 'choice' orientated educational system (Thapar-Björkert and Sanghera, 2010). Bilal reflected that his mother was a single parent, struggling alone and often absent for long periods of time in Pakistan, leaving him in the care of older siblings. It was not always realistic either for parents to be able to impose norms and values upon their children in respect of education, particularly in the face of dominant male peer cultures. Eshal, a mother in Slough whose 21-year-old son had dropped out of education after the first year of his 'A' level course, expressed fear and frustration over her lack of authority over her son:

> ... it's really frightening.... The 21 year old, all of his friends, his group, network, not one of them has turned out good... we've told him time and time again to stay away from these people, but on the whole, all of that sort of age group out of the boys, not one of them has turned out well. All they do is smoke and take drugs and take cars and sit around doing nothing. No education, their hearts are not in it.

What emerged from our analysis was some evidence for the picture of 'ethnic capital' constructed by Zhou (2000) which emphasises that the presence of dense co-ethnic networks, including cultural endowments, obligations and expectations, information channels and enforcement of social norms, can serve a distinct form of social capital. Our research suggested that while dense co-ethnic networks did work to produce competitiveness amongst parents and shared high aspirations, there were also limitations to these dense co-ethnic networks reducing the 'horizons of possibility' (Crozier and Davies, 2006: 688) for many young people from working-class Pakistani families. Thus it was families who had more middle-class orientations and greater cultural capital as well as more extended social capital networks that were often the most influential in enabling their children to do well. In summary then, we found variation in the forms of capital that British Pakistani parents mobilised to support their children's education. Better off or better educated Pakistani parents were able to mobilise economic resources as well as cultural capital to support their children's education. Limited economic capital and lack of cultural capital does not relegate all children from working-class families to underachievement. Those families able to mobilise 'ethnic capital', the cohesive family and community ties as well as provision of community educational resources, all of which reinforce norms and values regarding education, can support their children's education. However, we found that particularly within working-class families ethnicity interacted with gender to produce varying beliefs, values and norms in relation to educational performance and career/job choices among young British Pakistanis as we discuss below.

5. Intersections of ethnicity, gender and religion in the shaping of the educational outcomes

One of the most striking findings from our research was the role that gender played in shaping educational aspirations and experiences. While this finding is not perhaps at odds with a broader educational literature which highlights a growing gap between the successes of young women versus young men, particularly at GCSE level, it does suggest that the literature on British Pakistani young men and women has perhaps disproportionately focused on the assumed underachievement of young women.

5.1. Young women

As we have argued elsewhere (Dwyer and Shah, 2009) girls had higher aspirations and often outperformed boys in our sample.[4] Young women were outspoken in their desire to study and be successful. As Alia, an information systems student from Slough, explains:

> There's so much hype about Muslims at the moment. To get into an IT firm and get a job being a girl, I think that's going to be a big thing in itself for me... they reckon that we are oppressed and by showing that I've done the degree, and I've got a 2.1 and I'm going to come into the big, wide world and I'm going to do a job. It's going to be a big thing.

In this extract Alia challenges the dominant stereotypes about young Asian Muslim women ('they reckon we are all oppressed') cited in recent research (EOC, 2007) in her articulation of her future career trajectory. What was interesting about our research was that it was not only the high-fliers, those young women at university, who were this assertive, but these views were shared by other young women such as Huma, who left school with limited qualifications but was now gaining work experience at Slough Borough Council through the Modern Apprentice Scheme.

> If you don't have good GCSEs you won't get a good job anywhere. I've always liked office work and to be independent. I thought this is a good opportunity for me to go and get a good job, because once you've got your GNVQ Level 2 and 3 you get jobs that earn £15,000 a year. Basically, I've seen people work in retail, and I'm not saying it's bad, but I know I'm too good to work in retail, I've got the brains, and I've done my GCSEs... here I get experience, we work here like a full time employee and take on responsibilities. (Huma)

For the young women that we spoke to, education was important because it gave them the opportunity to be independent. Seventeen-year-old Abida, from Bradford, expresses this particularly strongly:

> I know people who from year 11, same age as me... who you study with for your GCSEs together and now they are married with kids. And I see that situation and I think I want to avoid it as much as possible. I don't want that to [happen to] me... and it's like they have to get married and then you know, they have problems with their husbands, they don't have

> an education to get out and get a job and support themselves and so you're just going to be reliant on that husband who is not treating you very well and I just want to be independent.

There was evidence from our respondents, intimated in the earlier research by Dale et al. (2002a, 2002b), Ahmad (2001) and Ahmad, Modood and Lissenburgh (2003), that as divorce rates increase there is a shift within Pakistani Muslim communities to recognise that investment in young women's education is a means by which her future is ensured. As Alia agrees:

> I've always got my degree to back me up, especially as the divorce rates are so high, they [her parents] know that if ever something like that happened to me, I've always got my degree to fall back on. Especially my dad, he always says to me 'God forbid, if anything ever happened to you, you've always got your degree to fall back on.'

This shift in the attitudes of some parents towards their daughters' education also reflects, as we discuss in greater detail below, the change in labour markets towards employment which valorises feminised 'soft skills'.

There has been considerable debate in the academic literature (see Dwyer and Shah, 2009) about how to interpret changing educational success for British Asian women. Certainly our research suggests that young women still face barriers and must negotiate normative gendered expectations of their parents or the wider community. Many respondents pointed out that they worked harder than boys at school, because they knew education represented an important opportunity for them (Thapar-Björkert and Sanghera, 2010). As Fauzia, a college student from Slough, explains:

> boys take it for granted as I said before and they just want to have a little bit of a laugh, and so they don't do as well as girls. Whereas girls want to impress their parents, especially their dads and say to them, 'look, we can be someone else'. Because they know that if they screw up, they will not get a chance to do it again,... they know that if we don't pass this time round, we're not going to get further and we're not going to get to uni.

This is echoed by Kamila, a 24-year-old student from Bradford:

> if you do well at school your parents aren't going to mind you going to college but if you mess about, and don't get on top of it, they are just going to pull you out, send you back to Pakistan to get married and that's what happened to a couple of girls I went to school with.

As other studies have suggested, local universities remain particularly important to students from working-class ethnic minority backgrounds and this was also particularly true for the female students we interviewed. It was evident that for those young women who had gone on to higher education or were working it was still important to maintain normative ideas of appropriate feminine behaviour. Young women were mindful both of the surveillance from the wider community (and their male peers) and that they needed to maintain the continued trust of their parents. As Rana explains:

> Some parents say 'if my daughter goes to college' or 'if my daughter goes to university, she might get into the wrong crowd and she might start doing things against Islam'... because I've built up that trust and they trusted me so they were fine, they supported me all the way.

The young women had to continually negotiate other peoples' expectations and manage their own behaviour. As Nasreen, a 17-year-old student in Bradford, explains:

> [you] have to hear what the people say... people's verbal stuff, like, 'Oh she's going off – she's to turn out like this, she'll be going on her own, she will be going to conferences on her own, she'll be going to other cities outside on her own' and people start thinking dodgy even though that person wouldn't be.

In Slough, Huma concurs:

> I've seen parents, like my own friends' parents, like N., they're really different, they don't give her that freedom, they did, but I think she broke their trust.

What emerges then is evidence for increasing education and independence for young Pakistani Muslim women although their educational aspirations are also contingent upon a careful negotiation of appropriate gender roles and 'respectability' (Dwyer, 1999). Many of the young women we interviewed were uncertain about the future and particularly if they would continue working after marriage and children:

> I want to get a good IT job, get a respectable job status, and just work my way up for a few years. For Pakistanis, it all comes down to marriage, it's such a big thing... they're [her parents] OK for me working for the next few... my dad's like 'you're not allowed to get married for another couple of years, like three or four years'. (Alia)

Respondents often looked to older sisters as models for charting new roles for educated young Pakistani women. Huma reflects on the likely future of her older married sister, who is the main breadwinner working as a hotel receptionist:

> I think she'll still have a career [when she has children], because there's people at her work, like, English people, they've got three or four children, they still made a career, they still manage, you can, and she'll always have her mum and dad to support her.

As Huma suggests, while attitudes might be changing, the extended family remains key in providing childcare amongst British Pakistani Muslim families (cf. Dale et al., 2002a, 2002b). Many of the young women we interviewed did not contest normative gender roles and often reiterated the importance of bringing up children in the future, or linked their educational success to better outcomes for their future children. Thinking about Pakistani Muslim girls, Rana reflects:

> No one should tell her what to do or how to do it, but then again she should understand that there's more to life than a career basically. You get more reward like bringing up children and things like that... women should work and you shouldn't make them stay at home [but] it's not inferior being a housewife.... I would class that as something good, at the end of the day you're nurturing your children, you're not just abandoning them and leaving them for the man to bring up, or the childminder or leaving them in a nursery.

Some interviewees were ambivalent about the possibility that 'too much' education could mean that marriage was deferred, or it became difficult to find a suitable marriage partner. Twenty-year-old university student Alia reflects:

> I've seen a lot of girls that have done Masters and stuff, they're 35 and not married, and they really regret it. When they should have got married they were just so into education and they looked for someone of the same match. And Pakistani men aren't really as educated as the women, then it's so difficult, and they'll just stay spinsters for the rest of their life, and then they regret it.

Further education for Pakistani Muslim women thus raises contradictions (Ahmad, 2001). Being well educated may give young women greater capital within the marriage 'market' but they may also find it difficult to find suitable partners amongst young men who are less well educated, particularly if they come from Pakistan.

In summary, the young women we interviewed often had high aspirations for education and employment, motivated by individual ambition and supported by changing norms and values within the wider Pakistani Muslim community. In this way we might argue that forms of 'ethnic capital' are emerging which support these processes even if the mechanisms might operate in complex ways. Thus norms about appropriate gender behaviour might operate to encourage young women to spend more time studying (and less time socialising outside the home) while education emerges as a 'safe' route for young women to negotiate greater autonomy and independence. As Ali (1992, cited in Dwyer, 1999: 19) argued:

> the good Muslim girl who shows unusual devotion of her faith may find it possible to express a desire for higher education or professional employment without risking her position or that of her family.

At the same time, however, shifts in labour markets and changing family dynamics are also operating to change dominant attitudes and values amongst Pakistani Muslims and to produce new forms of gender relations. We now turn to reflect on how the educational experiences and aspirations of young men were articulated illustrating how gendered norms and values played a role in shaping attitudes drawing on more extended discussions of Pakistani Muslim masculinities (see Sanghera and Thapar-Björkert, 2007a; Dwyer, Shah and Sanghera, 2008).

5.2. Young men

Our research revealed more diversity in the experiences and attitudes of young Pakistani Muslim men than of young women. Broadly speaking the young men might fall into two different groups; those who had conformed to parental expectations, studied at school and gone on to employment or further education and those who had left school with few qualifications. For the first group a number of factors seemed to be important in determining educational success. Certainly, as we suggested earlier, parental support was often very important in ensuring that young men were supported in their studies, particularly in the face of strongly oppositional masculine peer cultures which were often cited as reasons why young men neglected education. Reflecting on these peer cultures, Kamila, a 24-year-old from Bradford, explains:

> Pakistani Muslim young men and boys are so completely spoilt and so used to having everything there on a plate for them, they don't have to work for it... there's the obvious drugs issue, the selling of it is easy money to them and you know they go through all this gangster mentality that they have.... they don't want a job from 9–5 where they have to work to get a wage at the end of the month... selling drugs seem a lot cooler,

> faster money and is a lot better and you know [you] are a well respected person.... So it's quite frightening some of the role models that there are in Bradford....

Some of the young men we interviewed agreed that they had chosen different pathways from some of their less educationally orientated peers, often supported by parents with great social and cultural capital. As Naim explains:

> Our family have always been different, like the other ones, like our cousins they've always been low achievers in a way, well the ones in and around Bradford anyway... I think they feel safety within their own culture and with staying within the centre and stuff and not trying to move anywhere or do anything different.

For other young men, support for their achievements had come from a personal commitment to their faith:

> I mean now religion has more emphasis on knowledge, you know religious knowledge plus scientific knowledge... it comes from faith, there are lots of traditions that come from the Prophet, you know, like 'seeking knowledge from the Creator to the grave'. (Qasim, a 17-year-old 'A' level student from Bradford)

For Qasim his faith strongly influences his aspirations and also reflects his concerns about how Pakistani Muslims as a community are perceived:

> I mean like at present... Pakistani Muslims are the lowest of the low. I mean their aspirations for career-wise and all that is very low, keep reproducing the social vices and everything, and you know, it's partly to take the responsibility in that sense [and] show that there's the other side of the coin as well. That there are people in the Pakistani community that do want to achieve and they do want to raise standards.

It is possible to interpret both these examples of successful pathways into education as forms of 'ethnic capital' mobilising both familiar and broader ethno-religious networks. The most successful young men we interviewed often had parents with more middle-class orientations who had been able to deploy greater economic and cultural capital to support their sons and to impose stronger norms and values about education. Other young men had found these values outside their familial setting through their adherence to Islam. Often those young men who were active in religious groups cited the role of broader social networks gained through their religious activities as providing support for their career aspirations.

The influence of a negative masculine peer culture was important in shaping the experiences of some of those young men who had left school with few qualifications (Thapar-Björkert and Sanghera, 2010). Concentrated in neighbourhoods with lower performing schools, they reflected that school was primarily a social experience. 18-year-old Mohammad from Slough reflects:

> I think what I most enjoyed was seeing my friends and being in school and seeing everyone, once you leave it all, that's when you recognise that 'I could have done this, I could have done this, I could have done that', things that could have changed, or you could not change.

For some of these young men without formal qualifications the 'informal' or illegal economy, particularly drug dealing, was a means both to gain a significant income and also to gain respect amongst their peers through the valorisation of a 'hard', performative masculinity (Archer, 2003) measured in conspicuous consumption and sometimes violence. Zaki, from Bradford, points out that he knows plenty of people who have been successful in running their own businesses without qualifications:

> because I know the way life is now all I have to do is blag one good reference and I'll get a good job. That's how it works nowadays....

Many of these young men felt the pressure to be breadwinners demanded by their family but felt that there were few prospects for them. They reflected that employers already had stereotypical ideas about young Muslim men and would not want to employ them so that as Ali, from Slough, asserts:

> once you're on the streets, you're on the street, you ain't gonna get off the street.

These young men cited racism and Islamophobia as being significant obstacles which prevented them from doing well at school or accessing better jobs, issues we return to below. As Kamila suggests above, the gendered norms which operate within tight-knit, working-class Pakistani Muslim communities may work to valorise the rebellious behaviour of young men and reduce the influence which parents may have on their sons, producing a negative form of ethnic capital. This is not to suggest that there are not routes out of educational underachievement for young men. In both Bradford and Slough we met young men who had left school with few formal qualifications but had returned later to study. Bilal shared many of the attributes of his peers, believing personal contacts and a confident demeanour were important qualities in guaranteeing his success. For him college provided both opportunities. Formal educational qualifications and the social capital generated through his informal peer networks are all important to him:

> if I go to college, not only would I get a qualification, but I'll meet loads of new people, you know what I mean, and somebody opens the door for you all the time....

5.3. The influence of religion

By exploring the differential experiences of young men and young women we have suggested ways in which ethnicity intersects with gender in the production of shared norms and values which work to shape the attitudes and experiences of young people. In general, dominant discourses about appropriate Pakistani Muslim femininities seem to encourage the educational success of young women even if young women were subject to considerable restriction.[5] In contrast, shared discourses about appropriate Pakistani Muslim masculinities, while strongly orientated towards the role of male breadwinner, may allow space for young men to develop masculine subcultures within which 'street cred' is valued above educational success (Macey, 1999, 2007; Dwyer, Shah and Sanghera, 2008).

How does religion operate within this analysis of ethnic capital? The narratives cited suggest a Muslim religious identity was important to all our respondents although it was often articulated in different ways (Dwyer, Shah and Sanghera, 2008). For some young men and women, such as Qasim, Islam was a powerful force shaping their lives and they linked their educational aspirations to their religious conviction:

> What I have learnt from my religion is that you need to educate yourself, if you want to achieve anything. What I found is that people who are more religious have gone further in education so there is a kind of co-relation between people's religious kind of spirituality and their achievement. (Sara, 17-year-old student from Bradford)

At the same time, some respondents linked their education to helping them become better Muslims:

> Maybe my education has helped me, because obviously you need intellect, you need to be intellectual to look into your religion and look into what's right and wrong. It's not that [that is, because] I was born into a Muslim family that I've chosen my religion, basically I've actually looked at it and I thought 'this makes sense' so maybe if I wasn't educated I wouldn't have actually pondered on my purpose in life. (Rana)

Alia, a university student from Slough, makes a similar point:

> It's really important for Asians, because we have a lot of cultural and stuff in us, and it's important we understand our culture. And also because obviously I'm a Muslim, and there's so much hype in the media. And I think a lot of young people feel like they're just following the crowd, or like lost sheep following the rest of them because they are Muslims, and they've got to believe everything else. I think it's really important that they go to university, look at everything else around them and then understand why they're following their belief, and that's what's helped me.

This desire to challenge perceptions about Pakistani Muslims was also reflected in the desire to educate a wider society about Islam, in order to counteract negative stereotypes. Tayyas, a 24-year-old junior business analyst in Slough, pointed out that in his experience adherence to religious practice was not an impediment to his success:

> I don't think there's any way where, for example, my religion has hindered me to be working in any environment, for example, if I had to pray, it takes longer to smoke a cigarette than for me to say my prayer, so there are no compromises at all.

Other respondents, who might not necessarily be actively practising their faith, nonetheless saw their religion as a source they might draw on in the future. As Zaki, currently unemployed and involved in the illegal economy, in Bradford reflects:

> [I'm] hoping to become a better Muslim in the future, practising more of my Islam, you know, more of my religion... this year in December, my dad, he's retiring from work and everything, and he's going to Pakistan to live all his life, so I'm going to be living with my brothers and my sister. And so I want to, I'm going to work, and I'm going to be paying bills and looking after my family... so I know I need to settle down one day.

Thus, in different ways religious identifications emerge as important in the development of forms of ethnic capital for Pakistani Muslims. One very interesting way we saw this in operation was at the 'Slough Community School' which operated from the mosque in Slough, offering Saturday classes to children to support them with homework and GCSEs. Started by middle-class professional parents and staffed by volunteers including university and secondary school students, the school's Director explained that it was set up to provide children with supplementary education and to provide working-class children with some of the extra educational tuition which more middle-class parents 'buy'. In this way the school was a very good example of what Zhou (2005) calls an 'ethnic system of support' providing both academic input and forms of cultural capital such as peer mentoring, role models and raising aspirations.

6. Structural factors shaping achievement: racialised and generated labour markets

Finally we want to comment on the external factors shaping the experiences of young Pakistani Muslim men and women in gaining employment in order to address some of the limitations of focusing only on the mechanism of 'ethnic' capital. As we highlighted at the outset, the two case study sites offered contrasting economic opportunities. Although there was evidence in Slough for the operation of racialised youth markets (Bowlby, Lloyd Evans and Roche, 2004), a more buoyant service economy and active recruitment of young people by the Borough Council had opened up more employment possibilities. However, many believed that discrimination still existed:

> The jobs are available, but obviously I think to me there is a discrimination, if somebody is educated, few people, they've got the same education, same level but when it comes to the job, I don't know some sort of Islamophobia in this country .... (Aziz, Chair of Slough Pakistani Welfare Association)

In Bradford a depressed local economy meant that there were much more limited employment opportunities and even for graduates call centres often represented the only source of employment. Respondents in Bradford were much more likely to discuss the ways in which they felt discrimination shaped their labour market opportunities. Zaki, currently employed, says:

> they just think, yeah Asians, they're going to mess about, get out of this company in two weeks, don't employ 'em. That's the mentality they're thinking about us, isn't it?

Interviewees suggested that in a labour market where particular kinds of 'soft skills' or cultural attributes were important (Raffo, 2006) those from Pakistani Muslim backgrounds might be particularly discriminated against:

> An Asian guy wants to go for a call centre job, right. It might end up being that he can't speak properly or doesn't have that... I wouldn't say he can't speak properly. It is [a] type of dialect that just doesn't sound right or is not a proper telephone manner or even in an interview that is perceived in the wrong way, he might be a good worker, it's just by the way he comes across. (Khalid, university student, Bradford)

It is interesting to note that while most of the young women we interviewed were optimistic about their future job prospects, one of the young men reflected that it was easier for Pakistani young women than young men to gain jobs:

> I think it's still in the back of people's minds that may be hiring a Pakistani Muslim male is a lot more dangerous or a lot more risky than if you hired a Pakistani Muslim female. (Firoz, Bradford)

Firoz's comment suggests that the racialised, gendering of labour markets (McDowell, 2003) may favour young women over young men but it also implies the special 'risk' that young Pakistani Muslim males might pose. Dominant negative stereotypes about young Asian men (Alexander, 2000; Archer, 2001) became compounded after 9/11 and 7/7. Although conducted before the terrorist bombings in London in 2005 our research revealed how all our respondents were fearful of the ways in which the negative media portrayal of Muslims impacted upon them. As one young female respondent in Bradford explains:

> I think it's getting worse unfortunately, because of the media... and you've got the BNP kicking in as well... I mean like now my clothing [referring to her hijab]... now I'll get asked questions and funny looks that maybe I wouldn't have got asked three or five years back... things are not working for Muslims in the media and politics... now it's heightened [negativity towards Muslims], it's working more against Muslims.

It is important to recognise then that while young men and women operate as individual subjects, embedded within networks which might enable them to mobilise different kinds of economic, social and cultural capital to achieve their aspirations, external factors operate to structure the possibilities of education and employment. As the comments cited above suggest, the influence of racism and Islamophobia in shaping the life chances of our respondents should not be underestimated (EOC, 2007). Indeed studies published since our own research was completed (Berthoud, 2009; DCLG, 2010; IPPR, 2010) emphasise that Pakistanis and Muslims continue to be amongst the most disadvantaged groups in the country (NEP, 2010) and detail the range of ways in which racial discrimination continues in the labour market.

7. Conclusion

In this chapter we have discussed the findings from our research on the factors influencing educational achievement and career aspiration for young people from Pakistani Muslim immigrant backgrounds in Bradford and Slough. The theoretical framing for this chapter was provided by the concept of 'ethnic capital' (Modood, 2004). Drawing on the work of Zhou (2005), Modood asked whether particular forms of social and cultural capital (including the transmission of aspirations, strong social networks, enforcement of norms and values) could be identified as 'ethnic capital' within Pakistani Muslim communities. He postulated that such forms of 'ethnic capital' might work to militate against economic disadvantage for working-class families to produce higher educational outcomes for their children.

The research discussed here draws out the complex ways in which forms of 'ethnic capital' might operate (findings which are elaborated in greater detail in Shah, Dwyer and Modood, 2010). As we illustrate, our research found some evidence for the operation of processes which might be identified as 'ethnic capital'. British Pakistani parents emphasised the importance of higher education and had high career aspirations for their children, what Modood (2004; see also Archer and Francis, 2006) describe as 'ethnic capital'. We noted, however, that the extent to which such goals could be achieved varied across families. This was evidence for the complex ways in which 'ethnic capital' might be mobilised and the need to identify how mechanisms such as the enforcement of norms and values operate. Our research also suggested that class remains an important differentiating factor and families with more middle-class backgrounds were better able to operationalise positive ethnic capital (Shah, Dwyer and Modood, 2010). Existing literature, although rarely comparative, highlights differences between the aspirations and achievements of young Pakistani Muslim women and men. Our research suggested that gender was a significant factor shaping norms and values towards educational achievement. Despite popular assumptions to the contrary, our research provided evidence for trends noted by Dale et al. (2002a, 2002b) that young women were outperforming young men. While young women still face considerable barriers to accessing higher education and paid employment it was evident that young women in our study were strongly orientated towards educational achievement. In contrast, not all of the young men in our study saw educational achievement as a necessary means to success and instead ethnic masculine peer cultures were influential in persuading young men not to invest in their studies. Our research findings also provide evidence for the role which religious identities might play in shaping educational aspirations of young British Muslims. Religion proved to be a positive force in encouraging young people to study both by providing normative values and in some cases by enabling young men to develop important social and cultural networks beyond the immediate ethnic community. We also drew attention to the role of broader structural processes of disadvantage including poorer performing schools in inner-city neighbourhoods, the persistence of lack of opportunity for those trapped in depressed areas and the role of 'race' and Islamophobia.

Our research thus provides some evidence for the operation of 'ethnic capital'. We would contend that while class location, often identified as a key determinant of educational success (Reay, David and Ball, 2005), remains important, the components of 'ethnic capital' such as those identified by Modood (2004) and Zhou (2005) are also important. Our research suggests that familial adult–child relationships, transmission of values and aspirations related to education and enforcement of norms and sanctions can explain why many working-class Pakistani students enter higher education, particularly compared to their white working-class peers. However, it is clear that there is distinction between what Kao (2004) calls 'potential and actualised' ethnic capital, which might explain why siblings in a single household have different educational outcomes. The findings from this project suggest that gender, religion and structural disadvantages influence the level of ethnic capital that is actualised. Thus, following critiques of social capital (Edwards, Franklin and Holland, 2003; Anthias, 2007) we conclude that assessments of the utility of ethnic capital in achieving social mobility must be placed within wider debates about the social locations of individuals and groups.

Notes

1. This chapter reports on work undertaken for the project 'British Pakistanis: exploring differential outcomes in relation to gender and social capital' funded through the Leverhulme Trust programme on Migration and Citizenship. This chapter draws on some previous work including Modood (2004), Sanghera and Thapar-Björkert (2007a), Sanghera and Thapar-Björkert (2007b), Dwyer, Shah and Sanghera (2008), Dwyer and Shah (2009) and Shah, Dwyer and Modood (2010).
2. Figures from July 2005–June 2006, Government National Statistics, http://www.nomisweb.co.uk/reports/lop/la (accessed 27 June 2007).
3. All quotes are anonymised.
4. Although it is not a statistical quantitative study, and lower achieving girls may be absent from our study.
5. Although we do not want to exaggerate this finding. As we discuss in the methodological section our sample may not have included those young women who were outside the formal educational and work spaces in which we recruited participants. Indeed our research clearly shows evidence, in the words of many other participants, of young women who have been prevented from pursuing higher education because of restrictive parents.

References

Ahmad, F. (2001) 'Modern Traditions? British Muslim Women and Academic Achievement', *Gender and Education*, 13(2): 137–152.

Ahmad, F. Modood, T. and Lissenburgh, S. (2003) *South Asian Women and Employment in Britain: The Interaction of Gender and Ethnicity*. London: Policy Studies Institute.

Alam, M.Y. and Husband, C. (2006) *Reflections of Young British-Pakistani Men from Bradford: Linking Narratives to Policy*. York: Joseph Rowntree Foundation Report.

Alexander, C. (2000) *The Asian Gang*. Oxford: Berg.
Alexander, C. (2004) 'Imagining the Asian Gang: Ethnicity, Masculinity and Youth After the Riots', *Critical Social Policy*, 24(4): 526–549.
Ali, Y. (1992) 'Muslim Women and the Politics of Ethnicity and Culture in Northern England', in G. Sahgal and N. Yuval-Davis, eds. *Refusing Holy Orders*. London: Virago, pp. 101–123.
Allen, C. (2003) *Fair Justice – the Bradford Disturbances, Sentencing and the Impact*. London: Forum Against Islamophobia and Racism.
Anthias, F. (2007) 'Ethnic Ties: Social Capital and the Question of Mobilisability', The *Sociological Review*, 5(4), 1–18.
Archer, L. (2001) 'Muslim Brothers, Black Lads, Traditional Asians: British Muslim Young Men's Constructions of "Race", Religion and Masculinity', *Feminism and Psychology*, 11(1): 79–105.
Archer, L. (2002) 'Change, Culture and Tradition: British Muslim Pupils Talk About Muslim Girls' Post-16 "Choices"', *Race, Ethnicity and Education*, 5(4), 359–376.
Archer, L. (2003) *Race, Masculinity and Schooling*. Milton Keynes: Open University Press.
Archer, L. and Francis, B. (2005) 'They Never Go Off the Rails Like Other Ethnic Groups': Teachers' Constructions of British Chinese Pupils' Gender Identities and Approaches to Learning', *British Journal of Sociology of Education*, 26(2): 165–182.
Archer, L. and Francis, B. (2006) 'Challenging Classes? Exploring the Role of Social Class Within the Identities and Achievement of British Chinese Pupils', *Sociology*, 40(1): 29–49.
Ball, S. (2003) *Class Strategies and the Education Market: The Middle Classes and Social Advantage*. London: RoutledgeFalmer.
Ball, S., Bowe, R. and Gewirtz, S. (1995) 'Circuits of Schooling: A Sociological Exploration of Parental Choice of School in Social Class Contexts', *The Sociological Review*, 43(1), 52–78.
Ball, S., Reay, D. and David, M. (2003) '"Ethnic Choosing": Minority Ethnic Students, Social Class and Higher Education Choice', *Race, Ethnicity and Education*, 5(4): 333–357.
Basit, T.N. (1997) 'I Want More Freedom, but Not Too Much: British Muslim Girls and the Dynamism of Family Values', *Gender and Education*, 9(4): 425–439.
Berthoud, R. (2009) 'Patterns of Non-Employment, and of Disadvantage, in a Recession', Working Paper No. 2009-23, Institute for Social and Economic Research, University of Essex.
Bourdieu, P. (1997) 'The Forms of Capital', in A.H. Halsey, H. Lauder, P. Brown and A.S. Wells, eds. *Education: Culture, Economy, and Society*. Oxford: Oxford University Press, pp. 46–58.
Bowlby, S., Lloyd Evans, S. and Roche, C. (2004) 'Youth Employment, Racialised, Gendering and School-Work Transitions', in M. Boddy and M. Parkinson, eds. *City Matters*. Bristol: Policy Press, pp. 323–345.
Bradford Commission (1996) *The Bradford Commission Report*. Bradford: The Bradford Congress.
Brah, A. (1993) '"Race" and "Culture" in the Gendering of Labour Markets: South Asian Young Muslim Women and the Labour Market', *New Community*, 19(3): 441–458.
Burgess, S., Wilson, D. and Piebalga, A. (2009) 'Land of Hope and Dreams: Education Aspirations and Parental Influence Among England's Ethnic Minorities', Paper presented at Social Policy Association Conference, Edinburgh.

Cantle, T. (2001) *Community Cohesion: A Report of the Independent Review Team*. London: Home Office.

Coleman, J.S. (1988) 'Social Capital in the Creation of Human Capital', *American Journal of Sociology*, 94: S95–S121.

Connor, H., Tyers, C., Modood, T. and Hillage, J. (2004) *Why the Difference? A Closer Look at Higher Education Minority Ethnic Students and Graduates*. Research Report 532. London: Department of Education and Skills.

Crozier, G. and Davies, J. (2006) 'Family Matters: A Discussion of the Bangladeshi and Pakistani Extended Family and Community in Supporting the Children's Education', *Sociological Review*, 54(4): 768–795.

Dale, A., Shaheen, N., Fieldhouse, E. and Kalra, V. (2002a) 'Routes into Education and Employment for Young Pakistani and Bangladeshi Women in the UK', *Ethnic and Racial Studies*, 25(6): 924–968.

Dale, A., Shaheen, N., Fieldhouse, E. and Kalra, V. (2002b) 'Labour Market Prospects for Pakistani and Bangladeshi Women', *Work, Employment and Society*, 16(1): 5–26.

Darlow, A., Bickerstaffe, T., Burden, et al. (2005) *Researching Bradford: A Review of Social Research on Bradford District*. York: Joseph Rowntree Foundation.

Davies, N. (2004) 'Views, Voices and Visibility: Reflections on the Processes Involved in Realising the Achievement of Muslim Pupils of Pakistani and Kashmiri Heritage in Slough', *Raise Project Case Study*, RAISE, http://www.insted.co.uk/raise.html. Last accessed 6 June 2010.

Department of Communities and Local Government (2010) *Tackling Race Inequality – A Statement on Race*, http://www.communities.gov.uk. Last accessed 6 June 2010.

Dwyer, C. (1999) 'Veiled Meanings: British Muslim Women and the Negotiation of Differences', *Gender, Place and Culture*, 6(1): 5–26.

Dwyer, C. and Shah, B. (2009) 'Rethinking the Identities of Young British Pakistani Muslim Women: Educational Experiences and Aspirations', in P. Hopkins and R. Gale, eds. *Muslims in Britain: Race, Place and Identities*. Edinburgh: Edinburgh University Press, pp. 55–73.

Dwyer, C., Shah, B. and Sanghera, G. (2008) '"From Cricket Lover to Terror Suspect" – Challenging Representations of Young British Muslim Men', *Gender, Place and Culture*, 15(2): 117–136.

Edwards, R., Franklin, J. and Holland, J. (2003) *Families and Social Capital: Exploring the Issues*. London: Families and Social Capital ESRC Research Group, South Bank University.

Equal Opportunities Commission (2007) *Moving On Up? The Way Forward*. Report of the Equal Opportunities Commission's investigation into Bangladeshi, Pakistani and Black Caribbean women and work. London: EOC.

Francis, B. and Archer, L. (2005) 'British-Chinese Pupils' and Parents' Constructions of the Value of Education', *British Educational Research Journal*, 31(1): 89–108.

Haw, K. (1998) *Educating Muslim Girls: Shifting Discourses*. Milton Keynes: Open University Press.

Hopkins, P. (2004) 'Young Muslim Men in Scotland: Inclusions and Exclusions', *Children's Geographies*, 2(2): 257–272.

Hopkins, P. (2006) 'Youthful Muslim Masculinities: Gender and Generational Relations', *Transactions of the Institute of British Geographers*, 31: 337–352.

Hopkins, P. (2007a) 'Global Events, National Politics, Local Lives: Young Muslim Men in Scotland', *Environment and Planning A*, 39(5): 1119–1133.

Hopkins, P. (2007b) '"Blue Squares", "Proper" Muslims and Transnational Networks: Narratives of National and Religious Identities Amongst Young Muslim Men Living in Scotland', *Ethnicities*, 7(1): 61–81.

Hussain, Y. and Bagguley, P. (2005) 'Citizenship, Ethnicity and Identity: British Pakistanis After the 2001 Riots', *Sociology*, 39(3): 435–457.

Hussain, Y. and Bagguley, P. (2007) *Moving on Up: South Asian Women and Higher Education*. London: Treatham.

Institute of Public Policy Research (2010) 'Recession Leaves Almost Half of Young Black People Unemployed', http://www.ippr.org.uk/pressreleases/?id=3846. Last accessed 6 June 2010.

Kao, G. (2004) 'Social Capital and Its Relevance to Minority and Immigrant Populations', *Sociology of Education*, 7, 172–183.

Lewis, P. (1994) *Islamic Britain*. London: I.B. Tauris.

Macey, M. (1999) 'Class, Gender and Religions Influences on Changing Patterns of Pakistani Male Violence in Bradford', *Ethnic and Racial Studies*, 22(5), 845–866.

Macey, M. (2002) 'Interpreting Islam: Young Muslim Men's Involvement in Criminal Activity in Bradford', in Basia Spalek, ed. *Islam, Crime and the Criminal Justice System*. Devon: William Publishing, pp. 19–42.

Macey, M. (2007) 'Islamic Political Radicalism in Britain: Muslim Men in Bradford', in Tahir Abbas, ed. *Islamic Political Radicalism: A European Perspective*. Edinburgh: Edinburgh University Press, pp. 160–172.

McDowell, L. (2003) *Redundant Masculinities?* Oxford: Blackwell.

Modood, T. (1993) 'The Number of Ethnic Minority Students in British Higher Education', *Oxford Review of Education*, 19(2): 167–182.

Modood, T. (2004) 'Capitals, Ethnic Identity and Educational Qualifications', *Cultural Trends*, 13(2): 87–105; reproduced in D. Hoerder, Y. Hebért and I. Schmitt, eds. (2005) *Negotiating Transcultural Lives: Belongings and Social Capital Among Youths in Comparative Perspective*. Göttingen, Germany: V&R UniPress; and in R. Alba and M. Waters, eds. (2011) *New Dimensions of Diversity: The Children of Immigrants in North America and Western Europe*. New York: New York University Press, forthcoming; and in T. Basit and S. Tomlinson, eds. (2011) *Social Inclusion and Higher Education*. Bristol: The Policy Press, forthcoming,

Modood, T. and Shiner, M. (1994) *Ethnic Minorities and Higher Education: Why Are There Differential Rates of Entry?* London: Policy Studies Institute.

Modood, T., Berthoud, R., Lakey, J., et al. (1997) *Ethnic Minorities in Britain: Diversity and Disadvantage*. London: Policy Studies Institute.

Mohammad, R. (2001) '"Insiders" and/or "outsiders": Positionality, Theory and Praxis', in M. Limb and C. Dwyer, eds. *Qualitative Methodologies for Geographers*. London: Arnold, pp. 101–114.

Mohammad, R. (2005) 'Negotiating Space of the Home, the Education System and the Labour Market: The Case of Young, Working-Class, British Pakistani Muslim Women', in F. Ghazi-Walid and C. Nagel, eds. *Geographies of Muslim Women*. London: Guildford Press, pp. 178–202.

National Equality Panel (NEP) (2010) *An Anatomy of Economic Inequality in the UK*. London: Government Equalities Office.

Ouseley, H. (2001) *Community Pride not Prejudice*. Bradford: Bradford Vision.

Phillips, D. (2006) 'Parallel Lives? Challenging Discourses of British Muslim Self-segregation', *Environment and Planning D: Society and Space*, 24(1), 25–40.

Platt, L. (2005) 'New Destinations? Assessing the Post-migration Social Mobility of Minority Ethnic Groups in England and Wales'. *Social Policy and Administration*, 39(6), 697–721.

Ramji, H. (2005) 'Exploring Intersections of Employment and Ethnicity amongst British Pakistani Young Men', *Sociological Research Online*, 10(4), http://www.socresonline.org.uk/10/4/ramji.html.

Ramji, H. (2007) 'Dynamics of Religion and Gender Amongst Young British Muslims', *Sociology*, 41(6): 1171–1189.

Reay, D., David, M. and Ball, S. (2005) *Degrees of Choice: Social Class, Race and Gender in Higher Education*. Stoke-on-Trent: Trentham Books.

Salway, S. (2008) 'Young Bangladeshi Men in the UK L Market: Identity, Inclusion and Exclusion', *Ethnic and Racial Studies*, 31(6): 1126–1152.

Sanghera, G. and Thapar-Björkert, S. (2007a) 'Because I'm Pakistani and I'm Muslim ... and I am Political' – Gendering Political Radicalism: Young Femininities in Bradford', in T. Abbas, ed. *Islamic Political Radicalism*. Edinburgh: Edinburgh University Press, pp. 173–191.

Sanghera, G. and Thapar- Björkert, S. (2007b) 'Methodological Dilemmas: Gatekeepers and Positionality in Bradford', *Ethnic and Racial Studies*, 31(3): 543–562.

Shah, B. (2007) 'Place, Space and History in the Research Process: Reflections From Slough', Paper presented at the Panel on Feminist Research Methods at the American Sociological Association Meetings, New York, 11–14 August.

Shah, B., Dwyer, C. and Modood, T. (2010) 'Explaining Educational Achievement and Career Aspirations Among Young British Pakistanis: Mobilising "Ethnic Capital"?', *Sociology*: 44(6): 1109–1127.

Shain, F. (2002) *The Schooling and Identity of Asian Girls*. Stoke-on-Trent: Trentham Books.

Thapar-Bjorkert, S. and Sanghera, G. (2010) 'Social Capital, Educational Aspirations and Young Pakistani Muslim Men and Women in Bradford, West Yorkshire', *Sociological Review*, 58(2): 244–264.

Tyrer, D. and Ahmad, F. (2006) *Muslim Women and Higher Education: Identities, Experiences and Prospects: A Summary Report*. Liverpool: John Moores University and European Social Fund.

Zhou, M. (2000) 'Social Capital in Chinatown: The Role of Community-Based Organisations and Families in Adaptation of the Younger Generation', in M. Zhou and James V. Gatewood, eds. *Contemporary Asian America: A Multidisciplinary Reader*. New York: New York University Press, pp. 315–335.

Zhou, M. (2005) 'Ethnicity as Social Capital: Community-Based Institutions and Embedded Networks of Social Relations', in G. Loury, T. Modood and S. Teles, eds. *Ethnicity, Social Mobility and Public Policy: Comparing USA and UK*. Cambridge: Cambridge University Press, pp. 131–159.

Zhou, M. and Bankston, C.L. III (1994) 'Social Capital and the Adaptation of the Second-Generation: The Vietnamese Youth in New Orleans', *International Migration Review*, 28(4): 821–845.

10
Feeling and Being Muslim and British

Varun Uberoi, Nasar Meer, Tariq Modood and Claire Dwyer

1. Introduction

Great Britain was created through the 1707 Act of Union.[1] Few shared a notion of 'being British' at the time; but by the end of the Napoleonic Wars the British increasingly defined themselves against the French and through their belief in Protestantism and free political institutions (Colley, 1996: 58). Expanding empire and industrialisation enabled them to also see themselves as internationally powerful and economically dynamic (Davies, 1999: 876). But the Empire dwindled as did Britain's economic prowess. Protestantism became less salient and it was difficult for the British to see themselves as they once had. Familiar aspects of Britain began to disappear and unfamiliar ones emerged. Large numbers of racially and culturally distinct immigrants arrived and settled, Britain joined the European Economic Community and calls for the 'Break up of Britain' emerged (Nairn, 1977). Politicians, scholars and commentators began to discuss the nature and future of British nationhood and by the 1980s and early 1990s, these discussions were increasingly nuanced (Plamenatz, 1974; Swann, 1985; Gilroy, 1987; Powell, 1991; Miller, 1995). After devolution, it became clear that for some, their English, Scots and Welsh identities were more important than their British ones and this intensified these discussions (Curtis and Heath, 2000; Bechhofer and McCrone, 2007).

Yet current debates about Britishness are not restricted to national minorities and have instead come to focus on ethnic minorities. One influential articulation of British national identity in governmental policy and discourse, frequently discussed in the press, has sought its reinvigoration through the promotion of common civic values, as well as English language competencies; a wider knowledge of – and self-identification with – cultural, historical and institutional heritages, in addition to approved kinds of political engagement and activity (Meer and Modood, 2009). This may be cast as a sort of British civic national identity that remains embedded, as the Commission on the future of Multi-Ethnic Britain (CMEB) (2000) described, in particular cultural values and traditions that involve not only a rational allegiance to the state, but also intuitive, emotional, symbolic allegiances to a historic nation, even while the idea of the nation is contested and re-imagined.

This is not of course unique to British versions of civic nationalism. As Viet Bader (2005: 169) reminds us: 'all civic and democratic cultures are inevitably embedded into specific ethno-national and religious histories.' Were we to assess the normative premise of this view, however, we would inevitably encounter a dense literature elaborating the continuing disputes over the interactions between the civic, political and ethnic dimensions in the creation of nations, national identities and their relationship to each other and to non-rational 'intuitive' and 'emotional' pulls of ancestries and cultures and so forth. Chief amongst these is whether or not 'nations' are social and political formations developed in the proliferation of modern nation-states from the eighteenth century onwards, or whether they constitute social and political formations – or 'ethnies' – bearing an older pedigree that may be obscured by a modernist focus. What is most relevant to our discussion, however, is not the debate between different camps of 'modernist', 'ethno-symbolist' and 'primordialist' protagonists, amongst others, but the ways in which Muslims are conceived and portrayed in contemporary debates about Britishness.[2]

It is perhaps telling, however, that much of the literature on national identity in particular has tended to be retrospective to the extent that such contemporary concerns do not enjoy a widespread appeal in scholarly accounts of national identity (while the opposite could be said to be true of the literature on citizenship). This tendency is not limited to academic arenas and one of the curiosities in popular articulations of national identity is the purchase that these accounts garner from a recourse to tradition, history and the idea of a common past (Calhoun, 1994). One implication is that national identities can frequently reflect desires to authenticate the past, 'to select from all that has gone before that which is distinctive, "truly ours", and thereby to mark out a unique, shared destiny' (Smith, 1998: 43).

It was this very assessment which, at the turn of the millennium, informed the CMEB's characterisation of British national identity as potentially 'based on generalisations [that] involve a selective and simplified account of a complex history'. One in which '[m]any complicated strands are reduced to a simple tale of essential and enduring national unity' (cmmd 2.9, p. 16). Precisely this tendency informed the CMEB's alarm at how invocations of national identity potentially force ethnic minorities into a predicament not of their making: one in which majorities are conflated with the nation and where national identity is promoted as a reflection of this state of affairs (because national identities are assumed to be cognates of monistic nations). For in not easily fitting into a majoritarian account of national identity, or either being unable or unwilling to be reduced to or assimilated into a prescribed public culture, minority 'differences' may therefore become variously negatively conceived.

Britain has faced its own particular challenges in addressing issues of disadvantage tied to cultural difference experienced by a variety of ethnic and religious minorities. The most substantive response developed cumulatively during the final quarter of the last century and comprised a range of policies and discourses commonly known as multiculturalism. This has sought to engender equality of access and accommodate aspects of minority difference while promoting the social and moral benefits of ethnic minority related diversity in an inclusive sense of civic belonging (Modood, 2005; Meer and Modood, 2009). Indeed, at a public policy level Britain rejected the idea of integration being based upon a drive for unity through an uncompromising cultural 'assimilation', over 40 years ago, when the then Labour Home Secretary Roy Jenkins (1966) defined integration as 'not a flattening process of assimilation but equal opportunity accompanied by cultural diversity in an atmosphere of mutual tolerance'.

This has neither been a linear nor stable development and has frequently been subject to criticism not only from a variety of camps which – for different reasons – militantly resisted and opposed it, but also from those who 'accept[ed] multicultural drift grudgingly as a fact of life, regretting the passing of the good old days when, they believe, Britain was a much more unified, predictable sort of place' (CMEB, cmmd 2.2, p. 14). As the CMEB insisted:

> Britishness, as much as Englishness, has systematic, largely unspoken, racial connotations. (cmmd 3.30 p. 19).... Britain confronts a historic choice as to its future direction. Will it try to turn the clock back, digging in, defending old values and ancient hierarchies, relying on a *narrow English-dominated,* backward looking definition of the nation? (cmmd 2.3, pp. 13–14, emphasis added)

Seemingly misreading this and other passages, many in the media suggested that the report was anti-British and/or unappreciative of how contemporary Britishness was already inclusive of minorities (McLaughlin and Neal, 2004). But this does not detract from the fact that national identities usually reflect the culture of the majority and few scholars would deny this (Smith, 1988; Uberoi, 2007). British national identity is no exception, hence in the above passage, and elsewhere, the report suggested that 'many complicated strands' of British history are ignored. Those emphasised are usually taken mostly from the English majority who are privileged because they are dominant and it is difficult to justify why this dominance should continue. Excluding all minorities, national and ethnic, because they are seen as different not only encourages discrimination. It also increases pressure on those who are culturally distinct to assimilate and their loyalty may be questioned for not doing so (Modood, 1992). The CMEB thus suggested that Britishness must be re-imagined in a 'multicultural way' and shorn of its exclusionary elements (CMEB, 2000: 36–38).

Indeed, today whilst some on the far right still want cultural minorities to jettison all of their cultural particularities and assimilate, these are no longer desires that most, or even many, hold (Mason, 2010). But the loyalty of minorities and in particular Muslims to Britain is questioned by a great many (Gallup, 2009: 20). This may partly be due to irrational fears following 9/11 and 7/7 but, as Parekh (2008: 103) points out, fear in the West of the 'undemocratic nature' of Muslims and questions about their loyalty, predate the 'war on terror'. They stretch as far back as the toppling of the Shah of Iran and hinge in part on a belief that Muslims are loyal to the *ummah*, not the nation-state. But regardless of these and other reasons, fear of the loyalty of British Muslims seems unwarranted when the available evidence suggests that most Muslims have little difficulty identifying with Britain and feeling British. Using the 2005 Citizenship survey, Heath and Roberts (2008: 14) show that 43 per cent of Muslim respondents claim that they 'very strongly' belong to Britain and 42 per cent say that they belong 'fairly strongly'. These figures are corroborated both by earlier data, and reputable later surveys which suggest that British Muslims identify more strongly with Britain than the British public at large (Modood et al., 1997; Gallup, 2009). Nonetheless, we will show that leading politicians and journalists fail, at times, to recognise how the vast majority of Muslims identify with Britain. Instead, some Muslims are often conceived and portrayed as having difficulty *feeling* and *being* British, but what do we mean by this?

Parekh's recent work is helpful here because he suggests that when we talk about 'national identity' we often do so in an objective or a subjective sense (Parekh, 2008: 56). Objectively, one might refer to the identity of a political community; the history, the traditions, the values and the people that make it this political community and not another one. Subjectively, a national identity can be one of many identities that a person has and exhibits when they say things like they are 'British', 'French' or 'German'. When referring to those who discuss the ability of Muslims to *feel* British, we are interested in the subjective sense of national identity. Indeed, this interest highlights how a subjective sense of national identity also has an inter-subjective element because, as we will show, regardless of whether Muslims feel British, it is a subject of debate amongst others as to whether they do so. This inter-subjective element is also crucial when we are talking about those who describe the ability of Muslims to '*be* British'. This is because we will also show how some are deciding what it means to be British and suggesting that some Muslims cannot be placed in this category. But in doing so, it is not a subjective sense of national identity that is being invoked, but an objective one. Muslims are measured against the people, the values, the traditions and the history that makes Britain this community and not another one. These are the things that are thought to define 'the British' and Muslims are judged to either meet these criteria or not. When the ability of Muslims to 'feel British' is discussed, a subjective understanding of national identity is used, but when discussing their ability to 'be British', an objective understanding is used.

Feeling and being British are something that we will show leading politicians and journalists think and suggest are difficult for some Muslims, and the data to suggest this was gathered through a project entitled 'Religion, Citizenship and National Identity'. Aware that public debates about Muslims often featured discussions about Britishness and vice versa, we in part wanted to discern how those who contributed to these debates saw the relationship between Muslims and Britishness. So we examined the contributions of leading politicians and journalists who intervene in these debates and we interviewed some of them as well. Indeed, in light of the statistics cited earlier one might expect to see one of two things. First, there to be little or no mention of the ability of Muslims to feel and be British as their ability to do both is clear, or we might expect a willingness amongst *responsible* politicians and journalists to counter popular perceptions by suggesting that Muslims have little difficulty feeling and being British – instead we found the reverse. This is problematic because even theorists who disagree with one another suggest that politicians who control the state help through institutions like the public education system and the media to shape people's subjective sense of national identity (Gellner, 1983: 57; Smith, 1991: 100). Likewise, journalists on national newspapers like those we will cite have the power to convey information about, as well as an image of, the nation that many internalise and thus they too shape people's subjective sense of national identity (Anderson, 1983).

Between them, if leading politicians and journalists suggest that some Muslims have difficulty feeling and being British, it will be unsurprising if they are seen as outsiders in Britain. But a willingness by leading politicians and journalists to make such suggestions is also indicative of something else: that current debates about Britishness are not only, as many have written, about devolution, Britain's place in Europe, reconciling immigration and globalisation and the white working-class feeling like they no longer belong (Aughey, 2001; McLean and McMillan, 2005; Fenton, 2007; Hazell, 2008). If leading politicians and journalists suggest that Muslims have difficulty feeling and being British, then debates about Britishness are also about questioning whether Muslims feel attached to Britain as well as whether they have a place in it. Indeed to illustrate the former in the next section of this chapter we show how leading politicians in both the Labour and Conservative Parties conceive of and portray the ability of Muslims to *feel British*. Then to illustrate the latter we show how journalists portray the ability of Muslims to *be British* after which, we conclude.

2. Feeling British

In this section we examine how senior Labour and Conservative Party politicians conceptualise and portray the ability of Muslims to feel British and whilst we refer to a small amount of our interview data here, we managed to interview six members of the then government and four members of the then shadow cabinet for this part of the project. All interviewees had some ministerial or shadow cabinet responsibility for the policy area of community cohesion which since its introduction in 2001 has been intimately tied with issues relating to Muslims and Britishness (McGhee, 2003: 377; Brighton, 2007: 11; Dwyer and Uberoi, 2009). Indeed, this policy area was initially created to help prevent disturbances like those in 2001 in which young Muslims participated and the reports into these disturbances recommended a debate on 'the common elements of nationhood' (Home Office, 2001: 19). This seemed to suggest that those Muslims who participated in the riots had difficulty feeling British and this suggestion was supported by the then Home Secretary, David Blunkett, praising the reports for facing 'head on' how 'people in the Asian community help the second and third generation feel British...' (*Independent*, 9 December 2001). From its inception then, the policy area of community cohesion has been closely linked to issues of Muslims and Britishness and it is thus reasonable to explore how those politicians who are responsible for it conceptualise the ability of Muslims to feel British.

This was done by interviewing politicians like David Blunkett who believed that some Muslims had difficulty feeling British. For sure, he claimed, 'you can be first generation Pakistani and British...' (Interview with David Blunkett, 11 March 2008). But when asked which immigrant groups might have difficulty feeling British he said, 'I think there's a lip service to Britishness and the issue is if we get under the surface, do people really mean it, do they feel it?' He adds:

> you see Pakistani covers a lot of different backgrounds, Pashtun and all the rest of it, and so it's difficult and they don't always agree with each other. So I always have to find out who the community leaders are [laughs]...I think they would, I think all those groups would pay a lip service to being British.... (ibid.)

Unsure about whether *many* Pakistanis pay lip service to Britishness, Blunkett states: 'I don't have any authentic statistics on it, I don't have anything that is not just pure anecdote...' (ibid.). Indeed, here it is important to note that Blunkett was the Home Secretary who set up the Home Office Citizenship Survey which, inter alia, yielded the figures cited earlier. In establishing this survey, Blunkett reflected the turn towards 'evidence based policy' and the prevailing 'mood' in government of 'management by numbers' (Hood, 2010: 7–8). It is thus difficult to understand why despite requesting data on Muslims and despite a mood in government that favoured using it, Blunkett relies on anecdotal information. One possible reason that Blunkett felt he didn't have any '*authentic* statistics' on whether Muslims feel British is that may be for him, survey data on Muslims feeling British reflects the lip service that he thinks some are willing to pay to it.

But Blunkett does offer some explanation of why he holds these views: 'I just feel that the more economically successful people are, the more they actually coalesce and the more they feel they're committed to, this is just statistically the case...' (Interview with David Blunkett, 11 March 2008). Here Blunkett is aware of statistical evidence and whilst we are unclear about what evidence he is referring to, his comments on the subject of integration provide some additional insight:

> The Hindu community have managed not to be the focal point of bitterness and hatred...because there's a very much larger middle class, and wherever you have a larger middle class...then integration, social cohesion go hand in hand.... And therefore the answer to your question is those areas of inward migration, where people have been struggling at the very bottom end of the economic ladder, that obviously means Bangladeshi and to some extent Pakistani communities, although that is changing.... (ibid.)

Blunkett thus seems to think that some Muslims can have difficulty feeling British because some of those who are from Pakistan and Bangladesh are 'at the very bottom of the economic ladder' and he believes that there is a relationship between feeling British, integration and being economically successful.

As two of us have shown elsewhere, Blunkett's views were not necessarily shared by junior ministers who worked for and with him (Uberoi and Modood, 2010). But they are reflected in his public statements, no systematic and contextually driven analysis of which can be performed here. Nonetheless in 2003 Blunkett did claim, 'there will always be those...encouraging their followers to define their faith and their identity in opposition to outsiders rather than in positive terms.... It is a worrying trend that young second generation British Muslims are more likely than their parents to feel they have to *choose* between feeling part of the UK and feeling part of their faith...'. Blunkett thus suggests that a growing number of young Muslims feel that they have to choose between feeling Muslim and feeling British and similar claims were made by other leading government politicians. When Ruth Kelly was Secretary of State for Local Government and Communities and Liam Byrne was Minister of State for Immigration, they said in a Fabian pamphlet that 'there is a particular issue with a minority of second and third generation Muslims' ability to feel British' (Byrne and Kelly, 2007: 25). There are thus some senior Labour Party politicians who think that some Muslims have difficulty feeling British and, perhaps partly for this reason, they also portray young Muslims that way in their public statements. However, rather like the claims about Muslims in general, claims about the ability of *young* Muslims to feel British are at odds with the available evidence. In the Home Office's 2005 Citizenship Survey, Heath and Roberts (2008) show that 38 per cent of Muslim respondents aged 16–24 said that they belonged to Britain 'very strongly' and 45 per cent in the same age group say that they belong to Britain 'fairly strongly'. Indeed, the last figure is higher for Muslim respondents in this age group than it is for Christian respondents and those categorised as being of 'no religion'.[3] Regardless of such data, the willingness to portray young Muslims as having difficulty feeling British extends beyond members of the then government to those running public bodies that are accountable to it. Hence former head of the Commission for Racial Equality, Trevor Phillips, thought it necessary to tell young Muslims 'that they are British again and again and again' (*Times*, 3 April 2004).

Something similar is true about leading Conservative Party politicians. Hence we asked the current Security Minister, Pauline Neville-Jones, who in 2007 published a report on community cohesion, whether any particular 'types of people' might have difficulty feeling British. She answered, 'That's a very good question, and a kind of important question, actually. Umm, urr, what I'm about to say is not based on either work we've done or, or stuff I've read' (Interview with Pauline Neville-Jones, 17 October 2007). Without referring to studies on the subject she thought that there could be 'quite a lot of people who don't feel particularly British' and thus did not focus exclusively on Muslims. However, when asked whether some Muslims might have difficulty feeling British, Neville-Jones answered, 'yep' (ibid). Whilst this view and the rationale for it that we will describe below was not shared by all of Neville-Jones's colleagues, it was shared by former community cohesion spokesman and current Attorney General, Dominic Grieve. He also seemed unaware of studies about whether any group might have difficulty feeling British and whilst thinking that non-Muslims might also do so, he suggested that Muslims might have difficulty both being and feeling British. Hence with regard to the former he claimed:

> If looked at bluntly, I keep on meeting very pleasant people, not just Muslims, sometimes from other religious groups but I have to say principally Muslims, who seem to me to have views, and I have listened carefully to what they've got to say, which are certainly incompatible with development in our national and historical tradition. (Interview with Dominic Grieve, 18 September 2007)

In relation to Muslims feeling British, he claimed:

> It is true there are only a tiny number of people who want to blow themselves up on the underground killing people for the sake of their view of what the world should be like. But equally it seems to me that whilst there are large numbers of Muslims living in Britain who have very little difficulty reconciling their religious views with the advantages of living in a pluralist democratic society, there are actually quite a large number of them who, whilst they might be quite grateful for the fact that they are living in a pluralist society rather than being persecuted somewhere else, *actually want to live in a society that is very different*.... (ibid.)

'Large numbers' of peaceful Muslims are then glad to live in Britain and benefit from doing so, but they allegedly wish Britain to be a very different society and this stops them identifying with it. He thus suggests that aspects of what we described earlier as Britain's objective sense of national identity inhibit a subjective sense of national identity amongst some Muslims. Likewise, Neville-Jones referred to 'aspects of modern western British secular society' that 'are particularly unattractive. The violence, the lawlessness, the drunkenness, the, um, the vulgarity', these are all things that no 'sane person would actually want to join' (Interview with Pauline Neville-Jones,17 October 2007).

It is aspects of Britain's national identity in the objective sense that are thought to inhibit a subjective sense of national identity, but for Neville-Jones, another issue is also salient. When asked if some Muslims can have difficulty feeling British because of their socio-economic plight, religious reasons, perhaps something else, Neville-Jones said, 'I think it is a mistake to think that these things are purely associated with poverty', it was more about:

> whether you want to remain in the community, whether you want to get out of it, and how easy it is if you chance it, how easy it is to chance it into something else. And whether... your own... community accepts that. It's those things... which are... the issues that urr Muslims themselves need to confront.... And where they're entitled to help from the rest of society, and so – and the rest of society should create a framework in which everybody wants to feel part.

Here Neville-Jones seems to be suggesting that some Muslims are vulnerable to not feeling both British and rooted in the Muslim community. She is not advocating assimilation because she is suggesting that in order to encourage Muslims to become involved in the wider community, 'society should create a framework' of which Muslims want to feel part. Neville-Jones is thus suggesting that it is not only Muslims who need to change, British society must also do so.

Grieve and Neville-Jones thus seemingly think that some Muslims have difficulty feeling British, but for reasons that differ to Blunkett. They believe that some Muslims wish Britain to be more Islamic and less vulgar and this inhibits their ability to feel British as does a difficulty leaving their own communities. However, this has little to do with economic difficulties. Hence, at the launch of a report Neville-Jones authored called *An Unquiet World*, she stated that the challenge 'is not how you try to indigenise Islam ... which is important, but how you give British Muslims in this country the feeling that actually they are Brits, like any other British' (Conservative Party, 2007: 9). Some of her other colleagues make statements that suggest that most Muslims have no such difficulty (Warsi, undated: 2). But there are others who make claims that point in a similar direction to Neville-Jones, for example, Michael Gove. He claims, 'A rising generation has been encouraged by those Muslims most prominent in public life to put their Islamic identity ahead of their citizenship' (Gove, 2006: 106). If prominent Muslims are trying to make people's Islamic identities more significant than their British citizenship, then a conflict is portrayed between feeling Muslim and feeling British. David Cameron affirmed the ability of many Muslims to feel British but also suggested that it is problematic that some do not. In a speech at Cambridge University he claimed, 'the vast majority of families of recent immigrant origin do feel a strong sense of citizenship and what it is to be British. Indeed, my time in Birmingham ... showed that if we want to remind ourselves of British values ... there are plenty of British Muslims ready to show us what those things really mean. *The problem is some do not*' (Cameron, 2007: 7, emphasis added).

There are then leading politicians in both parties who believe that some Muslims have difficulty feeling British and they and their colleagues portray Muslims as such in their public statements. In the next section we will show that leading journalists also make a problematic link between Muslims and Britishness, but in slightly different way, by portraying the inability of Muslims to be British.

3. Being British

This apparent inability of Muslims to be British was articulated in the newspaper coverage that followed Jack Straw's controversial comments in 2006 about Muslim women who choose to wear the *niqab* (a face veil). In his weekly column in the *Lancashire Telegraph* (5 October 2006) Straw described how he asks Muslim women wearing the niqab to remove them when meeting him in his Blackburn constituency office for two reasons. First, he suggested that the removal of the face veil enables him to engage more effectively in a 'face-to-face' dialogue. He is more able to 'see what the other person means and not just hear what they say'. He then moved from a focus on the interpersonal to the societal, by describing face veils as 'a visible statement of separation and difference' that made 'better, positive relations between the two communities more difficult'.[4] He continued:

> It was not the first time I had conducted an interview with someone in a full veil, but this particular encounter, though very polite and respectful on both sides, got me thinking. In part, this was because of the apparent incongruity between the signals which indicate common bonds – the entirely English accent, the couple's education (wholly in the UK) – and the fact of the veil. Above all, it was because I felt uncomfortable about talking to someone 'face-to-face' who I could not see. (ibid.)

Straw has recently apologised for the 'problems' that such claims caused Muslims (*Daily Mail*, 27 April 2010) and as the above quote suggests, for Straw the veil, unlike other attributes of his interlocutors, is not 'wholly in the UK'. The niqab emphasises something other than the bonds that its wearer shares with other British citizens. More comfortable with the tradition of face to face conversation, the idea that those Muslims wearing the veil are antithetical to that tradition is obvious in Straw's claims. Reacting to the latter, leading journalists began to portray some Muslims as unable to be British and this section describes how they did so.[5]

Starting with the most widely read middle-market national newspaper, the *Daily Mail*, a publication that is widely recognised for focusing its coverage on controversial matters of ethnic minority difference, its leaders and editorials would frequently frame their discussion by juxtaposing British national identity with Muslim separatism (facilitated by multiculturalism), and the following extract provides a good illustration of how Muslims and national identity were often cast as mutually exclusive:

> [T]his Government has actively promoted multiculturalism, encouraged Muslim 'ghettoes' and set its face against greater integration. Anyone who dared to question this new apartheid was routinely denounced as a 'racist'. Britishness? Who cares? For New Labour yes, including Mr Straw, it became an article of faith for the ethnic minorities to celebrate their own languages, culture and traditions, at the expense of shared values. There could hardly be a more effective recipe for division. Is it really surprising... if they [Muslims] see Mr Straw's views on the veil as a juddering reversal of all that has gone before? (*Daily Mail*, 7 October 2005)

Several important ideas intermingle in this passage, but clearly Britishness is portrayed as the opposite to a government sponsored multiculturalism that encourages people to celebrate their differences. The latter has allegedly created a type of 'apartheid', especially amongst Muslims who were permitted, if not encouraged, to celebrate their differences under multiculturalism. Seen as a corollary of multiculturalism, Muslim difference is also juxtaposed with Britishness which occupies similar ideational space to shared values and integration. Like multiculturalism then, Muslim difference is conceived as a competitor to Britishness, but the latter is also seen as something that has been missing, something that can rectify the problems that multiculturalism has allegedly created, including 'Muslim ghettoes'. Seen as an opposite to multiculturalism and Muslim difference as well as a cure for their effects, Britishness is portrayed as antithetical to Muslims.

This position was supported by the newspaper's prominent columnists, amongst whom Alison Pearson articulated how she and other women feel a sense of ownership of Britain that is disturbed by those women wearing the niqab:

> It's not a nice sensation – to feel judged for wearing your own clothes in your own country. The truth is that females who cover their faces and bodies make us uneasy. The veil is often downright intimidating.... I just don't like seeing them on British streets. Nor do I want to see another newspaper provide, as it did this week, a cut-out-and-keep fashion guide to the different types of veil: 'Here we see Mumtaz, or rather we don't see Mumtaz because the poor kid is wearing a nosebag over her face, modelling the latest female-inhibiting shrouds from the House of Taliban.' (Pearson, 2006)

Again there is more at work here than national identity. In particular, there are clear intersections with gender and the discourse on female submission which belies the contested nature of what veiling signifies (Dwyer, 2008). But it is worth noting how similar Pearson's logic is to someone saying that they do not want to be 'judged' or 'intimidated' in their own home. Hence for Pearson, the 'country' belongs to those women who are willing *not* to cover their faces and bodies. Those who do the opposite are thus in some sense aliens, regardless of the fact that they may also be citizens. Adhering to alien traditions, they have the impudence to make those women who do not want to cover their faces and bodies uneasy in 'their own country', thus suggesting that this is not the country of those who want to wear face veils which being a garment from the 'House of Taliban' has no place on 'British streets'.

Perhaps surprisingly, journalists at the *Daily Telegraph*, in comparison, adopted a far more nuanced position with regards to the niqab. Hence Charles Moore (2006) did not endorse the idea of the veil as a symbol of oppression. Indeed, he noted how discussions about it amongst Muslims in Britain can at times signify autonomy. Hence Moore not only noted 'a struggle for control of Islam in this country, and for its political exploitation', he also continued:

> There is an attempt to 'arabise' Muslims from the Indian sub-continent, persuading them to wear clothes that are alien to their culture to show their religious zeal.... *For a few Muslim girls in this country, wearing the veil is a form of oppression imposed by their families; for more, it is a form of teenage rebellion, of showing more commitment than their parents* – a religious version of wearing a hoodie. (7 October 2006, emphasis added)

Likewise, there *seemed* to be a conscious attempt to de-couple criticism of the niqab for being 'different' (or 'exotic'), from it being 'unsettling' to others because it conceals the face. Again Moore is instructive, 'many non-Muslims find these veils a little unsettling... not because they are an exotic import to these shores... but because they conceal the face' (ibid.). Nonetheless Moore repeated a juxtaposition between British national traditions and the wearing of 'the veil' as 'a hostile statement about the society in which the wearer lives' (ibid.), and in so doing simultaneously portrayed Muslims who wear the niqab as being hostile to Britain and thus being unwilling to behave like other British people.

The Times columnist Janice Turner (2006) too described Straw's comments as 'no more than a quid pro quo' since 'we are as a culture deeply uneasy if we cannot see the faces of those we talk to' (*The Times*, 7 October 2006). This was supported by Simon Jenkins (2006) of the *Sun*day *Times* who cast the niqab as 'an assertion of cultural separateness' since 'to a westerner such conversation is rude. If Muslim women, and it is a tiny number, cannot understand this, it is reasonable to ask why they want to live in Britain' (*Sunday Times*, 8 October 2006). The first comment has an imperious tone and suggests that Turner speaks for a great many others. Indeed, she suggests that 'we' are a cultural group that are uneasy with those whose faces we cannot see and thus those who wear the niqab are not only people who 'we' are uncomfortable with, they are also not part of *our* cultural group. Not asking whether such cultural groups *should* request non-members to dress differently and why non-members should be unable to do likewise, Turner also suggests that such requests are merely a 'quid, pro, quo'. In doing so she conjures the notion of ungrateful outsiders who have been allowed to live amongst the cultural group but are unwilling to do what is necessary to enable others to accept their presence, and the second comment goes further. Unlike his colleague, Jenkins feels able to speak simultaneously for both those wearing the niqab and those not doing so. Hence, despite the fact that those who wear the niqab do so to facilitate public interaction across gender and thus also, at times, across culture, Jenkins says that the niqab is an assertion of cultural separateness. Then on behalf of those *not* wearing the niqab he says that they perceive those wearing it when in conversation as being 'rude', and any attempt to see this differently suggests an unwillingness to live in Britain, a corollary of which is not wanting to be British. Indeed, being British is thus portrayed not as it is, as something that is constructed and reconstructed over time and in different ways to suit new situations, but in a 'take it or leave it' way (Miller, 1995; Modood, 2007; Uberoi, 2008; Parekh, 2009). The *Sun*'s Martel Maxwell (2006) exemplifies this:

> [W]hat about championing British values? It's a question the nation is asking after Jack Straw's comments on Muslims covering their faces with veils. Yes, we can still be accepting of other beliefs. But it's time to put our own first and expect newcomers to respect us before being granted the same privilege. (*Sun*, 11 October 2006)

Maxwell thus sees Straw's comments as sparking a broader debate in which the nation's values are seen as having been ignored for too long, the beliefs of others can be accepted and thus also the beliefs perhaps of those Muslims who wear the niqab. But crucially, before the beliefs of others can be accepted, they must respect the beliefs of the nation. The nation's beliefs come first and reportage from the *Daily Mail*, *Daily Telegraph* and *The Times* suggest, albeit in different ways, that those Muslims who wear the niqab are not part of it. But what about more 'difference friendly' newspapers like the *Independent*?

With a reputation for balanced discussion, in which it is less predictable whether British national identity and examples of Muslim 'difference' will be cast as mutually exclusive, it is an interesting paper to examine. Indeed, in one leader entitled: 'Mr Straw Has Raised a Valid Issue, But Reached the Wrong Conclusion', it maintained that 'it [the niqab] is not the wearing of the headscarf.... Unlike in France, where the wearing of headscarves at school became a highly contentious political issue, the attitude to headscarves in Britain has been wisely liberal, which has kept the subject largely out of the political domain' (*Independent*, 7 October 2006). While another leader went as far as to contrast what it deemed as the negative contemporary press coverage of Muslims with that experienced by other groups in earlier periods:

> The shameful aspect is that we are repeating our mistakes, in standing by while certain ethnic or religious minorities – in this case, Muslims – are demonised. Britain may be seen abroad as having managed the transition to a multicultural society more successfully than some, but as a nation we have not overcome the tendency to suspect, even fear, 'the other'. (*Independent*, 6 October 2006)

This charge against a British national tendency to frame itself against a minority other rehearses some of the concerns by the CMEB mentioned earlier and makes the interesting distinction between national reality and international reputation. But as with the *Daily Telegraph*, these *Independent* editorials and leaders are particularly striking when contrasted with the ways in which its leading columnists use national identity to condemn those who wear the niqab and sometimes also the *hijab*. This included Richard Ingram (2006), Jemmima Lewis (2006), Deborah Orr (2006) and Joan Smith (2006). Most notably, it also included Yasmin Alibhai-Brown (2006); one of only two or three Muslim columnists in the national press, who stated:

> [W]hen does this country decide that it does not want citizens using their freedoms to build a satellite Saudi Arabia here? .... It [niqab] rejects human commonalities and even the membership of society itself .... It is hard to be a Muslim today. And it becomes harder still when some choose deliberately to act and dress as aliens. (Independent, 9 October 2006)

Wearers of the niqab are thus not only portrayed as those who deliberately reject British, or at the very least Western, society, they are also those who act and dress as aliens abusing their freedoms to make Britain more like Saudi Arabia. As the 'country' is asked to decide whether to accept the latter, the country does not include Muslims who wear the niqab, but Alibhai-Brown goes further. She assumes that the compatibility between being Muslim and not being an alien should be emphasised in a climate where it is difficult to be a Muslim in Britain, but those wearing the niqab do the reverse. They apparently illustrate how being a Muslim can at times involve being an alien in Britain and thus she accepts the proposition that being Muslim and British can, at times, conflict. This was nicely illustrated by the *Sunday Telegraph* columnist Patience Wheatcroft (2006) who characterised the niqab as

> [A] barrier that limits the creation of relationships. It unites those who nestle behind such garments and makes it harder for them to integrate .... It may be that there are many Muslims who choose to wear the veil but also want to play a full role in British society. They should realise that they are making that more difficult because of the uniform they choose to wear. (Sunday Telegraph, 8 October 2006)

Perhaps being less obvious than the politicians that we cited earlier, journalists working on papers that are traditionally thought to span the political spectrum are portraying some Muslims as having difficulty being British.

4. Conclusion

In this chapter we have shown that leading politicians and journalists conceive and portray some Muslims as having difficulty feeling and being British which supports a recent claim by Bhikhu Parekh that 'it is widely believed in many *influential circles* in Western Europe that its more than fifteen million Muslims pose a serious cultural and political threat.' This belief 'cuts across ideological and political divides and is shared, albeit in different degrees and for different reasons by right wing nationalists, conservatives, liberals and socialists' (Parekh, 2009: 51, emphasis added). If 'influential circles' in Britain conceive and portray some Muslims as having difficulty feeling and being British, they are conceived and portrayed as outsiders and it is not difficult to see how they can also be seen as a cultural and political threat. But the suggestion that Muslims have such difficulties also suggests that current debates about Britishness, whilst also focusing on other issues, are also about the attachments of Muslims to Britain as well as their place in it. But what precisely is at stake if some Muslims are conceived and portrayed as having difficulty feeling and being British?

With regards to the former, clearly politicians conceive of and are promoting an untruth about British Muslims: that they have difficulty feeling and being British. Indeed, as said, with statistical data being available since the 1990s to disprove this untruth as well as, as we described earlier, an inclination to use such data, it is hard to avoid the conclusion that some of these politicians should know better. More significant perhaps are the rationales for the beliefs of politicians. Blunkett's reasons were economic and whilst we certainly wouldn't want to deny that poverty may cultivate a sense of exclusion, it is important to note that such poverty is also experienced by certain white communities, but they are not typically thought to have any difficulty feeling British. Equally, for Neville-Jones and Grieve, some Muslims have difficulty feeling British because they want Britain to be more Islamic, less vulgar and they have difficulty leaving their own communities. All of these are empirical claims and we know of no empirical studies that support them, but given the high percentage of Muslims who feel British, even if true, these claims can only apply to a very small percentage of Muslims.

Turning to those minorities who are thought to have difficulty being British, an understanding of what it means to be British is being projected by senior journalists and it does not include certain Muslims. At times, those Muslims not included are just those wearing the niqab; at other times, other Muslims are excluded as well and it is difficult to know why leading journalists reach for such exclusive understandings of the nation. Indeed, we cited earlier that the CMEB outlined how such exclusive understandings of the nation are inaccurate, reflect a selective reading of British history and a privileging of the majority that is difficult to justify. More inclusive understanding of what it means to be British are available and indeed two of the authors of this chapter have separately suggested the need to accept them (Modood, 1992; Uberoi, 2007). But doing so would entail a willingness amongst journalists to accept a more inclusive form of Britishness, as a result of which 'space for Muslims' in the nation will be created (Modood, 2008). It is unclear whether journalists will accept either the former or the latter; certainly when the CMEB suggested recasting the national story, the media's reaction was hostile. But despite questions about both their attachment to and their ability to be a part of Britain, it is notable that the vast majority of Muslims still feel British. This not only suggests that the dangers of a self-fulfilling prophecy are remote, but also that even if others cannot envisage a conception of the nation that includes Muslims, Muslims can (Meer, 2010).

Notes

1. This chapter draws upon Meer, Dwyer and Modood (2010) and Uberoi and Modood (2010).
2. Though this concern perhaps relies on something from the cultural-imaginary form of 'modernist' argument most associated with Anderson (1983). Moreover, for a study of how this is happening in non-political urban contexts, see Kyriakides, Virdee and Modood (2009).
3. Indeed, Heath and Roberts data suggest that whilst young Muslims are less likely to say that they belong strongly to Britain than both young Christians and young people of no faith, young Muslims are more likely than their contemporaries in these groups to say that they belong fairly strongly to Britain (Heath and Roberts, 2008: 17).
4. It is also worth noting that throughout the article and subsequent interviews, Straw continually distinguished between the full face veil or *niqab*, and other types of Muslim coverings such as the headscarf or *hijab*.
5. For a discussion of methodology in this analysis, see Meer, Dwyer and Modood (2010).

References

Alibha-Brown, Y. (2006) 'We Don't Yet Live in an Islamic Republic, So I Will Say It – I Find the Veil Offensive', *Independent*, 9 October. Retrieved via *LexisNexis*.

Anderson, B. (1983) *Imagined Communities*. London: Verso.

Aughey, A. (2001) *Nationalism, Devolution and the Challenge to the United Kingdom*. London: Pluto Press.

Bader, V. (2005) 'Ethnic and Religious State Neutrality: Utopia or Myth', in H.G. Sicakkan and Y. Lithman, eds. *Changing the Basis of Citizenship in the Modern State*. Lewiston: The Edwin Mellen Press.

Bechhofer, F. and McCrone, D. (2007) 'Being British: A Crisis of Identity', *Political Quarterly*, 78(2), 251–260.

Blunkett, D. (2008) Interviewed by Varun Uberoi, 11 March.

Boycott, R. (2006) 'Does Wearing the Veil REALLY Oppress Women?', *Daily Mail*, 14 October. Retrieved via *LexisNexis*.

Brighton, S. (2007) 'British Muslims, Multiculturalism and UK Foreign Policy: "Integration" and "Cohesion" In and Beyond the State', *International Affairs*, 83: 1–17.

Bunting, M. (2006) 'Jack Straw has Unleashed a Storm of Prejudice and Intensified Division', *Guardian*, 9 October. Retrieved via *LexisNexis*.

Byrne, L. and Kelly, R. (2007) *A Common Place*. London: Fabian Society.

Calhoun, C., ed. (1994) *Social Theory and Politics of Identity*. Oxford: Blackwell Publishers.

Cameron, D. (2007) 'Islam and Muslims in the World Today', Conservative Party Press Release, 5 June.

Colley, L. (1996) *Britons*. London: Vintage Books.

Commission on the Future of Multi-Ethnic Britain (CMEB) (2000) *The Future of Multi-Ethnic Britain*. London: Profile Books.
Conservative Party National and International Security Policy Group (2007) Minutes of the launch of *An Unquiet World*. Chatham House, 26 July.
Curtis, J. and Heath, A. (2000) 'Is the English Lion about to Roar? National Identity after Devolution,' in *British Social Attitudes, The 17th Report*. London: Sage.
Daily Mail (2006) Editorial, 'A Risk Mr Straw is Right to Take', 6 October. Retrieved via *LexisNexis*.
Daily Mail (2006) Editorial, 'Whatever Happened to Free Speech Britain?', 7 October. Retrieved via *LexisNexis*.
Daily Telegraph (2006) Editorial, 'Integration Can't Be Achieved Behind the Veil', 7 October. Retrieved via *LexisNexis*.
Davies, N. (1999) *The Isles- A History*. Basingstoke: Macmillan.
Dwyer, C., (2008) 'Geographies of Veiling', *Geography*, 93(3), 140–147.
Dwyer, C. and Uberoi, V. (2009) 'British Muslims and Community Cohesion Debates', in ed. R. Phillips, *Muslims Spaces of Hope*. London: Zed Books, 201–222.
Eagle, A. (2007) Interviewed by Varun Uberoi, 15 October.
Fenton, S. (2007) 'Indifference Towards National Identity: What Young Adults Think About Being English and British', *Nations and Nationalism*, 13(2): 321–339.
Gallup (2009) The Gallup Coexist Index 2009: A Global Study of Interfaith Relations.
Gellner, E. (1983) *Nations & Nationalism*. Oxford: Blackwell Publishing.
Gilroy, P. (1987) *There Ain't No Black in the Union Jack*. London: Hutchinson.
Gove, M. (2006) *Celsius 7/7*. London: Weidenfeld & Nicholson.
Green, D. (2008) Interviewed by Varun Uberoi, 18 April.
Grieve, D. (2007) Interviewed by Varun Uberoi, 18 September.
Hague, W. (2001a) 'Vote for What You Value', the speech is undated, but from the text it was clearly given just before the 2001 General Election and just after the riot in Oldham.
Hague, W. (2001b) 'We Will Renew Britain's Civil Society', the speech is undated, but from the text the speech was clearly given just before the 2001 General Election.
Hague, W. (2001c) 'Spring Forum Speech 2001', 4 March.
Hazell, R. (2008) 'The Future of the Union', *Political Quarterly*, 78(1): 101–112.
Heath, A. and Roberts, J. (2008) *British Identity: Its Sources and Possible Implications for Civic Attitudes and Behaviour*. London: Department of Justice.
Heath, A. and Roberts, J. (2008) *British Identity, Its Sources and Possible Implications for Civic Attitudes and Behaviour*. London: Department of Justice, HMSO.
Heffer, S. (2006) 'Respect Works Both Ways', *Daily Telegraph*, 7 October. Retrieved via *LexisNexis*.
Home Office (2001) *Community Cohesion: A Report of The Independent Review Team*. London.
Home Office (2003) Press Release, 'Plans for Citizenship Ceremonies Welcomed', 9 December.
Hood, C. (2010) 'Measuring & Managing Public Services Performance', ed. V. Uberoi, A. Couuts, I. McLean and D. Halpern, Options for Britain II, Oxford: Wiley Blackwell, 7–19.
Independent (2006) Editorial, 'Mr Straw Has Raised a Valid Issue, but Reached the Wrong Conclusion', 7 October. Retrieved via *LexisNexis*.
Independent on Sunday (2006) Editorial, 'Britain Behind the Veil', 8 October. Retrieved via *LexisNexis*.
Ingram, R. (2006) 'I Do Not Often Agree With Jack Straw', *Independent*, 7 October. Retrieved via *LexisNexis*.

Jenkins, R. (1966) Address given by the Home Secretary to a meeting of Voluntary Liaison Committees, 23 May, NCCI, London.

Jenkins, S. (2006) 'Under Straw's Veil of Moderation a Fancy Piece of Political Footwork', *Sunday Times*, 8 October. Retrieved via *LexisNexis*.

Kavanagh, K. (2006) 'A Growing Number Use the Veil to Provoke Us', *Sun*, 9 October. Retrieved via *LexisNexis*.

Keating, M. (2001) *Nations Against the State*. Basingstoke: Palgrave Macmillan.

Kettle, M. (2006) 'It Isn't Enough to Say Anyone Can Wear Whatever They Like', *Guardian*, 7 October. Retrieved via *LexisNexis*.

Kyriakides, C., Virdee, S., and Modood, T. (2009) 'Racism, Muslims and the National Imagination', *Journal of Ethnic and Migration Studies*, 35(2): 289–308.

Lewis, J. (2006) 'The Veil is a Ghost From Our Collective Past', *Independent*, 7 October. Retrieved via *LexisNexis*.

Mactaggart, F. (2007) Interviewed by Varun Uberoi, 16 October.

Mason, A. (2010) 'Integration, Cohesion and National Identity: Theoretical Reflections on Recent British Policy', *British Journal of Political Science*, 40(4): 857–874.

Maudling, R. (1978) *Memoirs*. London: Sedgwick and Jackson.

Maxwell, M. (2006) 'British Values', *Sun*, 11 October. Retrieved via *LexisNexis*.

McGhee, D. (2003) 'Moving to Our Common Ground – A Critical Examination of Community Cohesion Discourse in Twenty-First Century Britain', *Sociological Review*, 51(3): 376–404.

McLaughlin, E. and Neal, S. (2004) 'Misrepresenting the Multicultural Nation, the Policy-Making Process, News Media Management and the Parekh Report', *Policy Studies*, 25(3): 155–174.

McLean, I. and McMillan, A. (2005) *State of The Union*. Oxford: Oxford University Press.

Meer, N. (2010) *Citizenship, Identity and Politics of Multiculturalism: The Rise of Muslim Consciousness*. Basingstoke: Palgrave Macmillan.

Meer, N. and Modood, T. (2009) 'The Multicultural State We're In: Muslims, "Multiculture", and the Civic Re-balancing of British Multiculturalism', *Political Studies*, 57(1), 473–479.

Meer, N., Dwyer, C. and Modood, T. (2010) 'Embodying Nationhood? Conceptions of British National Identity, Citizenship and Gender in the "Veil Affair" ', *Sociological Review*, 58(1), 84–111.

Miller, D. (1995) *On Nationality*, Oxford: Oxford University Press.

Mirror (2006) Editorial, 'Lifting the Veil Gently', 6 October. Retrieved via *LexisNexis*.

Modood, T. (1992) *Not Easy Being British: Colour, Culture and Citizenship*. Stoke-on-Trent: Trentham Books.

Modood, T. (2005) *Multicultural Politics: Racism, Ethnicity and Muslims in Britain*. Minneapolis and Edinburgh: University of Minnesota Press and University of Edinburgh Press.

Modood, T. (2008) 'Multicultural British Citizenship and Making Space for Muslims', *Cycnos*, 25(2): 81–100.

Modood. T. et al. (1997) *Ethnic Minorities in Britain*. London: Policy Studies Institute.

Moore, C. (2006) 'My Straw Poll: Extremists Must Be Seen for What They Are', *Daily Telegraph*, 7 October. Retrieved via *LexisNexis*.

Moore, K., Mason, P. and Lewis, J. (2008) 'Images of Islam in the UK, the Representation of British Muslims in the National Print News Media', http://www.irr.org.uk/pdf/media_muslims.pdf. Last accessed 22 December 2010.

Moore, S. (2006) 'The Veil Has No Place…in Kabul or Blackburn', *Mail on Sunday*, 8 October. Retrieved via *LexisNexis*.

Nairn, T. (1977) *The Break Up of Britain*. Edinburgh: Edinburgh University Press.

Neville-Jones, P. (2007) Interviewed by Varun Uberoi, 17 October.

O'Brien, M. (2007) Interviewed by Varun Uberoi, 30 October.

Observer (2006) Editorial, 'The *Niqab* is Not the Only Barrier to Integration', 8 October. Retrieved via *LexisNexis*.

Orr, D. (2006) 'Veils Turned Out to be Rather Provocative', *Independent*, 14 October. Retrieved via *LexisNexis*.

Parekh, P. (2008) *A New Politics of Identity*. Basingstoke: Palgrave Macmillan.

Parekh, B. (2009) 'Feeling at Home: Some Reflections on Muslims in Europe', *Harvard Middle eastern and Islamic Review*, 8: 51–85.

Pearson, P. (2006) 'Here's Why the Veil So Offends Me', *Daily Mail*, 11 October. Retrieved via *LexisNexis*.

Phillips, T. (2007) Interview in *The Times*, 3 April.

Plamenatz, J. (1974), 'Two Types of Nationalism', in E. Kamenka, ed. *Nationalism: The Nature of an Idea*. Canberra: Australian National University, pp. 123–137.

Porter, H. (2006) 'Jack Straw Should be Praised for Lifting the Veil on a Taboo: A Virulent Minority of Muslims is Turning its Face Against the Values of Liberal Democracy All Over Western Europe', *Observer*, 8 October. Retrieved via *LexisNexis*.

Powell, E. (1991) (20 April 1968) *Reflections of a Statesman, the Writings and Speeches of Enoch Powell*. London: Bellew.

Smith, A. (1991) *National Identity*, Nevada: University of Nevada Press.

Smith, A.D. (1998) *Nationalism and Modernism: A Critical Survey of Recent Theories of Nations and Nationalism*. London: Routledge.

Smith, J. (2006) 'The Veil is a Feminist Issue', *Independent on Sunday*, 8 October. Retrieved via *LexisNexis*.

Stotty, R. (2006) 'Jack and PC Correctness', 8 October. Retrieved via *LexisNexis*.

Straw, J. (2006) 'I Felt Uneasy Talking to Someone I Couldn't See', *Lancashire Telegraph*, 5 October.

Straw, J. (2007) Cyril Foster Lecture, 26 January.

Sun (2006) Editorial, 'Face to Face', 6 October. Retrieved via *LexisNexis*.

Sun (2006) Editorial, 'Religion is Not Above Criticism', 7 October. Retrieved via *LexisNexis*.

Sunday Express (2006) Editorial, 'Don't Draw a Veil Over Free Speech', 8 October. Retrieved via *LexisNexis*.

Sunday Telegraph, Editorial, 'Barefaced Truth', 8 October. Retrieved via *LexisNexis*.

Swann (1985) *Education For All, The Report of The Committee of Inquiry Into The Education of Children From Ethnic Minority Groups*. London: Her Majesty's Stationary Office.

The Times (2006) Editorial, 'Veiled Threat: Straw Should Not be Isolated for Speaking Out on Separation', 7 October. Retrieved via *LexisNexis*.

Turner, J. (2006) 'Why Mix? Parallel Lives Do Us Fine', *The Times*, 7 October. Retrieved via *LexisNexis*.

Uberoi, V. (2007) 'Social Unity in Britain', *Journal of Ethnic & Migration Studies*, 33(1): 141–159.

Uberoi, V. (2008) 'Do Policies of Multiculturalism Change National Identities?', *Political Quarterly*, 79(3), 404–417.

Uberoi, V. and Modood, T. (2010) 'Who Doesn't Feel British? Divisions Over Muslims', *Parliamentary Affairs*, 63(2): 302–320.

Warsi, S (undated) 'Race Equality Speech'. Warsi's speech was for the Guardian Race Equality Conference in London: Conservative Party Press Release.

Wheatcroft, P. (2006) 'Multiculturalism Hasn't Worked: Let's Rediscover Britishness', *Sunday Telegraph*, 8 October. Retrieved via *LexisNexis*.

11

'Our Own People': Ethnic Majority Orientations to Nation and Country

Steve Fenton and Robin Mann

1. Introduction

In this chapter we examine orientations towards nation and country with sole reference to the 'ethnic majority' in England. Drawing on extensive qualitative interview data collected as part of the Leverhulme Programme, we examine the nuanced ways in which majority people orientate to concepts of nation, country and multiculturalism. We illustrate the linkages between these specific national sentiments and the broader context of change in British[1] society, and changes in the life circumstances of our respondents as told in individual narratives. In doing so, we will argue that attitudes to ethnic or national identity and multicultural Britain are not traced solely through specific questions on those topics. These ideas, in themselves, we find to have little purchase amongst 'ordinary' people. We *did* ask respondents about 'national identity' and 'Englishness'. But we also asked people about their work and neighbourhoods, their sense of opportunity, merit and reward, and what they thought of Britain as a place to live. These questions and their responses allowed us to contextualise peoples' 'national orientations' within a wider set of social orientations to, for example, a sense of entitlement, security and stability in everyday life, and civility.

A key motivation for this research is that in all of the literature on the sociology of ethnicity and racism, much less attention has been paid to the identities expressed by the ethnic *majority*. For a long period, those writing on ethnic identities have for the most part focused on minority identities (see Smith, 2004 for a critique of 'minority ethnicity'). This has, in turn, unwittingly implied that it is they who are ethnic, whilst the majority are not. It was in the 1950s that Hughes and Hughes (1952), referring to White Anglo Saxon Protestant (WASP) identity in the USA, had noted the beginning of a tendency to refer to some people as not ethnic: 'If, in any community, *n* is the number of groups by the old definition, then *n* minus one is the number of groups by the new definition. There is one which is not ethnic, that is, the charter member ethnic group of the community' (Hughes and Hughes, 1952: 7). This tacit majority ethnicity, or unstated whiteness, is now acknowledged through the greater attention that is now devoted to white identities (Bonnet, 2000, Nayak, 2003; Garner, 2006), majority ethnicity (Karner, 2007; Jenkins, 2008), dominant ethnicity (Kaufman, 2003) as well as through the focus on the construction of ethnic and national identities 'from below' (McCrone et al., 1998; Condor, Gibson and Abell, 2006).

If this new academic focus poses a disjuncture between an unmarked whiteness and ethnically marked minorities, we are still left with the empirical question of why the majority should begin to view everyday life and national politics or themselves through an ethnic lens. Of course there are contexts and spaces both with Britain and elsewhere in which we would find majorities adopting a conscious sense of their own ethnicity, and subsequently conceived of as 'ethnic groups'. For example, Glazer and Moynihan (1975) refer to 'old Americans' as an ethnic group within a multiethnic New York. More recently, Baumann (1996), in his study of a multiethnic community in west London, refers to whites (English, Irish) as adopting a conscious sense of being ethnic vis-à-vis others. Yet these both represent contexts in which whites are numerical minorities within multiethnic localities or city-spaces. What remains largely problematic is how to conceive of the predominant population within a state whose internal variations (such as by class and region) appear at least as significant as their distinction from ethnic minorities. References to an ethnic majority in the singular are also problematised in that they may screen over important differences in identification amongst non-visible minorities, such as amongst second-generation Irish or Polish in England (see Hickman et al., 2005). It is also likely that a sizeable portion of the 'white English' could report, if they chose to stress it, a non-English national or ethnic heritage in some form.

In Britain it remains problematic as to whether and how the ethnic majority, and *their* 'cultural stuff', should enter into broader public policy debates concerned with Britishness, citizenship and multiculturalism. Moreover, the ambivalence in conceptualising the majority is also evident in how categories of 'English' and 'British' are used differentially within both pro-multiculturalist and anti-multiculturalist discourses. For instance, a reactionary 'little Englandism' or backward-looking Englishness can be viewed as representing a barrier to re-imagining British national identity (e.g., Parekh, 2000: 14). It can be also argued that Englishness refers to ethnicity or 'race', while Britishness refers to citizenship. For example, it is widely accepted that people of Caribbean and South Asian origin, but born in England, would see themselves as British. But whether they see themselves as English – or are defined by others as English – is less clear. As former Conservative politician Norman Tebbit, in conversation with Darcus Howe for the television documentary *White Tribe*, put it: 'We are both British, but only I am English' (cited in McCrone, 2006: 274). Thus, with respect to the distinction between Englishness and Britishness, whiteness appears important (see also Byrne, 2006). More recently there have been suggestions that some ethnic minority young people are inclined towards an English identity (Kenny, 2010).

Yet it does not necessarily follow that uses of the category 'English' as equating to 'whites' is antithetical to multicultural political projects. Ethnocultural understandings of the category 'English' are also evident in arguments in favour of multiculturalism. Bernard Crick (2008: 34) asserts that the adjective 'English' refers to a culture, as does Welsh, Scottish, but that British refers to 'an allegiance'. For Crick, this distinction is at its clearest in the case of the 'immigrant', whose 'allegiance is to the state' and thus 'rarely tries to become English'. Similarly, political theorists Kymlicka and Norman (2000) argue that in recognising the special status of minority groups within a state 'the majority' will 'have to distinguish more clearly than he (sic) had before between an ethnic English identity and a civic British identity' (Kymlicka and Norman, 2000: 30). These arguments are interesting because they both favour and endorse a pro-multiculturalist sense of Britishness which can represent its diverse citizenry, whilst simultaneously recognising an ethnicised English identity as referring to the ethnic majority and which sits beside other hybrid identities (e.g., Black British; Asian British) (see also Kaufmann, 2004: 2).

Thus while there are difficulties in conceiving the ethnic majority as an 'ethnic group', as something more than simply *not* ethnic minority, a case can be nevertheless be made for a *discursive majority*. As we will show, everyday discourses of the nation will often contain tacit reproductions of the discursive majority via the phrase 'our own people', or as a construction of 'we' or 'us', defined in opposition to ethnic (minority) others. Our respondents also discursively distinguish 'us' (as indigenous) from 'people coming in'. Similarly we know of the discursive majority that is also to be found in tabloid and right-wing media and political discourses to do with national identity, in headlines such as 'we're not allowed to be English anymore' and in reactions to immigration and multicultural citizenship. These public discourses can be and are reproduced within everyday discourse. Nonetheless, for all the media talk of the nation, many of our respondents did not find it easy to talk about Englishness or ethnic and national identity. And it is in the analysis of the broader discourse of lived contexts, often material contexts pertaining to housing, employment or access to services, talked about in a discourse of 'us', that the, typically resentful, vigour of discursive majoritarianism is revealed.

2. Orientations to nation and country: the research

In what follows we report on data collected for the 'nation, class and *ressentiment*' project (2004–06) which formed part of the Leverhulme programme on migration and citizenship. In total 120 respondents who, apart from two minority cases, were 'white English'[2] took part in qualitative interviews. Eight focus group discussions with members of community organisations were also held. The qualitative interviews were conducted across three research sites, including two sites in Bristol – *Southdown*, a multiethnic neighbourhood; *Northville*, a nearly all-white working-class estate; and *Westown*, a small town within commuting distance. In turn, we aimed to achieve class variation by targeting respondents in different parts of the site. Such a variation was particularly important given that there is a class basis to nationalist resentment (see Hewitt, 2005; Dench, Gavron and Young, 2006). Table 11.1 provides a simplified social class categorisation of our respondents, and the percentage of them in each of our research sites.

Our key theoretical rationale is to analyse majoritarian sentiments towards nation and country as embedded within, and emerging out of, peoples' broader narratives of their lives. Methodologically, this meant adopting a qualitative strategy of speaking to people about a wide range of topics before proceeding to ask more direct questions about 'being English', 'British' and 'their view of multiculturalism'. This approach can be distinguished from the quantitative analysis of national identity in Britain (Tilley and Heath, 2007). We draw much upon the work of Billig (1988, 1995) and other discourse analytical approaches (see Condor, 2000). In the work of these two scholars the focus is primarily upon 'talk' about the nation and its rhetorical construction within interviews. Our own conversations with respondents comprised of a wide range of topics to do with places lived, family, work and getting on, any of which could, we thought, evoke *sentiments* about the nation. Respondents spoke about their neighbourhoods and employment as well as more directly nation-oriented topics such as their view of changes in the country and their attitude to devolution, Europe and 'multicultural Britain'. What people said in response to these promptings certainly ranged more widely

Table 11.1 Respondents by social class

	Westown	Southdown	Northville	Total
1	9 (15%)	5 (15%)	1 (4%)	15 (13%)
2	18 (30%)	12 (35%)	7 (28%)	37 (30%)
3	20 (32%)	9 (26%)	9 (36%)	38 (31%)
4	4 (7%)	4 (12%)	3 (12%)	11 (9%)
5	3 (5%)	2 (6%)	2 (8%)	7 (6%)
6	2 (3%)	2 (6%)	3 (12%)	7 (6%)
7	5 (8%)	0	0	5 (4%)
Total	61	34	25	120

Note: 1 = Higher managerial/professional; 2 = Lower professional; 3 = Skilled/self-employed; 4 = Unskilled; 5 = Unemployed; 6 = Student; 7 = 'Housewife'.

than the narrow question of 'identity'. But there is no doubt that what people said was intimately relevant to how they viewed their relationship to 'the country', and how their view of the nation intersected with orientations towards civility, entitlement, fairness and historical change. At least as important as how people identified with being English or British is the 'tone' of this identification which varied from the mildest and most matter-of-fact to aggressive and assertive statements. In what follows we set out to describe and interpret some of the main themes which arise from the interviews.

3. Taken for granted Englishness-Britishness

In this section we describe the set of assumptions which people make about the national community. These assumptions are revealed in the phrases and cognitive frames which interviewees adopt in the interview conversation, rather than in what they say on specific subjects. On the one side, respondents frequently use phrases like 'us', 'our own country' and 'our own people' which mark out the ethnic majority. On the other side, they use phrases like 'people coming in' to mark out 'others'. This is unusually explicit in the following quote, an illustration of 'the English' being outside ethnic categorisation:

> No I'm not an ethnic group, I'm um I'm English, how can I be ethnic group, this is, this is England isn't it? So how can I be ethnic? (Respondent laughs) (Male, 70, retired production manager, Southdown)

This is to say that, in their tacit view of things, the whole public discussion of 'ethnicity', 'ethnic minorities' and 'multicultural Britain' is about *other people* and not about a diffusely defined 'us'. Respondents rarely made explicit mention of whiteness although many said that they ticked 'white English' and 'white British' in response to official forms which asked them to tick *something*. There was evidence that they saw ethnic reporting as an odd thing to be asked to do – perhaps as significant as anything else is the reporting of 'laughter' at that point in the interview quoted above. There is a subtlety here that ought to be observed. To be sure, whiteness may have been implicit in how respondents defined the majority, the 'English', and those who were not members of 'ethnic groups', counterposed to 'people coming in' or named groups such as Somalis or Muslims. Here is a respondent talking about the area in which she lived:

> Yes, yes yeah, very multiethnic, yeah. I mean, the children went to Greenfield Primary school which is I suppose, well very mixed. 50 per cent white and the rest are Asian, Chinese, West Indian perhaps like you know. Same with Whitfield school they go to, that's a very multiethnic school you know. Em, locally so they were brought up with it. I was brought

> up, well I went to primary school in the village and they're all white, they're all farmers, very much English you know. (Male, 50–59, engineer, Southdown)

However, it is likely that only a few regarded being white as an essential qualification for being *British*. Many of our respondents made statements which clearly accepted 'ethnic minorities' as British, as part of Britain and as a legitimate part of British society. This interpretation is certainly supported by survey findings that the great majority of British people do not regard 'being white' as an essential component of being British (IPSOS MORI, 2002).

Expressing a view that Britain is, or ought to be, 'a white nation' would be seen as an extreme position. Within our interview material, there are significant representations of 'moderate' opinion, as well as of resentful statements that are coupled with anti-immigration sentiments. 'Moderate' is perhaps an unsatisfactory summary term, but for our own purposes *moderate* would include statements which accept multicultural Britain and acknowledge the contribution of immigrants to British society. Furthermore, 'moderates' express critical opinions – about 'civility', benefits or 'declining Britain'– in *general* terms rather than in ways which are oriented to 'people coming in'. They speak about crime and social decline but they do not blame 'immigrants'. But when we do examine the responses (perhaps 35 per cent of all) which express a range of resentful attitudes, we find a clear dividing line between indigenous English-British and the incomers-minorities who make up multiethnic Britain. The first category – indigenous – is usually referred to by the use of terms like 'our own people' or 'our country' whilst the latter is referred to by the use of terms like 'people coming in' or 'people who come here and...' (e.g., 'expect us to change'). In this resentful discourse, there is sometimes no distinction made between 'people coming in' and (in effect) people who *came in* (who are descendants of immigrants from much earlier generations). We cannot be sure of this because it is rare for respondents to refer to specific groups, although we do find occasional mentions of such categories as Somalis, Muslims, Polish and Pakistanis.

Whilst the phrases such as 'our own people' define the category of belonging, rather than being a substantive theme, there are distinctive substantive themes which are connected to this category. That is, when our respondents do refer to 'our own people' it is very frequently connected with resentful comments where respondents refer to both material and symbolic disfranchisement. The following two quotations illustrate this:

> they just come straight into our country and claim everything straight away really. *And our own people are waiting for things.* (Female, 50–59, cleaner, Southdown)

> ...it is atrocious that we're not allowed to show *our flag*. The fact that this is our country...other religions and other communities have come into *this country* expecting to change it, the fact that it's not their country, if we went over there it's their country, they wouldn't accept us turning around saying 'burn your flag we want ours being put up', I think it is ridiculous how English has to change for other people. (Female, 20, student, Northville)

The first quotation above follows a format of statement commonly found in our interviews: 'they come in and get this.... *And we can't* get anything'. The second statement follows a similar format but with reference to *symbolic loss* rather than material loss: 'they can express their culture.... *But we're not allowed*' is the formula which these statements follow. Notably both sets of statements, of material loss and symbolic loss, have the same logic of 'they do...we can't or we're not allowed.' The same subjects, such as access to services and benefits, are also discussed by 'moderate' respondents but they discuss these things without the reference point of the exclusive use of 'we' or 'our own'. Thus, those with a 'moderate' or inclusive frame of reference also make statements which refer to undeserving recipients of benefits but these are not specifically associated with 'people coming in'. For them, the statement that people 'get along without working, without putting anything in' makes no reference to any claim that the 'undeserving claimants' are immigrants or minorities. Or there is an explicit denial that the statement refers to immigrants; they imply that *anybody* is capable of this 'living off the state'.

4. Civility – how people treat each other

Billig (1995) has described 'banal nationalism' as the un-noticed place of national symbols that are evident in everyday life. These symbols – or signs and names – remind us of national belonging without any direct language which asserts national identity. The banal reminder of national belonging is the 'limp flag resting in the corner of a room', rather than the flag aggressively waved in nationalist demonstrations or political rallies. Smith (1991) is describing something similar when he describes the everyday events, sights or comments which remind us of national belonging:

> ...flags, anthems, parades, coinage, capital cities, war memorials, ceremonies of remembrance for the national dead, passports, frontiers,... national recreations, the countryside, popular heroes and heroines, fairy tales, forms of etiquette, styles of architecture, arts and crafts, modes of town planning, legal procedures, educational practices and military codes...all those distinctive customs, mores, styles and ways of acting

> and feeling that are shared by the members of a community of historical culture.... (Smith, 1991: 77)

The 'flags, anthems, and ceremonials' are designed as overt reminders of the nation and so could hardly be described as 'banal'. Beyond these instances, Smith is largely referring to places and practices which have a kind of national resonance – and familiarity, like 'the countryside' and 'styles of architecture'. But when he speaks of 'forms of etiquette' and 'ways of acting and feeling', his point of reference is *everyday life* in which mannerisms and ways of acting are the barely noticed reminders of association with an imagined community. So it is that English 'reserve', politeness, understatement and ironic wit are taken to be marks of Englishness/Britishness which are not acquired by legal means (viz. naturalisation) but by being socialised into and attuned to an English/British way of doing things. We know of course that these things are not permanent. The public grieving at the death of a princess in 1997 was interpreted (and regretted) by some as a departure from the custom of English reserve (Freedland, 2007). Modes of behaviour associated with class deference have diminished with the diminution of deference itself. Nonetheless forms of etiquette and courtesy – like queuing – are identified (see below) as dimensions of national character and custom.

This makes it all the more understandable that our respondents frequently referred to 'etiquette' and everyday manners when they were asked about 'changing Britain'. Thus Britain was seen to have become 'coarser' and to have lost the decency and civility that respondents regarded as the familiar marks of an English-British way of life. Of course it is commonplace to hear people speaking of the 'good old days' and of the present as 'society in decline'. Even so the number of people who mentioned lack of civility as a mark of modern Britain suggests that everyday courtesy is an important part of how people think about 'the country'. There are good reasons for thinking that 'civility' and the 'nation' are connected. In the first place the emergence of common standards of behaviour which are recognised as 'civilised' is part of the emergence of the modern nation; and 'civility' has been taken as a particular mark of Englishness (Bryant, 1993). Secondly, as Miller (1995) has argued, national membership is predicated on a sense of mutuality and solidarity. We treat other people in a reasonable and respectful way because we regard them as belonging to us and as people to whom we owe something. Miller suggests that our sense of membership of a nation brings with it a sense of duty to fellow members:

> In acknowledging a national identity, I am also acknowledging that I owe a special obligation to fellow members of my nation which I do not owe to other human beings. (Miller, 1995: 49)

In this respect we often think of formal obligations such as respect for the law or the sentiments of mutuality which create support for general welfare policies. But it is possible to extend this idea of obligation to everyday life and the signifying of respect through the practice of 'good manners'. A *Daily Telegraph* editorial (2007) is close to this point when it concludes:

> in the building of an orderly society, a bus queue was a glory of our national character. Now it is on the verge of extinction. Manners make the nation. Without them, as we see, it becomes nasty and brutish.

Flint (2009), in a more critical analysis of prescriptions for proper social behaviour, makes the same connection in his analysis of 'civility' and the guidance offered to new migrants on 'how to behave in Britain'. These guidance documents indicate that the British authorities believe that conforming to British cultural expectations includes learning and respecting the rules that govern everyday life. Thus the state enters the arena of routine 'regulation of conduct' which is assumed to be guided by shared cultural norms. This is what Flint calls:

> ... a colonisation of civility through which the state inscribes itself deeper into daily social practices, based on imperially influenced imaginations of national communities. (Flint, 2009: 138)

Put more simply, this suggests that the state intrudes into everyday life by exhorting 'proper behaviour' among immigrants, a sign that good manners (or rather manners appropriate to Britain) are seen as necessary to successful adaptation. The list of 'daily social practices' of which immigrants are reminded include looking after your garden, saying please and thank you, and respecting the principles of queues (Flint, 2009: 131). However mundane, these practices are represented as being part of British values and failure to respect them endangers cohesion and integration. The fact that these cautions are delivered to migrants – whose 'integration' is deemed to be problematic – should not obscure the fact that a connection is being made between everyday practices, civility, social cohesion and the national community. The failures of civility are a constant theme for many of our respondents. We find this not attributed to 'migrants' but to a general decline of civilised values. This, in turn, is connected to their view of 'the country'. One of our respondents tells a story of opening a door for a woman with children in a pram:

> .... There's no thank you or please, they just push through and even on the ads on television, when they ask for things there's no 'well thank you very much'. Now when we were kids it was drummed into you, constantly. But that was a different era altogether. I think it was a happy era. It was a nicer society, a nicer way of life. (Male, 50–59, catering manager for council, Northville)

and another about the 'lack of respect':

> I'm horrified by what appears to be going on especially in the cities where you've got the larger population anyway, but I am horrified, this word respect I've been using it for several years now and as citizens we are not respectful of each other and that is dreadful. (Male, 60–69, farmer, Westown)

One respondent explained how in earlier years, neighbours helped each other as a matter of course – it was something people just did:

> .... You did it! And I think it was a much happier world. People want so much now, they are not so content. I think things have changed so much for the worse, I think people have got very selfish, very wanting.... (Male, 70–79, retired postman, Westown)

Such complaints about failure of manners and mutuality were accompanied by lots of references to loutishness, yobs and drunken behaviour. People talked about the English predilection for drunkenness and hooliganism as something that made them ashamed to be English – whilst recognising that drunken yobbishness might be seen as quintessentially English.

> Yeh people think we're hooligans and lager louts and typical English.... (Male, 30–34, carpenter, Southdown)
>
> I'm not very proud to be English, when I see, like, football fans behaving like, you know, hooligans and then when I go abroad and I see that nobody can speak any other languages apart from English, I feel really ashamed then.... (Female, 30–34, legal conveyancer, Southdown)

These hallmarks of Englishness were suggested in response to our questions about what respondents saw as being typically English – alongside some more conventional definitions of Englishness:

> *Interviewer: when you think about being English or Englishness what kind of images come to mind?*
>
> Football hooligans....Um the monarchy. (Female, 35–39, nurse, Northville)
>
> Oh Englishness....I think any tourist would say...is the stiff upper lip of an Englishman on his horse trotting through the countryside after the fox...not that they are allowed to do that a lot these days. You know the quaint tea in the afternoon it's those old traditions that are still there and people still expect to see it umm you know...I think other people look at

> Englishness as thugs and hooligans all over the country. (Female, 35–39, operations manager, Westown)

So, whilst references to 'our own people' are clearly predicated on a distinction with 'others', defined as 'people coming in', these references (above) to Englishness, belonging and civility have no clear reference to immigrants at all. It is of course more than likely that some of our respondents have images of class – rather than 'origin' – in mind. 'Yobs', 'hoodies' and 'chavs' (Haylett, 2001) are all terms to describe 'ill-mannered youth' who are associated with disorderly lives and unemployment. In the next theme which we examine – benefits, entitlement and welfare – the association with 'people coming in' was much more likely to be made.

5. Material resentment, entitlement, and 'our own people'

We have seen that in illustrating the theme of 'our own', the way people talked about 'us', we find it coupled with resentment about the distribution of resources. In speaking about housing, health care and jobs, people are indicating that they do not abstract their view of 'our own people' from ideas about access to material things. If we look carefully at what people say about 'this country' in relation to material resources we find a number of themes combined. One is the idea of *entitlement* – that people have 'paid in all their lives' and have a right to expect something back.[3] People who are perceived as 'just coming in' breach this rule. A second is the idea of *dis-privilege* – others get things that we don't or can't or are prevented from getting. A third is the *idea of scarce resources* – if 'people coming in' (the oft-used phrase in the responses of the interviewees) are using resources then there is less to go round. And a fourth is the idea of British *decline* – this is the view that there are all kinds of changes for the worse and we 'ordinary people, our own people' are displaced and neglected by these changes. We present data at a greater length here in order to illustrate these themes.

5.1. Entitlement

> ... people of my dad's generation that have *paid in all his life* but because he's got a pension can't get what these people seem, come in the country and get straight away. (Male, 50–59, electrician, Southdown)

5.2. Entitlement and scarce resources

> OK, a lot because um they're, they're, I don't want this to be, to sound as if I'm being really selfish, but they are they're actually, they're taking *all our... resources away* from us... um they're taking up the housing that people need it, they're using up all the um hospitals and all the money made for people who are sick um because *they're not putting anything back*

> into the country, they're not earning a living so they're not paying tax, they're not paying insurance um you know because they, they just want to come here. (Male, 50–59, bill poster, Southdown)

5.3. Dis-privilege

> .... One had carpeting didn't they, one had carpeting they didn't want it, or wood the other way round on the floors, they wanted, the next day they were in there putting carpet down. *Whereas the English can't get anything*.... (Male, 50–59, caretaker, Southdown)

> immigrants coming in asylum seekers.... Which are really *a drain on our resources*... (whilst others get everything) we can't even get the basics, apply for that, because he's got a pension but he *paid all his life* for that pension. So, I just yeah, I, [it's] just a working class man... from that point of view basically. (Male, 50–59, electrician, Southdown)

'People of my dad's generation have paid in': this statement is the classic formulation of what people deserve, of a sense of entitlement to those who have contributed. Other people get the things that 'we' can't get and they get them without waiting. For all the confusion or elision in the public imagination across 'minorities', recent immigrants and refugees, there is no convincing evidence that people are thinking of this entitlement as something that excludes minorities or excludes non-whites. The references are consistently to 'people coming in' and there are few specific references to British Asian and British Black people. This would fit with the MORI survey which found that there is widespread resentment towards those who 'come in' and get 'priority' for public benefits and services (IPSOS MORI, 2003).

A MORI (December 2003) poll found 46 per cent of respondents in the UK 'agree or tend to agree that others get unfair priority when it comes to public services and state benefits'. But when people were asked *who* got an unfair priority, 39 per cent mentioned asylum seekers or new immigrants and very few indeed mentioned 'minorities' (asylum seekers 20 per cent; new immigrants 19 per cent; lone parents 8 per cent). This loss of priority is seen as a drain on resources which should be available for all people ('they're taking all our... resources away from us'). The English, says one respondent, 'can't get anything'. These are all examples of our respondents speaking about 'entitlement' and the mundane concerns of health pensions and personal security. Indeed our electrician from Southdown above explicitly says he is speaking as 'a working-class man' and our retired factory worker from Northville below speaks about 'English workers'. There are repeated references to the need for government, the politicians or the authorities to address or do something about these problems. Indeed the government seems to be the initiator of the problem rather than its cure. Politicians and the government are usually, in this context, described as 'being too soft':

> *the authorities are too easy got over* you know cos people can pull the wool over their eyes you know as regards benefits, certain benefits and that, I think that is one of worst things in this country, we're a little bit soft you know... we seem to get people coming into the country and they don't never, not all of them but most, a lot of them don't have to work or, or, they don't seem to want to work.... I think a lot of people get, well there is a lot of people getting a hell of a lot more than they deserve, the fat cats that we call them, there's quite a lot of them about and er I think that perhaps you know some people don't get... what they should do but on the whole I think er you know apart from the scroungers and things like that um no it's not too bad, *I think just we're a little bit soft, I think politicians are soft, I* don't agree with a lot of their ways and things, I think they're soft. (Male, 60–69, council worker, Westown)

Finally, respondents made an association between a sense of grievance and national decline, and between national decline and the loss of symbols of Britishness or Englishness.[4] In the following quotation the points of reference are the industries and institutions which are lost to Britain and which are a loss of Britishness.

> All these industries being run down. Now we used to have ship building, car... building, big steel industries... also there were the mills for wool and cotton and all that sort of thing. Well the whole lot as you know has gone. They've got rid of all of it. Now it used to be more or less a self-supporting country except well, I know we used to import fruit, we used to import some meat and all that sort of thing but basically we were a self-supporting country. We made our own shoes and things like that and exported them. And they were a very good quality. Now what's happened to all those people who've been made redundant?... Because they had all the mines and all that sort of thing. But that's all gone. (Female 70–79, retired clerical assistant, Northville)

> And now today it's MG cars at Rovers and the government said they weren't prepared to back them up and they they're quite prepared to let it go on its basically. Which is dreadful really. Nobody seems to care about the English workers basically. As long as they line their pockets. Which is completely wrong basically. (Male 70–79, retired factory worker, Northville)

One woman identified the decline of Britishness in the behaviour of British people abroad – although she appears to put some of the blame on the media (note the effortless shift from Britain to England):

> And umm I think people have, people have lost a sense of pride in the country. They've had responsibility taken away from them by legislation

> and the government and... and I just don't think people give a shit anymore about you know about the reputation of the country, and you know, they treat themselves as individuals. I don't think people have a sense of British-ness anymore. Umm the media likes to group us all together and say you know, make, apply sweeping statements about Britain and Britons abroad and Britons' behaviour umm the type of people that represent us abroad umm put um England in a bad light. (Female, 40–44, doctor, Westown)

6. Multiculturalism and nationality identity

One of the strategies in our research was to ask respondents about a range of topics, some of them only indirectly connected to national identity, in the expectation that raising these topics would prompt conversation and opinions which would disclose how people felt about 'the country' and their sense of attachment to it. Many examples of this are found earlier in the chapter where, for example, people talk about industrial decline, welfare benefits and daily acts of (in)civility, and in doing so disclose sentiments about Britain and England. The topic of multiculturalism is more directly connected to questions of national identity, not least because part of the multiculturalist project is 're-thinking the national story'. Thus in tracing our respondents' comments on this question, we are looking to reveal what *they* think of the national story. Furthermore this question has a class dimension, partly because advocating the multiculturalist vision has been seen to be a class project (Haylett, 2001; Hewitt, 2005), and partly because antipathy to multiculturalism appears to be influenced by class situation (IPSOS MORI, 2009: 5).

Hewitt (2005: 11–14) in particular describes the rise of the 'new class' as the emergence of a professional, service and 'knowledge economy' class whose growth coincided with the diminished influence of traditional industrial working classes. Key elements of the 'new class', such as academics and public sector service providers, were the bearers of the multicultural message (see also IPSOS Mori, 2009 and references to 'middle class establishment and cosmopolitan liberals'). Haylett (2001) argues that the white working class – and certainly the white working-class poor – lie outside this 'neoliberal multicultural mainstream' (Haylett, 2001: 357). Portrayed as 'racist and sexist' the white working-class poor lose both 'material wherewithal and symbolic dignity' (2001: 352). This 'racialisation' of the working class leaves the poorest among them 'beyond the bounds of the British nation' (2001: 355).

Views and debates about multiculturalism can be found, we suggest, in three spheres: among intellectuals; in the media; and in popular discourse. In an assessment of popular views of 'multicultural Britain', we are least concerned with intellectual disputes. Even in the intellectual sphere, multiculturalism has been subject to many critiques (see, e.g., Barry, 2001; Michaels, 2007) so that one of its leading proponents has addressed the question 'Is multiculturalism dead?' (Modood, 2008). We are rather more concerned with the media since, as Hewitt has observed, there are close links between media and popular discourses about 'multicultural Britain' in the shaping of what he calls 'counter-narratives'. The dominant tendency in media commentary on multiculturalism is critical and sometimes vitriolic. At least four of the national dailies are hostile to almost anything connected to the word 'multicultural': the *Sun, Daily Mail, Daily Express* and *Daily Telegraph*.[5] The stories in these newspapers connect to popular stories. In our research, stories of 'not being allowed to fly the Union/St George's flag' were a case in point. The press carry many examples of this type of story.[6] Our respondents' accounts were usually told as something they knew about locally, or something that had happened to 'their uncle'; no doubt the press stories reinforce the local narratives.

Before turning to some examples from our interviews we can take a brief look at the evidence of opinion polls on 'multicultural' questions in the UK over the last few years. They provide strong support for the proposition that multiculturalism does not command public support in the UK. Furthermore, support appears to be falling, and sharply. One report of a survey, the BBC/MORI poll of August 2005, *does* show support for multiculturalism in Britain in the 'headline' question; 62 per cent of a national sample agreed that 'multiculturalism makes Britain a better place to live' (we should note that a national sample will include ethnic minorities whereas our focus is on the views of the ethnic majority). But this survey itself had secondary questions where the responses tended to run counter to the main message: 58 per cent agreed to the statement 'people who come to live in Britain should adopt the values and traditions of British culture.' Similarly in a Eurobarometer (1999) study, only 18 per cent agreed that 'governments should help minorities to preserve traditions' whilst 55 per cent agreed to the alternative that minorities should 'adapt into larger society'.

Subsequent surveys, including MORI's own repeat of the questions reported above, indicate much lower support for 'multiculturalism'. In 2009, MORI produced a briefing paper, based on research up to and including 2008, showing a clear downward shift in public support for multiculturalist statements. They report that:

> [These] trends in attitudes to immigration tie in with more general ambivalence about the merits of multiculturalism. When asked directly about multiculturalism, the British public is divided, but is more inclined to see multiculturalism as something which threatens the British way of life (38 per cent) than something which makes Britain a better place to live (30 per cent). Likewise, when forced to choose between developing a shared identity or celebrating diverse values and cultures, we are more

> in favour of the former (41 per cent) than we are the latter (27 per cent). However, a split is once again evident, with a third of people (30 per cent) not able to choose either. (IPSOS MORI, 2009: 3)

These findings confirm markedly lower support for 'multicultural Britain' in recent (2008 and just before) years. The report suggests that this lower support for multiculturalism runs alongside increased opposition to immigration. In 1999, 56 per cent responded agreeing that 'there are too many immigrants in Britain'. But by 2008, 70 per cent agreed to this statement. Again, we cannot be sure of the implications of peoples' responses for 'national identity' (since there are so many possible readings of the questions), but the question 'threatens the British way of life' seems to make the link more explicit. Of course these stark choices (makes Britain a better place to live versus threatens the British way of life) present difficulties. The option 'threatens the British way of life' is a harsh-sounding option; nonetheless in 2008 more chose this than its alternative. It is worth noting that Hjerm (2000: 366) has earlier noted similar patterns in Australia and Canada, often seen as the heartlands of multiculturalism. Asked whether 'ethnic minorities should be given government assistance to preserve their customs and traditions', 66 per cent disagreed in Australia (with 18 per cent 'neither agree nor disagree') and 58 per cent disagreed in Canada (with 22 per cent 'neither agree nor disagree'). These results are from the same International Social Survey Programme as the Eurobarometer results quoted above, though Hjerm's results are from the 1995 survey. This survey evidence of low support for multiculturalism, including in Britain, underlines Joppke's conclusion when he seeks to explain the 'retreat from multiculturalism in three states that had been prominently committed to them: Australia, The Netherlands and Britain'. Among the factors he cites as contributing to this retreat is a 'chronic lack of public support for multiculturalism policies' (Joppke, 2004: 237).

All this provides some quantitative context in which we can assess the qualitative materials in our 100 interviews in which we opened up the question of 'multicultural Britain'.

> *Researcher: Do you think multiculturalisms should be encouraged?*
>
> Yeah I think it should. Umm they've just started Bollywood dancing classes here and which is a great idea and mainly girls who go and they you know have the jewellery on and the makeup and things its really good. (Female, 40–44, teaching assistant, Westown)

The above is a good example of the 'celebration of diversity' model of multiculturalism. The respondent welcomes 'cultural diversity' and talks about her own participation in it. In the next (below quotation) there is an element of 'celebration of diversity' ('opens up children to other cultures') but it is accompanied by conditions ('it depends').

> I think *it depends on the way it's done* the local school here for example has been doing classes in Islamic art and that's a good thing because *it opens up the children to other cultures* and then they are aware from an early age of different cultural ways of life. I think if it gets to the point where you have to have a certain number of this people and a certain number of that people whether it be in a school or wherever else for the sake of *being politically correct* then you are bringing a whole other aspect to it. If it is going to be done then it has to be natural and *not forced on people*. (Male, 35–39, senior manager, Westown)

Another form of conditional statement is found where a respondent welcomes multiculturalism but adds something which hints at 'separatism', 'parallel lives' and failures to integrate.

> *Researcher: Britain is now seen as much more of a multicultural society – do you think it is a multicultural society?*
>
> Umm saying that it is multicultural – it is, *but umm they all stick to their own areas*. They don't amalgamate with us if you know what I mean. They stay in their own communities.
>
> *Researcher: Okay so what does multicultural – what does that mean to you?*
>
> Well different nationalities really, yes.
>
> *Researcher: Okay and how do you feel about that?*
>
> I don't mind anybody coming into England *as long as they're willing* to give something. You know work. But most people coming in now are just... I mean my dad worked on the buses years ago and some guy got on the bus and said to him 'where's the money shop?' You know? *So most of them just come over to live off our state really.* Handouts and not work.
>
> *Researcher: Okay so do you think it's a good thing for Britain then the way it's becoming more – more multicultural?*
>
> No – bad, really. I reckon our crime's gone up more since everybody's been coming in as well. *I mean you've got more drugs, more guns,* I mean going back to say Victorian times, you had sort of one murder a year in England. And that was terrible wasn't it. It's supposed to be about five every day now isn't it? (Female, 50–59, cleaner, Southdown)

The celebration of diversity in the next quotation, 'having Ramadan and stuff', is again accompanied by a condition of promoting 'English culture as well'

> *Researcher: Now seems to have become more of a, more of a multicultural kind of society, um do you think it is?*
>
> Yeah without a doubt, you know like even like I said in my little boy's school they do a lot of, like they do, like he's been having *Ramadan and stuff* like that which is fine *as long as they still do,* I think it's fine as long as they still do what our, cos my niece went to a school where they stopped doing the Christmas things which I didn't agree with because I think if they're going to do you know some cultures, they still should do, *you know, the English culture as well.* (Female, 25–29, administrative assistant, Southdown)

And lastly we have a response which takes the opportunity of a question about 'multiculturalism' to give a general assault on immigration.

> *Researcher: Britain is seen as a multicultural society and we have kind of already talked about this already, but do you think it is become more multicultural?*
>
> It is, ye, by the day.
>
> *How do you feel about that?*
>
> I feel it's wrong that we should let so many in. We should be like Australia and say no, we don't want you.
>
> *So we should have stricter immigration as well?*
>
> Ye.
>
> *And what about asylum seekers as opposed to . . . ?*
>
> Send them back. We don't want them do we? Again, why should we keep them on the money that's paid in by the people that work in this country? (Male, 60–69, battery operator, Northville)

As was shown, in the ethnic majority public it is very hard to be clear exactly what is being supported. There are any number of possibilities. Firstly, people (i.e., those who do support multiculturalism) may be giving a broad kind of assent to social and cultural diversity. They have no reason to oppose a Britain which is more culturally diverse, they see cultural diversity as 'interesting', and all this is underpinned by a folk morality of 'live and let live'. Secondly, people (supporting multiculturalism) may be reading multiculturalism as a code for a 'tolerant society' or a society which rejects racism and xenophobia and prohibits discrimination.

Thirdly, it is possible, but less likely, that they are giving assent to a more specific set of multicultural principles which might include, for example: cultural equality and inclusion predicated on 'a community of communities'; re-modelling British identity and the British national story; making changes to the law predicated on multicultural principles. Conversely, we cannot be sure what those who oppose 'multicultural Britain' are really opposing. Do they believe that multiculturalism equates to separate communities and Balkanises society? Are they irked by what they see as immigrants or minorities requiring 'us' to change, rather than 'them' adapting to our way of life? Do they equate multiculturalism with 'political correctness'? Or are they reading multiculturalism as a code for 'immigrants' and thus opposition to immigrants, or to immigration, is tacked on to and transposed into opposition to multiculturalism? These are all possible readings of attitudes to multiculturalism and in most surveys it is not easy to see which reading is intended or understood. The qualitative evidence suggests that 'formal acceptance' of multicultural Britain is commonly made 'conditional' by a number of qualifying statements which undermine the sense of approval.

7. Conclusion

We began this chapter with a discussion of the ethnic majority as an idea which has had little attention within the sociology of ethnicity. With specific reference to England/Britain, we considered difficulties in conceptualising the 'majority' population and how it relates to the more familiar concepts of nation, national identity and multiculturalism. Having provided this by way of introduction, we moved on to present the details of the research carried out as part of the Leverhulme Programme, highlighting key empirical themes. In presenting the material, we focused on orientations to nation and country both specifically in terms of different types of identification with being English and/or British, as well as the broader discursive contexts in which notions of 'English' and 'British' appear to have particular meaning for the ethnic majority.

Across the spectrum of respondents and responses, we find a number of ways in which people talk about 'the country' and 'the nation'. For some, it is a matter-of-fact statement of 'being British' or 'being English', accompanied by greater or lesser expressions of pride. Here we make a methodological point. While asking direct national identity questions has its use, they rarely have purchase amongst ordinary people themselves. People did not have much to say about being English or British and some respondents were 'stumped' by questions using ethnic and national categories. Rarely would people identify or describe themselves as white, although 'being white' was often associated with Englishness, but not with Britishness. This can be contrasted to an approach in which we ask questions about social change, or changing Britain, in order to understand what it is that people meaningfully associated with nation and country. Following this we argued that theoretical gains can be made from talking of national sentiments rather than national identities and of orientations towards nation and country rather than identification with nation and country.

For a large minority 'the country' and their own place in it is expressed with resentment – and is linked with specific symbolic and material grievances. In many cases this is characterised by grievances, and a sense of unfairness, over the symbolic domain (e.g., flags, national holidays). This is evident through phrases such as 'why can't we be English?', 'we're not allowed to be English anymore' or 'if they're allowed to celebrate their culture why can't we?'. To be sure these are discourses commonly found in sections of the media and tabloid press. But respondents also make references to personal and local experience. In other cases, symbolic and material grievances intertwine more closely, and are grounded in contexts of housing, employment and access to services. This theme is expressed through phrases such as 'what about us?'.

As this chapter shows, tacit majoritarianism is evident in the use of terms such as 'we', 'us' and 'our own people'. These could be references to 'the nation'; which in effect claim 'the nation' as 'our own'. There is a sense that what newcomers should be integrating into is not simply a detached shared community but something which is 'ours'. Conversely, there could be a reluctant admission that Britain is multicultural or multiethnic, and they are speaking for a group within it 'the white English'. These findings cast doubt over the viability of political, elite or intellectual attempts to re-imagine the nation in more plural forms. The evidence of the surveys we have discussed and the supporting evidence of the qualitative interviews indicate that the idea of multiculturalism as a project of cultural recognition or a 'community of communities' does not find broad-based popular support.

Notes

1. In qualitative research, it is impossible to sustain a fixed distinction between England and Britain. Where there is a reference to the 'system' and the state, Britain is the reference point (e.g., it is Britain which 'allows too many immigrants in'). Where there is a reference to 'us' and 'our way of life' England or English may be the referent. The two cannot be easily separated and we know from our research that respondents will talk interchangeably about England and Britain as 'their country', depending on context, and their choice.
2. With only two exceptions, our 120 respondents were 'white' and, of course, living in England. Most of them identified as being 'British' or 'English' or both. Several respondents mentioned other British nationalities in their ancestry – mostly Welsh or Irish parents, grandparents; and a very small number had some continental European ancestry.
3. Entitlement is a concept much discussed in Dench, Gavron and Young (2006).
4. The question that was asked was 'Do you think Britain is getting better or worse as a place to live?'. In other words, we used the term 'Britain' as the reference

for the social system as a whole. Nonetheless England and English enter into the replies.

5. These are four of the bestselling dailies, representing 68 per cent of daily sales and even this judgement requires classing *The Times* as pro-multiculturalist. See MAGFORUM: UK National Newspapers: at http://www.magforum.com/papers/nationals.htm (accessed 19 April 2010).
6. The *Daily Mail* is a regular carrier of this type of story. See, for example, Doughty (2010), 'England Branded Least Patriotic Nation in Europe, as Citizens Are Too Scared to Fly the Flag', http://www.dailymail.co.uk/news/article-1267230/England-branded-patriotic-nation-Europe.html (accessed 19 April 2010).

References

Barry, B. (2001) *Culture and Equality: An Egalitarian Critique of Multiculturalism*. Cambridge: Polity Press.

Baumann, G. (1996) *Contesting Culture: Discourses of Identity in Multi-Ethnic London*. Cambridge: Cambridge University Press.

Billig, M. (1995) *Banal Nationalism*. London: Sage.

Billig, M., Condor, S., Edwards, D. and Gane, M., eds. (1988) *Ideological Dilemmas: A Social Psychology of Everyday Thinking*. London: Sage.

Bonnett, A. (2000) *White Identities: Historical and International Perspectives*. Essex: Pearson Education.

Bryant, C.G. A. (1993) 'Social Self-Organisation, Civility and Sociology: A Comment on Kumar's "Civil Society"', *British Journal of Sociology*, 44(3): 397–401.

Byrne, B. (2006) *White Lives: The Interplay of 'Race', Class and Gender in Everyday Life*. London: Routledge.

Condor, S. (2000) 'Pride and Prejudice: Identity Management in English People's Talk About "This Country"', *Discourse and Society*, 11(2): 175–205.

Condor, S., Gibson, S. and Abell, J. (2006) 'English Identity and Ethnic Diversity in the Context of UK Constitutional Change', *Ethnicities*, 6(2): 123–158.

Crick, B. (2008) 'Citizenship, Diversity and National Identity', *London Review of Education*, 6(1): 31–37.

Dench, G., Gavron, K. and Young, M. (2006) *The New East End: Kinship, Race and Conflict*. London: Profile Books.

Doughty (2010) 'England Branded Least Patriotic Nation in Europe as Citizens are Too Scared to Fly the Flag', *Daily Mail*, 21 April.

Editorial (2007) 'Manners Make a Nation', *Daily Telegraph*, 2 June.

Fenton, S. and Mann, R. (2009) 'Introducing the Majority to Ethnicity – and Do They Like What They See?', in G. Calder, P. Cole and J. Seglow, eds. *Citizenship Acquisition and National Belonging: Migration, Membership and the Liberal Democratic State*. Houndmills, Basingstoke: Palgrave Macmillan, pp. 141–155.

Flint, J. (2009) 'Migrant Information Packs and the Colonisation of Civility in the UK', *Space and Polity*, 13(2): 127–140.

Freedland, J. (2007) 'A Moment of Madness', *Guardian*, 13 August.

Garner, S. (2007) *Whiteness: An Introduction*. London: Routledge.

Glazer, N. and Moynihan, D.P. (1975) *Beyond the Melting Pot*. Cambridge, MA: MIT Press.

Haylett C. (2001) 'Illegitimate Subjects?: Abject Whites, Neo-Liberal Modernisation and Middle Class Multiculturalism', *Environment and Planning D: Society and Space*, 19(3): 351–370.

Hewitt, R. (2005) *White Backlash and the Politics of Multiculturalism*. Cambridge: Cambridge University Press.

Hickman, M.J., Morgan, S., Walter, B. and Bradley, J. (2005) 'The Limitations of Whiteness and the Boundaries of Englishness: Second-Generation Irish Identifications and Positions in Multiethnic Britain', *Ethnicities*, 5(2): 160–182.

Hjerm, M. (2000) 'Multiculturalism Re-assessed', *Citizenship Studies*, 4(3): 357–381.

Hughes, E.C. and Hughes, H.M. (1952) *Where People Meet: Racial and Ethnic Frontiers*. Glencoe: Free Press.

IPSOS MORI (2002) 'Race is No Barrier to Being British', 16 May, http://www.ipsosmori.com/researchpublications/researcharchive/poll.aspx?oItemId=984. Last accessed 19 April 2010.

IPSOS MORI (2005) 'BBC Multiculturalism Poll', http://www.ipsos-mori.com/Assets/Docs/Archive/Polls/bbc050809.pdf. Last accessed 19 April 2010.

IPSOS MORI (2009) *Trend Briefing 1: Doubting Multiculturalism*, May. London: IPSOS MORI, http://www.ipsos-mori.com/_assets/pdfs/Multiculturalism-Briefing.pdf. Last accessed 19 April 2010.

Jenkins, R. (2008) *Rethinking Ethnicity*. London: Sage.

Joppke, C. (2004) 'The Retreat of Multiculturalism in the Liberal State: Theory and Policy', *British Journal of Sociology*, 55(2): 237–257.

Karner, C. (2007) *Ethnicity and Everyday Life*. London: Routledge.

Kaufmann, E. (2004a) 'Dominant Ethnicity: From Background to Foreground', in E. Kaufmann, ed. *Rethinking Ethnicity: Majority Groups and Dominant Minorities*. London: Routledge, pp. 1–14.

Kenny, M. (2010) 'Englishness: The Forbidden Identity', *Guardian*, 11 February.

Kymlicka, W. and Norman, W. (2000) 'Citizenship in Culturally Diverse Societies: Issues, Contexts and Concepts', in W. Kymlicka and W. Norman, eds. *Citizenship in Diverse Societies*. Oxford: Oxford University Press, pp. 1–43.

Mann, R. (2006) 'Reflexivity and Researching National Identity', *Sociological Research Online*, 11(4).

Mann, R. and Fenton, S. (2009) 'The Personal Contexts of National Sentiments', *Journal of Ethnic and Migration Studies*, 34(4): 417–434.

McCrone, D. (2006) 'A Nation That Dare Not Speak Its Name? The English Question', *Ethnicities*, 6(2): 267–278.

McCrone, D., Stewart, R., Kiely, R. and Bechhofer, F. (1998) 'Who Are We? Problematising National Identity', *Sociological Review*, 46(4): 629–652.

Michaels, W.B. (2007) *The Trouble With Diversity: How We Learned to Love Identity and Ignore Inequality*. New York: Metropolitan Books.

Miller, D. (1995) 'Reflections on British National Identity', *Journal of Ethnic and Migration Studies*, 21(2): 153–166.

Modood, T. (2008) 'Is Multiculturalism Dead?', *Public Policy Research*, 15(2): 84–88.

Nayak, A. (2003) *Race, Place and Globalization: Youth Cultures in a Changing World*. London: Berg Books.

Parekh, B. (2000) *The Future of Multi-Ethnic Britain: The Parekh Report*. London: Runneymede Trust.

Smith, A.D. (1991) *National Identity*. London: Penguin Books.

Smith, A.D. (2004) 'Ethnic Cores and Dominant Ethnies', in E. Kaufmann, ed. *Rethinking Ethnicity: Majority Groups and Dominant Minorities*. London: Routledge, pp. 17–30.

Tilley, J. and Heath, A. (2007) 'The Decline of British National Pride', *British Journal of Sociology*, 58(4): 661-678.

Wimmer, A. (2004) 'Dominant Ethnicity and Dominant Nationhood', in E. Kaufmann, ed. *Rethinking Ethnicity: Majority Groups and Dominant Minorities*. London: Routledge, pp. 50–58.

ZACAT Eurobarometer (2003) *Dataset: International Social Survey Programme 2003: National Identity II (ISSP 2003)*. Identification Number: ZA3910, http://zacat.gesis.org/webview/index.jsp?object=http://zacat.gesis.org/obj/fStudy/ZA3910. Last accessed 19 April 2010.

12
Global Migration, Ethnicity and Britishness

Tariq Modood and John Salt

1. Introduction

The chapters in this book confirm the need for scholars and policy-makers to take a holistic view of the migration process.[1] There is an almost seamless transition which takes us from the decision of the individual to move, through the process of movement and the roles of intermediaries to incorporation into the host labour market and society. The process then continues through a settlement process of varying lengths which is mediated by the attitudes of migrants, those of migrant background (which we sometimes call second or third generations) and the receiving society. When or whether the migration process ever ends is a moot point. What is certain is that the scale and nature of migration waves, short or long term, differentiated by age, gender, ethnicity or skill, largely determine social and geographical outcomes.

In addition to this complexity, there is little doubt that aggregate numbers of immigrants are important in determining their impact on the economy, service provision and society more generally. Their geographical distribution is uneven, though perhaps becoming less so in recent years as migrants from Eastern Europe have penetrated parts of the country which have hitherto experienced little adventitious foreign population (Bauere et al., 2007; IPPR, 2008). As is apparent from some of the projects reported here, the cultural make-up of the immigrant communities influences perceptions and identities of both majority and minority populations. What appears to be more significant than sheer numbers is the nature of the flows. While attention is often fixed on successive 'waves' of immigrants coming to settle, it is also the case that there is an ongoing 'base load' of often temporary migrants, coming mainly for economic reasons. The burgeoning of globalisation has created a flow of skills into and through the UK.

The research reported here has developed and tested a number of theories, most notably relating to the business model of migration, post-immigration forms of ethno-religious exclusion and resources, and to the meaning of national identity. New concepts have emerged, such as 'portfolios of corporate mobility', the meld of the corporate and academic worlds to create 'a new global elite', 'ethnic capital', 'ethno-religious groups' and the 'grumbling resentment' of the majority population. A variety of methodologies has been employed, the need for which reflects the complex nature of migration and its implications. Both quantitative and qualitative approaches have been used, both separately and combined. Methodologies range from innovative, using interviews with families to throw light on human smuggling, to more traditional but rigorous interview-based approaches elsewhere. Both web and face-to-face surveys were carried out and with different sorts of actors: individual migrants, opinion formers – including Cabinet and Shadow ministers – and employers. Policy discourses and the print media were closely analysed. A wide range of data sources has been employed: large datasets such as those of the Census and HESA; official sources; statistics provided by various migration actors relating to their own operations; policy documents, newspapers and political speeches.

2. Brief summary of main findings

The chapters of the book have provided major new insights into how migration to the UK occurs and its major implications, including ethnic hierarchies and sense of national identity 50 years after the migration. The main findings are briefly summarised here. Chapters 2 and 3 are largely contextual. The first demonstrates both the complexities of migration and the difficulty of categorisation and estimation of volumes. The second provides an overview of some of the key challenges to post-immigration integration given the fact and scale of ethnic diversity, a long-term phenomenon in the USA but new to Europe, and the valorisation of Muslim identity.

Chapter 4 shows that a combination of motivation, information, return and risk might begin to explain different migrant smuggling outcomes. The combination helps explain a migration decision that on the surface is irrational: why do people pay to undertake a migration that is risky at best and life-threatening at worst? In the case study described, the decision was shown in most cases to have been made in consultation with family members and in a deliberate and deliberative manner.

Chapter 5 shows that managing the mobility of expertise has become a key element in corporate globalisation. Companies formally develop and use different forms of movement, according to their needs and those of their employees, in doing so creating 'portfolios of mobility'. This new concept includes a range of different mobility types, from permanent recruitment, through various temporary moves such as secondments and business travel, to virtual mobility. They are employed in dynamic fashion according to business needs. It appears that mobility is traditionally regarded by global employers as a derived function, responding primarily to the type of business available, the time horizon of project planning, and client and market relationships.

The globalisation theme is developed further in relation to high-prestige research-rich university institutions in Chapter 6. Three interlinked processes seem to be at work which can be separated out as the elite university, the funding and the replacement labour models. The argument from the elite university model is that high-prestige universities attract staff because they are world-class universities through which 'high-flying' staff members circulate. The extent of research funding in these universities, however, creates a large number of fixed-term research assistant posts, not all of which can be filled by the domestic supply of postgraduates and postdoctorates, which are filled from overseas. For Britain, such researchers are replacement labour; for the researchers, such posts are an opportunity to develop strategically their future academic careers, though few initially see themselves as staying in the UK longer term. Overall, the UK seems to be a net beneficiary of brain circulation, with some highly rated 'magnets' that draw in overseas scholars on the basis of their perceived 'excellence' and research funding, including for posts at these and other universities where the UK is unable to produce sufficient graduates and postgraduates to meet both university and commercial demands for those skills.

The findings reported in Chapter 7 represent a very early phase in the analysis of a phenomenon, targeted recruitment of international students by employers, about which little is so far known. The study showed a growing awareness among university careers services of the practice. At the same time, employers saw the employment of international students as a way of increasing diversity in their staffing and inculcating a positive attitude towards mobility within their global human resources. It is part of the globalisation process in international labour markets and mobility and links two major elements in the international migration business: student mobility and corporate mobility. The two systems reinforce each other to create a more mobile global labour market and a more cosmopolitan internationally mobile population.

Part 3 focuses on some developments as migrants become settled citizens and gives special attention to Muslims both in relation to social mobility and wider questions about multiculturalism and national identity. Chapters 8 and 9 looked at aspects of how ethnic minorities, formed out of previous waves of migration, are placed in acquiring qualifications and benefiting from them in relation to jobs. Chapter 8 confirmed previous studies that post-immigration minority groups suffer an 'ethnic penalty', namely that they receive a lower occupational return on education than their white peers. It built on this knowledge in two ways. Firstly, it showed that the ethnic penalty was greater when individuals lived in areas with a concentration of co-ethnics. Secondly, that the penalty can be better calculated for a particular individual where religious affiliation is combined with ethnicity, improving our ability to predict the odds of success for a person. This is consistent with the argument that contemporary racial exclusion cannot be understood just in terms of 'colour racism', but also 'cultural racism' and the finding that some Muslim ethnic groups are amongst the worst disadvantaged in the labour market, and that in multi-faith ethnic groups, Muslims are worse off than their co-ethnics.

Chapter 9 found that while no one factor could explain why some working-class Pakistanis should achieve better qualification outcomes than their white peers, there is evidence of an 'ethnic capital' at work. This has three elements: familial adult–child relationships; transmission of values and aspirations related to education; and enforcement of norms and sanctions. It does not operate discretely and middle-class Pakistanis are able to mobilise forms of social and cultural capital not available to their working-class peers. Gender too is significant in shaping norms and values towards educational achievement. Young Pakistani Muslim women were strongly orientated towards educational achievement. In contrast, not all of the young men in the study saw educational achievement as a necessary means to success and instead ethnic masculine peer cultures were influential in persuading young men not to invest in their studies. Religion proved to be a positive force in encouraging young people to study both by providing normative values and in some cases by enabling young men to develop important social and cultural networks beyond the immediate ethnic community.

Chapter 10 deals with one of the important integration topics today, whether Muslims think of themselves as British and whether some of them behave in ways that others think is not consistent with being British. These matters exercise very senior politicians and are capable of being the top national media stories for days at a time. The chapter established that views on these issues are not clearly divided across the two main political parties. Rather there are two cross-party views in the two major parties. One view is that some young Muslims have difficulty feeling British. At the same time others of ministerial rank in each of these parties hold the opposite view. The intense national debate in the media following Jack Straw's remarks about the *niqab* contributing to a state of separation acted as a lightning rod for feelings against Muslims and multiculturalism in general. This flood of feelings, as dammed up emotions about the *niqab* in particular and Islam more generally burst their usual restraints, illustrates an important feature of nationhood. For such exclusionary, affective power, no less than imaginative inclusivity is a central feature of national belonging.

Chapter 11 demonstrates the difficulties in conceptualising the 'majority' population and how it relates to the concepts of nation, national identity and multiculturalism. For a large minority a sense was expressed that what newcomers should be integrating into is not simply a detached community but something which is 'ours'. The findings cast doubt over the viability of political, elite or intellectual attempts to re-imagine the nation in more plural forms. The evidence appears to indicate that the idea of multiculturalism, as a project of cultural recognition or a 'community of communities' has limited popular support.

3. The business model of migration

In Chapter 1 we indicated that a useful starting point for analysing international labour migration was to conceptualise it as a business, populated by a range of institutions, each of which has some influence on the processes, patterns and outcomes of movement. Migration outcomes result from the accommodations and compromises made by individuals and institutions as they seek to achieve their objectives. We pointed particularly to the role of employers and smugglers in using migration as a tool to maximise their revenues. The research findings in Part 2 of the book confirm the value of the business model as a major tool in explaining labour migration at opposite ends of both the legal and skill spectrum.

Human smuggling has been traditionally thought of as a form of migration which exploits migrants and places them at high and often deadly risk. This is undoubtedly the case in many circumstances and at the shady end of the smuggling business. Migrant smuggling can effectively degrade into human trafficking, where a migrant is moved without fully paying off his or her debt to a smuggler, thus opening up the possibility for exploitation until the balance is repaid (Koser, 2007). For those irregular migrants who do enter the labour market, a life on its margin may well be the norm for some, though for others there is a transition from precarious 'work' to a more settled 'job' (Ahmad, 2008a, 2008b). Yet there was evidence in Chapter 4 of a business which, while by no means legitimate, could be well organised, trusted and in many cases deliver satisfactory results for both the smuggled and smuggler. The decision of a migrant to use smugglers was shown in most cases within the sample studied to have been made in consultation with family members. A combination of high returns and low risks made the decision rational for those making it. For smugglers, their rationale is simple: it is very profitable. They offer a range of services, with packages costing differently because smuggling takes place at different times and to different destinations; and different smugglers apparently offer different deals. The smuggling business is underpinned by a network of contacts and information flows. As was pointed out in the chapter, the need to confront what is often a complex business organisation, which may operate legally in sending countries, presents new policy challenges for governments, not the least of which is obtaining cross national cooperation.

The business model applies particularly to large international employers engaging in what has become a global skills market.

3.1. Employer management of migration

One of the main themes emerging from our research is the growing influence of globalisation on the migration of skills. This has helped produce a highly skilled elite, often referred to as knowledge migrants. More specifically, we have identified two major elements in this growth. The first is the role of the recruitment and mobility practices of private companies and universities in attracting and retaining highly skilled migrants. The second is the interaction between industry and academia, through the recruitment of international students, in encouraging the development of a globally mobile elite. Although the moves engendered by these actions may result in settlement, for many – perhaps most – migrants the movement is temporary, the residence in the host country transitory.

Almost all governments wish to attract knowledge migrants because they are assumed to benefit national economies. However, with certain exceptions such as medical personnel for national health services, governments themselves do not recruit high-level skills internationally. That task is left to employers acting on their own perceived corporate requirements. Highly skilled migrants are thus largely managed by multinational corporations, through varied channels of movement which include recruitment to or moves between company 'centres of excellence' such as head office, regional and research centres, to newly established drilling, factory or office facilities or to open up new and emerging markets.

Subsumed within the various patterns of project-related and market development moves is a range of career-oriented moves that span from the most senior to younger potential leaders. In the past, international companies traditionally used a 'colonial' model to deploy and train their skills. Movement was based on expatriation of staff from the country of ownership or from a relatively small number of countries at similar levels of development. In the context of modern internationalisation, however, the historic preoccupation of international human resource management studies with expatriation has come to be challenged (Fenwick, 2004; Minbaeva and Michaelova, 2004; Collings, Scullion and Morley, 2007; McNulty, De Cieri and Hutchings, 2009). There are a number of reasons for this which are discussed in more detail in Chapter 5. They include variations in the strategic significance of expatriation, for example, between North American and European multinationals (Scullion and Brewster, 2001); wide variations in expatriation practice between sectors; and a marked shift towards developing local expertise to match international knowledge with national economic, political and cultural circumstances, including more joint ventures and alliances and small- to medium-sized firms offering specialist expertise (Morley and Heraty, 2004).

We saw in Chapter 5 that the new global 'diversity' model is designed to gain the best corporate advantage possible from all of the company's workforce, regardless of nationality and location. Conceptions of 'global work' and 'global business space' are valuable (Jones, 2008, 2009) in highlighting the multiple roles of global staff. Those with high-level skills, actual and potential, may expect to work wherever their expertise is required or where their career development may be maximised. Managing the international mobility of expertise has thus become a key element in corporate globalisation.

In order to bring this about, companies have developed a range of policies, backed up by detailed HR information systems and designed to identify those with talent, promote mobility and reduce the friction of distance. Career succession plans, corporate intranets and diversity policies are some of the tools used. They link together staff location, qualities and availability with corporate requirements as and when they arise, creating a symbiosis between the needs of the company and the career development of the individual.

Universities, too, are becoming increasingly global in outlook and staffing. The percentage of overseas academic staff in all types of institution, disciplinary areas and employment functions has increased. A relatively small number of universities with global reputations, mainly in the London-Oxbridge triangle, routinely recruit overseas staff, many of them on fixed-term contracts, others for permanent positions (Smetherham, Fenton and Modood, 2010). Frequently, university departments or research centres require highly specialised individuals, many of whom are chosen because of their international reputations. The attraction of UK institutions for overseas staff is the benefit to their career development, often in pursuit of long-term international careers. The main difference from commercial employers seems to be that the bulk of overseas academics are in the early career phase. Although this group is important for non-academic employers, expatriation and recruitment there extends more widely across the age spectrum.

3.2. Targeting of international students by employers

A new and unexpected research finding was the growing trend among large international companies to target international students at UK universities for recruitment into their global labour markets. This has major ramifications for universities because it increases competition within the global education system. Global companies do not recruit only in the UK. A consequence of this is that student fee levels and the quality of education provided are likely to be more heavily scrutinised, both nationally and internationally. Targeting of international students also creates pressures for domestic graduates entering the labour market. Preference for more culturally and linguistically experienced international students may affect the career chances of the home-grown.

The particular significance of this combination of an international education system and a global corporate system is that it links two major elements in the international migration business: student mobility and corporate mobility. The two systems reinforce each other to create a powerful combination that will inevitably lead to a more mobile global labour market and a more cosmopolitan, internationally mobile elite.

3.3. Government management of migration

The mobility requirements of large international employers and of large national employers which recruit internationally pose management problems for governments. Their desire to attract the high-level expertise needed to drive economic development is tempered by their need to protect domestic workers from what might be perceived as unfair competition. The perspective of employers is different. They have business models which require them to combine the training and career development of their staff with the placement of specific skills in locations which entail global employee mobility. Similarly, universities compete for global reputation and want to employ the best talent. In today's world, in which countries are competing for foreign investment and for jobs, employers usually have the upper hand. For the most part then, the strategies and procedures used to recruit specific skills are predominantly employer-led, with governments acting as facilitators. The consequence is often tension between governments and large employers as the former seek to manage migration through the identification of skill shortages, while also protecting the indigenous workforce, and employers seek the most efficient way of managing all their global human resources and optimising their use.

In Chapter 1 we suggested that government management of skilled labour immigration has two main drivers. The first is the attempt to increase the national bank of expertise through the acquisition of high-level human resources; the other is the development of policies to counter specific skill shortages. The new UK government points-based system (PBS) was developed from the old work permit system in order to achieve a better alignment of managed economic migration with economic goals. It is aimed at the citizens of non-EEA countries. Points are given to potential migrants according to a range of personal characteristics (such as language and age) and qualifications (educational and professional). For each tier, various conditions are attached.

Tier 1 of the PBS is supply led and is designed to attract those with the high-level skills perceived to benefit the UK economy to come to the country to seek and take up work. It also includes post-study international students, that is, those who have graduated at UK higher education institutions (mainly universities) and wish to stay and work in the country.[2] This group was the focus of Chapter 7. While it is possible for the government to curb the numbers of non-EEA international students staying on to work after graduation, they cannot prevent global employers from recruiting such students and then sending them to work in another – often their own – country. As we saw in Chapter 7, this is what some employers are now doing.

Tier 2 is the 'labour shortage' tier. There are three components. Firstly, intra-company transfers include those who move within the international labour markets of MNCs. This group particularly featured in Chapter 5. Secondly, those in officially designated labour shortage occupations. Thirdly, those in certain occupations which employers have found it impossible to fill, despite having carried out a resident labour market test. These two groups featured in Chapters 5 and 6. At the time of writing the UK government has indicated it will continue to allow the intra-company transfer system to operate as before. Even with a 'cap' on numbers of non-EEA skilled labour immigrants, employers will continue to press for the easiest possible access to the skills they profess to require.

Tier 4 relates to international students coming into the UK for educational purposes. Although none of the chapters dealt specifically with this group, its background importance for Chapters 6 and 7 is considerable. Universities want international students for their fees but they also want the best brains, the number attracted depending on institutional reputation. University reputations are enhanced by the successful attraction of high fee-paying international students and this, in turn, increases and improves the facilities that attract the best overseas researchers. That international employers wish to recruit overseas graduates from individual institutions further enhances their status, making it easier to attract more international students and also international researchers in a win-win situation.

3.4. The management of highly skilled migration

For all three of the institutional groups – employers, universities and government – global mobility and targeted recruitment presents management problems. These will grow in the face of continuing globalisation of education and labour markets. International labour mobility is a key component of the business models of UK plc, global corporations and the best universities. All have a vested interest in fostering that part of the migration business that best suits them; sometimes these interests coincide, at others they may conflict. For example, universities seek the best young research talent, train it up, then lose it to private enterprise. At the same time, those universities which are more successful at attracting the best overseas academic talent are likely to gain in reputation and thus financially compared to other institutions.

One of the key findings in Part 2 was the emerging relationship between employers and universities with respect to the targeting of international students. A key element in the operation of corporate labour markets is the ability to deploy expertise to whichever location it is needed in a timely fashion. Sometimes this is done for career development purposes, at others in relation to specific projects. The latter can be predominantly client orientated or associated with the opening up or development of new facilities and/or markets. In order for assignments to work well, companies need mobile staff able to work in different environments. By targeting international students they are recruiting staff who have already demonstrated an ability to move internationally and acclimatise themselves to different national and cultural situations. Hence there is a symbiosis between the mobility requirements of companies and the recruitment of young highly skilled international students from selected universities. The business models of both coincide. Furthermore, these universities themselves employ substantial numbers of overseas staff, from both EEA and non-EEA sources. But, as explained in Chapter 7, targeted recruitment of international students has the potential to lead to tensions between the main institutional actors that comprise the migration business: between global corporate managed migration and national government policies towards labour migration; between universities and employers; between individual universities; between government departments; and between university departments. What is now needed is detailed research into the policies and practices of these actors at the institutional level to examine the linkages between them and the tensions created.

4. Ethnicity, citizenship and national identity

In Part 3, we explored two aspects of the longer-term effects of migration that take place as the migrant generation rears to adulthood, a generation born in the new country (the second generation) or see their grandchildren grow up (the third generation). To study these effects our research programme included not just projects on new, economic migrants but on the ethnic minority groups who came as economic migrants in roughly the third quarter of the twentieth century, supplemented by family reunification and formation, as well as some later labour migrants. These were primarily people from the former British colonial territories and not of European descent. Coming primarily from places such as the Caribbean and South Asia they were 'racially' marked and, at least in the case of the Asians, perceived as culturally 'different'. The gradual recognition that they were not temporary migrants but settlers and fellow citizens led to their being conceived of as 'ethnic minorities'.

We studied two principal themes. Firstly, the aim of most international migrants is social mobility, measured by improvements in their standard of living. The key questions are does this happen and if not, why not? If it does happen, what resources might be available to and utilised by the migrants and subsequent generations to bring it about? We showed in Chapters 8 and 9 that education is central and that even some who seem to be disadvantaged in this respect may still have unexpected advantages. Secondly, migration on a large scale, followed by settlement of distinct groups of people, can lead to anxieties among both migrants and hosts about national heritage and cohesion, and indeed to national identity crises. Has this occurred and how is it manifested?

4.1. Exclusion by ethnicity

As each chapter of Part 3 shows in different ways, a post-immigration minority ethnicity can be a source of exclusion and disadvantage, whether at the level of equal opportunities in employment or of the national imaginary. Migrants arrive with the human capital that they bring with them. They have high levels of motivation and willingness to work hard and long hours and to take work for which they may be over-qualified. Many are highly qualified, yet the majority of the post-colonial immigration that is the focus here were not highly skilled in relation to the economy that they were entering. There was thus an expectation, both among themselves and in British society, that they were entering society near the bottom of the jobs and other hierarchies. This has been exacerbated in the case of the settlers from the former British Empire, who have in the main been non-white and identified as such. The data analysed in Chapter 8 show clearly that people who are not white get a lower occupational return on their qualifications. This has been the case for decades and continues to be the case, even though for at least some British-born, non-white individuals, in some contexts, especially in competition for professional jobs, this ethnic penalty may not be great (Heath and McMahon, 2005; Heath and Li, 2008; NEP, 2010: 225–226) – though even then they may suffer an ethnic pay penalty (Longhi and Platt, 2008). Our findings show that different groups may respond differently to this predicament; indeed, they may respond differently even within one group and even within one class. Aggregatively, Pakistani young working-class people, for example, respond by working harder than their class peers to achieve educational qualifications. Others, however, go down a different path, giving this group the highest proportion of persons leaving school with no qualifications.

The exclusion of ethnic groups may not be only in relation to material things and opportunities. Their 'colour', their non-whiteness may be a mark of their not being truly accepted as full members of the country in which they were born, raised and educated and with which they identify. At least that is how they may be perceived by many of the white British. Only a few decades ago most people would have assumed that to be British you had to be white. With most of the 5 million non-white people in Britain having been born and brought up in this country, it is now not the case that merely being of non-European appearance and descent will make you a foreigner in your own country (Kyriakides, Virdee and Modood, 2009).

Colour continues, however, to be a factor even if it becomes more the basis of exclusion when it is combined with a specific ethnicity, such as Pakistani or, especially potent currently, a religion, notably Islam. Survey data record that after the events of 9/11 in the USA and especially after the London bombings of 7/7, distrust and prejudice against Muslims, now commonly called Islamophobia, increased. As Chapter 10 showed, Muslims are the group that politicians and government ministers worry about most in relation to integration and attachment to Britain. Moreover, this is not just to do with security and international affairs. If media items are an indicator, it is the allegedly unacceptable practices of Muslims – the 'cultural threat' – rather than security and terrorism that occupy the media most in relation to Muslims. The *niqab* or the *burqa,* and the national debate that Jack Straw's comments on them ignited, was also a focus of Chapter 10. It is just one of a number of recent controversies in which the majority of the country, as represented by journalists but also by participation in radio phone-ins, letters to the newspapers, online comments and so on, seemed to feel the need to express loudly and fully the unacceptability of some Muslim practice or political demand. Muslim views on freedom of expression, on the use of aspects of *shar'ia* alongside the English legal system, and on gender relations and sexuality, amongst others, fall into this category.

Further analysis would show that in such discursive debates it is not only the boundaries of Britishness or what is culturally acceptable in Britain that are being marked out. The minority group in question, Muslims, is also being (re)constructed. As the debate becomes more intense and more emotionally charged the object of intolerance grows from certain practices and views to the very population group itself. Muslims are identified by non-Muslims, especially those suspicious or hostile to them, by their phenotypical appearance (typically South Asian or Middle Eastern) but also by their cultural appearance (for example, headdress or beards). As it is not possible to interrogate all Muslims to find out if they subscribe to Islamic doctrine, their appearance has to be the basis of identifying them. This means, as was argued in Chapter 3, that they are 'racialised'; but this is not merely a biological racialisation that sees the world in terms of 'blacks', 'whites', 'browns' and so on. Rather, because cultural attributes are part of the physical identification and the basis for hostility, it is better understood as a form of 'cultural racism' (Modood, 1997). Alternatively, one could speak of the ethnicisation of Muslims into an ethno-religious group. This process of ethnicisation or group formation is not all one-way. It does not merely come from non-Muslims. Muslims themselves may valorise their Muslimness and come together to both reinforce their Muslim identity and to resist hostility. In this they are not merely playing out an existing religious identity but, through discursive and political assertiveness they create a consciousness that did not previously exist to the same degree or with the same shape. One strategy is likely to be a growth in identification with fellow Muslims and participation in Muslim causes and networks, especially at times of conflict, regardless of the degree of one's own religiosity and in the absence of any firm religious belief. This then is a complementary dynamic in the process of making Muslims from varied associations of individual believers into a politicised ethno-religious grouping (Modood, 2005).

So, when we talk about ethnic minorities or post-immigration minorities we need to take care to avoid two misunderstandings. We must not think that minorities are mere constructions, that ethnic groups are fictions in the sense that they do not reflect social reality, how people really think and act. As we have seen in relation to the ethnic penalty in Chapter 8 and ethnic capital in Chapter 9 we understand certain social phenomena better when we see ethnicity at work. But it does not mean – and this is the second misunderstanding to avoid – that ethnic groups are biological givens (like sexual reproduction) and are present in the same form at all times. They are socially constructed and so subject to unevenness, change over time, economic fortunes, social interactions with other groups, political domination and resistance, encouragement and exclusion but no less real for all that. Any one of these things can make a group a more or less salient feature in society. The presence and social significance of a group cannot be taken for granted or ruled out in advance but is a matter of empirical inquiry. Moreover, as our studies make clear, ethnicity is not a discrete phenomenon but an aspect of complex situations in which issues of human capital, socio-economic structures, neighbourhoods, gender and so on are at play.

4.2. Ethnicity and social mobility

While ethnic minorities can be subject to disadvantage and exclusion, at the same time such ethnicities can be a source of norms and behaviour which can militate against exclusion and socio-economic disadvantage. Pakistani migrant families, many of which come from rural backgrounds with very limited education and understanding of the complexities of British society and little or no participation in dominant networks, can hardly be said to possess much by way of social or cultural capital (Bourdieu, 1997). Hence, it is not surprising that they suffer amongst the very highest levels of unemployment, poverty and related forms of deprivation of any groups in Britain (NEP, 2010). Yet our study of young Pakistanis in Chapter 9 found that while some coming from such disadvantaged households had poor scholastic careers and made little effort at school, others from those backgrounds were striving hard to make educational progress and succeeding. We postulated the presence of a non-economic, non-middle-class form of capital that was present in those families. As it is not present in the same way in white working-class families (as postulated by the relatively low rates of participation in post-compulsory education), nor in all migrants groups as such (for example, working-class black Caribbeans do not have this scholastic success), we hypothesised that it was to be found in some ethnic groups and not others and so could be thought of as 'ethnic capital'. This idea has been explained and evidenced in Chapter 9 and in the chapter summary above.

What is worth considering here, going beyond our study, are other ways in which certain ethnic minority groups may have norms, family and social structures or cultural orientations that may enable them to be successful in certain kinds of ways beyond others from equivalent socio-economic starting points. Beyond education, an example that has been studied is self-employment (Metcalf, Modood and Virdee, 1996). Many successful South Asian businessmen, of small business as well as those which mushroom into ones with multi-million pound turnovers, cite family cohesion that motivates and makes achievable the degree of personal and familial sense of purpose, hard work and deferred gratification as the basis of their success, despite some social scientists seeing such effort as poor economic return for the hours invested and predicting business failure (Jones, McEvoy and Barrett, 1994; Ram, 1994).

Another example of a resource based on an ethnic identification can be linked to the idea of 'a role model'. Role models are successful individuals who are members of a group that does not enjoy average rates of success and yet whose success, through its example, has a positive effect on other members of that group. In one sense there is nothing 'ethnic' about the role models. Successful women are often cited by other women as role models (or their absence bemoaned). Yet a role model can only be a causal factor in the success of the endeavours of other individuals if the latter identify with the model (and perhaps also vice versa). Women have to identify with the successful woman in order to be able to say to themselves 'someone like me can succeed against the odds'. Similarly, Barack Obama, can only be a role model of unimagined success to those who think that Obama is like them in background, in experience and opportunities and so on. The more deeply and emotionally they are able to identify with him the more capable his success is of being causally effective in motivating them. Hence ethnic minority role models depend upon ethnic identification. That sense of shared ethnicity makes an individual a role model as opposed to just another businessman or athlete or celebrity.

4.3. The national imaginary

As brought out in Chapters 10 and 11, the national imaginaries, British and English, are under severe strain as some politicians and elites expressly attempt to re-think them in order to make them more inclusive whilst worrying whether some Muslims can be integrated. At the same time, some white English people feel aggrieved by the perceived special attention – symbolic and material – they feel the minorities are receiving. It used to be said that British national identity is of an understated sort; that it's not British to be too demonstrative about national identity; that the British sense of self-confidence and indeed superiority looked down upon those countries which deck their public buildings with national flags. It was only the political right that emphasised nationhood, which it too readily identified with past military glories.

That undemonstrative self-assurance is now hard to find. Not only is there the loss of empire and the sense of a middle-ranking country that has to stick closely to the USA or to the European Union to have much weight in the world, but the delicate multi-nationality within the UK is experiencing difficult times. A confident Scottish nationalism has achieved devolution, which looks set to go further and in the estimation of some people threatens the very existence of Britain, accompanied as it is by similar if currently lesser developments in Wales. The English, who for so long had to suppress their own sense of nationality for the sake of the greater prize of being an imperial power, find themselves having to find or invent national symbols and narratives (Kumar, 2003). Scotland and Wales could conceivably get away with thinking of nationality as ethnicity writ large over a territory and a state but England cannot. Not only is there no such state, England being governed by the UK Parliament without any remainder, but urban England is multi-ethnic in a way not yet fully experienced by the rest of Britain. This not only creates problems – as much to do with the emotions of identity as with politics and policies – for the indigenous English in working out how they relate to England, let alone Britain. It also goes with a sense that some people – post-immigration minorities – are not sufficiently emotionally attached to Britain.

How such minorities should relate to England is not (yet) addressed by politicians and other elites but this question in relation to Britain is a live political issue, as was evident in Chapter 10. What this means in terms of policies is addressed in the next section. The point to be made here is that this question may not have clear answers but it is expressive of and surrounded by emotions. These emotions can be constructive and inclusive: they can be harnessed to support a shared citizenship and respect for cultural difference in the understanding that just as one can be Scottish and British, so one can be Indian and British or Muslim and British. Yet these emotions can also be sources of intolerance and boundary-drawing as was seen in the media storm in relation to the *niqab* (Chapter 10). They can also be a source of grievance and confusion. As Chapter 11 showed in relation to the difficulties posed by the uncertainties surrounding British and English national identity, including the shifts which we find in the attitudes to 'nation' among the ethnic majority. When the previous diffidence, complacency or arrogance among the majority are no longer so easily grounded, where might majoritarian attitudes to nation turn? In part there is the production of a strong counter-narrative, which rejects 'politically correct' and multicultural Britain. Recent surveys show falls in public support for multicultural values simultaneous with decline in identifying being British with being white. A strong sense of material and symbolic loss and unfairness is to be found in parts of the majority population, as detailed in Chapter 11. We are bound to fear that these sentiments could be translated into support for neo-nationalist and racist ideas or parties. Moreover, if minorities and their political champions were only to emphasise 'difference' as the basis of their 'identity', then the majority can play the same card – and indeed trump all minority bids. Hence even while all aspects of British, especially English life become more multicultural day by day, so does a festering resentment amongst some of the white majority in England. It is just as well that a leading scholar of these topics argues that the English, by their history and traditions, are well placed to exploit the globalisation and interconnectedness of all human activities, if they could resist a sulky withdrawal into a 'narrow and defensive nationalism' (Kumar, 2010: 482).

4.4. Multicultural policy drift

As pointed out in Chapter 3, Roy Jenkins, as Home Secretary, in 1966 signalled that assimilation would not be the government policy in relation to the large-scale 'coloured' migration that was taking place at the time. Rather, the policy would be integration. He defined integration in a way that to most people sounded like multiculturalism: 'not a flattening process of assimilation but equal opportunity accompanied by cultural diversity in an atmosphere of mutual tolerance'. While not all subsequent governments have been as enthusiastic about this policy (Mrs Thatcher was particularly opposed to it), no government has repudiated it. Even where the central government has used an alternative discourse or sought a more nationalist steer in, say, schools, many big city local authorities in England, professions such as social workers and teachers, the BBC and other parts of civil society and popular entertainment have created what has been called a 'multicultural drift' (CMEB, 2000). Thus while Britain, unlike say Canada, does not have a declaration or legislation that can be referred to as 'multiculturalism' this is a term used to characterise the British approach to integration and contrast it with that of some of its EU partners, such as France and Germany. The New Labour government that came into office in 1997 was particularly strong in this respect, embracing the emergent multicultural society as a key feature of its 'modernisation' of Britain.

It is widely argued that multiculturalism as a policy approach in fact reached its peak with that first New Labour administration. In responding to the urban disturbances of the summer of 2001, in which Muslim Asian youths battled in the streets with the far right and/or the police in several northern English towns, and to the events of 9/11, the government, it is said, gave up on multiculturalism, never to return to it (Meer and Modood, 2009). Instead, it identified self-chosen segregation and communalism as the new problems, with Asian Muslims and whites living in adjoining neighbourhoods but living 'parallel lives'. The policy solution was to encourage mixing, cooperation and shared activities across groups so as to encourage 'community cohesion' (Cantle, 2001). A number of government reports since then have built on these themes. Yet, this has not been instead of emphasising diversity but in addition to it. Even more remarkably, given how many commentators speak of the 'death of multiculturalism' – most of which is based on caricatures of multiculturalism – there has been little reversal as regards any policy associated with multiculturalism. There have indeed been new policies and laws which could be said to owe their origins to the events of 2001 but (and leaving issues of security and terrorism completely to one side) they are primarily in relation to naturalisation, citizenship, citizenship education and immigration controls, not integration per se. That is to say, they relate to the numbers and qualities of people entering Britain and becoming British citizens, not the relations between British citizens across 'difference'. In this respect, they follow a feature of British policy which goes back to the governments of which Roy Jenkins was a part, and which his colleague, Roy Hattersley, summed up as: 'Integration without control [of immigration] is impossible, but control without integration is indefensible' (Hattersley, 1965). It is by limiting immigration, not by directly challenging multiculturalist integration, that British governments respond to anxieties about 'race'. Hence the twenty-first century emphasis on community cohesion and Britishness (as in the speeches of Gordon Brown, for example, 2005) is best understood as a necessary 'civic re-balancing' of multiculturalism after a period of laissez-faire in relation to building commonalities between British citizens (Meer and Modood, 2009).

Chapters 10 and 11, on ethnic minorities and national identities, suggest that this civic rebalancing makes some sense. This is evident in the resentment amongst some of the white indigenous English, especially older people, in relation to the public importance that issues of minorities and equality have assumed. Approaches which bring different parts of the community together and which allow them, in their own way, to share Britishness and other forms of commonality are important. Multiculturalism must resonate with and be respectful of the majority English and this means it must engage with them and their concerns. At the same time, as our study of the place of Muslims in the national imaginary shows, there are real long-term dangers in stigmatising minorities, not least, those of self-fulfilling prophecies. People's sense of nationhood is not something that can be engaged with only, or even primarily, in terms of reason and policy, but enflaming emotions that cannot be controlled is a potent danger. It is also clear that even in relation to a group that gives primacy to its religious identity, as many Muslims do in ways that are no longer common in Britain (for the moment), issues of socio-economic disadvantage and inequality can be central to its place in society and is an area on which effective policies continue to be needed.

To accompany restrictive immigration legislation the Labour governments of the 1960s created laws against racial discrimination. These have been widened and tightened over time so today they are the strongest of their kind in Europe and beyond. In contrast, governments have argued that there was, outside Northern Ireland, no need for legislation against religious discrimination. In 2003, however, the government, following a European directive, created an offence of religious discrimination in employment. Within a few years it has been broadened in scope and depth, well beyond anything required by or existing within the EU and by 2010 was on a par with all other British laws on discrimination. This rightly notes the persistence of racial and religious discrimination, as is strongly indicated by our analyses of the ethnic penalty.

The government has in the same period also brought together all equalities bodies and created the Equality and Human Rights Commission on the understanding that different kinds of discrimination intersect with each other. This too is a sound perception and is supported by our ethno-religious penalty analysis. The analysis can also support the targeting of policies and resources on groups such as Pakistanis and Bangladeshis, of which the extensive report of the National Equality Panel (NEP) concluded: '[t]he particularly disadvantaged position of the Bangladeshi and Pakistani working age populations, cross-cutting with Muslim religious affiliation, was evident across each of the labour market outcomes we examined' (NEP, 2010: 400). The NEP report also shows that the economic inequalities amongst white people are of a much greater magnitude than the gaps between whites and non-whites and relatedly, that class-based factors are better predictors of inequality than, say, gender or ethnicity. However, it concurs with our findings that 'socio-economic structures or "objective" class factors do not fully explain the position of non-white minorities, either in terms of the distinctive disadvantages or of the advantages of specific minority groups' (NEP, 2010: 233). There may be reasons to avoid racial explicitness and the targeting of resources to meet the needs of specific ethno-religious groups. Avoiding the resentment of white working-class people may be such a reason. But it has to be acknowledged that the scale of disadvantage experienced by some ethnic, religious or ethno-religious minorities is such that their needs may not be effectively met by universalist policies alone.

A further feature of issues to do with Muslims, discrimination, socio-economic disadvantage and the boundaries of the national imaginary, is that religion is coming to have a renewed public significance in Britain and Europe more generally. The newness goes beyond the specificity of Muslims or even of Islam as a public force in Europe but also is characterised by religion becoming a feature of public policy and governmental activity in a context of secularism. For the issues that are to the fore, minorities and equality, are issues at the heart of the rights and goals of secular citizenship. Even more fundamentally, the polities in which these issues arise, like Britain, even if they were once, are not particularly religious societies or polities. The political culture is thoroughly secular and the dominant networks are of secular organisations and individuals. Individual politicians may be deeply religious and indeed their politics may be motivated by their faith but churches have little power in the political system or in economics or the national culture. To be sure, Christians have a cultural legitimacy, sometimes even a prestige, and an institutional infrastructure not true of the newly planted faiths such as Hinduism, Sikhism and Islam. This is what makes the new significance of public religion, as argued in Chapter 3, a triangular affair. What we have is not just a church-state or religion-politics binary but a set of discourses and controversies in which there are three sets of actors: those concerned to stem a decline in the status of Christianity, those seeking to institutionalise a new ethno-religious pluralism and those seeking to entrench secularism. This is not the place to speculate how this triangular relationship will develop and what will be the result but the re-opening of what one might call the European secular settlement may be one of the long-term unforeseen consequences of post-war migrations.

Notes

1. We are grateful to Steve Fenton for discussing this chapter with us.
2. The UK government announced in late 2010 that Tier 1, including the post-study element, would be abolished from April 2011, except for a maximum of 1,000 comprising investors and people of exceptional talent.

References

Ahmad, A. (2008a) 'Dead Men Working: Time and Space in London's "Illegal" Migrant Economy', *Work, Employment and Society*, 22(2): 301–318.

Ahmad, A. (2008b) 'Human Smuggling and Illegal Labour: Pakistani Migrants in London's Informal Economy', *Journal of Ethnic and Migration Studies*, 34(6): 853–874.

Bauere, V., Densham, P., Millar, J. and Salt, J. (2007) 'Migrants From Central and Eastern Europe: Local Geographies', *Population Trends*, 129(Autumn): 7–19.

Bourdieu, P. (1997) 'The Forms of Capital', in A.H. Halsey, H. Lauder, P. Brown and A.S. Wells, eds. *Education: Culture, Economy, and Society*. Oxford: Oxford University Press, pp. 46–58.

Brown, G. (2005) 'Roundtable: Britain Rediscovered' *Prospect Magazine*, 109: 20–25.

Cantle, T. (2001) *Community Cohesion: A Report of the Independent Review Team*. London: Home Office.

CMEB (2000) *The Future of Multi-Ethnic Britain: Report of the Commission on the Future of Multi-Ethnic Britain*. London: Runnymede Trust.

Collings, D.G., Scullion, H. and Morley, M.J. (2007) 'Changing Patterns of Global Staffing in the Multinational Enterprise: Challenges to the Conventional Expatriate Assignment and Emerging Alternatives', *Journal of World Business*, 42(2): 198–213.

Fenwick, M. (2004) 'On International Assignment: Is Expatriation the Only Way to Go?', *Asia Pacific Journal of Human Resources*, 42(3): 365–377.

Heath, A. and Li, Y. (2008) 'Period, Life-Cycle and Generational Effects on Ethnic Minority Success in the Labour Market', *Kölner Zeitschrift für Soziologie und Sozialpsychologie*, pp. 277–306.

Heath, A. and McMahon, D. (2005) 'Social Mobility of Ethnic Minorities', in G.C. Loury, T. Modood and S.M. Teles, eds. *Ethnicity, Social Mobility, and Public Policy*. Cambridge: Cambridge University Press, pp. 393–413.

Institute for Public Policy Research (2008) *Floodgates or Turnstiles: Post-EU Enlargement Migration Flows To (and From) the UK*. London: IPPR.

Jones, A. (2008) 'The Rise of Global Work', *Transactions, Institute of British Geographers*, 33: 12–26.

Jones, A. (2009) 'Theorizing Global Business Space', *Geografiska Annaler: Series B: Human Geography*, 91(3): 203–218.

Jones, T.P., McEvoy, D. and Barrett, G. (1994) 'Labour Intensive Practices in Ethnic Minority Firms', in J. Atkinson and D. Storey, eds. *Employment, the Small Firm and the Labour Market*. London: Routledge.

Koser, K. (2007) 'Irregular Migration', Chapter 4 in B. Marshall, ed. *The Politics of Migration*. London: Routledge

Kumar, K. (2003) *The Making of English National Identity*. Cambridge: Cambridge University Press.

Kumar, K. (2010) 'Negotiating English Identity: Englishness, Britishness and the Future of the United Kingdom', *Nations and Nationalism*, 16(3): 469–487.

Kyriakides, C., Virdee, S. and Modood, T. (2009) 'Racism, Muslims and the National Imagination', *Journal of Ethnic and Migration Studies*, 35(2): 289–308.

Longhi, S. and Platt, L. (2008) *An Analysis of Pay Gaps and Pay Penalties by Sex, Ethnicity, Religion, Disability, Sexual Orientation and Age Using the Labour Force Survey*. EHRC Research Report 9. London: EHRC.

McNulty, Y., De Cieri, H. and Hutchings, K. (2009) 'Do Global Firms Measure Expatriate Return on Investment? An Empirical Examination of Measures, Barriers and Variables Influencing Global Staffing Practices', *International Journal of Human Resource Management*, 20(6): 1309–1326.

Meer, N. and Modood, T. (2009) 'The Multicultural State We're In: Muslims, "Multiculture" and the "Civic Re-balancing" of British Multiculturalism', *Political Studies*, 57(3): 473–497.

Metcalf, H., Modood, T. and Virdee, S. (1996) *Asian Self-Employment: The Interaction of Culture and Economics in England*. London: PSI.

Minbaeva, D.B. and Michailova, S. (2004) 'Knowledge Transfer and Expatriation in Multinational Corporations: The Role of Disseminative Capacity', *Employee Relations*, 26(6), 663–679.

Modood, T. (1997) ' "Difference", Cultural Racism and Anti-Racism', in P. Werbner and T. Modood, eds. *Debating Cultural Hybridity: Multi-Cultural Identities and the Politics of Anti-Racism*. London: Zed Books, pp. 134–172.

Modood, T. (2005) *Multicultural Politics: Racism, Ethnicity and Muslims in Britain*. Edinburgh: Edinburgh University Press.

Morley, M. and Heraty, N. (2004) 'Global Careers and International Assignments', *Thunderbird International Business Review*, 46(5), 633–646.

NEP (2010) *An Anatomy of Economic Inequality in the UK: Report of the National Equality Panel*.(Chaired by Prof John Hills) London: Government Equalities Office.

Ram, M. (1994) *Managing to Survive: Working Lives in Small Firms.* Oxford: Blackwell.
Scullion, H. and Brewster, C. (2001) 'Managing Expatriates: Messages from Europe', *Journal of World Business*, 36: 346–365.
Smetherham, C., Fenton, S. and Modood, T. (2010) 'How Global is the UK Labour Market?', *Globalisation, Societies and Education*, 8(3): 411–428.

Appendix
Bristol-UCL Leverhulme Programme on Migration and Citizenship Publications

Publications in relation to Chapter 4

Petros, M. (2005) *The Costs of Human Smuggling and Trafficking, Global Migration Perspectives Series of the Global Commission on International Migration*. New York: United Nations.

Koser, K. (2007) 'Illegal Migration', entry in *New Oxford Companion to Law*. Oxford: Oxford University Press.

Koser, K. (2007) 'Migrant Smuggling', entry in *New Oxford Companion to Law*. Oxford: Oxford University Press.

Koser, K. (2007) 'Irregular Migration', Chapter 4 in B. Marshall, ed. *The Politics of Migration*. London: Routledge.

Koser, K. (2007) 'Strategies, Stories and Smuggling: Inter-Regional Asylum Flows and Their Implications for Regional Responses', 43–55 in S. Kneebone and F. Rawlings-Sanaei, eds. *New Regionalism and Asylum Seekers*. Oxford: Berghahn.

Ahmad, A.N. (2008) 'Dead Men Working: Time and Space in London's "Illegal" Migrant Economy', *Work, Employment and Society*, 22(2): 301–318.

Ahmad, A.N. (2008) 'Gender and Generation in Pakistani Migration: A Critical Study of Masculinity', in L. Ryan and W. Webster, eds. *Gendering Migration: Masculinity, Femininity and Ethnicity in Post-War Britain*. Ashgate, Aldershot, pp. 155–169.

Ahmad, A.N. (2008) 'The Labour Market Consequences of Human Smuggling: "Illegal" Employment in London's Migrant Economy', *Journal of Ethnic and Migration Studies*, 34(6): 853–874.

Ahmad, A.N. (2008) 'The Romantic Appeal of Illegal Migration: Gender, Masculinity and Human Smuggling from Pakistan', in M. Schrover, J. van der Leun, L. Lucassen and C. Quispel, eds. *Illegal Migration and Gender in a Global and Historical Perspective*. Amsterdam: Amsterdam University Press, pp. 126–150.

Koser, K. (2008) 'Why Migrant Smuggling Pays', *International Migration*, 46(2): 302–323.

Ahmad, A.N. (2009) 'Bodies that (Don't) Matter: Desire, Eroticism and Melancholia in Pakistani Labour Migration', *Mobilities* 4(3): 309–327.

Koser, K. (2009) 'The Global Financial Crisis and International Migration', Lowy Institute Analysis Paper. Sydney.

Koser, K. (2009) 'The Economics of Smuggling People', *Refugee Transitions*, Summer, 10–13.

Koser, K. (2010) 'Dimensions and Dynamics of Irregular Migration', *Population, Space, and Place*, 16: 181–193.

Ahmad, A.N. (2011) *Gender, Sexuality and 'Illegal' Migration: A Transnational Comparison of Pakistanis in Europe*. Ashgate, Aldershot.

Publications in relation to Chapter 5

Salt, J. and Millar, J. (2006) 'International Migration in Interesting Times: The Case of the UK', *People and Place*, 14(2): 14–24.

Salt, J. and Millar, J. (2006) 'Foreign Labour in the United Kingdom', *Labour Market Trends*, Office for National Statistics, October: 335–355.

Millar, J. and Salt, J. (2006) 'In Whose Interests? IT Migration in an Interconnected World Economy', *Population, Space and Place*, 13: 41–58.

Millar, J. and Salt, J. (2008) 'Portfolios of Mobility: The Movement of Expertise in Transnational Corporations in Two Sectors – Aerospace and Extractive Industries', *Global Networks*, 8(1): 25–50.

Salt, J. (2008) 'Global Corporate Labour Markets and the International Mobility of Expertise', in *Managing Highly Skilled Labour Migration Seminar, Amsterdam*. Paris: OECD.

Salt, J. (2008) 'Managing New Migrations in Europe: Concept and Reality in the ICT Sector', in C. Bonifazi, M. Okolski, J. Schoorl and P. Simon, eds. *International Migration in Europe*, Amsterdam: Amsterdam University Press, pp. 19–35.

Dobson, J. and Salt, J. (2009) 'Pointing the Way? Managing UK Immigration in Difficult Times', *People and Place*, 17(2): 16–29.

Salt, J., (2009) 'Business Travel and Portfolios of Mobility Within Global Companies', in B. Deruder, F. Witlox, J. Beaverstock and J. Faulconbridge, eds. *Business Travel in the Global Economy*. London, Ashgate, pp. 107–124.

Wood, P.A. and Salt, J. (2012) 'Shifting portfolios of international labour mobility among UK-based business consultancies', *Geoforum* (forthcoming).

Salt, J. and Wood, P.A. (2012) 'Recession and international corporate mobility', *Global Networks*, 12(4): 425–45.

Publications in relation to Chapter 6

Smetherham, C., Fenton, S. and Modood, T. (2010) 'How Global is the UK Academic Labour Market?', *Globalisation, Societies and Education*, 8(3), September: 411–428.

Publications in relation to Chapter 7

Millar, J. and Salt, J. (2007) 'Target Practice', *Graduate Recruiter*, p. 13, Association of Graduate Recruiters, December.

Salt, J. (2009) 'New Forms of Mobility in Europe: Global Corporate Labour Markets and the International Movement of Expertise', in M. Duszczyka and M. Lesinskiez, eds. *Wspolczesne Migracje: Dylematy Europy I Polski*. Warsaw, University of Warsaw Press, pp. 15–25.

Publications in relation to Chapter 8

Khattab, N. (2009) 'Ethno-Religious Background as a Determinant of Educational and Occupational Attainment in Britain', *Sociology*, 43(2): 304–322.

Johnston, R., Sirkeci, I., Khattab, N. and Modood, T. (2010) 'Ethno-Religious Categories and Measuring Occupational Attainment in Relation to Education in England and Wales: A Multi-Level Analysis', *Environment and Planning A*, 42: 578–591.

Khattab, N., Johnston, R., Modood, T. and Sirkeci, I. (2010) 'The Impact of Spatial Segregation on the Employment Outcomes Amongst Bangladeshi Men and Women in England and Wales', *Sociological Research Online*, 15:1(February), http://www.socresonline.org.uk/15/1/3.html.
Khattab, N., Modood, T., Johnston, R. and Sirkeci, I. (2011) 'Economic Activity in the South Asian Population in Britain: The Impact of Ethnicity, Religion and Class', *Ethnic and Racial Studies*, 34(9): 1466–1481.
Khattab, N., Johnston, R., Sirkeci, I. and Modood T. (2012). 'Returns on Education amongst Men in England and Wales: The Impact of Residential Segregation and Ethno-religious Background', *Research in Stratification and Social Mobility*, 30: 296–309.
Khattab, N. (2012, forthcoming) '"Winners" and "Losers": The Impact of Education, Ethnicity and Gender on Muslims in the British Labour Market', *Work Employment and Society*, 26(4).

Publications in relation to Chapter 9

Modood, T. (2004) 'Capitals, Ethnic Identity and Educational Qualifications', *Cultural Trends*, 13(2), no. 50, June; modified and updated versions also appeared in D. Hoerder, Y. Hebért and I. Schmitt, eds (2005) *Negotiating Transcultural Lives: Belongings and Social Capital Among Youths in Comparative Perspective'*. Göttingen: V&R UniPress; in R. Alba and M. Waters, eds. (2011) *The Next Generation: Immgrant Youth in a Comparative Perspective.* New York: New York University Press; and in T. Basit and S. Tomlinson, eds. (2012) *Social Inclusion and Higher Education.* Bristol: The Policy Press; 'Forme di capitale, identità etnica e percorsi formativi', *Sociologia e Politiche Sociali*, vol. 15–1: pp. 31–52, 2012.
Modood, T. (2006) 'Ethnicity, Muslims and Higher Education Entry in Britain', Debate Section, *Teaching in Higher Education*, 11(2): 247–250.
Sanghera, G. and Thapar-Bjorkert, S. (2007) '"Because I am Pakistani and I am Muslim, I am Political" – Gendering Political Radicalism: Young Masculinities and Femininities in Bradford', in Tahir Abbas, ed. *Islamic Political Radicalism: A European Perspective.* Edinburgh: Edinburgh University Press, pp. 173–191.
Sanghera, G. and Thapar-Bjorkert, S. (2007), 'Methodological Dilemmas: Gatekeepers and Positionality in Bradford', *Ethnic and Racial Studies,* 31(3): 543–562.
Sanghera, G. and Thapar-Bjorkert, S. (2007) 'Political Radicalism in Bradford, UK', Chatham House and ESRC, ISP/NSC Briefing Paper 07/01.
Dwyer, C. Shah, B. and Sanghera, G. (2008) 'From Cricket Lover to Terror Suspect' – Challenging Representations of Young British Muslim Men', *Gender, Place and Culture,* 15(2): 117–135.
Dwyer, C. and Shah, B. (2009) 'Rethinking the Identities of Young British Muslim Women', in P. Hopkins and R. Gale, eds. *Muslims in Britain: Race, Place and Identities.* Edinburgh: Edinburgh University Press, pp. 55–73.
Thapar-Bjorkert, S. and Sanghera, G. (2010) 'Social Capital, Educational Aspirations and Young Pakistani Muslim Men and Women in Bradford, West Yorkshire', *Sociological Review*, 58(2): 244–264.
Thapar-Bjorkert, S. and Sanghera, G. (2010) 'Building Social Capital and Education: The Experiences of Pakistani Muslims in the UK', *International Journal of Social Inquiry*, 3(2): 3–24.
Shah, B., Dwyer, C. and Modood, T. (2010) 'Explaining Educational Achievement and Career Aspirations Among Young British Pakistanis: Mobilising "Ethnic Capital"?', *Sociology*, 44(6): 1109–1127, December.

Publications in relation to Chapter 10

Modood, T. (2007) 'Britishness Out of Immigration and Anti-Racism', in B. Chandra and S. Mahajan, eds. *Composite Culture in a Multicultural Society*. New Delhi: Longman, pp. 32–49.

Modood, T. (2007) *Multiculturalism: A Civic Idea*. Cambridge: Polity.

Modood, T. (2007) 'Muslims, Religious Equality and Secularism', in G.B. Levey and T. Modood, eds. *Secularism, Religion and Multicultural Citizenship*. Cambridge: Cambridge University Press, pp. 164–185.

Uberoi, V. (2007) 'Social Unity in Britain', *Journal of Ethnic and Migration Studies*, 33(1): 141–157.

Dwyer, C. and Uberoi, V. (2009) 'British Muslims and Community Cohesion Debates', in R. Phillips, ed. *Muslim Spaces of Hope: Geographies of Possibility in Britain and the West*. London: Zed Press, pp. 201–221.

Meer, N. (2009) 'Identity Articulations, Mobilisation and Autonomy in the Movement for Muslim Schools in Britain', *Race Ethnicity and Education*, 12(3): 379–398.

Meer, N. (2010) *Citizenship, Identity & the Politics of Multiculturalism*, Basingstoke: Palgrave Macmillan.

Meer, N., Dwyer, C. and Modood, T. (2010) 'Beyond "Angry Muslims"? Reporting Muslim Voices in the British Press', *Journal of Media and Religion*, 9(4): 216–231.

Meer, N., Dwyer, C. and Modood, T. (2010) 'Embodying Nationhood? Conceptions of British National Identity, Citizenship and Gender in the "Veil Affair" ', *Sociological Review*, 58(1): 84–111.

Meer, N. and Modood, T. (2010) 'Diversity, Identity, and Multiculturalism in the Media: The Case of Muslims in the British Press', in Cheney, G., May, S., and Munshi, D., eds. *Handbook of Communication Ethics*. New York: Routledge, pp. 355–373.

Modood, T. (2010) *Still Not Easy Being British: Struggles for a Multicultural Citizenship*. Stoke on Trent: Trentham Books.

Uberoi, V. and Modood, T. (2010), 'Who Doesn't Feel British? Divisions Over Muslims', *Parliamentary Affairs*, 63(2): 302–320.

Meer, N. (forthcoming, 2012) 'Scales, Semantics, and Solidarities in the Study of Anti-Semitism and Islamophobia', *Ethnic and Racial Studies*.

Dwyer, C. and Parutis, V. (forthcoming, 2012) ' "Faith in the System?" State-funded faith schools in England and the contested parameters of community cohesion', *Transactions of the Institute of British Geographers*.

Uberoi, V. and Modood, T. (forthcoming, 2012) 'Inclusive Britishness – A Multiculturalist Advance', *Political Studies*.

Uberoi, V. (forthcoming, 2013) *Nation-Building Through Multiculturalism*. Basingstoke: Palgrave Macmillan.

Publications in relation to Chapter 11

Mann, R. (2006) 'Reflexivity and Researching National Identity', *Sociological Research Online*, 11(4), December.

Fenton S. (2007) 'Indifference to National Identity: What Young Adults Think About Being English and British', *Nations and Nationalism*, 13(2): 321–339.

Fenton, S. (2008) 'The Semi-Detached Nation: Post-Nationalism and Britain', *Cycnos*, 25(2): 29–45.

Fenton, S. and Mann, R. (2009) 'Introducing the Majority to Ethnicity: And Do They Like What They See?', in G. Calder, P. Cole and J. Seglow, eds. *Citizenship Acquisition and National Belonging*. Basingstoke: Palgrave Macmillan, pp. 141–155.

Mann, R. and Fenton, S. (2009) 'The Personal Contexts of National Sentiments', *Journal of Ethnic and Migration Studies*, 35(4): 517–534.

Mann, R. (2011) ' "It Just Feels English Rather than Multicultural": Local interpretations of Englishness and Non-Englishness', *Sociological Review*, 59(1): 128–147.

Condor, S. and Fenton, S. (2012) (eds) Class, Nation and Racism in England and Britain, *Ethnicities*, Special Issue, 12(4), August 2012.

Condor, S. and Fenton, S. (2012) 'Thinking across domains: Class, Nation and Racism in England and Britain', *Ethnicities*, Special Issue, 12(4), August 2012.

Fenton, S. (2012) 'Resentment, class and social sentiments about the nation: the ethnic majority in England', *Ethnicities*, Special Issue, 12(4), August 2012.

Mann, R. (2012) 'Uneasy Being English: The Significance of Class for English National Sentiments', *Ethnicities*, Special Issue, 12(4), August 2012.

Index

Note: Locators in **bold** type indicate figures or illustrations, those in *italics* indicate tables.